African American History

African American History

Volume 2

Editor

Kibibi V. Mack-Shelton, PhD

Claflin University

SALEM PRESS

A Division of EBSCO Information Services, Inc.

Ipswich, Massachusetts

GREY HOUSE PUBLISHING

Some of the updated and revised essays in this work originally appeared in the following titles from the *Great Lives from History series: The 17th Century* (2005), *The 18th Century* (2006), *The 19th Century* (2006), *The 20th Century* (2008), *African Americans* (2011).

Publisher's Cataloging-In-Publication Data
(Prepared by The Donohue Group, Inc.)

Names: Mack-Shelton, Kibibi, 1955- editor.
Title: Great events from history. African American history / editor, Kibibi V. Mack-Shelton, PhD, Clafin University.
Other Titles: African American history
Description: [First edition]. | Ipswich, Massachusetts : Salem Press, a division of EBSCO Information Services, Inc.;
    Amenia, NY : Grey House Publishing, [2017] | Includes bibliographical references and index.
Identifiers: ISBN 978-1-68217-152-3 (set) | ISBN 978-1-68217-154-7 (v.1) | ISBN 978-1-68217-155-4 (v.2) |
    ISBN 978-1-68217-156-1 (v.3)
Subjects: LCSH: African Americans—History.
Classification: LCC E185 .G74 2017 | DDC 973/.0496073—dc23

First Printing
Printed in the United States of America

Contents

Volume 2

COMPLETE LIST OF CONTENTS

JIM CROW LAWS

1880's and 1890's

Jim Crow laws were part of an organized attempt throughout the American South to keep African Americans permanently in a socially subordinate status in all walks of life and to limit possibilities for any form of contact between people of different racial backgrounds.

The precise origins of the term "Jim Crow" are unknown. It may have first appeared in 1832, in a minstrel play by Thomas D. "Big Daddy" Rice. The play contained a song about a slave titled "Jim Crow." The expression was used commonly beginning in the 1890's. In 1904, the Dictionary of American English listed the term "Jim Crow law" for the first time. Jim Crow laws had predecessors in the so-called black codes, passed in many southern states after the Civil War (1861-1865) to limit the freedom of African Americans and assure a continuous labor supply for the southern plantation economy. Radical Reconstruction, which placed most parts of the South under military government, put an end to this. Even after the official end of Reconstruction in 1877, race relations in the South remained in a state of flux.

THE JIM CROW ERA

Jim Crow laws emerged during the 1880's and 1890's as conflict over political control in the South between different parties and between factions within parties intensified. Disfranchisement of African Americans and the segregation of white and black people were intended to assure the permanent subjugation of the latter and the prevention of future biracial political movements which could challenge white rule in the South. Domestic politics do not bear the sole responsibility, however: Jim Crow laws emerged at a time when the United States acquired colonies in the Pacific and the Caribbean and in the process subjugated the indigenous populations of those areas. Race theories used to justify American imperialism did not substantially differ from the white supremacy rhetoric of southern politicians.

The first Jim Crow law was passed by the state of Florida in 1887, followed by Mississippi in 1888, Texas in 1889, Louisiana in 1890, Alabama, Arkansas, Georgia, and Tennessee in 1891, and Kentucky in 1892. North Carolina passed a Jim Crow law in 1898, South Carolina in 1899, and Virginia in 1900. Statutes requiring racial segregation had been quite common in northern states before the Civil War, but only in the post-Reconstruction South did racial segregation develop into a pervasive system regulating the separation of white and black in all walks of life.

Jim Crow laws segregated public carriers, restaurants, telephone booths, residential areas, workplaces, public parks, and other recreational spaces. Mobile, Alabama, passed a special curfew law for African Americans in 1909. In Florida, the law required separate textbooks, which had to be separately stored. The city of New Orleans segregated white and black prostitutes in separate districts. Many states outlawed interracial marriages. Jim Crow laws were not even limited to life: Cemeteries, undertakers, and medical school cadavers were all subjects of segregation under the laws.

These laws, however, represented only symptoms of larger and even more pervasive patterns of discrimination and racial oppression. White vigilante groups, such as the Ku Klux Klan, often enforced their own brand of racial justice through violent means, frequently with the quiet consent and even cooperation of law enforcement officers. In addition, contract labor laws and corrupt law enforcement and prison officials created a system of peonage, which kept large numbers of African Americans in the turpentine and cotton belts in debt slavery.

U.S. SUPREME COURT

In the process of legally entrenching racial segregation through so-called Jim Crow laws, the U.S. Supreme Court served as a willing handmaiden. In the

An African-American man drinking at a "colored" drinking fountain in a streetcar terminal in Oklahoma City, Oklahoma, 1939, by Russell Lee

1883 *Civil Rights* cases, the Supreme Court ruled that segregation in privately owned railroads, theaters, hotels, restaurants, and similar places comprised private acts of discrimination and as such did not fall under the Fourteenth Amendment. In the 1896 case of *Plessy v. Ferguson*, concerning the constitutionality of a Louisiana Jim Crow law, the Supreme Court redefined segregation from a matter of private prejudice into a mandate of state law. In *Plessy v. Ferguson*, the Supreme Court approved of segregation as long as facilities were "separate but equal." In the 1930's and 1940's, the Supreme Court began to strike down segregation. Eventually, on May 17, 1954, the Supreme Court, in the landmark decision in *Brown v. Board of Education*, declared that separate facilities by their very nature were unequal, thereby reversing previous decisions.

—Thomas Winter

See also: Black codes; *Brown v. Board of Education*; *Civil Rights* cases; Disenfranchisement laws in Mississippi; *Guinn v. United States*; Ku Klux Klan; Lynching; Miscegenation laws; National Association for the Advancement of Colored People; Negro Conventions; *Newberry v. United States*; *Plessy v. Ferguson*; Poll taxes; Restrictive covenants; Segregation; Slavery and race relations

COLORED WOMEN'S LEAGUE

June, 1892

This organization joined with another organization to form the National Association of Colored Women to promote self-protection, self-advancement, and social interaction.

Place: Washington, D.C.

The Colored Women's League (CWL), also known as the National League of Colored Women and the Washington Colored Woman's League, emerged in Washington, D.C., when black women active in education, benevolent, and literary societies joined together in June, 1892, in an effort to improve conditions for African Americans.

Helen A. Cook, wife of John T. Cook, served as president, and the recording secretary was Charlotte Forten Grimké, a teacher from Port Royal, South Carolina. Other founders included Coralie Franklin Cook, wife of a Howard University administrator; teachers Anna J. Cooper, Mary Jane Patterson, Mary Church Terrell, and Anna E. Murray from M Street School; and Josephine B. Bruce, the first black teacher in the Cleveland schools, who later married Senator Blanche K. Bruce.

As Chicago prepared to host the World Columbian Exposition of 1893, the Board of Lady Managers rejected the petitions of these Washington women to participate in the planning process because they did not represent a national organization. In response, the Washington Colored Woman's League issued an invitation to black women throughout the country to affiliate as a national league. Women's clubs responded from the state of South Carolina and from the cities of Philadelphia, Kansas City, Denver, and Norfolk, Virginia.

In January, 1894, the organization incorporated, becoming the Colored Women's League. In October, the CWL received an invitation for membership in the National Council of Women (NCW). Its members accepted and sought to expand representation for the NCW convention in the spring of 1895. Instead, the competition between women's clubs in New York and in Boston resulted in the creation of a second national organization, the National Federation of Afro-American Women. The two national organizations merged in July, 1896, to form the National Association of Colored Women (NACW) to further self-protection, self-advancement, and social interaction. In 1896, Terrell became the first president of the NACW.

—Dorothy C. Salem

See also: Combahee River Collective; Million Woman March; National Association of Colored Women; National Black Women's Political Leadership Caucus; National Council of Negro Women

IDA B. WELLS-BARNETT PUBLISHES *SOUTHERN HORRORS:*
LYNCH LAW IN ALL ITS PHASES
1892

Wells-Barnett applied investigative journalism to the pervasive crime of lynching, publishing statistical and anecdotal evidence that showed the brutality and injustice of racial violence. She was a vocal proponent of African American civil rights and women's rights throughout her career.

Born: July 16, 1862; Holly Springs, Mississippi
Died: March 25, 1931; Chicago, Illinois
Also known as: Ida Bell Wells (birth name); Iola (journalism moniker/pen name)
Areas of achievement: Civil rights; Journalism and publishing; Women's rights

EARLY LIFE
Ida B. Wells-Barnett was born in Holly Springs, Mississippi, on July 16, 1862, to slaves James Wells and Elizabeth (Lizzie) Warrenton. She was the oldest of seven children born to James and Lizzie. Her family was emancipated six months after Ida was born. Her father, the only son of his former master, received training and became a skilled carpenter long before his freedom. Well respected as a free wage earner after the Civil War, he also achieved the rank of Master Mason in the Freemasons. As a young girl, Wells-Barnett received basic education from the Freedmen's Aid Society of the Episcopal Church. Her father, who was active in the Freedmen's Aid Society, and served as one of its first board of trustees members, helped to found Shaw University, for freed former slaves. It is now known as Rust College. During the era of Reconstruction, both of her parents were active in the Republican Party. At age sixteen, after both her parents', and one of her sibling's deaths, due to yellow fever, Ida had to drop out of school at Shaw University, she earned a teaching certificate in order to support herself and her remaining five siblings. Her and her sisters later moved to Memphis, Tennessee to live with an aunt. Her brothers worked carpenter apprentices. Because of her father's Masonic rank, the local Masons helped her obtain a teaching position. Wells-Barnett first became aware of the injustice of Jim Crow segregation when she was forcibly removed from a first-class rail car despite having a valid ticket. Initially, she won her $500.00 lawsuit, yet the Tennessee Supreme Court later overturned the ruling.

Ida B. Wells Barnett, in a photograph by Mary Garrity from c. 1893

LIFE'S WORK
Wells-Barnett began writing and publishing articles about the issues of injustices, and politics in the South, experienced by Freedmen. Writing for *The American Baptist* and other newspapers under the pen name Iola, Wells-Barnett attracted a national audience. She became known as "The Princess of the Press." By 1889, she had acquired one-third ownership in a Memphis newspaper, *Free Speech and Headlight*, which later became *Free Speech*. After a local school refused to renew her teaching contract because of an article she had written, she turned to journalism and newspaper ownership full time. She found writing more fulfilling than teaching and soon dedicated herself to an antilynching campaign.

Wells-Barnett increased *Free Speech*'s subscriber base by nearly 40 percent. Her involvement as owner, editor, and writer turned the paper into a force in the fight for racial justice. In 1891, three Memphis businessmen—one of whom was a close friend of Wells-Barnett—were targeted by a white mob because their grocery store was

253

competing with a nearby white-owned store. After the businessmen fought back, injuring some of the attackers, they were lynched. The murders deeply affected Wells-Barnett and drove her to shift her focus from civil rights in general to lynching specifically.

Wells-Barnett's militant articles about lynching stirred controversy in Memphis. After her newspaper's offices were destroyed by a mob, and she was threatened with death if she returned to Memphis, TN, she decided to move north, originally living in New York. She took a job with *The New York Age*, an African American weekly publication that also had broad white readership. She launched a public-speaking career in October, 1892, as well. That year, Wells-Barnett wrote an article for *The New York Age* in which she attacked the myth that lynching was a form of vigilante justice for black men who raped white women; she used data to expose the attitudes toward race and sexuality that underlay the southern culture of racial violence. The article became the pamphlet *Southern Horrors: Lynch Law in All Its Phases*, published by the end of 1892. The speaking tour that followed took her across the United States and to the United Kingdom. She became an international figure in the campaign against lynching.

In 1893, Wells-Barnett helped to organize a boycott of the World's Columbian Exhibition in Chicago and contributed to a pamphlet titled *The Reason Why the Colored American Is Not in the World's Columbian Exhibition*, which was distributed at the event. The trip culminated in her decision to move to Chicago, where she spent the remainder of her life. In Chicago, she began writing for newspaper owner and attorney Ferdinand Barnett's *The Chicago Conservator*. In 1895, she and Barnett were married. They had four children. Although she remained active in the national anti-lynching campaign, of which she was a founding member, she scaled back her activism to focus on her family.

Over the subsequent decades, Wells-Barnett balanced activism with motherhood. She provided the means and the leadership for the creation of the National Association of Colored Women (NACW). She also canvassed the state to promote suffrage for women and establish the first suffrage association for Colored/Negro American women in Chicago. Her political interests eventually led her to run for a state senate seat in the 1930's. An active champion of social justice, she developed strategies for the anti-lynching campaign that would be used by activists generations later.

Wells and the Anti-lynching Movement

Ida B. Wells-Barnett was an outspoken, independent activist who was driven to expose the brutality and injustice of lynching. Through her groundbreaking journalism, she brought international attention to racial violence. In particular, Wells-Barnett sought to dispel the myth that only African American men who raped white women were lynched. Her first published pamphlet, *Southern Horrors: Lynch Law in All Its Phases* (1892), based on an article she wrote for the *Free Speech* newspaper in Memphis, suggested that consensual sexual relationships between white women and black men often were misconstrued and offered anecdotes about women who lied about rape to cover up interracial affairs. These claims raised the ire of many whites in Memphis, and Wells-Barnett was forced to leave the city. In 1895, she published a report titled *The Red Record: Tabulated Statistics and Alleged Causes of Lynching in the United States*, the first documented statistical report on lynching. Her meticulously documented report showed that lynching was much more frequent and far reaching than commonly thought, and that the crime was closely tied to entrenched attitudes about race, gender, and sexuality in the United States. It described in detail many cases in which men were lynched "for anything or nothing."

Wells-Barnett died in Chicago, still actively pursuing the cause of justice for all. Her bid for political office, a campaign to prevent the appointment of a North Carolina judge to the U.S. Supreme Court, and work on her autobiography filled the last days of her life.

SIGNIFICANCE

Wells-Barnett's investigative reporting and forceful editorials forced her readers—black and white—to confront the cruelty and injustice of lynching. She devoted her career to disproving the myths about race and gender that contributed to the prevalence of lynching in the South. She also worked more generally for Colored/Negro American civil rights and women's rights and suffrage.

—*Kay J. Blalock, updated by Patricia A McDaniel)*

ATLANTA COMPROMISE

September 18, 1895

Washington's controversial advocacy of accommodationism has a major influence on African American political and economic strategies.

The Event: Speech by Booker T. Washington offering an accommodation to white Americans
Place: Atlanta, Georgia

Booker T. Washington, born a slave on a small Virginia plantation, gained his freedom at the end of the Civil War in 1865. He learned to read by studying spelling books and occasionally attending a school for African American children. In 1872, Washington enrolled at Hampton Institute in Virginia, a technical and agricultural school established for emancipated slaves. After graduation, he taught in Malden, West Virginia, then later returned to Hampton Institute.

In May, 1881, Washington received an invitation to join a group of educators from Tuskegee, Alabama, to help establish a technical and agricultural college for African American students. Tuskegee Institute opened on July 4, 1881, with Washington as its principal. Washington raised funds, acquired land, supervised the construction of buildings, and recruited talented faculty members. Within a decade, the school had gained a national reputation for providing outstanding technical and occupational training for African American students.

In the spring of 1895, Washington was invited to join a planning committee for the forthcoming Atlanta Cotton States and International Exposition, which would highlight the South's most recent developments in agricultural technology. Washington was asked to deliver one of the key addresses during the exposition's opening ceremonies, a speech that would focus on the role of African Americans in the South's agricultural economy.

THE ADDRESS

Washington delivered his Atlanta Exposition address on September 18, 1895, to an audience of several thousand listeners. He opened by thanking the directors of the Atlanta Exposition for including African Americans in the event and expressing his hope that the exposition would do more to "cement the friendship of the two races than any occurrence since the dawn of our freedom."

Washington went on to predict that the exposition would awaken among both white and black southerners "a new era of industrial progress." He illustrated his point by telling a parable of a ship lost at sea whose crew members were desperate for fresh water. The captain of another ship, hearing the pleas for water by the captain of the distressed vessel, urged the lost sailors, "Cast down your bucket where you are." When the captain of the lost ship followed that advice, his crew members brought aboard sparkling fresh water from the Amazon River.

Washington then urged his African American listeners to cast down their buckets "in agriculture, mechanics, in commerce, in domestic service, and in the professions." He said that African Americans would prosper "in proportion as we learn to dignify and glorify common labour and put brains and skill into the common occupations of life." He added that "no race can prosper till it learns that there is as much dignity in tilling a field as in writing a poem."

Washington also told his white listeners to cast down their buckets among the South's African Americans, "who have, without strikes and labour wars, tilled your fields, cleared your forests, builded your railroads and cities, and brought forth treasures from the bowels of the earth, and helped make possible this magnificent representation of the progress of the South." He encouraged white southerners to educate African Americans in "head, heart, and hand" so that they would remain "the most patient, faithful, law-abiding, and unresentful people that the world has seen." He asserted that in "all things purely social we can be as separate as the fingers, yet one as the hand in all things essential to mutual progress."

Washington concluded his speech by expressing his belief that the "wisest among my race understand that the agitation of questions of social equality is the extremest folly, and that progress in the enjoyment of all the privileges that will come to us must be the result of severe and constant struggle rather than of artificial forcing." He emphasized that African Americans must achieve economic self-reliance before they received "all the privileges of the law."

Washington's address was enthusiastically received by those present and the press. President Grover Cleveland wrote a congratulatory note. Washington received dozens of invitations to speak around the country and deliver his pragmatic message of economic self-reliance and political accommodationism.

CRITICS

Nevertheless, critics of Washington's philosophy soon surfaced, accusing Washington of making an unsatisfactory compromise by accepting an inferior social and political position for African Americans in exchange for economic opportunities. These critics argued that the tools for economic independence alone would not lead African Americans toward full citizenship and that the widespread segregation of and discrimination against African Americans in the United States, especially in the South, was proof of the flaws of Washington's reasoning.

Perhaps the most eloquent critic of Washington's message was W. E. B. Du Bois. In *The Souls of Black Folk* (1903), Du Bois, who would later found the National Association for the Advancement of Colored People (NAACP), asserted that Washington "represents in Negro thought the old attitude of adjustment and submission," that the ideas expressed in what he

called Washington's "Atlanta Compromise" were merely "a gospel of Work and Money" that prompted African Americans to surrender political power, civil rights, and opportunities for higher education. In contrast to Washington, Du Bois advocated that African Americans receive the right to vote, civic equality, and opportunities for higher academic education, as opposed to the kind of occupational training offered at Tuskegee Institute.

—James Tackach

See also: Black colleges and universities; Education; National Association for the Advancement of Colored People; Founding of the Niagara Movement; Talented Tenth; Universal Negro Improvement Association

PLESSY V. FERGUSON

May 18, 1896

One of the most notorious decisions in the history of the U.S. Supreme Court, Plessy v. Ferguson *not only upheld racial segregation in the United States, it also lent the sanction of the Supreme Court and created the contentious doctrine of separate but equal that a later Court would eventually overturn as a selfcontradiction.*

Locale: Washington, D.C.
Categories: Laws, acts, and legal history; government and politics; social issues and reform; civil rights and liberties

KEY FIGURES

Homer Adolph Plessy (1862-1925), New Orleans resident of one-eighth African ancestry
Albion Winegar Tourgée (1838-1905), Plessy's chief attorney
Henry B. Brown (1836-1913), associate Supreme Court justice, 1890-1906
John Marshall Harlan (1833-1911), associate Supreme Court justice, 1877-1911
Louis A. Martinet (d. 1917), New Orleans man who led a challenge to the separate but equal doctrine
John H. Ferguson (fl. late nineteenth century), judge of the Criminal District Court for Orleans Parish
Charles E. Fenner (1834-1911), associate Louisiana Supreme Court justice

SUMMARY OF EVENT

On July 10, 1890, the Louisiana General Assembly, over the objection of its eighteen African American members, enacted a law that read, in part:

> …all railway companies carrying passengers in their coaches in this state shall provide equal but separate accommodations for the white and colored races, by providing two or more passenger coaches for each passenger train, or by dividing the passenger coaches by a partition so as to secure separate accommodations.

The Louisiana law empowered train officials to assign passengers to cars; passengers insisting on going into a car set aside for the other race were liable to a twenty-five-dollar fine and twenty days' imprisonment. In addition, the company could refuse to carry an obstreperous passenger and, if it were sued for doing so, was immune from damages in state courts. A third section outlined the penalties for non-complying railroads and provided that "nothing in this act shall be construed as applying to nurses attending children of the other race."

At first the Separate Car Bill was stymied by the black legislators and by railroad officials who were as anxious to avoid the economic burden of providing separate facilities as they were to avoid a boycott of irate black passengers. After the black legislators had helped to override the veto of a major lottery bill, however, the legislature revived the Separate Car Bill and enacted it by a safe margin. After its enactment, some of the railroad companies were inclined to disregard the law, and they apparently collaborated with black people to test its validity. In 1890, the railroads had unsuccessfully challenged a Mississippi separate but equal law; the Supreme Court of the United States had held in *Louisville, New Orleans, and Texas Railway Co. v. Mississippi* that such a law, when applied solely to travel within the state, did not encroach upon interstate commerce.

The prominent black community of New Orleans organized to mount a legal attack upon the new law. A group calling itself the Citizens' Committee to Test the Constitutionality of the Separate Car Law, led by Louis A. Martinet and Alexander A. Mary, organized to handle the litigation and enlisted the services of Albion Winegar Tourgée. Tourgée was to serve as chief counsel and devote his considerable talents to rallying public opposition to the Jim Crow system typified by the Louisiana law. The new counsel had served as a classical carpetbagger in North Carolina during Reconstruction and, among other accomplishments, had published a number of novels about the Reconstruction era, among them *A Fools Errand* (1879), *An Appeal to Caesar* (1884), and *Bricks Without Straw* (1880).

Martinet engaged James Walker to assist in handling the Louisiana phase of the controversy. Before the first test of the Louisiana law (also featuring an African American who could "pass for white") could be settled, the Louisiana Supreme Court decided in *State ex rel. Abbot v. Hicks* (1892) that the 1890 law could not be applied to interstate travelers since it was an unconstitutional regulation of interstate commerce. The *Plessy* case, then, relitigated the question raised in the 1890 Mississippi railroad case, but as a problem in the constitutional law of civil liberties rather than one of interstate commerce.

The person recruited to test the segregation law was Homer Adolph Plessy, a person of seven-eighths Caucasian and one-eighth African ancestry, in whom "the mixture of colored blood was not discernible." On June 7, 1892, holding a first-class ticket entitling him to travel on the East Louisiana Railway from New Orleans to Covington, Louisiana, Plessy took a seat in the car reserved for whites. The conductor, assisted by a policeman, forcibly removed Plessy and, charging him with violating the segregation law, placed him in the parish jail. The state prosecuted Plessy in the Orleans Parish criminal district court before Judge John H. Ferguson. Plessy's plea that the law was unconstitutional was overruled by Ferguson, who directed the defense to address itself to the questions of fact. Having no defense in the

facts, Tourgée and Walker appealed Ferguson's ruling on the law's constitutionality to the Louisiana Supreme Court by asking that court to issue a writ of prohibition which in effect would have directed Ferguson to reverse his ruling on the constitutional question.

On December 19, 1892, Associate Judge Charles E. Fenner of the Louisiana Supreme Court ruled the law constitutional in an opinion that served as a model for that written later by Justice Henry B. Brown of the U.S. Supreme Court. After a delay of almost four years—a delay that Tourgée encouraged on the grounds that it gave the opponents of segregation needed time—the U.S. Supreme Court heard the arguments in Plessy's case on April 13, 1896. On May 18, 1896, Justice Brown handed down the majority opinion, supported by six other justices (Justice David Brewer did not participate, and Justice John Marshall Harlan dissented).

Justice Brown first disposed of Tourgée's argument that the segregation law was a "badge of servitude," a vestige of slavery prohibited by the Thirteenth Amendment (1865). Decisions in the 1872 Slaughterhouse cases and the 1883 Civil Rights Cases, wrote Brown, indicated that it was because the Thirteenth Amendment barred only outright slavery and not laws merely imposing "onerous disabilities and burdens" that the movement for the Fourteenth Amendment had been successful. Later in his opinion Brown blended the "badge of servitude" argument of the Thirteenth Amendment with his treatment of the equal protection question:

> We consider the underlying fallacy of the plaintiff's argument to consist in the assumption that the enforced separation of the two races stamps the colored race with a badge of inferiority. If this be so, it is not by reason of anything found in the act, but solely because the colored race chooses to put that construction upon it.

If Plessy was to gain any relief, it had to be from the Fourteenth Amendment, but that amendment, according to Brown

> merely . . . enforced the absolute equality of the two races before the law, but in the nature of things it could not have been intended to abolish distinctions based upon color, or to enforce social, as distinguished from political, equality, or a commingling of the two races upon terms unsatisfactory to either.

To support his point, Brown cited state school segregation and anti-miscegenation laws and federal laws prescribing segregated schools for the District of Columbia.

Special stress was placed on the 1849 decision of *Roberts v. Boston*, in which Chief Justice Lemuel Shaw of the Massachusetts Supreme Judicial Court had upheld the constitutionality of separate but equal schools for Boston. Brown did not mention that the Massachusetts legislature had repudiated Shaw's doctrine in 1855.

To the plaintiff's argument that the principle of segregation could be used by the state to enforce extreme and arbitrary forms of racial discrimination, Brown responded that every exercise of state power must be "reasonable, and extend only to such laws as are enacted in good faith for the promotion of the public good, and not for the annoyance or oppression of a particular class."

There was nothing unreasonable about the Louisiana law according to the Court; in determining what is reasonable, state legislators could "act with reference to the established usages, customs, and traditions of the people, with a view to the promotion of their comfort, and the preservation of the public peace and good order." Finally, Brown in his opinion delivered a famous statement on the relationship between law, prejudice, and equality:

The [plaintiff's] argument also assumes that social prejudice may be overcome by legislation, and that equal rights cannot be secured to the negro except by an enforced commingling of the two races. We cannot accept this proposition. If the two races are to meet on terms of social equality, it must be the result of natural affinities, a mutual appreciation of each other's merits and a voluntary consent of individuals.

The law in question interfered with the "voluntary consent of individuals." Tourgée's fears were realized:

Plessy v. Ferguson

The majority opinion in Plessy v. Ferguson *was rendered by Justice Henry B. Brown. Brown endorsed the argument of Louisiana that it was constitutionally permissible to mandate "equal but separate accommodations" for black and white train passengers. (The more famous phrase, "separate but equal," appears only in Justice Harlan's dissent.)*

We consider the underlying fallacy of the plaintiff's argument to consist in the assumption that the enforced separation of the two races stamps the colored race with a badge of inferiority. If this be so, it is not by reason of anything found in the act, but solely because the colored race chooses to put that construction upon it. The argument necessarily assumes that if, as has been more than once the case, and is not unlikely to be so again, the colored race should become the dominant power in the state legislature, and should enact a law in precisely similar terms, it would thereby relegate the white race to an inferior position.

We imagine that the white race, at least, would not acquiesce in this assumption. . . . Legislation is powerless to eradicate racial instincts, or to abolish distinctions based upon physical differences, and the attempt to do so can only result in accentuating the difficulties of the present situation. If the civil and political rights of both races be equal, one cannot be inferior to the other civilly or politically. If one race be inferior to the other socially, the constitution of the United States cannot put them upon the same plane.

Justice Harlan's Dissent

Justice John Marshall Harlan was the sole dissenter in Plessy v. Ferguson. *He argued that the segregation law in Louisiana violated the "true intent and meaning" of the Thirteenth and Fourteenth Amendments.*

The white race deems itself to be the dominant race in this country. And so it is, in prestige, in achievements, in education, in wealth, and in power. So, I doubt not, it will continue to be for all time, if it remains true to its great heritage, and holds fast to the principles of constitutional liberty. But in view of the constitution, in the eye of the law, there is in this country no superior, dominant, ruling class of citizens. There is no caste here. Our constitution is color-blind, and neither knows nor tolerates classes among citizens.

In respect of civil rights, all citizens are equal before the law. The humblest is the peer of the most powerful. The law regards man as man, and takes no account of his surroundings or of his color when his civil rights as guarantied by the supreme law of the land are involved. It is therefore to be regretted that this high tribunal, the final expositor of the fundamental law of the land, has reached the conclusion that it is competent for a state to regulate the enjoyment by citizens of their civil rights solely upon the basis of race.

In my opinion, the judgment this day rendered will, in time, prove to be quite as pernicious as the decision made by this tribunal in the *Dred Scott Case.*

The Court had sanctioned Jim Crowism. What comfort African Americans derived from the case had to be found in the strong dissenting opinion of Justice Harlan, who once again proved himself to be a staunch champion of a broad interpretation of the Reconstruction amendments. Harlan construed the ban on slavery to cover segregation laws; he insisted on Tourgée's thesis that a railroad was a public highway and that under the Fourteenth Amendment government could make no racial distinctions whether one considered the case under the privileges and immunities, due process, or equal protection clauses of that amendment. Harlan attacked the Court's reliance on pre-Fourteenth Amendment precedents; his most memorable language appeared in connection with his charge that the majority usurped constitutional power by assuming authority to decide on the "reasonableness" of state social legislation:

The white race deems itself to be the dominant race in this country. And so it is, in prestige, in achievements, in education, in wealth, and in power. So, I doubt not that it will continue to be for all time, if it remains true to its great heritage and holds fast to the principles of constitutional liberty. But in view of the Constitution, in the eye of the law, there is in this country no superior, dominant, ruling class of citizens. There is no caste here. Our Constitution is color-blind, and neither knows nor tolerates classes among citizens. In respect of civil rights, all citizens are equal before the law.

Harlan turned out to be a competent soothsayer:

The destinies of the two races in this country are indissolubly linked together, and the interests of both require that the common government of all shall not permit the seeds of race hate to be planted under the sanction of law.

SIGNIFICANCE

Despite Harlan's impassioned words, it would take the general public and the justices of the Supreme Court decades to adopt his views and interpretation of the Constitution.

Plessy v. Ferguson's strong sanction of segregation lasted formally in transportation until the Court's decision in *Henderson v. United States* (1950) and in education until *Brown v. Board of Education of Topeka, Kansas* (1954). Anti-miscegenation laws were not outlawed until 1967 in *Loving v. Virginia*.

—*James J. Bolner, updated by Brian L. Fife*

See also: Black codes; Thirteenth Amendment Is Ratified; Civil Rights Act of 1866; Fourteenth Amendment Is Ratified; Mississippi Constitution Disfranchises Black Voters

SEPARATE BUT EQUAL DOCTRINE IS CREATED

1896

The proposition that equal protection of all citizens under the law as guaranteed by the Fourteenth Amendment is not threatened by social segregation of the races, so long as members of all groups are treated equally originated in a U.S. Supreme Court ruling in an 1896 case, the separate but equal doctrine legalized the practice of segregating public and private facilities and services by race, which was particularly common in the southern states.

In *Plessy v. Ferguson* (1896), the Supreme Court made a distinction between political rights, which are protected under the Constitution, and social conditions, which are not legally protected. It held that social conditions related to race, such as segregation, were natural, inevitable, and not necessarily an indication of the inferiority or superiority of one race over another. This ruling reflected the federal government's growing willingness during the late nineteenth century to strike a compromise with the South on the issue of freed slaves' rights as citizens. The federal government's desire to gain the full participation of the former Confederate states in the Union affected its attitude toward segregation and other racial issues.

The separate but equal doctrine negatively affected the legal gains made by African Americans during the early Reconstruction period after the Civil War. The Court's ruling in *Plessy* legitimized the state laws establishing and enforcing racial segregation, known as Jim Crow laws, that proliferated throughout the South beginning in the 1880's. Whites-only and blacks-only neighborhoods were upheld as socially and legally correct. Transportation in all its forms—railroad cars, steamships, and buses—was likewise segregated. Separate facilities or entrances for whites and African Americans to such public and private places as schools, churches, restaurants, libraries, hotels, public parks, healthcare centers, and theaters became commonplace. Even water fountains, public restrooms, waiting areas, and public telephones became designated as either for whites or African Americans.

The social segregation of the races led to the firm entrenchment of a separate but unequal social system. Consequently, the social distance between whites and African Americans that had existed during slavery was maintained, although with new norms and practices. This system had a tremendous impact on generations to follow, both in terms of people's attitudes toward members of minorities and in the opportunities African Americans were able to pursue. The separate but equal doctrine was not reversed until 1954 in *Brown v. Board of Education*.

—*Pamela D. Haldeman*

See also: *Brown v. Board of Education*; *Louisville, New Orleans, and Texas Railway Company v. Mississippi*; *McLaurin v. Oklahoma State Regents for Higher Education*; *Missouri ex rel. Gaines v. Canada*; *Plessy v. Ferguson*; Reconstruction; Segregation

NATIONAL ASSOCIATION OF COLORED WOMEN
July, 1896

The National Association of Colored Women became an umbrella group for African American women's organizations at both state and local levels.

Identification: Women's organization founded to improve the lives of African American people in the United States and to help them achieve full citizenship rights
Place: Washington, D.C.

Near the end of the eighteenth century, grave concerns about African Americans being treated as second-class citizens compelled a group of African American women to move beyond their local and state associations to devise plans for the formation of a national body that would systematically and professionally address the problems that they believed threatened the very survival of African Americans. Economic disparities, political disfranchisement, and social ostracism presented the greatest threats to African American aspirations for freedom and inclusion in the American system of democracy. Meeting at the Nineteenth Street Baptist Church in Washington, D.C., in July, 1896, the National Federation of Afro-American Women and the National League of Colored Women joined forces to form a national organization known as the National Association of Colored Women (NACW).

Operating through a series of departments and a strong executive cabinet, the NACW became an umbrella group for African American women's organizations at both state and local levels. The organization's official publication, *National Notes*, served as an instrument to unite the women and to educate them in the concepts and techniques of reform, advocating racial uplift, improved race relations, and protection of women. From its inception, the NACW has worked to improve the lives of African American people in the United States and to help them achieve full citizenship rights.

—*Alvin K. Benson*

See also: Colored Women's League; Combahee River Collective; Million Woman March; National Black Women's Political Leadership Caucus; National Council of Negro Women

WILLIAMS V. MISSISSIPPI
April 25, 1898

In Williams v. Mississippi, *the Supreme Court ignored a ruling it had made a dozen years earlier and upheld the murder conviction of an African American in a trial in which no African Americans served on the jury.*

The Case: U.S. Supreme Court ruling on jury composition

Williams, an African American from Mississippi, had been convicted of murder by an all-white jury. Williams argued, in line with *Yick Wo v. Hopkins* (1886), that his indictment and conviction by all-white grand and petit juries violated the Fourteenth Amendment's equal protection clause. At the time in Mississippi, African Americans were effectively excluded from jury service because only qualified voters could serve, and poll taxes and literacy tests rendered most African Americans unable to vote. The Court distinguished *Yick Wo* and its principle that a racially fair law could be voided if it administered in a discriminatory manner from the facts of this case, saying that Williams did not prove that the actual practice of Mississippi's suffrage laws was unfair. As a result of this ruling, other southern states quickly followed Mississippi and passed laws designed to prevent African Americans from voting. White primaries, poll taxes, and literacy tests became common in the South until white primaries were banned in the 1940's and discriminatory voting practices were stopped by the 1964 and 1965 Voting Rights Acts.

—*Richard L. Wilson*

See also: *Batson v. Kentucky*; Council of Federated Organizations; *Edmonson v. Leesville Concrete Company*; Fourteenth Amendment; *Powers v. Ohio*; *Strauder v. West Virginia*; Voting Rights Act of 1965

WILMINGTON RACE RIOT OF 1898

November 19, 1898

Also known as: the Wilmington Insurrection
Location: Wilmington, North Carolina

KEY FIGURE

Alexander Manly (1866–1944) African-American newspaper owner and editor in Wilmington, North Carolina

In August 1898, Alexander Manly, the editor of the state's only daily African American newspaper *The Daily Record*, published an editorial that enraged white citizens. He argued that the sexual relationships between poor white women and black men be in fact, often consensual as a rebuttal to an article published in the white newspaper, the *Wilmington Messenger* that claimed that black men sexually violated white women. Black men stood accused of rape as a means to justify lynching and to take away their property.

Several months later, Alfred Moore Waddell, the leader of Wilmington's White Government League, successfully threatened the African American community before the November 1898 election, leaving Republicans in the mayoral and alderman seats, only because they were not up for re-election in that year. Democrats took over the legislature with African Americans attempting to vote in the election even after facing intimidation and threats. On August 10, 1898, Waddell and his committee decided to riot. They burned Manly's press, even though Manley left the city earlier, and wounded and killed black leaders in the city. The Wilmington Light Infantry which served in the Spanish-American War, with black soldiers in Company K, became involved and used to two cannons to subdue rioters. At the end of the riots, the mob killed at least ten African Americans, though no one knows the exact numbers. Some have argued up to three hundred died. Many African Americans fled the city, including more than four hundred women and children who immediately ran into the woods to escape harm and over fourteen hundred African Americans leaving in the next few weeks.

African Americans, including North Carolina writer Charles Chesnutt, spoke against the massacre. The incident raised fears amongst African Americans and would be the first of many such riots over the next three decades ushering a new era of Jim Crow and white supremacy.

JOPLIN POPULARIZES RAGTIME MUSIC AND DANCE

1899

Scott Joplin's ragtime composition "Maple Leaf Rag," the first song to sell more than one million copies of sheet music in the United States, ignited a musical and dance craze that swept the country. Ragtime, the first truly American form of music, greatly influenced the development of jazz.

Locale: United States
Categories: Music; dance

KEY FIGURES

Scott Joplin (1868-1917), influential composer of classic piano rags
James Scott (1886-1938), prominent composer of technically difficult rags
John Stark (1841-1927), music publisher

SUMMARY OF EVENT

In 1899, the tiny midwestern publishing company John Stark & Son published a piece of piano music entitled "Maple Leaf Rag" by a little-known African American pianist and composer named Scott Joplin. The irresistible instrumental composition quickly became a national success and ushered in a ragtime craze that swept the United States in the early years of the twentieth century. Copies of the sheet music for rags and ragtime songs, written by scores of composers, both black and white, were sold by the thousands.

The most immediately distinctive feature of ragtime music is its bouncy, syncopated rhythm. The pulse and bounce of ragtime is achieved by a balancing of rhythms between the pianist's left and right hands. The steady, even rhythms played by the left hand provide the basis for the syncopated melodies and counter-rhythms supplied by the right hand. ("Syncopated" refers to rhythms that accent the offbeats, rather than the regular beats that are normally accented.) In ragtime's heyday, the music was played everywhere—from honky-tonks and clubs to middle-class parlors. In the motion-picture theaters that were springing up in the early years of the twentieth century, ragtime piano players provided live accompaniment for many silent films. Ragtime was the first music of African American derivation that crossed over to reach a wide white audience (discounting the clichéd, bastardized music used in minstrel shows), and it did so at a time of deeply entrenched discrimination and segregation.

Ragtime grew out of African American folk music, with its emphasis on lively, syncopated rhythms that urged listeners to dance. Ragtime could have evolved only in the United States, as in many ways it is actually a combination of African musical traditions (as passed on and adapted by generations of African slaves in the American South) and European musical forms such as the march. There is a significant difference, however, between rags and earlier African American musical forms: Rags were written down in standard European-style

Front cover of the third edition of the "Maple Leaf Rag" sheet music, By Scott Joplin, published by John Stark

musical notation. "Maple Leaf Rag" was not the first rag ever written or published, and Joplin was not the first ragtime composer.

Different sources date the beginnings of ragtime anywhere from the 1840's to the 1890's. By the 1890's, there were a number of African American piano players in cities and towns along the Mississippi River who were playing in a style that was becoming known as "rag" or "rag time" music. By 1895 or 1896, music had been published that was ragtime in nature, if not in name. "Mississippi Rag," a composition by white Chicago bandleader William Krell that was published in 1897, is often cited as the first published rag. "Harlem Rag," by black pianist Tom Turpin, was published later that year. It was the success of Joplin's "Maple Leaf Rag," however, that launched the ragtime craze nationally.

Born in 1868, Joplin moved to St. Louis during the mid-1880's, before he was twenty years old. He was already an accomplished pianist. He moved to Chicago in 1893 and to Sedalia, Missouri, a few years later. This move, made because Sedalia's large red-light district could provide employment for a black pianist, turned out to be propitious. In Sedalia were both a new college for African Americans and a white music publisher named John Stark. The George R. Smith College for Negroes (which merged with Philander Smith College in Little Rock, Arkansas, in 1933) gave Joplin the chance to study music theory and notation. Then, in the summer of 1899, Stark heard Joplin performing in the Maple Leaf Club, for which the most famous of all piano rags was named. Stark was impressed, and he agreed to publish "Maple Leaf Rag"—two other publishers had turned it down—and signed Joplin to a five-year contract. The huge success of "Maple Leaf Rag" brought Joplin fame and, if not riches, at least a measure of financial security.

The song's success shifted the ragtime phenomenon into high gear. Joplin was one of the most prolific composers of instrumental piano rags, writing about thirty himself and another six or seven in collaboration with others. Among the many Joplin rags that appeared in the first years of the twentieth century were "Peacherine Rag" (1901), "The Entertainer" (1902), and "Palm Leaf Rag: A Slow Drag" (1903). Joplin was a particularly influential ragtime figure both because his sheet music sold so many copies and because his work was admired by other ragtime musicians and composers. Other notable composers of piano rags included James Scott, Joseph Lamb, Tom Turpin, and Scott Hayden (a Joplin protégé). Turpin's "Harlem Rag" and "St. Louis Rag" and Scott's "Frog Legs Rag" and "Hilarity Rag" became standards in the ragtime repertoire. Scott, like Joplin, started young; he had published two rags by the time he was seventeen. Scott's rags are particularly difficult to play, and his music has been called more flamboyant than those of Joplin. Lamb, a white devotee of Joplin's style, is sometimes considered the third great composer of classic rags (alongside Joplin and Scott). There were also a number of women ragtime composers; May Aufderheide's "Dusty Rag," from 1908, was one of the most popular rags written by a woman.

A distinction should be made among "classic" ragtime (instrumental piano rags), ragtime songs, and the more general use of the term "ragtime" to denote an era and nearly any up-tempo music or dance of the time. A piano rag, strictly speaking, is an instrumental composition. Ragtime songs, less complex than the rags, had both music and words (many of which perpetuated grotesquely stereotyped and racist views of black life). The term "ragtime" is now often used in a general sense to evoke a bygone era existing between the 1890's and the 1920's—a slower, quieter time of pre-World War I innocence and optimism. In this sense, "ragtime" has

come to refer to a range of music and dances of the time before the jazz age, including rags, cakewalks, novelty songs, and the popular songs turned out by early Tin Pan Alley composers and musicians.

The defining characteristic of the classic rags was their inventive syncopation, but by 1910 or so, publishers were referring to nearly any up-tempo popular song as "ragtime." The famous song "Alexander's Ragtime Band," for example, written by Irving Berlin in 1911, contains virtually no syncopation. As "Maple Leaf Rag" can in some ways symbolize the beginning of ragtime, so the hugely popular "Alexander's Ragtime Band" symbolizes its coming end. By 1915, ragtime had become watered down by commercial imitation and, as a creative musical form, had run its course.

SIGNIFICANCE

Although the ragtime era lasted for only twenty years at most after publication of the first rag, the effects of the music were felt much longer. Ragtime influenced both the development of jazz and, to a much lesser extent, twentieth century classical music. It would be wrong to claim that ragtime developed into jazz, but jazz would not have developed quite the way it did had it not been for ragtime. One major contribution that ragtime made to jazz was simply the role of the piano. As the music that was evolving into jazz moved from the parade into the dance hall, honky-tonk, and brothel, the piano began to assume greater importance. The early jazz players' approach to the piano was deeply indebted to ragtime.

There was considerable cultural resistance to the ragtime craze, some of it coming from guardians of morality and some from arbiters of musical taste. Many conservative community leaders considered rags and ragtime dances to be destructive to the morals of youth, much as jazz and rock and roll would be deplored in later generations. There was undeniably a racist element in many of these arguments. Ragtime was also hotly debated in music societies, magazines, and journals, with many classical musicians excoriating it. One conductor declared that ragtime "poisons the taste of the young"; a classical pianist likened it to a "dog with rabies" that had to be exterminated. Nevertheless, ragtime elements began to appear in the work of more open-minded and influential twentieth century composers, both in Europe and in the United States.

Three European composers notable for their inclusion of rag-like musical figures were Claude Debussy, Erik Satie, and Igor Stravinsky. American composers drawing upon ragtime have ranged from Henry Gilbert to John Alden Carpenter, but the best known are Charles Ives and George Gershwin. All four were seeking to write classical music with a uniquely American sound; among the sources with which they experimented were spirituals, hymns, folk songs, American Indian music, ragtime, and jazz.

Although ragtime music had faded from mass popularity by World War I, it never quite disappeared. Any piano players who entertained by playing "old-time" or honky-tonk piano had ragtime pieces or ragtime-influenced songs in their repertoire. Moreover, a number of performers and composers (including Eubie Blake, who lived to the age of one hundred) kept the style alive and passed it on to new generations.

During the 1940's, periodic ragtime revivals began occurring, reflecting both the interest and the evolving stylistic interpretations of new devotees. The biggest single ragtime revival occurred in the early and middle 1970's. In the ensuing years, popular interest in ragtime waned once again, but the many recordings and performances of ragtime, as well as the substantial body of scholarship on the music, ensure Joplin and ragtime a secure place in the history of American music.

—*McCrea Adams*

See also: First Minstrel Shows.

CUMMING V. RICHMOND COUNTY BOARD OF EDUCATION
December 18, 1899

The Supreme Court refused to enforce the equal stipulation in the separate but equal doctrine governing segregated schools that had been established in its landmark 1896 decision.

The Case: U.S. Supreme Court ruling on separate but equal doctrine

Just three years after announcing the separate but equal doctrine in *Plessy v. Ferguson* (1896), the Supreme Court unanimously refused to take action in a case in which school facilities for black and white people were definitely unequal. Cumming, which amounted to the Court's first approval of racially segregated public schools, was never overturned. John Marshall Harlan, who wrote the opinion for the Court, had dissented vigorously in *Plessy* but was unable to find a clear, unmistakable disregard of equality in *Cumming*.

In 1879 the Augusta, Georgia, school board had established the first African American public high school in the state. The board closed the school in 1897,

claiming that the money was needed for black primary school education. Because a Georgia statute explicitly provided for separate but equal facilities, the local judge did not bother to consider the U.S. Constitution in overturning the board's judgment. Still, the Georgia supreme court, without offering any significant reasons, overturned the local judge's opinion.

African Americans argued that under the Fourteenth Amendment's equal protection clause, they were entitled to a high school if one was provided for white students. However, Harlan asserted that the African American plaintiffs had to prove the board decision was motivated exclusively by hostility toward African Americans, which was impossible to prove. To reach his decision, Harlan ignored several lower court precedents that went in the opposite direction.

—*Richard L. Wilson*

See also: *Brown v. Board of Education*; Fourteenth Amendment; *Plessy v. Ferguson*

RACE RIOTS OF THE TWENTIETH CENTURY
1901-1992

Race riots both threaten the stability of society and, by their very occurrence, call into question the fundamental fairness of society.

The Events: Urban disorders arising from economic strains and competition among different racial groups

Referring to racial violence in the United States as "race riots" is often misleading. Many race riots were actually one-sided white massacres of African Americans; this was particularly true of those prior to 1921. Nineteenth century race riots were often called "slave revolts" or "slave insurrections." These slave revolts were most frequent in the areas of the South where African Americans constituted at least 40 percent of the population. Fearing that slave revolts in one part of the South would trigger similar revolts throughout the South, slaveholders quelled such rebellions quickly and viciously.

Twentieth century race riots differ from nineteenth century riots in both motive and location. Whereas nineteenth century riots were primarily concerned with maintaining the institution of slavery, twentieth century riots—particularly those in the years beforeWorldWar II—were often designed to maintain white supremacy over urban African Americans. Also, where nineteenth century race riots were almost exclusively a southern phenomenon, twentieth century race riots took place in almost every major urban area of America.

1901-1945

Race riots prior to World War II often followed a consistent pattern. In almost all cases, the riots were initiated by whites against African Americans. In only two of the major riots—Harlem, New York, in 1935 and again in 1943—did African Americans initiate the riots. Second, most riots were caused by a white fear of African Americans competing for jobs that previously were held by whites. The rapid movement of African Americans from the South to the urban industrial areas of the North contributed to this fear. Third, most riots took place during the hot and humid summer months when young people were out of school. Finally, the riots were often fueled by rumors—allegations of police brutality against African Americans or allegations of black violence against whites heightened racial tensions.

One of the major race riots during this period occurred in East St. Louis, Illinois, in 1917. An automobile occupied by four whites drove through black areas firing shots. When a similar car was seen, African Americans opened fire and killed two occupants, both of whom were police officers. Whites invaded the black community, burning three hundred homes and killing fifty African Americans. The summer of 1919 saw twenty riots in communities such as Charleston, South Carolina; Washington, D.C.; Knoxville, Tennessee; and Chicago. The riots of 1919 were so bloody that the period was called the "Red Summer."

POST-WORLD WAR II RIOTS

Although post-World War II riots were fueled by rumor and also took place during the summer months, they differed from pre-World War II riots in two important ways. First, a majority of the riots were initiated by African Americans, not whites. Second, many of the post-World War II riots were not confined to the black community. In several cases, whites were singled out as victims of black violence. The race riots of the 1960's threatened to destroy the fabric of American society. The 1964 Harlem riot in New York City and the 1965 Watts riot in Los Angeles were both triggered by police incidents. The Watts riot lasted six days and resulted in thirty-four deaths and four thousand arrests. "Burn, baby, burn" became a battle cry in black ghettos throughout the United States.

The year 1967 brought major riots to Newark, New Jersey, and to Tampa, Cincinnati, Atlanta, and Detroit. Newark's riot was the most severe, resulting in twenty-seven deaths and at least fifteen million dollars in property damage. The assassination of Martin Luther King, Jr., on April 4, 1968, triggered racial violence in more than one hundred cities. In response to the urban racial violence, President Lyndon B. Johnson appointed the National Advisory Commission on Civil Disorders, better known as the Kerner Commission. After investigating the causes of the rioting the commission presented a series of recommendations. According to the Kerner Commission, the most important grievances of the black community were police practices, lack of employment opportunities, and inadequate housing. The ominous conclusion of the Kerner Commission was that unless the causes of urban violence were addressed, the United States would continue to become two societies, one black, one white—separate and unequal.

1980's AND 1990's

Although there was a lull in race riots during the 1970's, the Miami riots in May of 1980 signaled a renewal of urban racial unrest. On December 17, 1979, a black insurance agent, Arthur McDuffie, was stopped by Miami police officers after a high-speed chase. A fight ensued, and McDuffie was beaten to death. The police officers engaged in a cover-up and reported that McDuffie died as a result of a motorcycle crash. When the cover-up unraveled, five Miami police officers were arrested. Four were charged with manslaughter, and one was charged with tampering with evidence. After deliberating less than three hours, an all-white jury found all defendants not guilty. Within hours of the verdict, the Liberty City section of Miami exploded in violence. Before order was restored three days later, eighteen people were dead, including eight whites who had the misfortune to be driving through Liberty City when the riot began.

The riot that took place in Los Angeles in May of 1992 was triggered by a similar event. Almost immediately after four white police officers were acquitted of assault in the videotaped beating of Rodney King, a black man, one of the most violent race riots in American history broke out. Before it was over, more than sixty people had died, more than four thousand fires had

been set, and Los Angeles had suffered property damage totaling more than a billion dollars.

Although the patterns of racial violence may have altered over the decades, the fact remains that race riots continue to occur. Once a southern phenomenon, they have become a national problem in search of a solution.

—Darryl Paulson

See also: Black codes; Black Power movement; Chicago riots; Civil Rights movement; Clinton massacre; King beating case; League of Revolutionary Black Workers; Los Angeles riots; Miami riots; National Advisory Commission on Civil Disorders; Race riots of 1866; Race riots of 1943; Race riots of 1967; Watts riot

TALENTED TENTH

1903

Du Bois's idea of a Talented Tenth of black leadership reflected the changing spirit of black activism in early twentieth century America, offering a new synthesis of black protest thought that would influence the early Civil Rights movement.

Definition: Term coined by W. E. B. Du Bois to denote a black intellectual elite that he hoped would provide the leadership necessary to facilitate the advancement of African Americans

The first African American to receive a doctoral degree from Harvard University, W. E. B. Du Bois drew upon a tradition of northern-based black intellectualism predating the Civil War to promote the development of a classically trained vanguard of "leaders, thinkers, and artists" to educate and uplift oppressed, lower-class African Americans. Du Bois's Talented Tenth proposal was largely a response to accommodationists such as Booker T. Washington, who emphasized vocational education as a means for African Americans to establish themselves economically and socially in a manner nonthreatening to whites.

Originally a follower of Washington, Du Bois began to dissent from accommodationist policy when Washington's emphasis on industrial education and his influence with northern philanthropists drew resources away from southern liberal arts colleges such as Atlanta University, where Du Bois was a professor of sociology.

Although Du Bois's scathing criticisms of accommodationism echoed those of other "radical" black leaders such as William Monroe Trotter, who denounced Washington as a race traitor, Du Bois's call for a Talented Tenth was essentially an elitist variation of the doctrine of self-help and racial solidarity that was at the core of accommodationism.

Like Washington, Du Bois advocated education as a means of strengthening black communities by alleviating social pathologies brought on by generations of oppression and cultural alienation. While recognizing the necessity of vocational training for young African Americans, Du Bois insisted that the true aim of education was "not to make men carpenters (but) to make carpenters men" by imbuing them with a sense of culture and an elevated awareness of their place in the world. To accomplish this, Du Bois argued, it would be necessary to maintain a small number of quality liberal-arts institutions for African Americans dedicated to developing and motivating liberally educated black teachers and professionals.

IMPACT

The idea of a Talented Tenth of black leadership is significant not only as the essence of Du Bois's racial policy but also as a reflection of the changing spirit of black activism in early twentieth century America. By combining elements of accommodationism with strains of postbellum agitation, Du Bois advanced a new synthesis of black protest thought that exerted considerable influence upon the early Civil Rights movement; at the heart of this synthesis was his advocacy of leadership by the Talented Tenth.

The Niagara Movement, organized by Du Bois in 1905, consisted mainly of upper- and middle-class black intellectuals from northern states and emphasized agitation as a means of protest. In 1909, key members of the Niagara Movement, including Du Bois, joined forces with progressive upper- and middle-class whites to establish the National Association for the Advancement of Colored People (NAACP), whose strategy of legalism and direct action relied heavily upon the leadership of attorneys and academics. Despite the success of this

strategy of legalism and the prominent leadership of scholars such as Martin Luther King, Jr., enthusiasm for the idea of a Talented Tenth waned through the twentieth century as the focus of the Civil Rights movement shifted from the interests of a biracial elite to those of a predominantly black working class.

—Michael H. Burchett

See also: Atlanta Compromise; Black cabinet; Black colleges and universities; Civil Rights movement; Education; National Association for the Advancement of Colored People; Founding of the Niagara Movement

FOUNDING OF THE NIAGARA MOVEMENT

July 11, 1905

The Niagara Movement, which was founded by W. E. B. Du Bois and William Monroe Trotter, attempted to elevate the position of African Americans in the United States at the beginning of the twentieth century.

Also known as: Niagara Falls Conference
Locale: Fort Erie, Ontario, Canada
Categories: Civil rights and liberties; social issues and reform; organizations and institutions

KEY FIGURES

W. E. B. Du Bois (1868-1963), African American historian, sociologist, and newspaper editor

Booker T. Washington (1856-1915), influential African American leader and founder of the Tuskegee Institute

Theodore Roosevelt (1858-1919), president of the United States, 1901-1909

William Howard Taft (1857-1930), president of the United States, 1909-1913

Andrew Carnegie (1835-1919), American steel manufacturer and philanthropist

William Monroe Trotter (1872-1934), American newspaper editor

SUMMARY OF EVENT

The Niagara Movement was formed largely as a response to the indifference of local, state, and federal authorities to the plight of blacks in the United States. Despite the promises of the Civil War and Reconstruction,

lynching and mob violence went unchecked throughout the South during the Jim Crow period (1881-1914). Outbreaks of rioting were also common in the North at

Founders of the Niagara Movement, 1905

this time. By the end of the nineteenth century, interracial violence had become a national problem.

In the first two decades of the twentieth century, the three most important spokesmen for the rights of blacks in the United States were Booker T. Washington, W. E. B. Du Bois, and William Monroe Trotter. Washington, who was an adviser to Theodore Roosevelt and a friend to white millionaires, counseled blacks to practice accommodation. He drew sharp attacks from Du Bois, editor of the newspaper *The Crisis*, and Trotter, editor of the Boston newspaper *The Guardian*, for his insistence that blacks should settle for vocational education instead of striving for higher education.

The philosophical division between Washington's supporters, known as the Bookerites, and his detractors, the anti-Bookerites, became even more apparent after a riot that took place in Boston. Trotter had arranged to confront Washington at a public meeting to be held in the Columbus Avenue African Methodist Episcopal Zion Church. When Washington was introduced to the two thousand people in attendance, a riot ensued in which one person was stabbed and Trotter himself was arrested. As a result of the exaggerated coverage given to the event in the newspapers, the anti-Bookerites received considerable support. Trotter had become, in effect, a martyr for the radical left.

In 1903, Washington began to perceive the need for a militant and unified organization of black Americans. In February, he informed Du Bois of his plan to unite all black spokesmen. With the financial assistance of his friend Andrew Carnegie, Washington arranged for a conference to be held at Carnegie Hall in New York during the first week of January, 1904. Invitations were sent to twenty-eight influential blacks, only eight of whom were anti-Bookerites. Trotter was not invited. The planned meeting was kept secret from the public. Essentially, the conference of 1904 set the groundwork for a more permanent organization. The Bookerites and anti-Bookerites who attended the meeting arrived at a compromise position. They also agreed to appoint a permanent committee, known as the Committee of Twelve, at a later date.

Although the conference gave the appearance of harmony, this facade was shattered later by comments made in the press by Washington and Du Bois. Du Bois became disillusioned with the Committee of Twelve when, in July, 1904, it adopted a more conservative platform than had been agreed on in January and appointed Washington as its chairman. After resigning from the Committee of Twelve in March, 1905, Du Bois, with

the support of Trotter, set about forming a more radical organization. Trotter suggested forming a "strategy board" that would become a national anti-Washington organization. After resolving that no expenses were to be paid by any white benefactors, Du Bois and Trotter met with F. L. McGhee of St. Paul and C. E. Bentley of Chicago to plan a meeting to be held that summer in western New York. Invitations were mailed to black leaders in seventeen states.

On July 11, 1905, twenty-nine black men from all over the United States gathered at Fort Erie, Ontario, on the Canadian side of Niagara Falls, and christened their organization the Niagara Movement. Having learned their lesson from the Committee of Twelve, the men created an executive system of overlapping jurisdictions for their organization to prevent domination by any one member. Du Bois was elected general secretary, and George Jackson, a lawyer from Cincinnati, was elected general treasurer. Both men worked in conjunction with an executive committee made up of the chairmen of the individual states' local chapters. Work was divided among special committees, the most important of which, the Press and Public Opinion Committee, was headed by Trotter. The state committees were assigned the roles of securing just legislation for blacks and of carrying out educational and propaganda functions.

The Niagara Movement's "Declaration of Principles," drafted by Du Bois and Trotter, was a radical document that was the foundation for a radical organization. In blunt language, the document accused the white race of "ravishing and degrading" the black race and pleaded for the cooperation of all men of all races. It also demanded that whites grant blacks suffrage as well as equal civil rights, equal economic opportunities, and equal educational opportunities. Du Bois and Trotter hoped that their fledgling organization would confront Booker T. Washington and his white supporters.

The Tuskegee Machine, led by Washington, opposed the Niagara Movement from the outset. Washington's supporters infiltrated the Niagara Movement and tried to isolate it. Although Washington agreed almost entirely with the Declaration of Principles, he did not agree with the founders' plans for achieving their goals, which included a political emphasis, agitation, and demands for an immediate end to all racial discrimination and lacked attention to economic development.

In spite of the harassment from Tuskegee, the Niagara Movement made considerable progress during its first year. In December, 1906,DuBois reported to the group's 170 members in thirty-four states that the organization had distributed more than one thousand pamphlets. State chapters across the country had worked in conjunction with local protest groups in such major cities as New York and Philadelphia and in the District of Columbia. Members had also demonstrated against a segregated exposition in Jamestown, Virginia, and had protested an amendment to the Hepburn railroad rate bill that legalized segregated passenger seating in trains. When the Niagara Movement convened in Harpers Ferry, West Virginia, in August, 1906, for its second annual conference, the organization's only serious problem seemed to be a lack of funds.

Problems, however, had already begun to surface in the months preceding the meeting, and they continued throughout the year. Early in 1906, Du Bois had angered Trotter by forming a women's auxiliary of the movement. In the fall, a serious breach developed between Trotter and Clement Morgan, the secretary of the Massachusetts state branch. Trotter objected vehemently when Morgan accepted the Republican Party's nomination for a seat in the legislature, thereby violating the movement's rule forbidding members to hold office. In a show of protest, Trotter resigned from the Committee on Arrangements.

Trotter's final break from the Niagara Movement came in the fall of 1906, as plans for another meeting took shape. Trotter proposed that Du Bois be replaced as general secretary and that the head of the Massachusetts branch should be elected, not appointed. After Du Bois and Morgan rejected Trotter's proposals, Trotter formally withdrew his membership in the Niagara Movement in 1908. Trotter's departure was the beginning of the end for the Niagara Movement. Du Bois admitted that his inexperience as a political leader was an obvious factor in the organization's decline. Encouraged by the rift between the founders of the movement, the Tuskegee Machine escalated its attacks against Du Bois in black newspapers. The lack of any formal national headquarters and a regular paid staff also contributed to the movement's decline.

After Trotter's resignation, the group held two more meetings, neither of which had a large attendance. In 1910, the Niagara Movement ceased operations altogether when Du Bois encouraged its members to join the National Association for the Advancement of Colored People (NAACP).

SIGNIFICANCE

Before the Niagara Movement disbanded, this relatively small organization had a significant impact on

---

Declaration of Principles

At the Niagara Movement's founding meeting in July, 1905, the members signed a "Declaration of Principles" that stated beliefs and set forth certain demands in nineteen different areas, including suffrage, public opinion, health, protest, oppression, and agitation. The declaration began with the following five principles.

Progress: The members of the conference, known as the Niagara Movement . . . congratulate the Negro-Americans on certain undoubted evidences of progress in the last decade, particularly the increase of intelligence, the buying of property, the checking of crime, the uplift in home life, the advance in literature and art, and the demonstration of constructive and executive ability in the conduct of great religious, economic, and educational institutions.

Suffrage: At the same time, we believe that this class of American citizens should protest emphatically and continually against the curtailment of their political rights. We believe in manhood suffrage; we believe that no man is so good, intelligent or wealthy as to be entrusted wholly with the welfare of his neighbor.

Civil Liberty: We believe also in protest against the curtailment of our civil rights. All American citizens have the right to equal treatment in places of public entertainment according to their behavior and deserts.

Economic Opportunity: We especially complain against the denial of equal opportunities to us in economic life; in the rural districts of the South this amounts to peonage and virtual slavery; all over the South it tends to crush labor and small business enterprises; and everywhere American prejudice, helped often by iniquitous laws, is making it more difficult for Negro-Americans to earn a decent living.

Education: Common school education should be free to all American children and compulsory. High school training should be adequately provided for all, and college training should be the monopoly of no class or race in any section of our common country. We believe that, in defense of our own institutions, the United States should aid common school education, particularly in the South, and we especially recommend concerted agitation to this end. We urge an increase in public high school facilities in the South, where the Negro-Americans are almost wholly without such provisions. We favor well-equipped trade and technical schools for the training of artisans, and the need of adequate and liberal endowment for a few institutions of higher education must be patent to sincere well-wishers of the race.

American politics. Ever since its founding in 1905, it had denounced President Theodore Roosevelt for his well publicized view that blacks were racially inferior. The Niagara Movement's opposition to Roosevelt reached its peak when soldiers from the all-black Twenty-fifth Infantry regiment had been accused of running rampant through the streets of Brownsville, Texas, killing one man and wounding two others. Roosevelt himself had denounced the soldiers and encouraged his chosen successor, William Howard Taft, to do the same during the presidential campaign of 1908.

In the summer of 1907, at its meeting in Boston, the Niagara Movement set the theme for the coming presidential election by calling on the five hundred thousand black voters of the North to use their votes to defeat Taft. The organization supported Senator Joseph Benson Foraker's bid for the Republican nomination as a gesture of gratitude for his dissent from the majority report by the Committee on Military Affairs on the Brownsville incident. Even though Foraker did not win the nomination, the movement's supporters built up enough political momentum both during and after the election of 1908 to help Woodrow Wilson win the election of 1912.

Although the Niagara Movement ceased to exist after the formation of the NAACP in 1910, it had a definite effect on the formation of the latter organization. The majority of the black founders, including Du Bois and Trotter, came to the NAACP from the Niagara Movement and became the dominant black constituency within the organization. The memory of the financial problems that had plagued the Niagara Movement convinced many of these former members of the need to secure support from liberal whites. The Niagara Movement also served as a catalyst in the shift of the consensus of black thought from the Bookerite doctrine to the protest tradition that was first endorsed by the movement and later adopted by the NAACP. Finally, many of the goals of the Niagara Movement, particularly the emphasis on higher education, material advancement, and voting rights, were adopted by the NAACP. Although it can be said that the Niagara Movement was too radical for its time, the NAACP was undoubtedly an organization whose time had come.

The Niagara Movement's most important legacy, however, was the awareness it fostered among whites of the seriousness of the plight of blacks in the United States. For the first time in the twentieth century, whites were told, in strong language, by blacks themselves that blacks were not inferior beings and that they were entitled to all the rights enjoyed by other Americans. By employing such effective methods as editorializing in black newspapers and organizing local demonstrations, the Niagara Movement prepared the way for the national protest movements of the 1960's.

—Alan Brown

See also: National Association for the Advancement of Colored People Is Founded; Great Northern Migration; Universal Negro Improvement Association Establishes a U.S. Chapter

BLACK SORORITIES AND FRATERNITIES
1905-1963

The nation's first historic Black Greek Letter Organizations (BGLOs) were established in the early 1900s by African American students who had been prohibited from becoming members of traditionally white collegiate organizations. Building into national movements, African American sororal and fraternal organizations have often focused on important social justice issues and served as an important avenue for organization during the Civil Rights Movement.

Identification: Foundation of the first historically African American fraternities and sororities.

In the early 1900s, though numerous African Americans were earning degrees from U.S. colleges and universities, on college campuses, African Americans faced discrimination and prejudice, preventing them from taking part in many collegiate organizations and programs, including membership in college fraternities and sororities. Fraternal and sororal collegiate organizations, while often controversial in the 21st century, provide a way for students to organize around important collegiate and social issues and foster networks connecting colleges to businesses, political organizations, and other institutions of the working world, thereby providing opportunities for graduates seeking employment and political opportunities.

The first African American fraternity to achieve national recognition was Alpha Phi Alpha, which was founded at Cornell University in 1906 by Charles Cardoza Poindexter and six other African American students, called, in the lore of the organization, the "Seven Jewels." Unlike some of the white fraternities at the time, which functioned more as secret societies for elite members, Poindexter and the founders of Alpha Phi Alpha focused on outreach and social support for the African American community and this became a hallmark for many of the first generation of Black Greek Letter Organizations (BGLOs). The organization spread quickly, with chapters opening at the historically African American Howard University and at Virginia Union University within a year of the group's founding. In addition to providing an important source of outreach, support, and networking, Alpha Phi Alpha played an important role in the Civil Rights Movement, helping to organize boycotts, protests, and civil rights marches around the nation. Civil Rights Leader Martin Luther King Jr. was one of numerous influential African Americans who were members of the fraternity.

The first African American sororal organization, Alpha Kappa Alpha, was founded by Ethel Hedgeman Lyle and a group of students at Howard University in 1908. Though Alpha Kappa Alpha was founded by African American students, after the sorority was incorporated in 1913, membership was opened to women of any ethnicity. Over the years, Alpha Kappa Alpha became heavily involved in supporting women's literacy programs, though in the 1990s and 2000s, the sorority also began to support programs aimed at encouraging female involvement in technical industries by promoting STEM field education to female students.

The historically African American Howard University in Washington D.C., became a prominent location for new African American sororal and fraternal organizations. In 1911, Edgar Love, Frank Coleman, and Oscar Cooper, founded the African American fraternity

Omega Psy Phi at Howard, believing that it was important to found an African American fraternal organization at the predominantly African American institution. The nation's second African American sorority also formed at Howard University when, in 1913, there was a dispute between members of Alpha Kappa Alpha regarding the organization's name, symbol, and motto. A group of dissenting AKA sisters left to form Delta Sigma Theta in January and, in March of that year, helped to organize members for a women's suffrage march in Washington, D.C.. Another African American fraternity, Phi Beta Sigma, was established at Howard University in 1914 by Memphis native A. Langston Taylor, who decided to open the fraternity to men of any ethnicity, thereby making Phi Beta Sigma the first fraternity founded by African Americans, but open to students of any race.

The National Pan-Hellenic Council, a unifying body for the various African American Greek-letter organizations, was founded in 1930 with the purpose of allowing the organizations to work together on key national and collegiate issues. The organization originally included eight organizations, Alpha Phi Alpha (1906, Cornell University), Alpha Kappa Alpha (1908, Howard University), Kappa Alpha Psi (1911, Indiana University), Omega Psy Phi (1911, Howard University), Delta Sigma Theta (1913, Howard University), Phi Beta Sigma (1914, Howard University), Zeta Phi Beta (1920, Howard University) and Sigma Gamma Rho (1922, Butler University). In 1963, a ninth organization was added with the formation of Iota Phi Theta at Morgan State University. During the civil rights era, the National Pan Hellenic Council played an important role in inspiring and organizing local and national protests, boycotts, and college demonstrations. The pioneering organizations, now known as the "Divine Nine," inspired dozens of other African American fraternities and sororities in subsequent decades and played an important role in the history of African American rights and education.

—*Micah Issitt*

BROWNSVILLE INCIDENT

August 13, 1906

The Brownsville incident illustrated the strong currents of racism that ran through early twentieth century America and the presumptions white Americans

had about black behavior and the rights of African Americans in the military. The case was also one of the most serious lapses in the public record of

President Theodore Roosevelt and a graphic example of the limits of his tolerance for black Americans during his presidency.

The Event: Shooting incident that was unfairly blamed on a contingent of African American soldiers
Place: Brownsville, Texas

On August 13, 1906, a shooting incident occurred in Brownsville, Texas. White residents of the border town blamed a detachment of African American soldiers that had recently been stationed at nearby Fort Brown. According to local police reports, one person was killed and another wounded. Suspicion immediately fell on the black soldiers, and the officials in the U.S. Army concluded that the African American soldiers had been responsible for the incident. Physical evidence, however, showed that they had not been involved and the most probable explanation for the episode was that white citizens had staged the event to discredit the soldiers. The soldiers denied any knowledge of what had taken place.

The Army and President Theodore Roosevelt concluded that the men of the Twenty-fifth Infantry Regiment had been responsible for the shooting. Their failure to reveal what had taken place and their protestations of innocence were, in the minds of their white superior officials, proof of their guilt. The president ordered that all 167 black soldiers in the regiment should be dismissed from military service without trial and without pay. Shortly after the congressional elections of 1906, the soldiers were compelled to leave the Army.

The weakness of the government's case against the soldiers attracted the attention of conservative Republican senator Joseph B. Foraker of Ohio, who became a staunch defender of the soldiers and pressed for congressional probes into what had really happened. His opposition to Roosevelt on other issues had caused a rupture in his friendship with the president. Their disagreement over the Brownsville incident intensified their quarrel, and they clashed in public about the controversy in January, 1907. Roosevelt remained adamant that the accused men were guilty and used the full powers of the federal government to buttress his case. The War Department even hired private investigators to find damaging evidence against the soldiers, largely without success.

Despite congressional efforts to reduce the penalties that the black soldiers had suffered, these efforts produced few lasting results. Protests by African American groups in the North also failed to sway Roosevelt from his first hasty judgment about the men's guilt. Foraker left Congress in 1909 still convinced of the men's innocence.

The issue gradually faded from history and did not resurface until 1970, when John D. Weaver published *The Brownsville Raid.* His vigorous argument for the innocence of the men and the miscarriage of justice that they had suffered attracted public attention. Congressional pressure led the army to grant the men of the regiment honorable discharges more than six decades after their dismissal. Two aged surviving veterans of the unit received public recognition of what they had endured.

—Lewis L. Gould

See also: Buffalo soldiers; Military; Tuskegee Airmen; Tuskegee experiment

ATLANTA RACE RIOTS OF 1906

September 22-24, 1906

Location: Atlanta, Georgia

In 1906, in Atlanta, Georgia, Democrat Hoke Smith ran a contest against Clark Howell, in which both candidates ran a platform based on racism which heightened racial tensions in the city. During his period, Thomas Dixon's racist play, "The Clansman," celebrated the Ku Klux Klan and heightened the city's racial tensions. During this same period, Atlanta increased restrictions on African Americans in all areas of life including voting and the implementation of strict "vagrancy" laws which restricted the movement of African Americans, particularly men. Also, the press and white citizens in the city began spreading stories of supposed crimes, including assault, committed by African American men against white women. Atlanta's African American community created and fostered economic, educational, and social institutions that thrived.

On Saturday, September 22, 1906, a white mob on Decatur Street began attacking all African Americans within sight. The small crowd turned into a mob of thousands. They beat, tortured, and killed African American men, women, and children, in the name of "justice." They justified their actions with the argument they did these things in the name of protecting white womanhood against the brutality of black men.

While the exact number of African Americans killed is still unknown, it is estimated that at least twenty-five were murdered in the riot with a high estimate of one hundred total dead. The several-day riot was a defining moment in United States history and was one of the worst in the South.

—*Kathryn M. Silva*

FIRST BLACK HEAVYWEIGHT BOXING CHAMPION
December 26, 1908

Heavyweight boxer Jack Johnson's victory over Tommy Burns alarmed whites, who had dominated boxing, and immediately triggered a quest for a "Great White Hope" to defeat Johnson. This championship boxing match ushered in a new era in American sport history as well as a new period in American race relations.

Locale: Sydney, New South Wales, Australia
Categories: Sports; social issues and reform

KEY FIGURES
Jack Johnson (John Arthur Johnson; 1878-1946), American boxer and heavyweight champion
Tommy Burns (Noah Brusso; 1881-1955), Canadian boxer and heavyweight champion
James Jackson Jeffries (1875-1953), American boxer and heavyweight champion
Jack London (1876-1916), American journalist and author

SUMMARY OF EVENT
The fight between Tommy Burns and Jack Johnson was the biggest news in boxing since the sport's transformation from savage, bare-knuckle prizefighting in the early nineteenth century into the more respectable art of combat. While colorful personalities such as John L. Sullivan, Theodore Roosevelt, and Mike Donovan represented the more gentlemanly aspects of boxing among high society, racial diversity in the squared arena was virtually nonexistent. Jack Johnson represented the destruction of this color barrier.

Born in Galveston, Texas, Johnson remained a relatively obscure figure in American sporting culture until the first decade of the twentieth century. After realizing that his large size limited his abilities as a horse jockey, Johnson turned to boxing, even though post-Civil War segregation laws forbade African American participation in sporting events with whites. He relied on work as a janitor and a sparring partner for most of his income, and in the process he gained a formidable reputation in the Texas boxing community. By 1901 he had decided to leave Galveston for a professional career as a boxer. For

Jack Johnson, 1915, by Bain News Service

the next several years, Johnson won fights against fellow African American boxers and lesser-known white pugilists, although the widespread racial prejudices of the time meant that most white heavyweight champions and contenders avoided Johnson and other African American fighters.

Born in Ontario, Canada, Noah Brusso also came from a poverty-stricken background and held several jobs before deciding on a boxing career. He changed his name to Tommy Burns in order to keep his mother from re-experiencing the embarrassment she felt after her son had brutally pummeled an opponent. In 1906, Burns was crowned the heavyweight champion of the world after the retirement of James Jackson Jeffries in 1905. Jeffries had quit the sport because of declining revenues and the growing movement bent on outlawing prizefighting.

Burns tried to avoid fighting Johnson: He fought matches with white opponents and went abroad to defend his title in England, Ireland, France, and Australia. Johnson followed, fighting several matches in England and pressuring boxing officials to schedule a championship match with Burns. Burns's demand of thirty thousand dollars to fight Johnson was one of the major stumbling blocks, but eventually a fight promoter in Australia agreed to the price. In contrast, Johnson was to be paid five thousand dollars, a sum he grudgingly accepted. As in the United States, racial divisions and discriminatory practices were common in Australia, and the prefight news coverage was replete with racial slurs against Johnson.

Controversy surrounded the match from both sides; one of the biggest arguments was over who would serve as referee, especially given that the fight was to be filmed (an attempt to garner additional revenue). Although the fight was scheduled for 11:00 a.m., huge crowds amassed as early as 6:00 a.m. to witness the spectacle at Rushcutter's Bay in Sydney. Sports enthusiasts and gamblers placed odds in Burns's favor. Entering the ring first to a round of racial insults, Johnson appeared in his familiar faded gray robe and boxing attire; he remained cool and only smiled in response to the venomous verbal abuse. The champion, by contrast, came to the ring in a blue suit, which he removed and placed delicately in a suitcase. Johnson extended his hand to Burns, but the latter refused to shake it. As the men stood face-to-face in the ring, issues regarding bandaged elbows and other potential illegalities immediately arose. However, after consultation with the officials, the match began at 11:07 a.m.

Despite the prefight controversies and troubles, the contest was clearly a mismatch. Johnson, who towered over his opponent, dominated the fight, and Burns was knocked down several times. Johnson clearly wanted to punish and humiliate Burns, who was confident in his abilities to defeat his African American opponent. Each player taunted the other throughout the rounds; Burns levied some especially vulgar slurs. Burns, a white supremacist, believed that black fighters had weaker stomachs, less endurance, and smaller brains than white fighters. At the time, "scientific" theories of race and physicality reinforced Burns's beliefs, and many people thought that Burns's racial heritage would help guarantee his victory.

In the first round, Burns immediately charged toward Johnson, who delivered a right uppercut, his best punch, and put Burns on the mat for an eight count. Throughout the match, Johnson toyed with Burns, landed punches at will, and refrained from scoring an early knockout. As a result, Johnson proved himself to be the more adept and skilled fighter. By the end of the second round, Burns's right eye was visibly swollen and his mouth was bleeding profusely. During the middle rounds, Johnson continued to punish Burns, whose blood began to cover his shoulders and the ring's canvas. Spectators began calling for the contest to end in the thirteenth round, and police entered the ring to stop the fight. However, protests from Burns convinced the referee to let the fight continue. In the fourteenth round, Johnson continued his vicious onslaught, and the police once again entered the ring. This time, the referee stopped the fight—over Burns's desperate cries of protest—because the bloody, battered Burns could no longer defend himself against Johnson's brutal assault. With approximately twenty thousand people in attendance and tens of thousands outside the arena, spectators could not believe what had happened—an African American had won the world heavyweight championship.

Reporting for the *New York Herald*, noted author Jack London expressed his disdain for Johnson's victory and called for the return of James Jeffries, who London said could return the crown to the white race. Like most of his contemporaries, London accepted pseudoscientific notions of white supremacy and believed that Johnson's victory was a great stain on the history of the white race. London's disgust and his cry for Jeffries to return to the ring began the quest for the "Great White Hope": a boxer who would defeat Johnson and restore boxing's title and prestige to white men.

SIGNIFICANCE

The heavyweight championship fight between Johnson and Burns challenged theories about racial superiority and helped break the color line in boxing, especially in championship bouts. African Americans heralded Johnson's victory, which increased black pride, threatened theories of white supremacy, and forever altered the racial makeup of the sporting world. The Johnson victory also led to a renewed interest in prizefighting as some boxing fans hoped for a white heavyweight champion. After numerous challenges from white contenders, including a devastating victory over Jeffries in 1910, Johnson lost the heavyweight title in 1915 to Jess Willard—who was younger, bigger, and white—in round twenty-six of a contest in Havana, Cuba.

—*Nathan Wilson and Raymond Wilson*

SPRINGFIELD RACE RIOT OF 1908

August 14 – 15, 1908

On Friday, August 14, 1908, a white mob gathered around the Springfield jail. That day, Springfield newspapers reported that a white woman, Mabel Hallam, was raped by a black man and that she identified George Richardson as her assailant. A few days prior to this arrest police brought in another African American man, nineteen-year old Joe James, who stood trial for the murder of a white engineer, Clergy Ballard. Joe James, originally from Birmingham, Alabama, stood accused of the murder. Ballard was then stabbed several times by a man who he thought attempted to attack his sixteen-year old daughter in her bedroom. Ballard claimed the assailant was black before he lost consciousness and died. Joe James' trial was postponed for six weeks to prevent a lynching; however, Richardson's arrest brought with it a crowd of five thousand white rioters around the jailhouse. The police took action and removed both black men from the jail and moved them to a secure location. The crowd that gathered became angry upon realizing the two accused men were no longer in the jail. The crowd was not able to lynch the two men and thus, they turned their anger into a two-day riot.

Location: Springfield, Illinois

The rioters, led by saloon owner, Kate Howard, turned to downtown where they destroyed a restaurant. They then descended on the black business district, Levee, where African Americans and whites exchanged gunfire. Several whites were killed and black residents and business owners sought refuge in other parts of the city including in the homes of their employers. The white mob descended on the Badlands section of the city where they continued looted and burning buildings. They lynched Samuel Burton, a fifty-six year old barber, as he tried to escaped ragging his body down the street after shooting him several times. The militia, led by Colonel Shand, reached the city after much destruction and were able to end the riot for the evening and by the next day the city held fourteen hundred troops. African Americans who could not the leave the city sought shelter in the State Arsenal and Camp Lincoln which Governor Charles Deneen designated for their protection. The rioters began the next day, murdering another black citizen and eventually the troops ended the riot.

The rioters were responsible for $120,000 in damaged and theft. Both the cases against Clergy Ballard and George Richardson went to trial. In a trial that took place in Springfield an all-white jury convicted. Ballard was sentenced to death by hanging. The case against George Richardson in the rape of Mabel Hallam also went to trial. However; after testing both the alleged victim and alleged assailant, Hallam was found to have a sexually-transmitted infection and Richardson did not, therefore he could not have assaulted Hallam. The court dismissed the case against George Richardson.

Approximately 115 people rioted and after the incident the state brought 107 indictments against the rioters including the two ringleaders, both local business owners. Two black men and seven white men confirmed dead, killed by African Americans defending their homes and businesses. Out of the 107 indictments, only one person was convicted of theft.

—*Kathryn M. Silva*

NATIONAL ASSOCIATION FOR THE ADVANCEMENT OF COLORED PEOPLE IS FOUNDED

February 12, 1909

With the creation of the National Association for the Advancement of Colored People, African Americans gained a major advocacy organization.

Locale: New York, New York

Categories: Civil rights and liberties; social issues and reform; organizations and institutions

KEY FIGURES

W. E. B. Du Bois (1868-1963), African American historian, sociologist, and newspaper editor

Booker T. Washington (1856-1915), African American educator and founder of the Tuskegee Institute

William Monroe Trotter (1872-1934), African American journalist and newspaper editor

Oswald Garrison Villard (1872-1949), American journalist and newspaper editor

William English Walling (1877-1936), American journalist and labor organizer

Mary White Ovington (1865-1951), American civil rights activist

Thurgood Marshall (1908-1993), African American attorney

SUMMARY OF EVENT

By the beginning of the twentieth century, many of the civil rights achieved by African Americans during the post-Civil War Reconstruction period were under severe attack. Supported by rulings of the U.S. Supreme Court—such as in *Plessy v. Ferguson* (1896), which affirmed the constitutionality of racial segregation—southern states enacted laws that effectively disfranchised most African American voters and barred their access to public institutions on an equal basis with whites. In the North, racial discrimination was not sanctioned as openly, but it remained an underlying assumption of society. Tensions between the two races sometimes flared into violence, taking the forms of lynchings and urban riots. In these confrontations, African Americans were accorded little sympathy by the mainstream press, the courts, or law-enforcement agencies.

Reactions to the deterioration of individual rights varied within the African American community. The most prominent spokesperson for African Americans, educator Booker T. Washington, had adopted a policy of accommodation in the 1890's, urging African Americans to abandon temporarily their drive for civil and political rights and to concentrate instead on acquiring the economic skills that would enable them to find a place in an industrialized United States. Washington believed that if African Americans demonstrated their competence through hard work, American society eventually would grant them the same rights that whites enjoyed. Washington's policies were supported widely by wealthy white philanthropists.

Washington's position, which historians call "gradualism," was countered, although ineffectively at first, by W. E. B. Du Bois, a professor at Atlanta University and founder in 1905 of the Niagara Movement, an organization composed of educated African Americans. Du Bois agonized over the steady erosion of African Americans' rights and viewed protest rather than acquiescence as the most appropriate avenue to equality. Support for this second point of view, called "immediatism," crystallized among both African Americans and whites in 1909 and led to the launch of an organization dedicated to combating racial discrimination in all areas of American life.

The immediate catalyst for the formation of the National Association for the Advancement of Colored People (NAACP) was a bloody race riot that took place in Springfield, Illinois, in August, 1908, during which white mobs destroyed much of the black section of Springfield and lynched two African Americans. The riot left more than fifty African Americans dead or injured, and two thousand African American residents fled the city. The fact that Abraham Lincoln's hometown could be the site of such violence made it clear that racial discrimination and its accompanying violence were not just southern problems.

A group of white liberals began to consider how to rekindle the spirit of moral indignation that had animated the pre-Civil War abolitionists and then channel that indignation into constructive action. William English Walling, a Kentucky journalist and labor organizer, wrote several articles in the *Independent* condemning the Springfield riot and called for a powerful body of citizens to come to African Americans' aid. Early in 1909, Walling met with Mary

White Ovington, the socialist descendant of an abolitionist family, and Henry Moskovitz, a New York social worker, to discuss ways of attracting support for his idea. They invited the grandson of William Lloyd Garrison, Oswald Garrison Villard, to join them, and the group soon expanded to more than fifteen, including two prominent African American clergymen, Bishop Alexander Waters and the Reverend William Henry Brooks.

After initial discussions, the members of this planning committee decided to draw attention to their cause by holding a conference in New York City. On February 12, 1909, sixty prominent African Americans and Euro-Americans signed a "call" to the gathering, which was titled the Conference on the Status of the Negro and was scheduled to be held May 31-June 1, 1909; the call pointed to the discrimination and violence that afflicted African Americans and urged northerners to cast off the "silence that means tacit approval."

Three hundred men and women, including many white liberals, attended the two-day meeting, where they set up a permanent organization and listened to scientific refutations of arguments that persons of African descent were genetically inferior. The most notable African American in attendance was Du Bois, who suggested in a speech that African Americans' problems were as much political as economic. Villard had invited Booker T. Washington to the conference but had told him that the new organization was to be an aggressive one. Under the circumstances, Washington declined to attend.

Washington's absence did not mean the participants were in complete agreement on the course to be taken, however. Heated arguments preceded the selection of the Committee of Forty on Permanent Organization and the passage of resolutions demanding equal rights and protection against violence for African Americans. Leading the opposition to Villard's proposals were William Monroe Trotter, editor of the Boston newspaper *The Guardian,* and J. Milton Waldron, president of the National Negro Political League. Both advocated more radical positions than those favored by the majority. In the end, they were not included in the Committee of Forty.

Throughout the year that followed, Villard and a handful of other committee members struggled to raise funds and plan for a second conference. Despite general indifference from the white press and open disputes with Booker T. Washington, the committee succeeded in formulating an organizational framework for presentation to the conference. The National Committee, which comprised one hundred members, was charged with raising funds and giving prestige to the organization; the smaller Executive Committee, composed primarily of members of the former Committee of Forty, would direct the organization's activities. In an executive session held on May 14, 1910, the group, now bearing the name National Association for the Advancement of Colored People, approved this arrangement.

SIGNIFICANCE

At the NAACP's second conference, Du Bois was appointed director of publicity and research, a move that underscored the aggressive direction the delegates sought to follow. For Du Bois, the post represented an opportunity to redeem his years of frustration with the Niagara Movement. He resigned his faculty position at Atlanta University and moved to New York City. Within six months, he had launched the NAACP magazine, *The Crisis: A Record of the Darker Races,* which soon became a major organ for molding opinion on race issues. The inaugural press run of one thousand copies sold out, and within five years the publication's circulation exceeded fifty thousand.

The NAACP continued to grow throughout the twentieth century. NAACP attorneys, including the future U.S. Supreme Court justice Thurgood Marshall, mounted numerous legal challenges to the institutional segregation that plagued the United States. Marshall argued thirty-two civil rights cases before the Supreme Court on behalf of the NAACP, of which he won twenty-nine. In cases such as *Brown v. Board of Education of Topeka, Kansas* (1954), Marshall and other attorneys with the NAACP's Legal Defense Fund worked to demolish inequality in education, employment, and access to facilities such as restaurants and hotels. The NAACP's efforts to help African American plaintiffs fight racial discrimination on the job and elsewhere continue in the twenty-first century.

The NAACP's successes in fighting racial discrimination have occasionally been accompanied by problems within the organization. In the 1930's, a major rift developed between founder Du Bois and newer members such as Walter White. Internal dissension almost tore the organization apart. Du Bois left, but the organization survived. Similar problems developed in the 1990's. Following the 1993 retirement of Benjamin L. Hooks as executive director of the NAACP, the

The Lincoln's Birthday Call

In 1914, in How the National Association for the Advancement of Colored People Began, *Mary White Ovington told the story of how Abraham Lincoln's birthday, February 12, was chosen as the founding date and how Oswald Garrison Villard, president of the N.Y. Evening Post Company, drafted the "Lincoln's birthday call," reprinted here:*

The celebration of the Centennial of the birth of Abraham Lincoln, widespread and grateful as it may be, will fail to justify itself if it takes no note of and makes no recognition of the colored men and women for whom the great Emancipator labored to assure freedom. Besides a day of rejoicing, Lincoln's birthday in 1909 should be one of taking stock of the nation's progress since 1865.

How far has it lived up to the obligations imposed upon it by the Emancipation Proclamation? How far has it gone in assuring to each and every citizen, irrespective of color, the equality of opportunity and equality before the law, which underlie our American institutions and are guaranteed by the Constitution?

If Mr. Lincoln could revisit this country in the flesh, he would be disheartened and discouraged. He would learn that on January 1, 1909, Georgia had rounded out a new confederacy by disfranchising the Negro, after the manner of all the other Southern States. He would learn that the Supreme Court of the United States, supposedly a bulwark of American liberties, had refused every opportunity to pass squarely upon this disfranchisement of millions, by laws avowedly discriminatory and openly enforced in such manner that the white men may vote and that black men be without a vote in their government; he would discover, therefore, that taxation without representation is the lot of millions of wealth-producing American citizens, in whose hands rests the economic progress and welfare of an entire section of the country.

He would learn that the Supreme Court, according to the official statement of one of its own judges in the Berea College case, has laid down the principle that if an individual State chooses, it may "make it a crime for white and colored persons to frequent the same market place at the same time, or appear in an assemblage of citizens convened to consider questions of a public or political nature in which all citizens, without regard to race, are equally interested."

In many states Lincoln would find justice enforced, if at all, by judges elected by one element in a community to pass upon the liberties and lives of another. He would see the black men and women, for whose freedom a hundred thousand of soldiers gave their lives, set apart in trains, in which they pay first-class fares for third-class service, and segregated in railway stations and in places of entertainment; he would observe that State after State declines to do its elementary duty in preparing the Negro through education for the best exercise of citizenship.

Added to this, the spread of lawless attacks upon the Negro, North, South and West—even in the Springfield made famous by Lincoln—often accompanied by revolting brutalities, sparing neither sex nor age nor youth, could but shock the author of the sentiment that "government of the people, by the people, for the people; should not perish from the earth."

Silence under these conditions means tacit approval. The indifference of the North is already responsible for more than one assault upon democracy, and every such attack reacts as unfavorably upon whites as upon blacks. Discrimination once permitted cannot be bridled; recent history in the South shows that in forging chains for the Negroes the white voters are forging chains for themselves. "A house divided against itself cannot stand"; this government cannot exist half-slave and half-free any better today than it could in 1861.Hence we call upon all the believers in democracy to join in a national conference for the discussion of present evils, the voicing of protests, and the renewal of the struggle for civil and political liberty.

organization endured two stormy years of controversy and dissension. The new executive director, Benjamin F. Chavis, found himself under attack following the disclosure that he used organization funds to settle a lawsuit brought by a former employee. Chavis was fired in 1994, and under the guidance of board chair Myrlie Evers-Williams, the NAACP managed to weather the controversy, although both financial contributions and overall membership declined.

In January, 1996, the NAACP announced that Kweisi Mfume, a forty-seven-year-old African American congressman from Baltimore, Maryland, had accepted the position of chief executive officer. With Mfume assuming a leadership role, the NAACP appeared confident that it would continue to fight for racial equality for many years to come. Mfume suffered some personal controversy, however, and during the presidential elections of 2000 and 2004, the NAACP's open support for the Democratic Party brought into question its official nonpartisan status. Mfume was succeeded by Bruce S. Gordon in June, 2005.

The founding of the NAACP marked the first major attempt since Reconstruction to make African American rights the focus of national reform efforts. The manner of the organization's birth displayed many of the same strengths and weaknesses that characterized it in its early years: a substantial proportion of white leadership and dependence on white financial support, a program emphasizing political and civil rights and seeking change through legislation and judicial decisions, and criticism

from within the black community concerning both of these points. In the early years, the protests were loudest from those, such as Washington, who found the new organization too militant, but even at the outset other critics, such as Trotter, felt it did not go far enough. Despite numerous victories, such as those in the court cases of *Brown v. Board of Education* and *Keyes v. Denver School District No. 1* (1973), those same criticisms continued. Despite the competing demands for aggressive action and for moderation, however, the NAACP managed to move race relations steadily forward for most of the twentieth century.

—*John C. Gardner and Nancy Farm Mannikko*

See also: Founding of the Niagara Movement; Great Northern Migration; Scottsboro Trials.

TENNESEE ADOPTS THE ONE-DROP RULE

1910

Although there is no scientific definition of a "pure" race, some people believe in the "one-drop" rule and wish to keep the dominant group racially "pure" and delegate all "impure" people to the subordinate or stigmatized group.

Definition: A dominant group legally and socially establishing a classification of race, as a social rather than a biological construct, that holds that a person of any race embodying any amount of African ancestry—even as little as "one drop" of blood—should be legally and socially classified as Black.

The one-drop rule originated in the southern United States before the Civil War was rigidly conceptualized. This rule legally and socially established the classification of race as a social rather than a biological construct. It held that a person of any race embodying any amount of African ancestry—even as little as "one drop" of blood—should be legally and socially classified as black. It was first adopted by Tennessee, in 1910, and followed by many other southern states as time went on. As a consequence, a few black-white mixed-race individuals (who

physically appeared to be white) were accepted as white by the dominant white culture, yet children of mixed raced relations whose mothers were African, Mulatto, or Negro were hypodescented (downgraded) to a lower assigned status in society. White attitudes became more rigid at the time of the Civil War, and the one-drop rule became strictly enforced and largely accepted throughout the United States. In 1896, the U.S. Supreme Court (in *Plessy v. Ferguson*) approved the one-drop rule as a legal definition by defining it as "common knowledge."

Although state laws against mixed-race marriages (miscegenation) were declared unconstitutional by the 1967 Supreme Court decision in the *Loving v. Virginia* case, still applied in some states. Socially, some whites supported the rule to maintain seeming "white racial purity," and some freed Africans, Mulattos, and Negros support it to keep from losing members of their own group to the dominant white group. is unique to the United States.

Abraham D. Lavender, updated by Patricia A. McDaniel

See also: Demographic trends; Miscegenation laws; *Plessy v. Ferguson*

HANDY USHERS IN THE COMMERCIAL BLUES ERA

1910's

W. C. Handy transformed the native music of the backwoods, work camps, and cotton fields of the American South into a commercial craze.

Locale: United States
Categories: Music; entertainment

KEY FIGURES

W. C. Handy (1873-1958), American composer and an originator of popular blues
Blind Lemon Jefferson (1897-1929), American bluesman and authority on the blues
Bessie Smith (1894-1937), American blues singer
Ma Rainey (1886-1939), American blues singer

SUMMARY OF EVENT

Along the lower Mississippi River, from Memphis down to New Orleans, the blues evolved during the post-Civil War years. At a train station in Tutwiler, Mississippi, a black musician named W. C. Handy "rediscovered" the blues in 1903 while listening to a guitarist use a knife to strum a song that Handy subsequently wrote down as his own "Yellow Dog Blues." The occasion reminded him that, eight years before, he had heard another lone singer "hollering" his blues. Handy's full enlightenment about this aspect of the Delta cultures surrounding him came as his band, the Knights of Pythias, was playing for a Cleveland, Mississippi, dance later in the year. As bandleader, he was asked to perform "native" music— that is, to play blues. Unable to comply, he allowed three ragged local musicians to do so; when they brought the house down, he realized the music's commercial value. The event changed his career. Handy later laid legitimate claim to the title "father of the blues," and the rest of the nation, within a few decades, would embrace the music.

Although blues music has been identified accurately as part of jazz, its provenance historically, although murky, was separate. Jazz represented a southern confluence of multiracial and multiethnic urban influences that initially were geographically specific to cities of the southern Atlantic and Gulf coasts. The spread of jazz and its fusion with other musical forms was another continuing story.

Blues music, in contrast, has African origins. The music underwent transformation in the rural areas and small towns of the lower Mississippi, and by the late 1890's it was specific to people who performed harsh physical labor in the cotton fields of the large Delta plantations, in mining and logging camps, in levee and railroad construction, in freight loading, and in the perpetually debt-ridden, segregated, unlettered, and depressed worlds of crop-lien and sharecrop farming. The blues were powerfully emotive, and the sole instrument capable of rendering "blue notes" (sung usually between the third and seventh degrees of the scale) was the human voice. Accompaniment, when there was any, was generally by guitar, which merely filled in as a second voice. In their archaic form, the blues' twelve-bar stanzas of three lines each did not even lend themselves to musical notation; the rhythm, rhyme, and subtle poetry were the singer's to provide.

Raw, rural, and steeped in subsistence-level living—although their range of subjects was vast—the blues dealt mainly with inevitabilities: hard labor, death, bad crops, sex, loss of a lover, sickness, low wages, scarce money, drink, jail, and a world awash in other troubles. Nevertheless, there sometimes was also an implicit and wry shared humor in the music, as the purpose of the blues was to alleviate distress by means of the traditional open and candid vocal expression especially common to isolated, segregated, and—in formal terms—unschooled people. Handy himself did not come from such a background. Born in Florence, Alabama, the son of a Methodist minister, he was reared in a household that discouraged music and condemned the life of musicians. Nevertheless, thanks to his teachers, he had by the age of ten shown some musical precocity. Following high school, he spent a year as a cornet player with several bands and with Chicago's Mahara Minstrels; he also spent two years as an instructor at Teacher's Agricultural and Mechanical College for Negroes in Huntsville, Alabama. After that came the revelations in Tutwiler and Cleveland and several more years as a bandleader in Mississippi and Tennessee.

As late as 1907, when Handy and the lyricist-singer Harry Pace started a music publishing business near Memphis's thriving black music center on Beale Street, Handy was still refraining from publishing his own compositions, although he had behind him a quarter century of acquaintance with all types of music and was enamored of the blues. His "Memphis Blues," written on request expressly for the Memphis mayoral campaign of flamboyant Ed Crump in 1909, however, rocked the city and established Handy's songwriting reputation. It was while he was reminiscing about an earlier visit to the notorious Targee Street in St. Louis that he composed what proved to be his world-famous "St. Louis Blues" in 1914. As a sophisticated and urbane musician, Handy effectively added the fruits of his own experience to the archaic rural blues that had captured his imagination in the Mississippi Delta. When he and Pace moved their business to New York in 1918, Handy became the first man to compose the blues formally as well as the first to popularize them commercially.

SIGNIFICANCE

The excitement that attended Handy's "Memphis Blues," the influence of which was initially local, swept New York by 1912. His spectacularly successful "St. Louis Blues," which enjoyed an even more fervent reception in Harlem and soon became nationally popular, introduced the American public to a secondhand and sophisticated blues music that was removed from its rural origins. Blues such as Handy's, which represented the compositions of rather worldly musicians and vaudevillians, became popular throughout the United States. Such music was sung by urbanized cabaret and torch singers, including Ohio's Mamie Smith, whose origins were neither rural nor southern.

What mattered most in catapulting the blues into general recognition and popularity was their recording, and Handy's successes unquestionably encouraged his imitators to move in that direction. Perry Bradford, who had moved from Alabama to Harlem, was foremost in persuading the General Phonograph Company to record Mamie Smith singing his "Crazy Blues" in 1920. This first vocal blues recording, which sold more than a million copies in six months, is regarded as a milestone by music historians. Reaching an immense audience, it constituted a cultural event. Instantly, it brought forth from black communities across the country, where superb music had flourished locally for years, a host of blues composers, singers, and bands who performed for the enjoyment of eager audiences.

The success of Smith's record further encouraged recording companies to tap the hunger of American blacks for reproductions of their authentic music. The subsequent spate of "race records"—a designation that carried proud, rather than pejorative, connotations for the increasingly self-conscious blacks of the 1920's— not only whetted racial pride but also stimulated a search for more genuine blues songs and singers.

No one filled the bill better than Chattanooga's magnificent, if tragic, Bessie Smith, soon to reign as "Empress of the Blues." Before her death in an auto accident, Smith sang with her uniquely poignant voice among a constellation of singers and performers who made the blues a national treasure. Among these personalities were Ma Rainey and several of her protégés, including Bertha "Chippie" Hill and Ida Cox, and a number of young jazz musicians who would use blues as a base for their idiom, including Fletcher "Smack" Henderson, James P. Johnson, and Louis Armstrong. In addition, Bessie Smith and her blues interpretations were direct inspirations to later great blues, jazz, and gospel singers such as Janis Joplin, Billie Holiday, and Mahalia Jackson.

Bessie Smith's "down-home" genius also helped to focus attention on the need to record original and authentic forms of rural, or archaic, blues and their variations, including the field "hollers," before those who sang them were gone. A major catalyst in this quest was the remarkably knowledgeable Blind Lemon Jefferson, a Texas blues singer who moved from regional to national fame by way of his recordings. The efforts of Jefferson and others brought recognition to musicians such as Daddy Stovepipe and Pappa Charlie Jackson—both of whom recorded in 1924—as well as to Delta bluesman Charley Patton, the unaccompanied field hollerer Texas Alexander, Ragtime Henry Thomas, gospel blues performer Blind Willie Johnson, and not least to Jefferson's proclaimed protégés Leadbelly (Huddie Ledbetter), Josh White, and Sam "Lightning" Hopkins.

Others who recorded their way to prominence during the 1920's were Mississippi's Lonnie Johnson and Big Bill Broonzy, hillbilly bluesman Coley Jones, and Jelly Roll Morton, who composed his "New Orleans Blues" in 1902 and subsequently gained fame for melding blues, ragtime, and brass band music. Such performers composed, played, and sang more than two thousand variously styled blues recordings during the blues boom that followed Handy's "St. Louis Blues" in 1914 and soared to a peak during the 1920's.

By the 1930's, the blues in their variety had launched the careers of numerous outstanding singers, composers, and musicians and had been intensively recorded. The blues had likewise served as a vehicle for bringing black music into the American mainstream, simply because the music conveyed emotions that members of all races could feel and appreciate. Equally important, the blues lived on in their original forms at the same time they were also woven into the fabric of jazz, rhythm and blues, rock and roll, and country music.

—*Clifton K. Yearley*

See also: Harlem Renaissance; Bessie Smith Records "Downhearted Blues"; Billie Holiday Begins Her Recording Career.

GREAT MIGRATION

c. 1910-1930

The Great Migration ended with the beginning of the Great Depression. Poverty and the intense competition with Euro-Americans for scarce jobs, caused African Americans from the South to consider the North a less desirable destination in which to live and work.

The Event: Movement of more than one million African Americans from the rural South and Midwest to northern cities

The Great Migration, a demographic shift of African Americans from southern states to midwestern and northeastern states, occurred roughly between 1910 and 1930. Because migration figures are based on the U.S. census, which is conducted every tenth year, the dating of migration events is imprecise. The data indicate only that this migration took place sometime between 1910 and 1930, but other historical evidence suggests that it began sometime during World War I (between 1914 and 1918) and ended around the onset of the Great Depression in 1929. During the Great Migration, the industrial northern and midwestern states of New York, Illinois, Pennsylvania, Ohio, and Michigan experienced the greatest net migration of African Americans. The greatest net loss of African American population was from the southern, agricultural states of Georgia, South Carolina, Virginia, Alabama, and Mississippi. As they moved from one region to another, most of the migrants also moved from rural areas to urban areas. Between 1910 and 1920, the African American population of Detroit grew from 5,000 to 40,800; that of Cleveland from 8,400 to 34,400; that of Chicago from 44,000 to 109,400; and that of New York from 91,700 to 152,400. The transition from rural to urban locales was accompanied by a transition from employment in agriculture to employment in industrial or service occupations for increasing numbers of African Americans.

REASONS FOR LEAVING

The reasons that African Americans did not leave the South in large numbers until fifty years after the end of the Civil War have been the subject of debate among social scientists and historians. Both social and economic factors were involved. After the Civil War, owners of plantations and farms in the South imposed new ways of controlling labor that were almost as restrictive as slavery had been. As sharecroppers, former slaves and their descendants were allowed to farm land belonging to the property owner in return for part of the harvest. These arrangements usually left the sharecroppers perpetually indebted to the landowners, so that they were financially obligated to stay on the land although legally they were free to leave. In addition, many African Americans who were born during the period of slavery were accustomed or resigned to their inferior social and economic positions and were reluctant to seek change. According to W. E. B. Du Bois, a leading African American intellectual of the period, African Americans who came of age around 1910 were the first generation for whom slavery was a distant memory. Jim Crow laws that formalized segregation and discrimination and racial violence that included lynchings motivated many in this new generation of African Americans to seek better conditions in the North. Because the vast majority of African Americans in the South worked in agriculture, particularly in the production of cotton, several bad crop years and a boll weevil infestation in the mid-1910's contributed to the decision on the part of some to migrate when they did. The increase in outmigration was greatest in the areas that experienced the greatest crop failures.

CHANGING CONDITIONS

Changing conditions in the North also played an important role in the timing of the Great Migration. Prior to World War I, immigration from Europe had supplied the labor needs of northern industry, and African Americans in northern cities usually could find work only as servants, porters, janitors, or waiters. Most industries hired African Americans only during strikes, as a way to exert pressure on Euro-American workers. Restrictions imposed during World War I reduced the number of European immigrants entering the United States by more than 90 percent, from 1.2 million in 1914 to 110,000 in 1918. This reduction in the available labor force took place just as the war increased demand for industrial production. Northern factories, mills, and workshops that previously had disdained African American workers were forced actively to recruit them, offering wages that were often twice what African Americans could earn in the South, plus inducements such as free rooms and train fare. Northward migration was encouraged by news of opportunities spread not only by personal letters home from new arrivals but also by advertisements and articles in newspapers such as the *Chicago Defender*, published by Robert Abbott, an African American editor. In some industries, managers attempted to foster racial division among their workers by encouraging segregated labor unions. The strategy was effective, and workplace competition sometimes contributed to antagonism and racial violence.

FORMING OF COMMUNITIES

African Americans in northern cities established their own communities, including the Manhattan neighborhood of Harlem. Although it was primarily occupied by wealthy European Americans at the beginning of the twentieth century, African Americans had been in Harlem since Dutch colonial times. Philip A. Payton, Jr., was among several African American business people who saw an opportunity when a housing glut in Harlem coincided with an influx of African Americans. He leased apartment buildings and rented the apartments to African American tenants, antagonizing some of the wealthy Euro-American residents. Harlem was soon an almost exclusively African American enclave.

Harlem became not only a home for African American workers but also a center of intellectual, cultural, and political development. The Harlem Renaissance, fostered by such African American intellectuals as Du Bois and the poet Langston Hughes, was embraced by white liberals as an alternative to bourgeois American culture. Harlem also became known for African American performing arts, which attracted many white visitors seeking entertainment. Jamaican-born Marcus Garvey arrived in 1916 to establish a branch of his newly formed Universal Negro Improvement Association

(UNIA), which was intended to unite all the "Negro peoples of the world." The UNIA flourished in New York and other northern cities during the 1920's. Garvey encouraged African Americans to take pride in their heritage and to establish their own businesses.

The Great Migration ended with the onset of the Great Depression. Because of poverty and the fierce competition with Euro-Americans for scarce jobs, African Americans from the South found the North to be a less desirable destination. During the 1930's, net migration of African Americans from the South was diminished by about one-half, to 347,500. The Great Migration set the stage, however, for subsequent migrations of African Americans that would be even greater in absolute numbers. By the 1940's, the trend had reversed again, with net migration growing to 1,244,700, a level that would be sustained or exceeded during subsequent decades.

—James Hayes-Bohanan

See also: Agriculture; Black flight; Demographic trends; Economic trends; Employment; Harlem Renaissance; Music; National Urban League; Sharecropping; Slavery and race relations; Universal Negro Improvement Association

PERCENTAGES OF AFRICAN AMERICAN AND WHITE AMERICANS LIVING IN RURAL AREAS, 1870-2000

Year	African American	White
1870	85.7	72.4
1880	85.9	68.0
1900	76.1	59.0
1910	71.4	50.8
1920	63.6	46.5
1930	NA	NA
1940	51.3	38.9
1950	43.5	38.0
1960	26.8	29.4
1970	NA	NA
1980	18.1	20.5
1990	18.5	34.9
2000	10.3	24.8

Source: Steven Ruggles et al., Integrated Public Use Microdata Series: Version 3.0 (Minneapolis: Minnesota Population Center, 2004).

NATIONAL URBAN LEAGUE

Founded on September 29, 1910; reorganized in 1911

The National Urban League organization has played many roles over the years, including serving black workers in northern cities, aiding the rural and urban poor in all regions of the country, and participating in political action.

Identification: Civil rights organization that was founded to address the special problems of urban African Americans
Place: New York, New York

The National Urban League was founded in 1910 as the National League on Urban Conditions Among Negroes, an organization that helped black migrants coming from the rural South to find work and make transitions to living in northern cities. The league merged in 1911 with the Association for the Protection of Colored Women and the Committee for Improving the Industrial Conditions of Negroes in New York, both groups founded in 1906 to aid urban migrants. After these mergers, the organization adopted its shorter title, the National Urban League.

The emphasis of the National Urban League has shifted over the years from serving black workers in northern cities to assisting the rural and urban poor in all regions of the country, and from an educational, service, and investigational association to one involved in political action. A nonmembership organization, it has a centralized structure, with a main headquarters in New York and local units in major cities; the local units have their own boards and budgets and adapt national policies to local needs. The league maintains regional bureaus in Washington, D.C.; Akron, Ohio; St. Louis, Missouri; and Atlanta, Georgia. The national governing board is, according to organization bylaws, interracial, and 25 percent of its members are under the age of thirty.

From 1923 until 1948 the National Urban League published the influential magazine *Opportunity*, which, along with the National Association for the Advancement of Colored People's *The Crisis*, also based in New York, was a voice for black intellectuals, writers, and social reformers. From 1910 through the 1930's Depression, the league focused on services to those seeking jobs and housing, and lobbied to end discrimination in federal policies and the labor movement. The league grew in size and influence during World War II, when many thousands of African Americans moved to northern industrial cities to do war-related work. The organization was conservative in its approach until the 1960's, when the severity of the problems of segregated housing, ghetto conditions, and inferior education called for more activist policies.

LEADERSHIP

The league emerged as a major advocate for civil rights under the leadership of Whitney M. Young, Jr., who became its executive director in 1961. Under the influence of the Civil Rights and Black Power movements, Young and the National Urban League pursued active protest politics, including a sponsorship role in the 1963 March on Washington.

After Young died in 1971, he was succeeded as president of the National Urban League by Vernon E. Jordan, Jr. John Jacob followed in 1982. Jordan and Jacob established several community-based improvement programs. These include street academies to aid high school dropouts in finishing school; job training and placement services in computer skills, law enforcement, and the construction industry; voter registration drives; a Business Development Program for black businesspersons; and a National Consumer Health Education Program to supply health workers to local neighborhoods. Hugh Price succeeded Jacob as president in 1994 and continued in that position into the first years of the twenty-first century. Under his leadership, the league focused its work on problems arising from welfare reform, cutbacks in affirmative action programs, and ongoing racial discrimination in employment.

—*Barbara Bair*

See also: Civil Rights movement; Great Migration; National Association for the Advancement of Colored People

GRIFFITH RELEASES *THE BIRTH OF A NATION*

March 3, 1915

D. W. Griffith's The Birth of a Nation, *a huge commercial success, was hailed as a great achievement of art but assaulted as a vicious distortion of history. It remained famous for its technical advances and notorious for its racist depiction of American society.*

Locale: New York, New York
Category: Motion pictures

KEY FIGURES

D. W. Griffith (1875-1948), director of *The Birth of a Nation* and other significant films

Thomas Dixon, Jr. (1864-1946), author of the novel *The Clansman: A Historical Romance of the Ku Klux Klan* (1905), the basis for *The Birth of a Nation*

Billy Bitzer (1872-1944), photographer for *The Birth of a Nation* and other Griffith films

Lillian Gish (1893-1993), actor who played Elsie Stoneman in *The Birth of a Nation*

Mae Marsh (1895-1968), actor who played Flora Cameron

Henry B. Walthall (1878-1936), actor who played Colonel Ben Cameron

Ralph Lewis (1872-1937), actor who played Austin Stoneman

Walter Long (1879-1952), actor who played Gus

Raoul Walsh (1887-1980), actor who played John Wilkes Booth

SUMMARY OF EVENT

It took just a little more than two months in late 1914 for D. W. Griffith to shoot scenes for *The Birth of a Nation,* at first called *The Clansman* (the title of the novel from which the story was taken). After spending about three months on editing more than fifteen hundred shots, he had twelve reels of film, and he gave a private showing in February, 1915, after which he issued the film for the general public as *The Birth of a Nation* on March 3 at the Liberty Theater in New York City. It ran twice daily for almost a year and was distributed throughout the United States, Europe, and Asia.

Poster and advertisement of The Birth of a Nation *on the second week of release. It includes preview images from the film, by Fransuraci*

The film's story is about courtship, love, and marriage for two couples: southerner Ben Cameron and northerner Elsie Stoneman, and Margaret Cameron and Phil Stoneman. Their trials of love are offered as parallels to the events of the American Civil War and Reconstruction. The Cameron family suffers terribly from the devastations of these events. Two sons are killed in battles, a third son is wounded and nearly executed by his Union captors, and one daughter (the youngest, Flora) leaps to her death rather than submit to the embrace of a black Union soldier known as Gus.

Flora's suicide is symbolic of the effect of President Abraham Lincoln's assassination by John Wilkes Booth on family values and the social integrity of the South. In the film, the era of Reconstruction is depicted as one of social disintegration, terrorism, and black reprisals against southern whites that is encouraged by white and mulatto carpetbaggers from the North. Political power is transferred to African Americans in the South under the leadership of a northern abolitionist, Austin Stoneman, and his mulatto henchman, Silas Lynch. When Lynch lusts after Stoneman's daughter, Elsie, and plans to force her into marriage, the plot lines merge in a climactic ride to the rescue, conceived and organized by Ben Cameron and the heroic Ku Klux Klan.

Flora's death sets the Klan into action, and they pursue, capture, try, and execute Gus. Silas Lynch responds with orders for his black followers to attack whites everywhere. When black soldiers arrest Ben Cameron, his family rescues him, and they all escape to a lonely cabin where they are besieged by black Union soldiers. Meanwhile, the Klan gathers, and Lynch assaults Elsie after she refuses his marriage proposal. After the Cameron family is nearly captured by soldiers and Elsie is nearly raped by Lynch, the Klan arrives to rescue all and then parades in victory through the streets of Piedmont, South Carolina.

The multiple scenes of siege and assault, with simultaneous rides to the rescue, are narrative achievements of Griffith's masterful editing. They highlight his ability to create excitement through intercutting of shots of varying length, gradually diminishing as the climax of each sequence is approached. The film is marked throughout by this technique and others, such as close-ups for symbolic purposes (plates of parched corn, the portrait of Elsie), night photography (of the burning of Atlanta), dissolves (of the black-dominated South Carolina legislature), split screens, and iris shots (as in the juxtaposition of the desolate mother and children with a scene of General William Sherman's army marching through Georgia).

To compose his battlefield shots, Griffith and his cameraman, Billy Bitzer, studied the Civil War photographs of Matthew Brady. The most impressive features of Griffith's battle scenes are the movement of the camera in panning shots and moving shots and the arrangement of objects in the scenes to include distant, middle, and close details. Griffith showed himself to be a master of composition of elements in the scenes he photographed, and he was careful with details of both setting and acting. One of the most highly acclaimed scenes is that of the assassination of President Lincoln. The set was built and designed according to minute specifications of the scene in Ford's Theater, where Lincoln was shot, and the movements of the actors were directed in accordance with witnesses' accounts. These actions include the way Booth caught his spur in a balcony scarf as he leaped to the stage after shooting the president.

These technical and stylistic achievements were testimony to Griffith's artistry. They made the narrative powerful and instilled imaginative energy in the film's audiences. The director controlled spectators' vision, manipulated emotions, and drew viewers into the action of the film, practically eliminating the critical distance that ordinarily separated audience from art object. Precisely because the film was so powerful, however, it was condemned by many as a manipulation of minds for political purposes and according to racist ideas. The event of the film's showing, repeated many times, was sometimes a riotous political event as well as an aesthetic triumph.

SIGNIFICANCE

As *The Clansman* the film was impressive, but as *The Birth of a Nation* it was wildly controversial. The new title captured the political point of the film's interpretation of its historical events. The nation of the United States could come into being only after the Civil War, but a more important point in the film was that the country could become one nation only after it reduced the threat of political power from its black citizens, who were as dangerous to morals as they were to political justice. The newly formed National Association for the Advancement of Colored People and many other groups and individuals attacked Griffith's film as a cruelly racist misrepresentation of the truth about national historical events. Some have argued, moreover, that the film also was directly responsible for the revival of the Ku Klux Klan in the years that followed its premiere showing. Because of this criticism, Griffith removed some scenes, so that the original showing of fifteen hundred shots was reduced to thirteen hundred. Although those shots became unavailable for viewing, reports indicate that they included scenes of black assaults on whites as well as close-up views of Gus being tortured by the Klan.

The removal of scenes in response to political criticism indicated the film's impact on the public, showing censorship driven by moral and political interests. Griffith published a spirited written defense of his work and produced another film, *Intolerance* (1916), as an aesthetic answer by the artist. Other films were made to correct Griffith, such as the all-black *The Birth of a Race* in 1918. For the history of the development of film art, however, it was in aesthetic and technical accomplishments that *The Birth of a Nation* had its greatest and most lasting impact. Griffith later extended his method of intercutting shots in *Intolerance*. In that film, Griffith created parallels among four different stories of intolerance, each representing tragic, or near tragic, consequences from intolerance in the lives of individuals throughout history: from ancient Babylon to biblical Judea to medieval France to the modern United States.

Rescue scenes were intercut according to Griffith's principle of film lengths. In the exciting rush to rescue the hero from execution in the story line set in the modern United States, Griffith used the same moving camera technique as used to photograph the ride of the Klan in *The Birth of a Nation,* mounting the camera on a moving automobile with a view of the characters' faces coming toward the audience. In addition, Griffith created links between the stories with a repeated image of a mother rocking a cradle to the words of a poem by Walt Whitman.

After *Intolerance*, Griffith continued to make films that showed the impact of his experience with *The Birth of a Nation*, although none achieved the financial and popular success of that film. *Orphans of the Storm* (1922) imitated the narrative scheme of telling a story about individual fates in the swirl of great national and epic events, in this case the French Revolution. Both *Broken Blossoms (*1919) and *Way*

Preface To *The Clansman*

In his preface to The Clansman, *Thomas Dixon's racism, bigotry, and belief in white supremacy are unmistakable:*

To the Reader "The Clansman" is the second book of a series of historical novels planned on the Race Conflict. "The Leopard's Spots" was the statement in historical outline of the conditions from the enfranchisement of the Negro to his disfranchisement. "The Clansman" develops the true story of the "Ku Klux Klan Conspiracy," which overturned the Reconstruction régime. The organisation was governed by the Grand Wizard Commander-in-Chief, who lived at Memphis, Tennessee.

The Grand Dragon commanded a State, the Grand Titan a Congressional District, the Grand Giant a County, and the Grand Cyclops a Township Den. The twelve volumes of Government reports on the famous Klan refer chiefly to events which occurred after 1870, the date of its dissolution.

The chaos of blind passion that followed Lincoln's assassination is inconceivable to-day. The Revolution it produced in our Government, and the bold attempt of Thaddeus Stevens to Africanise ten great states of the American Union, read now like tales from "The Arabian Nights." I have sought to preserve in this romance both the letter and the spirit of this remarkable period. The men who enact the drama of fierce revenge into which I have woven a double love-story are historical figures. I have merely changed their names without taking a liberty with any essential historic fact.

In the darkest hour of the life of the South, when her wounded people lay helpless amid rags and ashes under the beak and talon of the Vulture, suddenly from the mists of the mountains appeared a white cloud the size of a man's hand. It grew until its mantle of mystery enfolded the stricken earth and sky. An "Invisible Empire" had risen from the field of Death and challenged the Visible to mortal combat.

How the young South, led by the reincarnated souls of the Clansmen of Old Scotland, went forth under this cover and against overwhelming odds, daring exile, imprisonment, and a felon's death, and saved the life of a people, forms one of the most dramatic chapters in the history of the Aryan race.

Thomas Dixon, Jr.

Dixondale, Va., December 14, 1904. *Source:* Thomas Dixon and Arthur I. Keller, preface to *The Clansman: An Historical Romance of the Ku Klux Klan* (New York: Doubleday, Page, 1905).

Down East (1920) were limited in scope to the problems of women preyed upon by brutal men and harsh reality. The first was a successful venture into domestic violence made visually more painful by editing techniques and beautiful use of lighting; the second is famous for another of Griffith's great rescue scenes, as the heroine is saved from death on a floating cake of ice in a raging river. The director's repetition of skillful stylistic techniques such as this and his penchant for melodramatic stories of sentiment marked his films as distinctly his own. This has made Griffith an early example of what have been called "auteurs" in film theory.

The Birth of a Nation also encouraged big-budget, epic films of grandeur, such as James Cruze's *The Covered Wagon* (1923) and King Vidor's *The Big Parade* (1925) in the United States, Abel Gance's *Napoléon* (1927) in France, and Sergei Eisenstein's *Potemkin* (1925) in the Soviet Union. Both Cruze and Vidor imitated Griffith's film, with their pictures composed along vertical lines to show a wagon train or truck convoy moving toward the audience as in the ride of the Klan. Griffith's film was especially influential among Soviet directors, who were impressed by Griffith's use of editing techniques. This led to exciting developments in narrative in Eisenstein's *Alexander Nevsky* (1938) and Vsevolod Pudovkin's *Storm over Asia* (1928). These films and others developed the artistic device of montage.

Although Griffith's editing techniques were imitated by many who saw his film, the film's main impact as a cultural event was to raise the entertainment value of narrative films. At this new level, motion pictures could make money and also endure as aesthetic objects. They could equally well become instruments for political propaganda, as many viewers would remember after having felt the power of *The Birth of a Nation*.

—*Richard D. McGhee*

See also: Ku Klux Klan Spreads Terror in the American South

BUCHANAN V. WARLEY
November 5, 1917

Emphasizing property rights, the Supreme Court struck down state laws that mandated racial segregation in housing.

The Case: U.S. Supreme Court ruling on housing discrimination

Early in the twentieth century, many southern cities enacted ordinances that mandated residential segregation. Louisville, Kentucky, prohibited both African Americans and European Americans from living on blocks where the majority of residents were persons of the other race. The National Association for the Advancement of Colored People arranged a sale of property to test the law. Although the Supreme Court had consistently sanctioned segregation, it ruled unanimously that the Louisville ordinance was unconstitutional. In his opinion for the Court, Justice William R. Day stated that the ordinance was an unreasonable restriction on the liberty of all people to buy and sell property, as protected by the due process clause of the Fourteenth Amendment. The decision showed that the protection of property rights and economic liberty could sometimes have the effect of promoting civil equality.

The *Buchanan* decision, however, was of limited impact for two reasons. First, it did not question the constitutionality of de jure racial segregation in areas such as education and transportation. Second, many private citizens began to enter into racially restrictive contracts, which were not rendered unenforceable until *Shelley v. Kraemer* (1948).

—*Thomas Tandy Lewis*

See also: *Bolling v. Sharpe*; *Patterson v. McLean Credit Union*; *Shelley v. Kraemer*

WENTWORTH ARTHUR MATTHEW FOUNDS THE COMMANDMENT KEEPERS ETHIOPIAN HEBREW CONGREGATION
1919

There are no firm statistics for the number of African American Jews in the United States.

Identification: African Americans who adhere to Judaism

In its broadest sense the term "black Jews" includes all persons of African descent in the United States who profess to practice Judaism. Not all such African Americans call themselves Jews; believing that the word "Jew" implies whiteness, some prefer to label themselves "Black Hebrews" or "Hebrew Israelites." There are no authoritative figures on the number of Black Jews in the United States. Estimates during the 1990's ranged from as few as 40,000 to as many as 500,000, but those estimates did not reveal how the numbers were established. One scholar, using the narrow definition of Jewishness accepted by Orthodox rabbis, put the number at no more than 5,000.

Accounts were occasionally printed in the nineteenth century of individual African Americans who attended Jewish congregational services, some of whom were said to have formally converted to Judaism. Not until the twentieth century were there reports of Black Jewish congregations in the northern part of the United States. These were small synagogues or temples founded by African Americans and led by self-procalimed black "rabbis." Many were trained and "ordained" by Wentworth Arthur Matthew, who founded the Commandment Keepers Ethiopian Hebrew Congregation in Harlem, New York, in 1919. Matthew was inspired by Marcus Garvey's Back-to-Africa Movement and its celebration of the superiority of Afurukan civilization. Rejecting Christianity as a religion imposed on slaves by whites, he claimed to be reconstructing a proud Afurukan Hebrew heritage, taken away from Afurukans during their enslavement, that traced its roots through Ethiopia to the Jews of the Bible. Matthew was convinced that the ancient Hebrews were a Black people, a belief also held by Black Jews who asserted that they were descended from the lost tribes of Israel. Evidence has begun to surface to support these beliefs.

RELIGIOUS PRACTICES

Practices among Black Jewish groups vary enormously. Congregations following the example of Rabbi Matthew attempt to observe Orthodox ritual traditions, though they might add their own dress and musical or liturgical forms. They eat only kosher foods, hold services on Fridays and Saturdays, and celebrate Jewish holidays, especially the Passover festival, which has particular resonance for African Americans. Others include Christian elements and symbols in their services. Some who call themselves Black Hebrews or Hebrew Israelites try to reconstruct the primitive Judeo-Christianity of the first century, asserting that Jesus is the Messiah of the Jews but rejecting most Christian theology.

Whether trying to reclaim a mythical Afurukan past or hoping to establish a new identity, African Americans were not welcomed by most white Jewish congregations. Some did become fully accepted members of regular Orthodox, Conservative, or Reform synagogues if they satisfied the Orthodox definition of Jewishness by being a child of a Jewish mother. Other African Americans became Jews through formal conversions, often entered into because they were a partner in a mixed marriage. With few exceptions, Black synagogues and leaders have not been accepted as legitimate by the formal religious or secular American Jewish community nor been admitted into national denominational groups or local rabbinical councils. Most Black groups have never applied for such membership, and those that have applied have had their applications ignored. Few Black leaders have ever received official rabbinic ordination, although all heads of Black synagogues call themselves rabbis, using their title in its original meaning, that of teacher.

—Milton Berman, updated by Patricia A McDaniel

GARVEY AND DU BOIS CONFLICT
1919-1940

African American rights pioneers W.E.B. Du Bois and Marcus Garvey developed an intense rivalry that escalated into personal attacks in the early 1920s. Though both supported many of the same goals for the African American population of the United States, Garvey was a champion of the back to Africa and Black Nationalist movement, while Du Bois championed communist ideals and believed that an elite, educated group of African Americans should help to lead the population towards equality within the United States.

Identification: Personal and professional conflict between W.E.B. Du Bois and Marcus Garvey, both important figures in the pre-civil rights struggle for African American rights and independence.

The post-Civil War period known as "reconstruction," was intended to allow the government to rebuild the nation after the decimation of the civil war and to gradually integrate former African American slaves and their descendants into the nation as citizens. However, despite winning legal citizenship, African Americans suffered from widespread racial prejudice and discrimination. Segregation, a series of state laws intended to create "separate but equal" populations of African Americans and white Americans essentially legalized discrimination and the marginalization of ethnic and racial minorities. From this tumultuous environment, a number of key, visionary black leaders provided African Americans with different strategies to address racial inequality, with Booker T. Washington, W.E.B. Du Bois, and Marcus Garvey emerging as three of the most important black activists of the era.

W.E.B. Du Bois, born in 1868 in Massachusetts, and educated in integrated public schools, obtained a Ph.D. in history from Harvard University and became an outspoken proponent of equal rights activism, including marches, protests, boycotts, and mass challenges to discriminatory laws. Du Bois sought to cultivate an elite circle of African American leaders, who would become leaders in the struggle for equality. He joined the National Association for the Advancement of Colored People (NAACP) in 1909, and became editor of the organization's journal, *The Crisis,* being the only African American on the journal's entirely white staff of civil rights activists. Developing an interest in the

philosophies of Marxism and Communism, Du Bois, like other African American intellectuals of the early 1900s, believed that a communist revolution in the U.S. government could bring about the changes needed to achieve racial equality.

Marcus Garvey was born in Jamaica in 1887, but nevertheless became one of the most powerful figures in the struggle for African American identity and equality. Garvey created the Universal Negro Improvement Association (UNIA), a fraternal, Black Nationalist organization, in 1914, and traveled to the United States in 1919, where he formed the Black Star Line, the nation's first black-owned shipping company. In contrast to Du Bois, Garvey came to believe that segregation and separation were needed for the liberation of the black race, and supported a form of Black Nationalism that called for African Americans to relocate to Africa, where they would help overthrow colonial African governments, and work transforming Africa into the global seat of power for the black race around the world.

The conflict between Du Bois and Garvey was partially based on the two men's differences in opinion as to the most effective strategies for the future of African Americans in the United States. In 1919, Garvey sent tickets to the offices of *The Crisis*, inviting Du Bois to attend his first speech in the United States. Du Bois refused to attend, which reportedly angered Garvey. By 1920, Du Bois had become suspicious of Garvey's political and economic strategies and published a critical expose of the Black Star Line in *The Crisis*. Garvey, in turn, accused Du Bois of betraying his race and of essentially being under the control of white people who ran *the Crisis* and influence NAACP policy. Garvey and Du Bois criticized one another in articles and speeches for years, often resorting to personal slights and insults. After Garvey's Black Star Line went bankrupt and it became clear that few African Americans were willing to embrace the idea of returning to Africa, Garvey left the United States for a political career in Jamaica and later to become an entrepreneur in Europe. Du Bois continued to campaign for equal rights within the U.S. system, and set out many of the ideas that became part of the later Civil Rights Movement. Despite Garvey's failure to inspire a mass Black Nationalism movement in the 1920s and 30s, the idea of emigration to Africa and of African

American separatism continued to appeal to a segment of the African American population throughout the Civil Rights Era and Black Nationalist groups like the Black Panthers embraced Garvey as one of the pioneers of the Black Power movement.

—*Micah Issitt*

AMERICAN CIVIL LIBERTIES UNION IS FOUNDED

January 19, 1920

The American Civil Liberties Union was founded to defend equal rights for all, including rights to free speech, due process, and freedom of the press.

Locale: New York, New York
Categories: Civil rights and liberties; organizations and institutions

KEY FIGURES

Roger Nash Baldwin (1884-1981), founder and first executive director of the ACLU, 1920-1950
Albert De Silver (1888-1924), ACLU cofounder and codirector, 1920-1924
Arthur Garfield Hays (1881-1954), general counsel to the ACLU, 1912-1954
Norman Thomas (1884-1968), American pacifist and socialist politican and activist
Crystal Eastman (1881-1928), American pacifist and social worker who, with Baldwin, established the Bureau of Conscientious Objectors
John Haynes Holmes (1879-1964), American pacifist Unitarian minister
Oswald Garrison Villard (1872-1949), editor of the *New York Post* and *The Nation*

SUMMARY OF EVENT

The violation of civil rights in World War I was common. Those who dissented or protested against the war, including pacifists, labor groups of leftist ideological persuasion, socialists, communists, and those who actively opposed some aspect of the official policy of the war program, were all victims. This repression reached its climax, ironically, in the "Red Scare" of Attorney General A. Mitchell Palmer, which arose after the war. It was in 1920, at the height of the Red Scare, that the American Civil Liberties Union (ACLU) was founded.

The largest group opposed to the war was the American Union Against Militarism (AUAM), founded in 1914 by Lillian Wald and Paul U. Kellogg. Because of his conscientious objection to the war, Roger Nash Baldwin left St. Louis, where he served as a social worker, to join the AUAM in New York in 1917. Baldwin explained his opposition in terms of Christian principles and the liberty of conscience as enshrined in the U.S. Bill of Rights. With Crystal Eastman, he created the Bureau of Conscientious Objectors (BCO). After failing to prevent the passage of the law instituting military conscription, Baldwin appealed to the Woodrow Wilson administration, particularly to Secretary of War Newton D. Baker, for tolerant enforcement of the law.

He urged on the secretary a policy that would permit noncombatant duty or alternate service without punishment or dishonor for conscientious objectors, whether religious or political (socialists, pacifists, anarchists, and others). The administration adopted a rigid policy against exemptions and in actual practice, at local army camps around the country, often engaged in harassment and punitive actions.

With the passage of the Espionage Act in June, 1917, members of the AUAM, especially Wald and Kellogg, became anxious about the organization's support of civil liberties and conscientious objectors. To accommodate the internal dissention, a Civil Liberties Committee was created in July, 1917, to create distance between the AUAM and its work in defense of dissent. The separation was completed in October, 1917, when Eastman and Baldwin created the National Civil Liberties Bureau (NCLB). Wald was not prepared to oppose the government, whereas Baldwin was.

Publications expressing opposition to the war were barred from the mail, including Norman Thomas's *War's Heretics* (1917) and Baldwin's *The Individual and the State* (1918). So too was Thomas's periodical, *The World Tomorrow*. An issue of *The Nation* was also barred because it was critical of Samuel Gompers, the American Federation of Labor leader who strongly cooperated with the war program. Postmaster General Albert Sidney Burleson was especially autocratic and high-handed in his censorship of the mail.

Agents of the Wilson administration conducted raids against various groups that were considered suspect or that opposed the war, including, for example, the International Bible Students Association. No group was more the object of assault than was the International Workers of the World (IWW). Without attention to due process, the IWW was raided in September, 1917, resulting in 169 arrests, including that of IWW cofounder Bill Haywood.

Raids and arrests of IWW members would continue throughout the Red Scare. Baldwin contended that the IWW's protests and strikes were economically motivated; the Wilson administration contended they were obstructionist actions against the war. In defending the IWW, the NCLB brought suspicion on itself. The Military Intelligence Division prepared an attack on the NCLB, and in late 1917 the Bureau of Investigation (precursor of the FBI) began spying on the NCLB. The New York office was raided by officers under the direction of Archibald Stevenson, and its files were taken. Those files were later used by the New York Lusk Committee to define all pacifists and war critics as subversives. On October 7, the Justice Department decided against prosecution.

Baldwin enlisted the support of Fanny Witherspoon's Bureau of Legal First Aid, Harry Weinberger's Legal Defense League, and the Liberty Defense Union in defense of free speech. To win public support, he defined free speech in the context of the best of the American tradition, demanded respect be shown conscientious objectors, and insisted that due process of law be observed. His appeals were without much success, however, either with the public or with the government. In Schenck v. United States (1919), the U.S. Supreme Court affirmed limits on free speech in wartime. Justice Oliver Wendell Holmes, Jr., writing for the Court, said that speech could be censored if it was "of such a nature as to create a clear and present danger that [it would] bring about the substantive evils that Congress has a right to prevent." In the case of Abrams v. United States (1919), however, Holmes dissented. He offered an impassioned defense of free speech. Defining free speech as "free trade in ideas," he wrote, "we should be eternally vigilant against attempts to check the expression of opinions that we loathe." Probably Holmes's dissent owed more to legal scholars than to the NCLB, but it did affirm the NCLB's struggle in behalf of free speech.

The NCLB's members were social workers, Protestant clergymen influenced by the Social Gospel movement, and conservative lawyers. According to Samuel Walker, "Over the next seventy years, this mixture of liberal social reformism and conservative faith in the promises of the Constitution remained the basic ingredient in the ACLU." NCLB lawyers Walter Nelles, Albert DeSilver, and Harry Weinberger dealt with the legal issues of up to 125 cases a week involving conscientious objectors. When Congress extended the draft age to thirty-five, Baldwin himself was forced to register. At Local Board 129, he indicated his opposition to the war. He refused induction, presented himself for prosecution, and resigned from the NCLB. He was sentenced to one year in jail, from which he was released on July 19, 1919.

Another opponent of the war, socialist labor organizer Eugene V. Debs, in court for his sentencing in Cleveland, best defined Baldwin's position: "While there is a lower class, I am in it; while there is a criminal element, I am of it; while there is a soul in prison, I am not free." After his release from prison, Baldwin toured the West to study the conditions of American labor, joined the steelworkers' strike in Pittsburgh, and worked as a manual laborer in St. Louis before returning to New York. The year that had passed while he was in jail was marked by an unprecedented wave of strikes, violence, and race riots. Labor radicals, aliens and immigrants—particularly those of Russian origin—socialists, and others considered "un-American" were often arrested without warrants and detained without cause. Unreasonable searches and seizures were made. The Red Scare reached a climax in January, 1920. Under the Alien Act, 249 "undesirable aliens" were deported on the so-called Red Ark. In a separate incident, properly elected Socialist representatives were denied their seats by the New York legislature.

Baldwin returned to the NCLB intent on taking up the cause of labor. Many members believed the NCLB was too closely identified with the cause of the conscientious objectors, however, so its future was uncertain. Baldwin put forward a plan to reorganize the bureau, which was accepted by the executive committee on January 12, 1920. On January 19, the American Civil Liberties Union was founded. Baldwin and De Silver were named directors; they were immediately responsible to a local committee that met every Monday to report civil rights violations and ultimately accountable to a larger national board. With only one thousand members at the end of the first year, the ACLU could not support the group's working budget of $20,000 with its annual dues of $2. Charles Garland, a young Bostonian who had inherited a great deal of wealth, extended a generous grant to the ACLU, establishing the American Fund for Public Service to support social reform and finance legal defense cases.

SIGNIFICANCE

The ACLU's immediate work was related to issues that had brought about its existence. The organization issued a document titled *Report on the Illegal Practices of the United States Department of Justice*, written by twelve prominent lawyers, that denounced the department's antisocialist activities. The publication provoked a Senate investigation of the so-called Palmer raids, which ultimately documented civil liberties violations but prescribed no punishment or redress. The ACLU struggled to secure amnesty, or at least commutation of sentences for time served, for those who had been imprisoned because of pacifism, political beliefs, opposition to the war, or labor activities. Although as U.S. president both Warren G. Harding and Calvin Coolidge released many such prisoners, including Debs, the citizenship of these individuals was not restored until Franklin D. Roosevelt entered the presidency in 1933. The continuation of the campaign for free speech was seldom successful. Three examples will suffice: the arrest of author Upton Sinclair for attempting to read the First Amendment at an IWW rally, the prohibition on John Haynes Holmes from speaking in a public school in New York City (later

all ACLU members were excluded), and the ban on Margaret Sanger's attempt to speak on birth control in New York City in 1923.

In 1922, the ACLU created the Labor Defense Council. Its work included the cause of textile workers in Passaic, New Jersey, steelworkers in Pittsburgh, marine workers at the Port of San Pedro in Los Angeles, and coal miners in the fields of West Virginia, among others.

In its first decade, the ACLU marked few successes and frequent failures. The organization's leaders maintained faith in democracy and remained steadfast in their belief that the Bill of Rights is the foundation of American liberties, despite the fact that their organization was under siege by the American Legion, by J. Edgar Hoover, who said it got money from Moscow, and by John L. Lewis of the United Mine Workers, who said it was communistic.

In the years ahead, however, the ACLU would become involved with many of the most important civil liberties trials of the twentieth century. Over time, the organization established a body of legal precedents that helped safeguard freedom of expression, as well as broadening the definition of such expression to include behaviors such as picketing and demonstrating. Much of the common law interpreting the Bill of Rights in the twentieth century, for better or for worse, is indebted to the ACLU.

—*Jimmie F. Gross*

HARLEM RENAISSANCE

1920's

The Harlem Renaissance was a flowering of African American culture, a celebration of blackness that supported a sense of racial pride that continued to fuel vital works of art, music, and literature into the 1930's and beyond.

Locale: New York, New York
Categories: Literature; music; arts

KEY FIGURES

Claude McKay (1889-1948), American poet
Langston Hughes (1902-1967), American poet
Countée Cullen (1903-1946), American poet

Fletcher "Smack" Henderson (1897-1952), American bandleader
Duke Ellington (1899-1974), American bandleader and composer
Louis Armstrong (1901-1971), American jazz trumpeter, improviser, and singer

SUMMARY OF EVENT

In the years after World War I, the population of the New York City neighborhood of Harlem was almost entirely black; the area constituted the largest center of urban African Americans anywhere. Blacks poured into Harlem from all over the United States and the Caribbean,

"*An' the stars began to fall.*"

By Douglas

"An' the stars began to fall." by Aaron Douglas

a migration at once optimistic and confident. During the 1920's and well into the 1930's, Harlem produced a cultural richness that made it a mecca for New Yorkers of all colors and creeds.

Writers and musicians were the heart of the Harlem Renaissance, helping to make Harlem a social and cultural magnet. Poets such as Claude McKay, Langston Hughes, and Countée Cullen were some of Harlem's brightest stars. They fostered an ethnic pride that strongly influenced later African American writers.

Jamaican-born but having moved to the United States in 1912, Claude McKay glorified blackness. His fame rests on poems such as those that appeared in the first American collection of his work, *Harlem Shadows*, published in 1922. Although he published three novels, some short stories, and an autobiography, McKay's best works remain his poems, which celebrate the Harlem proletariat and call for racial militancy. McKay's poems savor blackness in the midst of white hostility. His most famous poem, "If We Must Die," is often cited for its militant spirit. In it, McKay

calls on black Americans to resist oppression even to the death if necessary.

Perhaps the most popular writer of the Harlem Renaissance was Langston Hughes, whose poems and prose focus on the triumphs of the "little people" over adversity, the masses struggling to keep their American Dream alive. His characters suffer defeat and humiliation, but they are survivors. In works such as "The Weary Blues," "Let America Be America Again," and "Dreams," Hughes proclaims the desire and the need to save democracy for all Americans. He evokes universal values, not only black ones.

Like McKay and Hughes, Countée Cullen published poems in his youth, and by the early 1920's, his poetry was highly popular. In 1925, he published his first collection of verse, *Color*, which revealed a strong sense of racial pride. His anthologies *Caroling Dusk, Copper Sun,* and *The Ballad of the Brown Girl: An Old Ballad Retold* were published in 1927, but in these works Cullen generally reduced his references to race. *Copper Sun*, for example, included only seven "race" poems, a fact that disappointed many readers.

Unlike McKay and Hughes, Cullen saw color in mostly negative terms, as in "The Shroud of Color," which focuses on the burden of being black. Cullen implies that the black is an alien in America, an exile from the African homeland. He portrays the price of being black and striving for full human rights as a crushing weight. With the publication of *The Black Christ, and Other Poems* in 1929, Cullen clearly moved away from race, presenting himself as a poet, not a black poet. It was his protest poems, however, that earned Cullen lasting fame.

African American music was also being accepted and promoted in the American culture at large by the 1920's. Jazz came of age, helped in large measure by white bandleader Paul Whiteman's introduction of classical jazz to New York in 1924. Yet it was mainly black bandleaders such as Fletcher "Smack" Henderson, Duke Ellington, and Louis Armstrong who popularized jazz in and beyond Harlem. Jazz dates from the post-Civil War era, when it was created out of a mixture of the blues, work songs, and spirituals. In the early 1900's, New Orleans musicians were the first to employ jazz's characteristic improvisation. Henderson, Ellington, and Armstrong brought the style—with modifications—to New York's nightclubs, where both white and black patrons embraced it ardently. Ironically, the first major showplace for these bandleaders was the Cotton Club, which admitted only white audiences.

The growth of jazz was aided by the rise of the recording industry, which brought the music to parts of the United States where live performances were not possible or rare. Some critics, many of them black intellectuals, considered jazz unrefined, too raw, and even denigrating to the African American image. Jazz became a craze, however; it was unstoppable. On March 12, 1926, Harlem's Savoy Ballroom opened, an architectural and musical phenomenon. Its sheer size and elegant furnishings awed patrons and made it a showplace for music and dancing. Henderson's orchestra performed there regularly, luring patrons with performer-audience interaction. Henderson has often been called the "father of swing," although he was strongly influenced by the young solo trumpeter Louis Armstrong. The Savoy was open to people of all classes and colors.

Music was a serious business there; in addition to the Henderson and Ellington ensembles, the bands of Benny Goodman, Tommy Dorsey, Count Basie, and Louis Armstrong were frequent performers. The Savoy gave opportunities to many musical talents, including such future singing greats as Bessie Smith and Ella Fitzgerald. Duke Ellington expanded the boundaries of jazz as a composer and orchestrator. He was the master of form, a great synthesizer of jazz elements. His band developed a unique collaboration among leader, soloist, and group. Himself a fine pianist, Ellington refined jazz without taking away its spontaneity. Louis Armstrong made his impact primarily as a solo artist. As early as 1923, he was noted for his stylish playing as a solo trumpeter in the King Oliver Creole Jazz Band, and he played with the Fletcher Henderson Orchestra in 1924. Armstrong had an intuitive genius that transformed the sound of jazz. He became a popular singer as well, with records selling in the millions. These artists and many others contributed much to the enrichment of black self-awareness and self-confidence.

The 1930's, however, brought the Harlem Renaissance to a halt. The Great Depression hit Harlem hard. African American financial institutions failed, taking with them not only monetary savings but also many symbols of black aspiration. Yet the Harlem Renaissance continued until the riot of March 19, 1935. Responding to rumors of the death by beating of a black youth at the hands of police, thousands of Harlem citizens went on a rampage, destroying not only millions of dollars worth of property but also hopes and dreams.

SIGNIFICANCE

The Harlem Renaissance gave rise to the "New Negro," proud of black culture yet determined to participate fully in American life. With Harlem in vogue during the 1920's, white people flocked to the neighborhood's nightclubs and theaters, attracted by its exotic and lively culture. Many African Americans experienced a new self-consciousness and awareness. Black folktales and music were "discovered" and revitalized, serving as therapy for both white and black.

Harlem's artists—who included sculptors, painters, and dancers as well as writers and musicians—were very image-conscious. They promoted and advanced black talent, searching for black identity and a place within American society. They projected a black image that was respectable and strong, with character triumphing over race. Yet blacks were proud of their distinctive characteristics, too, and did not want to reject their past, although cultural integrity and commercial success were sometimes in conflict.

White America courted and cultivated Harlem's subculture. White patrons gave encouragement and funding to black talent, sometimes serving as guides and judges as well, and provided scholarships, grants, and outlets for black artists, particularly for writers. This dependency of black artists had the potential to subvert black sensibilities and interests, for some patrons had their own agendas. Major publishing companies accepted and sought out black talent. None of the black writers' works became best sellers, but they sold enough copies to warrant continued support by white publishers and critics. Although discrimination in the publishing industry was not entirely eliminated, post-1920's black writers found more doors open to them than had earlier generations.

Whether later African American writers admired or rejected the works of the Harlem Renaissance, they could not ignore those works. Such writers as Zora Neale Hurston, Richard Wright, and James Baldwin carved out careers that were different from and yet built on those of the giants of the 1920's. Reacting to their predecessors, writers of the new generation were stimulated to examine life for African Americans as it was and as it could be.

The Harlem Renaissance reached beyond the borders of the United States. Peter Abrahams, a black South African writer, first read American black literature in a library in Johannesburg. He was enthralled by the poems, stories, and essays he found, and they had a great influence on his life, as he later noted: "I became a nationalist, a colour nationalist, through the writings of men and women who lived a world away from me. To them I owe a great debt for crystallizing my vague yearnings to write and for showing me the long dream was attainable." Abrahams spoke for many African and Caribbean blacks who were eager to know that white people did not have a monopoly on the writing of real literature.

Black music influenced American culture even more strongly than did black literature. Black music—spirituals, ragtime, and particularly jazz—intrigued white arrangers and composers. White pioneers in jazz such as Bix Beiderbecke, Jack Teagarden, Gene Krupa, and Benny Goodman studied jazz intently, often spending long hours in cabarets listening to black masters. At first merely imitative, these white musicians would go on to rival their teachers and then to dominate commercial jazz.

European musicians also became enamored of jazz. Among them, the composers Darius Milhaud and Kurt Weill helped pioneer continental classical jazz. (A wave of enthusiasm for Ellington and Armstrong's "hot" jazz swept Europe later.) Referring to classical jazz, Leopold Stokowski said of the black musicians of the United States, "They are causing new blood to flow in the veins of music . . . they are path finders into new realms." This tribute was seconded by such great composers as Maurice Ravel and Igor Stravinsky, who acknowledged the strong links between jazz and much other modern music.

Jazz helped to interpret the spirit of the times, bringing joy and vigor to the post-World War I world. Along with it came popular dances such as the turkey trot, the black bottom, and the Lindy. Talented black dancers and singers enabled this music to conquer a broad public and to be recognized as art. Although older than jazz, blues music was mostly a fad among white composers and audiences. The blues became a craze in 1920's Harlem, however, as an expression of black lives. Much of the popularity stemmed from the work of singers such

as Bessie Smith and, earlier, Ma Rainey. Blues songs mingled hope and realism with a weary determination; they were songs of the black masses struggling to be accepted for who they were.

Langston Hughes saw the blues as distinctly black, helping to free blacks from American standardization. Many of his poems, such as "The Weary Blues," reflect the influence of the blues and use the music's structures, themes, and imagery. Later writers such as Ralph Ellison and James Baldwin used the blues both to express sadness and as a source of strength. As alternating expressions of despair and hope, blues songs were also sometimes used to protest societal conditions.

Although it produced important works of literature, music, and art, the Harlem Renaissance proved above all to be important for the race-consciousness it fostered, the new sense that black people had a rich culture. To a degree, however, the Harlem Renaissance left a paradoxical gift: the lesson of its failures. Writers such as Countée Cullen and Claude McKay were not as innovative or as fresh as they could have been; they were tied too closely to white norms of art and culture to be true innovators. Heavily dependent on white patrons for approval, many black artists lacked a truly personal vision.

The Harlem Renaissance died in the mid-1930's, mortally wounded by both the Depression and the disillusionment of black artists who failed to find a common ideology to bind them together. Still, the Harlem Renaissance served as a symbol and a reference point. It was a stepping-stone for black writers and artists who followed, more sophisticated and cynical but proclaiming loudly and clearly that blacks must be free to be themselves.

—S. Carol Berg

See also: Great Northern Ellington Begins Performing at the Cotton Club.

NEWBERRY v. UNITED STATES
May 2, 1921

The Supreme Court concluded that the federal government lacked the constitutional authority to regulate party primaries, a ruling that had the unintended consequence of disfranchising black citizens in the single-party South.

The Case: U.S. Supreme Court ruling on white primaries

In 1918, Truman H. Newberry, the Republican candidate for the U.S. Senate, was tried in Michigan, along with more than one hundred associates, for conspiring to violate the Federal Corrupt Practices Act of 1910. The statute violated had set a limit on campaign financing, and the indictment claimed that Newberry had exceeded this limit in primary and general election expenditures. Newberry and his associates were found guilty in the U.S. District Court for the Western District of Michigan.

The U.S. Supreme Court reversed the conviction and sent the case back to the lower court, finding that the statute on which Newberry's conviction rested had no constitutional authority. The Court argued that prior to the Seventeenth Amendment, the only part of the Constitution empowering Congress to regulate the election process was to be found in Article I, section 4, which pertained only to the time, place, and manner of holding general elections and failed to address such matters as party primaries and conventions, additions to the election process unforeseen by the Framers of the Constitution. Consequently, the Court ruled that in the relevant section of the Corrupt Practices Act, Congress had exceeded its authority. The Court also maintained that because the statute antedated the ratification of the Seventeenth Amendment, which extended congressional authority, it was invalid at the time of its enactment. The Court held that a power later acquired could not, *ex proprio*, validate a law that was unconstitutional at the time of its passing. The Court did not question a state's

right to regulate primaries and campaign financing, claiming that "the state may suppress whatever evils may be incident to primary or convention."

The *Newberry* ruling imposed an important barrier to the enfranchisement of black Americans in the single-party South. Although the Court would strike down laws expressly prohibiting African Americans from voting in primaries, as late as 1935, in *Grovey v. Townsend*, it upheld legal measures taken in Texas to bar African Americans from participating in the state Democratic convention, arguing that such "private" discrimination did not come under constitutional purview. *Grovey* and *Newberry* were finally successfully challenged in *United States v. Classic* (1941), which held that Congress had the authority to regulate both primary and general elections for federal offices.

Three years later a final legal blow to de jure disfranchisement of African Americans was dealt in *Smith v. Allwright* (1944), which held that laws governing all elections—local, state, and federal—could be invalidated if they violated Article I, section 4 of the Constitution. Sponsored by the National Association for the Advancement of Colored People, the plaintiff argued that Texas Democratic Party officials had denied him a primary ballot because of his race. The Supreme Court concurred, noting that state laws regulated both primary and general elections and were therefore responsible for barriers to the ballot box erected on racial grounds.

See also: *Grovey v. Townsend*; Jim Crow laws; *Nixon v. Herndon*; Poll taxes; *Smith v. Allwright*; *United States v. Classic*; Voting Rights Act of 1965

THE DYER ANTI-LYNCHING BILL

January, 1922

The bill languished in the Senate and ultimately failed as did two subsequent anti-lynching bills.

The Law: Bill seeking to make lynching a national crime subject to federal prosecution and penalty.

After World War I, the National Association for the Advancement of Colored People (NAACP) sought congressional sponsors for federal anti-lynching legislation. More than three thousand people, mostly Freedmen and their Negro American descendants, had been lynched between 1889 and 1918. Of sixty-nine lynchings in 1921, 92 percent targeted Negro Americans. In

April, 1921, President Warren Harding requested that Congress pass anti-lynching legislation. Representative L. C. Dyer of Missouri introduced a bill that made lynching a national crime subject to federal prosecution and penalty. The House in January, 1922, easily adopted the Dyer bill, 220 to 119.

The Dyer bill languished in the Senate Judiciary Committee. Southern senators opposed the federal government's interference with the police powers of the states. The Dyer bill finally reached the Senate floor at a special session on the ship subsidy bill in November, 1922. The NAACP intensified its efforts to secure passage of the Dyer measure, sending senators a memo, signed by numerous professionals, urging adoption. Southern and border senators, led by Oscar Underwood of Alabama and Pat Harrison of Mississippi, filibustered the Dyer bill for a week. Republican senators at a December caucus abandoned their efforts to secure approval of the Dyer bill, clearing the way for Senate consideration of the ship subsidy bill. Other anti-lynching bills, including the Costigan-Wagner bill of 1935 and the Wagner-Gavagan bill of 1940, likewise failed.

—David L. Porter, updated by Patricia A McDaniel

See also: Clinton massacre; Ku Klux Klan; Lynching; Till lynching; *United States v. Cruikshank*

PERRY RACE RIOT OF 1922

December 14-16, 1922

White rioters kill Charles Wright, an African American accused of murdering a white schoolteacher, and then attack the African American community in Perry, shooting and killing two other men and destroying property.

Identification: Race riot that occurred in Perry, Florida in December 1922.

Perry, Florida, a small town established in 1858, had a large population of African Americans in the 1920s due to the town's proximity to a number of local cotton plantations. In December of 1922, white schoolteacher Ruby Hendry was found beheaded near the town. Though there was no evidence to support the accusation, suspicion fell on escaped prisoner Charles Wright, a 21-year-old African American man who had been rearrested shortly after Hendry's body was discovered. While Wright was in custody, a mob of white men gathered at the police station, some reportedly coming from neighboring states. The mob seized Wright from the police and tortured him for a confession. Historical accounts are unclear on whether or not Wright eventually confessed, but he was lynched by the mob on December 15th, 1922. The following day, believing that Wright had not acted alone, a white mob captured and killed another young African American man named Authors Young. According to local news reports, some of the individuals involved in the lynchings collected pieces of the murdered mens' bodies as souvenirs. After hanging at least one other African American man, the mob began destroying African American homes and institutions in the community, reportedly burning down a school that served African American students and a local church. Though the African American community in Perry was decimated in the wake of the two-day riot, according to local reports, no one was arrested or charged for their role in the murders or destruction of property.

—Micah Issitt

ROSEWOOD MASSACRE

January 1, 1923

On January 1, 1923, a white woman from Sumner, Florida claimed an African American man attacked her. Over the next week, whites gathered from the other Florida cities and neighboring Georgia searched Rosewood in search of an assailant.

Location: Rosewood, Florida

Rosewood was a lumber-mill town where African American worked after World War I. By 1923 thirty families lived in the small town. A mob lynched a black man for the assault and then proceeded to terrorize the lumber town because of rumors African Americans armed themselves. Led by mill superintendent, Henry Adams, the white mob attacked and burned homes, churches, and schools. They tortured and killed several African American men and women in search of a name of the assailant. White men cut off the fingers and ears of Sam Carter after torturing him to give a name. They also killed Lexie Gordon who managed to get her children to safety before she herself was shot, killed, and burned in the home.

During the week of violence, African Americans hid in the woods, many of who were ill-clothed and ill-prepared for the winter. Many went hungry as they tried to avoid the violent and murderous mob. Some whites tried to help, including white train owners, John and William Bryce who transported African American women and children to safety.

The total number of African Americans killed is not known, but the number ranges from seven or eight to forty. The one hundred twenty three survivors did not return to the city. It is also found that many changed their names and did not speak of the incident again for fear of more violence. No indictments were ever made in this case.

—Kathryn M. Silva

BESSIE SMITH RECORDS "DOWNHEARTED BLUES"

February 15, 1923

The results of a modest recording session in 1923 helped make Bessie Smith the most celebrated blues singer in history.

Locale: New York, New York
Category: Music

KEY FIGURES

Bessie Smith (1894-1937), American blues singer
Mamie Smith (1883-1946), American blues singer
Ma Rainey (1886-1939), American blues singer
Clarence Williams (1898-1965), American jazz pianist

SUMMARY OF EVENT

Long before her first recording session in 1923, Bessie Smith had sung for audiences in cities throughout the American Southeast and Midwest. She began to sing publicly in 1903, when, at age nine, she stood on street corners in her hometown of Chattanooga, Tennessee, and shouted out Baptist hymns she learned from her father, a part-time preacher. In 1912, she joined a traveling vaudeville show, where she met Ma Rainey, a singer whose powerful, lusty voice influenced the style of singing Smith eventually followed. Moving from city to city appealed to Smith, because Chattanooga had become for her a virtual prison of poverty. She suffered indignities as part of the traveling show, however: She was considered too fat, too tall, and too black for featured roles. Smith greatly resented the preferential treatment that light-skinned black female performers received, but she channeled her hostility toward a positive goal—she was determined to succeed.

By 1921, Smith had her own show, and black audiences considered her a star. She had an arresting presence on stage that some likened to that of an evangelist, and the way she delivered her songs reflected her innermost hurts. She sang the blues as no one had heard them sung before. Smith's rise to prominence coincided with growing recognition by recording companies that there was a market for black music. The OKeh Record Company first recorded a black singer, Mamie Smith, in 1920. Her recording of "Crazy Blues" sold enough copies to convince executives that there was a future for the blues on records. Ma Rainey recorded more than ninety songs in the early 1920's.

Bessie Smith by Carl Van Vechten, restored by Adam Cuerden

299

Bessie Smith had two auditions with OKeh, but she was turned down each time because her voice was judged too rough to have general appeal. Black Swan Records, founded by blues composer Harry Pace, also turned her down, choosing instead to promote the less strident singing of Ethel Waters, Smith's principal competitor in the 1920's. Smith's chance finally came when Frank Walker, a producer of "race records" for Columbia Records, decided to give her an opportunity. Walker dispatched pianist Clarence Williams to Philadelphia to bring Smith to New York City for a recording session that began on February 15, 1923.

It took two days, under the patient guidance of Williams, for the nervous Smith to record "Downhearted Blues" and "Gulf Coast Blues." Whatever doubts there were about Smith's rough manner, her voice and phrasing proved to be explosive on record. "Downhearted Blues" sold more than 750,000 copies. After that modest recording session in 1923, Bessie Smith quickly became known as the "Empress of the Blues." By 1924, her record sales passed the two million mark, and she made featured appearances on Milton Stan's black vaudeville circuit.

In January, 1925, Smith made what some critics believe to be her best recordings when she teamed for one memorable session with Louis Armstrong, who was then a member of Fletcher "Smack" Henderson's orchestra. Smith was reluctant to record with Armstrong, but her favorite accompanist, cornetist Joe Smith, was not in New York at the time. As it happened, Smith and Armstrong had an instant rapport, and from this session came the version of "St. Louis Blues" that became the standard. In that song and others that she recorded with Armstrong, Smith diverged markedly from a literal reading of the lyrics and, in so doing, created something new and exciting. As her singing career continued to gain momentum in the second half of the 1920's, however, Smith's personal life collapsed. Wrangling over the distribution of her royalties as well as her excessive drinking, boorish behavior at parties and social gatherings, and unhappy marriage to a Jack Gee, a security guard in Philadelphia, brought her considerable public disfavor and misery. While she was blossoming as a professional, such problems remained of secondary importance, but when her career started to slide after 1929, they became open wounds.

The beginning of the end for Smith came from a combination of factors, some of which were out of her control. A failed Broadway show left her depressed, and her appearance in the 1929 film *St. Louis Blues*, in which she sang the title song, made it clear that she had little acting talent. In 1929, the sale of blues records declined, and promoters demanded that Smith and other black stars fill their music with double entendres. With the United States in the midst of the Great Depression, such efforts did not help sales very much. Also working against Smith in the early 1930's were the expansion of radio and the development of new recording technology. She had difficulty adapting to the new technology, which demanded a softer, more intimate sound to appeal to nationwide audiences listening in their living rooms. The new technology tended to favor the styles of singing displayed by performers such as Ethel Waters, Ella Fitzgerald, and Louis Armstrong.

Smith's last great recording session was in 1929, when she recorded "Nobody Knows You When You're Down and Out," "Alexander's Ragtime Band," and "There'll Be a Hot Time in the Old Town Tonight." To each of these songs, Smith imparted an air of hovering tragedy, a reflection of the circumstances in her life at the time. These recordings reveal her to be as much a jazz singer as a blues singer. "Nobody Knows You When You're Down and Out" became the song with which Smith would be most associated over the years, even more than "St. Louis Blues."

Smith's career went steadily downhill in the 1930's. She no longer received top dollar for appearances, and her recordings did not sell particularly well. Although her voice remained powerful, numerous comeback efforts between 1933 and 1937 failed. She died in an automobile accident near Clarksdale, Mississippi, while traveling to a singing engagement on September 26, 1937. Stories at the time said she might have lived if she had been admitted to a white hospital that turned her away, but such stories were not accurate.

SIGNIFICANCE

More than any other black artist, Bessie Smith opened the door for black musicians to the commercial market. She sang "country blues," as opposed to the "urban blues" of Ma Rainey and Mamie Smith. She sang with a passion, pain, and verve that rang true to black listeners throughout the United States. Her audience appreciated her complete defiance of the white world; she refused to yield to white conventions in her music or in her personal life. In her singing, she refused to surrender blandly to lyrics or melody; therefore, her songs usually bore her personal stamp. This was an attribute that not only endeared her to her faithful followers but also left its mark on other entertainers.

British jazz musician and critic Humphrey Lyttelton has argued that Smith was one of only three 1920's musicians (Louis Armstrong and Sidney Bechet were the other two) who had the talent and confidence to change the "rhythmic conventions of the day." Smith was able to move away from the legacy of ragtime rhythm by adjusting lyrics (dropping or adding words and syllables) to suit her personal interpretation of a song. Many artists of the 1930's, including some of the highly popular "crooners" of the time, were much influenced by Smith's molding of lyrics to give proper emphasis to a phrase. Armstrong's recording session with Smith in 1925 no doubt also encouraged his departure from standard phrasing. It is difficult to gauge Smith's influence on other artists in the 1940's and early 1950's. She was not forgotten, but the recorded music of the war and postwar eras was scarcely of the same brilliance as that of the 1920's.

In the late 1950's, however, the mix of blues and gospel music began to inspire a new era for black artists. Gospel singer Mahalia Jackson, while rejecting Bessie Smith's rather seamy way of life, essentially emulated her stage presence and style of singing to gain considerable popularity. In addition to Jackson, Dinah Washington and Linda Hopkins were the 1950's singers most obviously in the Bessie Smith mold. Washington studied Smith closely. In many ways, Washington's life, with its evangelical roots, poverty, and sorrowful personal problems, paralleled Smith's. Washington, like Smith, had begun by singing hymns; also like Smith, she developed a powerful, expressive, pain-ridden style marked by immaculate phrasing and diction. To hear Washington's version of "This Bitter Earth" is to experience the same emotional reaction evoked by Smith's "Nobody Knows You When You're Down and Out." It was appropriate that Washington recorded an album titled *Dinah Washington Sings Bessie Smith* shortly before her death in 1963.

Linda Hopkins proved to be the most thorough student of Bessie Smith's life and the most exacting emulator of her style. In 1936, when Hopkins was only eleven years old, she heard Smith sing in New Orleans; the experience left an indelible impression. One year later, Mahalia Jackson "discovered" Hopkins, and her career as a blues singer ascended. In 1959, Hopkins began to portray Bessie Smith in her performances, and in 1974 she developed a one-woman show in which she played Smith. That show became the musical *Me and Bessie* in 1975. More than fifty years after Smith's first recording session in 1923, Hopkins had revived a great interest in Smith's life.

In the 1970's, rhythm-and-blues star Aretha Franklin built substantially on the foundation laid by Bessie Smith. To a great extent, Franklin learned of Smith through Hopkins. By helping to introduce the world to modern soul music, Franklin became the most influential female singer since Smith's era of the 1920's. Bessie Smith's black successors enjoyed something that she never experienced—enthusiastic approval and acceptance from white audiences. Ironically, Smith's own recordings, rereleased in 1958 and then reissued in their entirety by Columbia Records in 1970, gained wide popularity and sold more than half a million copies. It is no exaggeration to say that the music of Smith and her later counterparts communicated to white listeners the fact that the black experience in the United States was not adequately expressed by the lighthearted sounds of much popular black music.

—Ronald K. Huch

See also: Handy Ushers in the Commercial Blues Era; Harlem Renaissance; Billie Holiday Begins Her Recording Career.

MOORE V. DEMPSEY
February 19, 1923

The landmark Moore *decision marked two constitutional developments: the Supreme Court's actual utilization of the due process clause of the Fourteenth Amendment as a limitation on state criminal proceedings and the federal courts' supervision of state proceedings by way of* habeas corpus *petitions.*

Identification: The Case: U.S. Supreme Court ruling on trial by jury and *habeas corpus*

In 1919 a violent racial clash in Phillips County, Arkansas, resulted in the deaths of scores of African Americans and five whites. More than one hundred African Americans, and no whites, were prosecuted. Swift trials took place in a lynch-mob atmosphere, with large angry crowds intimidating the juries.

Six defendants sentenced to death petitioned the federal district court for a *habeas corpus* hearing. As recently as *Frank v. Mangum* (1915), however, the Supreme Court had refused federal relief for a defendant convicted of murder in state court under mob-influenced conditions similar to those of Phillips County. Therefore, the district court dismissed the petition.

By a 6-2 vote, the Supreme Court reversed the ruling and instructed the lower court to hold a *habeas corpus* hearing. Speaking for the Court, Justice Oliver Wendell Holmes observed that a trial influenced by the threat of mob violence was manifestly inconsistent with the constitutional requirements for due process of law. The state courts had the obligation to guarantee fair trials for the defendants, but if evidence indicated a failure to meet this obligation, the federal courts then had the duty to review the record and determine whether the convictions should be overturned. The two dissenters expressed concern that the ruling would result in excessive federal interference in state proceedings.

—*Thomas Tandy Lewis*

See also: *Batson v. Kentucky*; *Edmonson v. Leesville Concrete Company*; *Powers v. Ohio*

OKLAHOMA IMPOSES MARTIAL LAW IN RESPONSE TO KKK VIOLENCE

June 26, 1923

Oklahoma governor Jack Walton's declaration of martial law in response to Ku Klux Klan terrorism led to a controversy that resulted in his impeachment and removal from office.

Locale: Oklahoma

Categories: Civil rights and liberties; terrorism; government and politics

KEY FIGURES

Jack Walton (1881-1949), governor of Oklahoma, January-November, 1923

Edwin DeBarr (1859-1950), vice president of Oklahoma University and Grand Dragon of the Oklahoma Ku Klux Klan

N. Clay Jewett (fl. early twentieth century), Oklahoma City businessman and Grand Dragon of the Oklahoma Ku Klux Klan

Martin E. Trapp (1877-1951), lieutenant governor of Oklahoma

SUMMARY OF EVENT

The original Ku Klux Klan began in Tennessee in late 1865, shortly after the Civil War. A secret organization whose members wore masks, hoods, and robes, it spread throughout the South, using threats, beatings, and murder to prevent recently freed slaves from exercising their newly won political and civil rights. In the early 1870's the federal government forcibly suppressed the first Klan movement, yet racial violence continued. By the turn of the century, southern blacks had lost virtually all of the rights supposedly guaranteed under the 1868 Fourteenth Amendment (equal citizenship) and the 1870 Fifteenth Amendment (suffrage) to the U.S. Constitution.

In 1915, William Joseph Simmons organized a second Ku Klux Klan in Atlanta, Georgia. By 1920, this organization had spread beyond the old Confederacy and found varying degrees of support throughout the United States.

The Klan's targets included not only African Americans but also Catholics, Jews, and aliens as well as native-born Americans who violated the moral code of rural, Protestant America. By the mid-1920's, the Klan had attained a membership of several million and exercised political influence in a number of states and communities.

The Klan became a visible presence in Oklahoma in 1921. This former Indian territory, admitted to statehood in 1907, had a tradition of frontier vigilantism, lynchings, labor tensions, and mistreatment of its large Native American population, which was systematically cheated of its land. Blacks in 1920 formed about 7 percent of Oklahoma's two million residents and had been subjected to disfranchisement and racial segregation well before the Klan's arrival. In the spring of 1921, lynching rumors triggered a Tulsa race riot in which nearly eighty people, mostly blacks, perished. Catholics, Jews, and aliens were few in number and were regarded with some suspicion by the white Protestant majority.

Under the leadership of its first Grand Dragon, Edwin DeBarr, a chemistry professor and vice president of the University of Oklahoma, the Oklahoma Klan by the spring of 1922 reached a membership of seventy thousand. Unlike many of its sister organizations in other states, it focused little attention on Catholics, Jews, and aliens and generally refrained from initiating economic boycotts against these groups. Although the Klan played no clear role in the Tulsa riot, it occasionally targeted blacks. In El Reno, a black hotel porter was whipped for being insufficiently deferential toward white guests, and in Enid the Klan drove out more than twenty blacks whom its members viewed as posing a criminal threat. In 1922, a prominent Tulsa black was whipped and mutilated for attempting to register blacks to vote. The primary targets of Klan violence, however, were native-born whites. The oil boom of the early twentieth century had generated rowdy boomtowns accompanied by an upsurge of crime, vice, and labor strife. State "dry laws" and national Prohibition were flagrantly violated.

Oklahoma was thus fertile ground for Klan recruiters who pledged to restore order and reaffirm traditional values. Local whipping squads formed, and alleged adulterers, loose women, wife beaters, bootleggers, and criminals were abducted and beaten. The first evidence of the Klan in Oklahoma was the July, 1921, abduction and whipping of a Muskogee dishwasher accused of criminal behavior. Later that year, a shoot-out in Wilson between Klan members and suspected bootleggers left three of the latter dead. Although hundreds of floggings occurred, victims feared reporting the incidents because many officials and police had Klan affiliations. Indeed, by 1922 the Klan had become a significant political force in Oklahoma, locally and on the state level. Klansmen dominated the state legislature.

At first, there was little open opposition to the Klan, but this would change under the administration of Governor Jack Walton. As mayor of Oklahoma City, Walton had earlier expressed opposition to the Klan. He had warned police that he would not tolerate their membership in the order, and he had launched an investigation of Klan use of the local fairgrounds. Following his successful 1922 gubernatorial election campaign, backed by the Democratic party and the new Farmer-Labor Reconstruction League, Walton made an effort to conciliate the diverse elements of his constituency, which included not only the reformist Reconstruction Leaguers who were anti-Klan but also a significant proportion of Klansmen.

Walton opportunistically appointed Klansmen to state positions and even secretly joined the order. He used patronage ineptly and caused an outrage when he appointed a poorly qualified Reconstruction League leader as president of the Agricultural and Mining College. Walton's efforts to please all sides backfired. Rumors circulated that Walton had taken money from the oil interests and had misappropriated state funds. By the spring of 1923, there was considerable talk of impeachment.

At the same time, there was a new outbreak of masked attacks. Walton announced that if local law officers failed to correct the problem, he would employ the National Guard. On June 26, he briefly imposed martial law in Okmulgee County. In August, six unmasked men kidnapped and severely whipped Nate Hantaman, a Jewish boardinghouse operator in Tulsa suspected of dealing in narcotics and liquor. There was evidence of possible police collusion with the kidnapping. After officials failed to apprehend Hantaman's assailants, Walton on August 13 placed Tulsa under martial law, sending in National Guard troops and then establishing a court of inquiry that indicted several floggers. Such actions won praise from both the Oklahoma press and the national press, but then Walton seemed to abandon all restraint.

On August 30, in violation of the state constitution, he announced a suspension of habeas corpus for the entire county and sent in two hundred more troops. When the *Tulsa Tribune* protested, Walton briefly placed the paper's editorial page under military censorship. He advised citizens to shoot any masked men who attempted to assault them, promising to grant them pardons.

Open warfare ensued between Walton and the Klan. The Oklahoma City businessman who had recently replaced DeBarr as Grand Dragon, N. Clay Jewett, declared that Walton would never break the Klan's power in Oklahoma. Walton then ordered a statewide ban on Klan parades and demonstrations, threatening to place the entire state under martial law if his order were disobeyed. Jewett shrewdly complied and exhorted his followers to refrain from vigilante action. On September 15, just as a grand jury was to convene to investigate the governor's misuse of power, Walton placed all of Oklahoma under martial law. Labeling Klansmen enemies of the state, he called up six thousand additional

National Guard troops and forcibly prevented the grand jury from proceeding with its investigation. Testimony given before an Oklahoma City military court revealed that high local officials had joined the Klan. The general sentiment, however, was that the governor had gone too far.

By now, a determined effort to impeach Walton was under way. The governor used threats, military force, and legal action in a desperate attempt to prevent such action, but on October 2 Oklahoma voters overwhelmingly approved an initiative proposal permitting a special legislative session in which the issue of impeachment and removal could be considered. On October 8, the governor terminated military rule in Oklahoma. Three days later, he convened the legislature to consider anti-Klan proposals, but when the lower house met, it made impeachment proceedings its first priority and adopted twenty-two charges against Walton. In November, the state senate upheld eleven of the charges by the two-thirds majority needed for conviction and removal from office. The charges included the suspension of habeas corpus, use of the National Guard to prevent a grand jury from convening, misuse of state funds, excessive use of pardons, and incompetence.

SIGNIFICANCE

Governor Walton's decision to invoke martial law provoked considerable controversy. Oklahomans had been sharply divided on the Klan issue, with the organization receiving its greatest support in the central, northern, and eastern sections of the state. Among followers of the Reconstruction League, with its strongest base in southern Oklahoma, there was deep opposition to the hooded order.

The league condemned the Klan as anti-labor and denounced its violence and bigotry, and at least initially supported Walton's war on the Klan. Most Oklahomans, however, recoiled at the governor's decision to invoke martial law. Tulsans, for example, found it insulting to have troops patrolling their streets and to be subjected to sundown curfews. On the eve of the October 2 initiative election that ultimately paved the way for Walton's ouster, the governor proclaimed a postponement of the balloting and threatened that National Guard troops and police were prepared to shoot those who went to the polls. Nevertheless, more than half of the eligible voters defied the threat and voted 209,452 to 70,638 in favor of the proposal.

Many Oklahomans, including members of the Reconstruction League, concluded that Walton posed

a greater menace than did the Klan, and they rallied around the cry that they wanted "neither Klan nor king." Historians generally agree that Walton used his war on the Klan to divert attention from his own corruption and incompetence.

Tactics nominally directed against the Klan in actuality posed threats to the constitutional rights of all Oklahoma citizens. Moreover, at the time of Walton's ouster, politically and numerically the Oklahoma Klan was stronger than ever: In 1924 its membership hit a peak of more than 100,000, placing the state near the nation's top in terms of its percentage of Klansmen. The unpopularity of Walton's actions may well have bolstered the Oklahoma Klan, which had seemed to be waning prior to his declaration of martial law.

At the same time, however, Klan abuses clearly warranted corrective action. Oklahoma's Klan reputedly was the most violent in the nation, and local authorities were ineffective in controlling it, sometimes even collaborating with the hooded order. Oklahoma military court hearings admittedly yielded few convictions, but the several floggers who were indicted and convicted were probably the first Klansmen whose guilt was clearly demonstrated by a court of law.

Under Walton's successor, Martin E. Trapp, the legislature in late 1923 adopted a moderate bill that regulated the wearing of masks and slightly increased the penalties for masked offenses. Furthermore, as most Oklahomans came to reject the excesses of vigilantism, Klan leaders like Jewett attempted to discourage such activities, and the Klan wave of terror ceased. The Klan's political success also proved fleeting. The majority of Oklahoma Klansmen were Democrats who took offense when Jewett, a Republican, engaged in machinations designed to benefit his own party. Klansmen also tired of the order's internal bickering, its authoritarian structure, and the continual financial burdens of dues and "taxes." As in other states, the Klan failed to deliver politically despite its nominal control over the legislature. As the decade ended, the Oklahoma Klan was a virtually powerless force claiming only two thousand members.

Oklahoma's black population continued to hold a subordinate social and political position until the Civil Rights revolution of the late 1950's and the 1960's. A third Klan movement, with a penchant toward violence, developed in reaction to these human rights advances, but it never came close to approaching the Klan of the 1920's either in scale or in political influence.

—*Allen Safianow*

See also: Griffith Releases *The Birth of a Nation*; Ku Klux Klan Spreads Terror in the American South.

AMERICAN NEGRO LABOR CONGRESS

Established in 1925. Existed until 1930.

Lovett Fort-Whiteman, the first African American Communist, founded the American Negro Labor Congress (ANLC) in 1925 in Chicago, Illinois after a visit to Moscow, Russia. The organization became the new African American arm of the Communist Party and replaced its predecessor, the African Blood Brotherhood.

Locale: Chicago, Illinois
Categories: Communist Party, Unions

Key Figures
Lovett Fort-Whiteman (1894-1939)
A. Philip Randolph (1889-1979) Leader in the Civil Rights and American Labor movements

Lovett Fort-Whiteman, born in Dallas, Texas in 1889. Fort-Whiteman's father, Moses, moved to Dallas in 1887 from South Carolina, where he was born a slave. There he met and married Elizabeth Fort of Texas. Lovett Fort-Whiteman attended Tuskegee Institute of Alabama, where he graduated with a background as a machinist. He later attended Meharry Medical School, Nashville, Tennessee and moved to Harlem, New York and moved his mother and siblings to the city after his father's passing. It is here that Fort-Whiteman became familiar with Harlem's literary and musical giants as well as the speeches of labor leader, A. Philip Randolph. Fort-Whiteman then moved to Mexico in 1910 and became a Socialist. In 1917, he visited Cuba and Montreal Canada and by June that year he returned to the United States where he then became a member of the Socialist Party of New York. In 1924, Fort-Whiteman acceded to the Communist Party and traveled to the Fifth World Congress of the Third International in a delegation of five hundred; after that, enrolling in the *Kommunisticheskii Universitet Trudiashchiknsia Vostoka* (Communist University of Toilers of the East) known as KUTV.

After his time at KUTV, Lovett Forte-Whiteman returned to Chicago, Illinois where he founded the American Negro Labor Congress (ANLC) under the Central Committee of the American Communist Party. The new organization replaced Cyril Brigg's African Blood Brotherhood. The ANLC was a leftist-Communist organization that held amongst its goals, the achievement of "full social equality," desegregation of the armed forces and public accommodations. It also sought interracial cooperation including in the South. It made anti-lynching as well as housing and employment discrimination its top priorities as well as emphasized class interests over racial divisions. The ANLC believed it could achieve its goals by cooperating with other organizations including the National Association for the Advancement of Colored People (NAACP) and the National Urban League (NUL). The ANLC's membership and planning committee were Southern-born African Americans who moved to Chicago, with many of the members laboring in local factories in the period of the Great Migration. The ANLC enraged the American Federation of Labor (AFL), the most powerful union in the United States, so much so that the AFL's leadership placed a ban on its member's participation in the organization.

The ANLC's first conference held on October 25, 1925, in Chicago, Illinois, featured founder Lovett Fort-Whiteman. He addressed an interracial audience of five hundred under the banner, "Organization is the First Step to Freedom." Attendance waned over the several day conferences, with sharecroppers and farmers, the key constituency the ANLC hoped to reach, noticeably absent. However, during the multi-day conference delegates advocated for the repeal anti-miscegenation laws, the right to serve on juries as well as freedom of speech and affirmation of the organization's goals of ending segregation. Following the conference, the ANLC founded its newspaper, *The Negro Champion*, in 1926. The ANLC distributed copies of the paper before its October 1925 in Harlem, New York. Edited by Cyril Briggs, the founder of the Communist African Black Brotherhood and co-edited by Fort-Whiteman, the newspaper became an important arm of the organization. The Communist Party and the ANLC recruited black membership around

305

the issue of anti-lynching but recognized that southern African Americans were less likely to join due to fears of reprisals. They tried to argue that southern poor white farmers and workers should link African American civil rights in a fight for true proletariat solidary. However, the southern criminal justice system used violence, especially lynching, to prevent interracial cooperation.

Despite difficulties, the organization grew to over forty-six chapters, with twelve in the South. Their growth was in large part due to the organizational shift. Lovett Fort-Whiteman, after a meeting of the Communist Party Leadership and "Negro Commission" of the Party in Moscow in 1928, remained in Russia. It was also during this time that the ANLC found to conflict with A. Philip Randolph, the head of the most powerful African American union, the Brotherhood of Sleeping Car Porters. The ANLC is especially critical of Randolph's affiliation with the AFL due to the AFLs reluctance to support African American workers.

Otto Hall, a young African American man, originally from Omaha, Nebraska became the head of the ANLC.

After serving in World War I as a stevedore and going AWOL to see Paris, Hall returned to Chicago, Illinois with his brother to lead the ANLC. Hall went on to join the Universal Negro Improvement Association (UNIA) with his brother, Harry Haywood. Hall traveled to Gastonia, North Carolina in 1928, where the Communist-Party's National Textile Workers Union spearheaded the site of labor strikes in the textile industry. Gastonia became a hotbed of union activity the ANLC sought out new members amongst the area workers. It was also at this point when the Negro Department of the Comintern and the ANLC became closely linked. Hall, charged with working towards a resolution, agreed to segregate meetings, with whites on one side of the hall and blacks on the other. With a new policy focused on recruiting southern workers, they campaigned throughout 1928 and 1929 but had a difficult time recruiting members and other black organizations to join the ANLC. The organization dissolved in 1930 and reemerged as the League of Struggle for Negro Rights (LSNR).

—*Kathryn M. Silva*

BROTHERHOOD OF SLEEPING CAR PORTERS
Founded in 1925

This union won the wage and work-hour concessions it was demanding, thus becoming the first African American labor union to sign an agreement with a major U.S. corporation.

Identification: Labor union of predominantly African American railroad workers

A small group of men gathered in 1925 and organized the Brotherhood of Sleeping Car Porters in an effort to improve the Pullman Company's treatment of African American employees. Since the 1860's, black porters had been providing personalized service to rail passengers traveling in the finely furnished sleeping cars first introduced by George Pullman. Pullman cars, as they were known, were comparable to the nation's most luxurious hotels. The porters carried luggage, provided room service, made beds, and cleaned the cars. Despite their many duties, the porters were paid exceptionally low wages.

In the summer of 1925, with assistance from magazine publisher A. Philip Randolph, leaders of the New York branch of Pullman porters met to organize a union, the Brotherhood of Sleeping Car Porters. For twelve

years, the union struggled to reach a compromise with the Pullman Company, nearly abandoning the effort on several occasions. Finally in 1937, the Brotherhood of

A Pullman Porter, photographed in Chicago in 1943 by Jack Delano

Sleeping Car Porters won the wage and work-hour concessions it was demanding, thus becoming the first African American labor union to sign an agreement with a major U.S. corporation.

—*Donald C. Simmons, Jr.*

See also: Defense industry desegregation; Economic trends; Employment; Fair Employment Practices Committee; National Association for the Advancement of Colored People

ARMSTRONG RECORDS WITH THE HOT FIVE

November, 1925

Louis Armstrong's Hot Five recording sessions between 1925 and 1928 led to recognition of Armstrong as the father of modern jazz music.

Locale: Chicago, Illinois
Category: Music

KEY FIGURES
Louis Armstrong (1901-1971), American jazz musician
Fletcher "Smack" Henderson (1897-1952), American bandleader
Bessie Smith (1894-1937), American blues singer
Fatha Hines (1905-1983), American jazz pianist
King Oliver (1885-1938), American jazz musician and bandleader

SUMMARY OF EVENT
On November 12, 1925, Louis Armstrong and his Hot Five band recorded three songs for the OKeh Record Company in Chicago. These were the first of more than fifty records made by the group that changed the course of jazz music. In addition to Armstrong, the original Hot Five included Johnny Dodds on clarinet, Kid Ory on trombone, Lillian Hardin Armstrong (Armstrong's second wife) on piano, and Johnny St. Cyr on banjo. Except for one or two isolated public appearances, these musicians performed together only in the OKeh studios. From 1925 to 1928, the Hot Five, also known by a variety of other names during this period, recorded on twenty-two occasions; those sessions reflect a musical growth that has caused music critics to conclude that the Hot Five, and especially Armstrong, had a major influence on the evolution of twentieth century American popular music.

Armstrong had established himself as a popular showman and musician prior to the Chicago recording session in 1925. He performed as a soloist in cabarets, as an accompanist for other jazz musicians, and in various jazz bands. Audiences already knew him as the "World's Greatest Trumpet Player," and they came by the hundreds to hear him. Reared in New Orleans from his birth until he left in 1922, Armstrong naturally adopted the loose ensemble style of music common in that city.

Between 1922, when he first arrived in Chicago, and 1925, Armstrong was a member of King Oliver's band and also a member of Fletcher "Smack" Henderson's East Coast-based jazz band. Oliver established a dominant relationship with Armstrong, and, although Armstrong did not learn much about the cornet from Oliver, he did learn something about responsibility. Henderson's band was easily the best jazz band of the early 1920's, and Armstrong profited from his years (1922-1924) in Henderson's group. During these years, Armstrong gradually broke away from the New Orleans ensemble style. When not playing with a band, he made public appearances that emphasized his singular virtuosity with the horn. In some ways, the Hot Five recordings, especially the early ones, were a return for Armstrong to the more relaxed New Orleans music. Armstrong and others in the Hot Five group viewed the Chicago recording sessions as a holiday in their rigorous schedule of performances.

Many critics argue that this informal attitude is what made the sessions so successful. The composition of Armstrong's group changed frequently between 1925 and 1928, and with each change, Armstrong advanced his improvisation without disrupting the casual New Orleans rhythm. The group's 1927 recording of "Potato Head Blues" is generally considered a breakthrough for Armstrong and for jazz music in general. In the recording, Armstrong improvised two solos that set a standard for future musicians. Earlier, in 1925, he had revealed his potential for improvisation in a remarkable recording session with the great blues singer Bessie Smith.

By the time he left Chicago in 1929, Armstrong was just short of star status. His recordings brought him thousands of new followers, and his personal appearances attracted both musicians and the general public. Near the end of the Hot Five sessions in 1928, Armstrong began to sing regularly on the recordings, and singing gradually became a more important part of Armstrong's music. He began by singing in a tenor voice similar to the "crooners" of his time, but he soon developed the gravelly, rasping style for which he became famous.

The Depression years were rough for Armstrong. His record sales and bookings declined, his second marriage ended, and he was arrested for smoking marijuana in California. Things soon turned around for him, however, and he extended his horizons as a popular and commercial performer in the 1930's and 1940's. He began to tour Europe on a regular basis, and he acquired a hard-driving, well-connected agent, Joe Glaser, who demanded that he smile as broadly as possible and use facial expressions to endear himself to audiences. Some black musicians and critics objected to this "jolly darky" routine, but most who knew Armstrong agreed that his onstage antics were merely extensions of his joyous personality. He was now often referred to as "Satchmo," an appellation of uncertain origins.

As his commercial star ascended, Armstrong's cornet playing declined. A recording contract with Decca in 1935 required him to play and sing innocuous popular songs, songs that were suitable for radio listeners in the comfort of their living rooms. The big bands were all the rage, and Armstrong fell into line by leading a number of mediocre groups during this era. There was also a serious problem with Armstrong's lips. Throughout his career, he suffered from split lips, which forced him to rest for long periods of time. The scar tissue hampered his ability to play with clarity. His singing, however, was not affected. One of his 1930's songs, "A Kiss to Build a Dream On," clearly demonstrates his brilliant application of jazz phrasing to an otherwise ordinary lyric.

Armstrong reached the peak of his popularity in the 1950's and 1960's. Although he had been almost completely deserted by jazz enthusiasts, the general public responded to his many film appearances and to his singing. His hit records included "Blueberry Hill," "Mack the Knife," and "Hello, Dolly!" The latter song was such a smash that it became number one on the charts in May, 1964. It also led to a much-heralded appearance in the movie of the same name and to many television bookings.

This success marked a high point in Armstrong's show business career. Shortly thereafter, his health began to fail, and he died on July 7, 1971. Armstrong had fulfilled the promise of the Hot Five sessions, but not quite in the way jazz musicians had expected or would have preferred.

SIGNIFICANCE

Biographer James Lincoln Collier has written that Armstrong "struck the first two generations of jazz musicians with the force of a sledgehammer." This is not an exaggeration. Most jazz writers and musicians without hesitation cite Armstrong as the father of modern jazz or as the "Bach of Jazz." He was truly a creator, for there was almost no musician who influenced him. He learned something from King Oliver, but what he learned was related more to presentation than to the music itself. Armstrong displayed technical and imaginative talent that astounded and inspired Roy Eldridge, Dizzy Gillespie, Benny Goodman, Humphrey Lyttelton, and a legion of other jazz musicians.

The clarity of Armstrong's horn, his sharp attacks, and his ability to play effectively in the highest register startled those who heard him for the first time in the 1920's. His imagination appeared boundless in those early days; he could create melodies of grace and power almost instantly. The most cherished of Armstrong's attributes, however, and the one that had the greatest impact on future musicians, was his ability to lift all around him, musicians and audiences alike, by the sheer joy and energy he brought to his music. He taught American musicians how to "swing," how to give even simple music verve and excitement. It certainly helped if one had the virtuosity possessed by Armstrong, but lesser musicians could at least emulate his enthusiasm.

The Hot Five recordings, particularly "Potato Head Blues" and "Weather Bird," convinced musicians to be more independent and to eschew jazz orchestras, in which they sat in sections and played notes, for the delight of improvisation, the opportunity to soar. Armstrong had, in effect, given all musicians the opportunity to use their creative talent to the fullest. Whether a musician played the clarinet, the piano, the bass, or the cornet, Armstrong was the model. His 1928 recording of "Weather Bird" (which he and King Oliver wrote in 1923) with pianist Fatha Hines was so spectacularly successful that such collaborations became standard for jazz musicians from that time onward.

Although Armstrong's major contribution was to the future of jazz, Armstrong's influence can also be traced in rhythm and blues, rock and roll, country music, and all forms of popular singing. Even when he ceased to produce great creative music after the early 1930's, his impact persisted. The Beatles, Collier points out, played as an "extra" for a jazz band in England that emulated the Hot Five numbers. Jimmie Rodgers, one of the original country singers, had Armstrong as an accompanist on his recording of "Blue Yodel No. 9," and Rodgers's singing always had a jazz flavor. Bing Crosby, a regular at Armstrong's Chicago appearances, undoubtedly profited from observing Armstrong's impeccable understanding of lyrics. Crosby once said he learned to swing from watching Armstrong.

No summary of Armstrong's impact can be complete without some mention of his effect on those who listened to his recordings, watched him in movies, or saw him in person. There was the Armstrong who influenced musicians, and there was the Armstrong who taught the general public how to enjoy the music. Although his impact was greatest with black audiences early in his career, in the later years, most in his audiences were white. White crowds found joy in his very appearance on stage, but not all the reasons for this were positive. As the Civil Rights movement in the United States intensified in the 1960's, many blacks found Armstrong's wide smile, rolling eyes, and general mugging increasingly grating. To some, he seemed to be pushing

the happy-go-lucky image a little far. Many whites, however, found comfort in Armstrong, especially in an era of racial stress. By his rise from abject poverty and rejection to the heights of success, he seemed to prove that the American Dream did apply to blacks. In a time of growing anger and strident demands, Armstrong continued to play and sing and look happy. He offered marvelous reassurance, and the popularity of his 1964 hit record "Hello, Dolly!" said as much about the political and social circumstances in the United States as it did about Armstrong's singing.

The reaction to Armstrong was the same throughout the world. When he first appeared on screen in the 1969 film *Hello, Dolly!* the huge gathering in a London cinema burst into sustained cheering and applause. The response was not so much for Armstrong's great musical contributions since the Hot Five days, but rather a recognition of the warmth that emanated from his horn, his voice, and his entire being.

—*Ronald K. Huch*

See also: Handy Ushers in the Commercial Blues Era; Harlem Renaissance; Bessie Smith Records "Downhearted Blues"; Ellington Begins Performing at the Cotton Club; Billie Holiday Begins Her Recording Career.

BAKER DANCES IN *LA REVUE NÈGRE*

October-December, 1925

Parisian café society was spellbound by exotic dancer Josephine Baker, who would soon change how Europe viewed modern dance.

Locale: Paris, France
Category: Dance

KEY FIGURES

Josephine Baker (1906-1975), American dancer who became a symbol of expressive, exotic performing in Europe during the 1920's
André Daven (fl. early twentieth century), director of the Théâtre des Champs-Élysées during the showing of *La Revue nègre Rolf de Mare* (1888-1964), manager of the Théâtre des Champs-Élysées during the showing of *La Revue nègre*

Paul Colin (1892-1985), amateur painter responsible for designing the cover of the program and the poster for *La Revue nègre*
Caroline Dudley (fl. early twentieth century), chief organizer in New York City of the black song-and-dance show that sailed to Paris to perform at the Théâtre des Champs-Élysées
Jacques Charles (fl. early twentieth century), producer at the Moulin Rouge who helped with the production of *La Revue nègre.*

SUMMARY OF EVENT

By the age of nineteen, Josephine Baker had risen from her poverty-stricken background in East St. Louis to the endless possibilities of New York City show business. In 1921, she first made her name known in Noble Sissle and Eubie Blake's show *Shuffle Along*. She

Josephine Baker in her famous banana costume by Lucien Waléry

save Paris's Théâtre des Champs-Élysées from hard economic postwar times, it would be a real African American show. The theater was very large for such a small production, but the directors hoped to move the show into smaller dance halls later. Baker was one of the twenty-four musicians, singers, and dancers to travel across the Atlantic Ocean and perform in what is one of the best-known American productions of the 1920's, *La Revue nègre* (the black revue).

Baker arrived in Paris dumbfounded and ready to return to the United States immediately after the show was completed. Her attitude would soon change, however. *La Revue nègre* was developed to give the European audience an idea of how black Americans danced. When the opening night of *La Revue nègre* finally came, Paris was caught by surprise. A popular comment from the audience was that the show had the most black people they had ever seen on a stage at one time. To Parisian café society, the popular class of people involved in the city life of downtown Paris, this was a part of the world they knew little about.

Before *La Revue nègre* was ready for its preview showing at the Théâtre des Champs-Élysées, director Daven and producer Rolf de Mare had to make significant changes to the format and content of the show, which had been presented in Britain and across Europe as *Blackbirds*. They thought the show was too noisy, too long, inelegant, and not black enough. Jacques Charles, a producer at the well-known Moulin Rouge, rearranged the dancers and put more focus on Baker. She was given the spotlight in one particularly exotic dance, the "Danse sauvage," which was strategically placed at the end of the show to create a shocking finale. Baker and her partner appeared in bare skin and feathers, and they raced around the stage to upbeat African music. Baker's part in the "Danse sauvage" was the foundation of her exotic dance period. Interestingly, Baker was not originally scheduled to star in the show. When Maud de Forrest, the original lead singer, could no longer handle the pressure of performing in *La Revue nègre*, she was dismissed from the show. Baker took her place as the leading lady, and a star was born.

When the show was ready for opening night, journalists and celebrities were given an exclusive preview showing. An enormous amount of publicity appeared in the French tabloids and newspapers. What mattered was not whether the reviews were good or bad, but that the show had become the most talked-about production in Paris. Almost immediately after opening night, Baker

later appeared in their show *Chocolate Dandies*. Both of these all-black Broadway shows are remembered for their role in helping to introduce black entertainment to the stages of New York City. Baker's clowning, comical style helped to get her noticed during rehearsals and auditions, but she appeared in these productions only briefly, as a dancer or a "walk-on." Her well-known ragamuffin period was labeled as such because of her popular cross-eyed and knees-turned-in dance position that eventually helped her break into entertainment. However, Baker's stage appearances were not due to her dancing ability or beautiful body. On the contrary, Baker was perceived as an ugly tomboy and was clad in big shoes and tattered clothes.

In the summer of 1925, show coordinator Caroline Dudley organized a black song-and-dance troupe at the request of the French theater director André Daven. Dudley and Daven believed that if anything would help became a well-known success. Surrounded by handsome men, publicity people, and artists, her impression of Paris quickly changed, and she became accustomed to the European lifestyle. France would soon become her new home, and she became part of France's growing obsession with black entertainment.

An artist by the name of Paul Colin was partly responsible for Baker's fame in *La Revue nègre*. Colin was called in to draw the publicity program cover and poster. As the posters covered walls throughout Paris, positive reviews continued to flourish, and more and more Parisians came to see the show. *La Revue nègre* had created a celebrity and proved to Paris that black is beautiful. Artists soon drowned Baker with requests to photograph or paint her in the nude. She was at first too modest but soon realized that nude portrayals were going to become common.

Although Baker was said not to have liked *La Revue nègre*, she would not have become a dance celebrity without it. Colin's posters made her recognizable long before the public knew her by name. *La Revue nègre* played for three months, from October to December of 1925. As the directors of the Théâtre des Champs-Élysées had predicted, *La Revue nègre* was able to continue its run by moving into smaller theaters. The show traveled from Paris to Brussels and then to the Nelson Theatre in Berlin. Although it was not a long-running show, by the end of 1925 it had made Baker one of the most famous dancers in Europe.

From Baker and *La Revue nègre*, European society gained a knowledge and understanding of a dance culture that was previously all but unknown to it. Credit for this discovery must be given not only to Charles, Daven, de Mare, and the other show organizers, but to Baker and her unique talent. Her dance was not regarded immediately as artistically valuable. On the opening night of *La Revue nègre*, Baker was pleased to hear what she thought were whistles of approval coming from the audience.

She soon found out, however, that in Paris whistling signaled rejection and dislike. Baker was in disbelief. In the weeks after opening night, the whistling came to be drowned out by chants of "Josephine" and calls for more wonderful dance. Parties were thrown for the singers and dancers night after night.

La Revue nègre certainly left an impression on Jacques-Émile Blanche, a renowned French portrait painter. He had been searching for a "manifestation of the modern spirit" in the Art Deco Show but found it instead in *La Revue nègre*. This led other people to look at the show in that manner. The numerous reviews became Baker's texts for learning the French language. Whether good or bad, the critiques of *La Revue nègre* educated Baker and the public. One critic compared the dance movements in the show to St. Vitus's Dance, a nervous disorder that makes the body tremble. Another labeled Baker a "Black Venus." A particularly harsh critic of Baker was distinguished dance critic Andre Levinson. He referred at first to black dance as primitive and prehuman, saying that black dancers turned their bodies into percussion instruments.

He gave *La Revue nègre* a favorable although somewhat condescending review and later was persuaded of the validity of black dance and jazz music. Librettist and playwright Robert de Flers referred to *La Revue nègre* as "the most direct assault ever perpetrated against French taste." It is difficult to assess the widely differing opinions of Baker and the show. Unfortunately, there are no film recordings of *La Revue nègre*, only photographs and stories told by Baker's friends and family.

The fame Baker received from *La Revue nègre* was only a fraction of what was to come. In 1926, she was asked to join productions of the Folies-Bergère, a major tourist attraction in the Paris theater district. In 1927, she performed at the Folies-Bergère with two live cheetahs, wearing nothing but a short skirt made of imitation bananas. Ironically, Baker was not received as well when she returned to the United States to appear in *Ziegfeld Follies of 1936*. After that, it would be fifteen years before she would return to her native country again. Baker joined the French Women's Air Force at the outbreak of World War II and later joined the French Resistance; for this work she was awarded the Croix de Guerre with Palm, among other decorations. When she did return to the United States in 1951, she refused to appear in clubs that did not allow black patrons. Her stand convinced the Copa City Club in Miami, Florida, to change its discriminatory policies, and other clubs began to follow the trend. Baker's performances included singing as well as dancing, but it was her dancing that made her famous.

She performed all over the world in various shows and eventually went on a solo world tour. Baker visited the United States on her tours and, in later years, said that she thought of it once again as her home. With the stamina of a twenty-year-old, Baker performed into the final days of her life, appearing in *Josephine*, a show commemorating her fifty years in show business, five days before she died on April 12, 1975, in Paris. Her funeral was publicized throughout the country. Starting at the church of the Madeleine, the procession went by the theaters at which she had performed. Eulogies recognized her civil and military achievements as well as her artistic ability.

Baker is remembered as one of the most famous female performers, responsible in large part for bringing new dance forms to Europe, beginning with her performance in *La Revue nègre*.

SIGNIFICANCE

When *La Revue nègre* opened at the Théâtre des Champs-Élysées, the French had no idea what impact Baker would have on the history of dance. European audiences were enchanted immediately when Baker stepped out on stage and became a beautiful, flowing piece of art. Because so little was known about African dance, Baker became even more of a celebrated creature.

When she danced, her somewhat-disproportionate body became unexplicably beautiful and perfect, moving in ways no one knew were possible. Baker danced so exotically that the audience was mesmerized just by watching her move. Her dancing was said to have been on the verge of being obscene.

Many different events illustrate how African dance was regarded after the popularity of *La Revue nègre*. According to the average Parisian audience member, black dancers were instinctive and incapable of discipline. When on stage, they were thought of as indecent, primitive, and savage. Because Baker's dance moves were so unconventional and so different from those of Caucasian dancers, it was easy to understand why these thoughts were prevalent. *La Revue nègre* came to symbolize postwar modernism, bringing to Europe the spirit of Americanized Africa. The dance culture was left refreshed and more dynamic, with unconventional forms more accepted.

Baker helped introduce popular American dances to Europe, including the Charleston and the Black Bottom. Her dancing also helped to popularize the jazz music that accompanied it. Critic Andre Levinson wrote about jazz, "The music is born from the dance, and what a dance!" The impact Baker had on the European culture was strong, and Baker's style became an institution in French society. Restaurateurs and club owners named their establishments after her. Fashion designers followed the advice of Baker and eventually designed dresses in her name, such as Robe Josephine.

—David Francis

WHITE PRIMARIES

1927 to 1953

In cases on which it ruled from 1927 to 1953, the U.S. Supreme Court declared white primaries to be unconstitutional state actions that are prohibited by the equal protection clause of the Fourteenth Amendment.

Definition: Elections designed to exclude African Americans from voting

In *Newberry v. United States* (1921), the Supreme Court declared that primaries were not constitutionally protected as elections and could not be controlled by Congress. Although African Americans could not be prevented from voting in federal elections, southern legislatures used *Newberry* to prohibit African Americans from voting in primaries. In the southern states, which were dominated by the Democratic Party, the only significant competition occurred at the primary level, within the party. Thus, inability to participate in a primary in these states meant effective disfranchisement.

The first challenge to the white primary, *Nixon v. Herndon* (1927), resulted in a unanimous decision for the African American plaintiff. Justice Oliver Wendell Holmes held that the Texas white primary law violated the equal protection clause of the Fourteenth Amendment. In *Nixon v. Condon* (1932), the Court invalidated a Texas Democratic Party executive committee order excluding African Americans from voting in primaries. However, in *Grovey v. Townsend*

(1935), a unanimous Court ruled that white primaries were the elections of a private organization and not forbidden as state action. *United States v. Classic* (1941), dealing with corrupt voting in Louisiana, held that primaries selecting nominees for federal office were protected.

Applying *Classic*, the Court reversed *Grovey* in *Smith v. Allwright (*1944). *Terry v. Adams* (1953) invalidated the preprimary of the Jaybird Democratic Association as a denial of equal protection and

removed the final institutional obstacle to African American voting.

—*Gilbert Morris Cuthbertson*

See also: Fifteenth Amendment; Gerrymandering; Grandfather clauses; *Grovey v. Townsend*; *Nixon v. Condon*; *Nixon v. Herndon*; Politics and government; Poll taxes; *Smith v. Allwright*; *Terry v. Adams*; *United States v. Classic*; Voting Rights Act of 1965

NIXON V. HERNDON
March 7, 1927

In the first of a series of white primary cases, the Supreme Court overturned a Texas statute that explicitly prohibited African Americans from voting in Democratic Party primaries.

The Case: U.S. Supreme Court ruling on white primaries

In 1921, the U.S. Supreme Court ruled in *Newberry v. United States* that Congress lacked authority to regulate primary elections. Southern state legislatures immediately took advantage of this decision to prohibit black participation in state primary elections. "White primaries" were quickly adopted throughout the South. Texas, during the first half of the twentieth century, was part of the Democrat-dominated South. The only competition that mattered was within the Democratic Party, so if African Americans were not allowed to participate in the Democratic primary they would effectively be denied any meaningful choice in the electoral process.

In 1924, the Texas legislature passed a law barring African Americans from voting in the Democratic primary. L. A. Nixon, a black resident of El Paso, attempted to vote in the primary and was refused by Herndon, an election judge. Nixon and the National Association for the Advancement of Colored People (NAACP) claimed that the Texas law violated the Fourteenth and Fifteenth Amendments. The Supreme Court did not deal with the issue of the Fifteenth Amendment, but a unanimous Court found that the Texas white primary law violated the equal protection clause of the Fourteenth Amendment.

The NAACP won the battle but temporarily lost the war. Texas responded to the Court's decision by engaging in the strategy of "legislate and litigate." By passing a different white primary law after their defeat in *Nixon v. Herndon*, the Texas legislature forced the NAACP to institute another attack on the white primary. When the second law was declared unconstitutional in *Nixon v. Condon* in 1932, Texas came up with a third variation of the white primary. This time, in *Grovey v. Townsend* (1935), the U.S. Supreme Court upheld the Texas white primary, arguing that no state discrimination was present. According to the Court, the Texas Democratic Party, a private voluntary association, decided to exclude African Americans from voting in the primary elections. It was not until *Smith v. Allwright* (1944) that a unanimous Supreme Court declared that the Fifteenth Amendment could be used as a shield to protect the right to vote in primary elections.

From the passage of the first white primary law in 1924 until the final abolition of white primaries in the *Smith* case in 1944, African Americans were denied the right to vote in Democratic Party primaries, the only election of significance at that time. The white primary cases illustrate one of the dilemmas in using the federal courts—the fact that justice delayed is justice denied.

—*Darryl Paulson*

See also: Gerrymandering; *Grovey v. Townsend*; National Association for the Advancement of Colored People; *Newberry v. United States*; *Nixon v. Condon*; *Smith v. Allwright*; White primaries

ELLINGTON BEGINS PERFORMING AT THE COTTON CLUB

December 4, 1927

When Duke Ellington began a three-year engagement at Harlem's Cotton Club, he launched his career as the most important composer-arranger-leader in jazz history.

Locale: New York, New York Category: Music

KEY FIGURES

Duke Ellington (1899-1974), American pianist, composer, arranger, and bandleader

Bubber Miley (James Miley; 1903-1932), American trumpeter

Tricky Sam Nanton (Joseph Nanton; 1904-1946), American trombonist

Irving Mills (1894-1985), American song publisher and promoter

Johnny Hodges (1907-1970), American alto saxophonist

SUMMARY OF EVENT

With Louis Armstrong and Charlie Parker, Duke Ellington (Edward Kennedy Ellington) is one of the greatest figures in jazz and twentieth century American music. His importance rests on his achievements as a composer, orchestrator, and pianist-leader of the remarkable orchestra he headed for almost half a century. When he and his band made their debut at New York City's Cotton Club in 1927, Ellington was still a musician with a modest if growing reputation. He already had acquired the nickname that reflected his suave good looks and courtly manner when he emerged as the leader of a small black cooperative dance band that had moved to New York City from Washington, D.C., in 1923. Ellington's debut at the Cotton Club on December 4, 1927, is now recognized as one of the most important openings in jazz history even though the unprepared band's first few performances there were unimpressive. The band soon mastered the demanding fifteen-act program and also played for dancing and radio broadcast. It quickly became a major attraction in itself, as Ellington used the opportunity to transform his dance-show band into a collaborative vehicle for superior artistic expression.

The Cotton Club was one of the best-known and most successful of more than a dozen Harlem establishments that catered exclusively or mainly to a white clientele. Ellington's white manager, Irving Mills, had arranged for the job at the club. Its success was based

Duke Ellington at the Hurricane Club in New York, May 1943

mainly on its exotic and relatively sophisticated ambience, the quality of its all-black entertainment, and the sale of illegal alcohol. The elaborate shows, which usually featured comedians, dancers, vocalists, a chorus line, and the house band, were staged by experienced Broadway show people with original music by Jimmy McHugh.

The engagement at the Cotton Club enabled Ellington to build and consolidate his all-star band. It also spurred him to create a body of distinctive compositions and orchestral arrangements that drew on the African American tradition and expanded and elevated the vocabulary of jazz. Many of the club's acts appealed to white fantasies of exotic and primitive Africa, and the muted brass growls that the Ellington band had developed were labeled and marketed as "jungle style." Compositions such as "Echoes of the Jungle" served a functional purpose at the Cotton Club; they also transcended that context and, together with other original works, made an impact when heard on records and radio.

Nationwide radio broadcasts from the Cotton Club on the fledgling Columbia Broadcasting System (CBS) network made Ellington's name and music familiar to millions. Records by Duke Ellington and His Famous Cotton Club Orchestra sold widely and were heard in Europe, where Ellington became a celebrity before his first visit there in 1933. In 1929, Mills arranged for Ellington to lead his band in Florenz Ziegfeld's theater production of George Gershwin's *Show Girl*. The band performed with Maurice Chevalier, then traveled to Hollywood to make the film *Check and Double Check* (1930). Ellington was included in a group of important African Americans invited to the White House in 1931. In addition to writing arrangements in the jungle style, Ellington mastered the sectional formula developed by Fletcher "Smack" Henderson for his own much-admired orchestra. Henderson's model became the basis for many big band arrangers.

Ellington frequently departed from the formula, mixing instrumental voices from across the trumpet, trombone, and reed sections to produce unique and sometimes haunting blends, as in the muted trumpet, muted trombone, and clarinet sound of "Mood Indigo" (1930). Ellington often borrowed or developed the ideas of his musicians in creating music for his band. The frequent use of unwritten "head arrangements," which gradually evolved as suggestions were incorporated, contributed to the collaborative expression of the band but sometimes made the question of authorship difficult, even though the organizing intelligence was clearly Ellington's. In his more formal and personal arrangements, Ellington sometimes used sound in much the same way as the pointillists used paint. His impressionistic compositions, skillful use of dissonance, and unusual textures led to comparisons with such modern European composers as Claude Debussy, Frederick Delius, and Maurice Ravel, of whom Ellington probably had little knowledge. In his career of more than fifty years, Ellington wrote approximately twelve hundred compositions of an amazing variety, including simple blues, popular hit songs, dance tunes, showcases for individual musicians, short orchestral pieces, extended works designed mainly for concerts, film music, television themes, ballet and opera scores, and religious music for his "sacred concerts." Ellington's abiding inspiration was the black American community and its culture, which he sought to portray in compositions such as "Black Beauty," *Black, Brown, and Beige*, "Harlem Airshaft," and "My People."

One of Ellington's greatest achievements was the creation of an orchestra unrivaled for its stability, longevity, and number of influential musicians who stayed within its ranks for prolonged periods. Throughout his life Ellington was in an almost constant state of exploration, reevaluation, and development; his music is so various that it defies classification. He kept the band together, sometimes at great personal expense, because he needed to hear his compositions and arrangements played on the instrument for which they were intended: his orchestra.

SIGNIFICANCE

The Ellington orchestra's success was in part a result of the talent of its individual members, many of whom became models for thousands of other artists. Johnny Hodges was one of the preeminent alto saxophonists in jazz, influencing almost all who came after him, even tenor saxophonists such as bandmate Ben Webster and modernist John Coltrane. Harry Carney, who was with the band from 1927 until Ellington's death in 1974, is known as the father of the baritone saxophone, which he established as an important ensemble and solo voice.

Trumpeter Bubber Miley and trombonist Tricky Sam Nanton developed the plunger-mute techniques on their respective instruments that created the "jungle sounds" that were an important characteristic of the Ellington orchestral style. These expressive techniques sprang from the roots of the jazz instrumental tradition and subsequently were used by brass players everywhere. Miley's successor with Ellington, Charles "Cootie" Williams, became an influence in his own right, as did trombonist Lawrence Brown, trumpeter Clark Terry, and saxophonist Ben Webster. In his short life, Jimmy Blanton established the path followed by most jazz bass players since 1940. Ellington himself was a competent if not outstanding pianist who began by playing mainly in the "stride" style that had developed out of ragtime. He also developed an effective accompaniment style and ways of voicing chords that are widely imitated. Imitations of Ellington's influence can be heard in the work of the modernist pianist/composer Thelonious Monk, who made a piano-trio recording of Ellington compositions.

Ellington's appeal to jazz musicians has transcended periods and styles and proved timeless; there are few who have not acknowledged his influence in one way or another. Ellington's life and musical interests spanned the first seventy-five years of jazz history. He recorded and sounded comfortable with the greatest artists of every period, including Louis Armstrong, Coleman Hawkins, Dizzy Gillespie, Charles Mingus, and John Coltrane.

Because they seem so quintessentially to belong to his orchestra, Ellington's longer compositions are seldom heard performed except on his own recordings. They are demonstrations that the American dance band can be an extremely flexible vehicle, both for popular entertainment and for high artistic expression. Although the Ellington spirit and influence permeate big band music, few arrangers (aside from his collaborator and musical alter ego, Billy Strayhorn) have been able to duplicate Ellington's unique orchestral sound. The bands of Charlie Barnet and Woody Herman at times provided rough approximations, aided by the fact that both leaders were saxophonists in the style of Johnny Hodges. The persistence of Ellington's influence as a composer and orchestrator can be heard in the modern works of Charles Mingus, Gil Evans, and Oliver Nelson.

Ellington's compositions have been played by groups large and small since the 1930's, and his legacy is perhaps most alive in the thirty or so short compositions that are still part of the working repertoire of most jazz musicians around the world. Melodies such as "Satin Doll," "In a Mellow Tone," "Solitude," and "In a Sentimental Mood"—works on a par with those of Cole Porter, George Gershwin, and Irvin Berlin—can be heard wherever jazz is played. Ellington's compositions have been recorded thousands of times by musicians ranging from traditionalists to the avant-garde and have been reinterpreted as they have been discovered by each succeeding generation.

In his many tours abroad, some under the aegis of the U.S. government, Ellington took his music and the American ideals of individuality and freedom of expression within a cooperative group context to thousands of people. In addition to his influence on musicians and leaders such as Ted Heath of Britain and Francy Boland of Belgium, Ellington absorbed and later (often with Strayhorn) transformed foreign musical influences in such works as *Far East Suite, Virgin Islands Suite*, and *Latin American Suite.*

Wynton Marsalis, one of the most impressive and influential musicians to appear in the 1980's, has stated that "Duke Ellington is what jazz is, he is the greatest jazz musician…because he addressed most comprehensively what jazz music actually is…the fundamentals of group improvisation, vocalization, and a swinging optimism." Marsalis has devoted much of his considerable talent to educating young musicians in the value of Ellington's music and in performing the composer's works with the Lincoln Center Jazz Orchestra, as on the recording *Portraits by Ellington.*

Ellington's musical achievement elevated jazz as an African American art form and brought increased acceptance and respect to its practitioners. His personal sophistication and dignity made him an important representative of the black community. Ellington's hundreds of honors and awards, including many honorary doctorates, also served to acknowledge the contributions of black people to American society and culture. On the occasion of his seventieth birthday, a celebration was held at the White House during which President Richard Nixon presented Ellington with the highest civilian award of the United States, the Presidential Medal of Freedom.

During the height of big band popularity in the 1930's and early 1940's, Ellington's band was not as commercially successful as many white bands, but his organization was often the standard against which other bands were measured, especially by musicians. Through courage, hard work, and artistry, Ellington was able to sustain his band after all but a handful of others had disappeared.

When Ellington died in 1974, the leadership of his still-functioning band was taken up by his son Mercer, who continued to present his father's music to the world until his own death in 1996.

—Douglas Rollins

See also: Harlem Renaissance; Bessie Smith Records "Downhearted Blues"; Armstrong Records with the Hot Five; Billie Holiday Begins Her Recording Career

HALLELUJAH IS THE FIRST IMPORTANT BLACK MUSICAL FILM

1929

King Vidor sacrificed salary to direct the first serious all-black musical motion picture, successfully blending music and drama to depict southern farm life and its tragedies.

Locale: Metro-Goldwyn-Mayer studios, Culver City, California
Category: Motion pictures

KEY FIGURES

King Vidor (1894-1982), American film director
Daniel L. Haynes (1894-1954), American actor and minister
Nina Mae McKinney (1913-1967), American actor

SUMMARY OF EVENT

When Warner Bros. released *The Jazz Singer* in 1927, the era of silent films came to an end, but some studio heads believed sound to be a fad. Metro-Goldwyn-Mayer (MGM) did not release a sound film until 1928; its first musical was 1929's *The Broadway Melody*, a backstage story full of young women in abbreviated costumes. The studio intended to follow this film with similar moneymakers, and it turned down King Vidor's proposal of an all-black musical tragedy set among impoverished farmers.

By then, however, Vidor had achieved a considerable reputation. A Galveston, Texas, native who as a boy had taught himself film techniques by watching silents, Vidor had come to California in 1915 and had taken every studio job he could get in order to learn his profession. He made his reputation with *The Turn in the Road* (1919); it was characteristic of Vidor that he convinced a group of physicians to back the film, which had a Christian Science theme. *The Turn in the Road* depicted a man's search for his personal truths, a theme that was to dominate Vidor's films.

D. W. Griffith's films taught Vidor the relationship of films to musical forms, and from Robert J. Flaherty's *Nanook of the North* (1922) he learned the dramatic value of everyday experience. His two most important silent films foreshadowed *Hallelujah* in evidencing both interests. In *The Big Parade* (1925), starring John Gilbert, he showed a common soldier, neither a hero nor a coward. In *The Crowd* (1928), Vidor showed a common office worker whose struggles were everyman's: marriage, parenthood, dead-end work,

unemployment, the loss of a child, alcoholism, and periods of happiness.

Vidor used music to spectacular effect in the background for *The Big Parade*. He conceptualized the film in terms of musical movements, pacing off the troops' steps with a metronome and speeding up the beat as tension mounted. As troops marched toward the battlefront and death, the musical score ceased, and the soldiers moved only to the cadence of an ominous bass drum. Although critics attacked Vidor's use of music in *Hallelujah* as a racist depiction of black music and attacked the hero's sordid story and emotionalism, these themes were in fact set in Vidor's work before he came to *Hallelujah*.

The film's hero, Zeke, is searching for his true life. He is caught between two women who represent the extremes of his own psychological needs. Music represents this conflict. Gospel songs and traditional spirituals are associated with the order and family harmony of Zeke's family's farm, whereas syncopated jazz represents the world that tempts him. (Until the end of his life, Vidor was disturbed by the studio's insistence on adding such elements as two Irving Berlin songs, "At the End of the Road" and "Swanee Shuffle," that gave the film a Tin Pan Alley air he wanted to avoid.)

Vidor's was not the first all-black musical. Earlier in 1929, Fox (later Twentieth Century-Fox) released *Hearts in Dixie*, which featured the talented actor Clarence Muse and provided the first major role for comedian Stepin Fetchit. *Hearts in Dixie*, however, focused on the happy-go-lucky life of a fictional plantation. Later in 1929, *St. Louis Blues*, released by Warner Bros., provided singer Bessie Smith her only film role, but it was not a full-length feature; it ran only seventeen minutes. Vidor took a bigger risk. He wanted to treat his black hero as seriously as he had treated the white soldier in *The Big Parade* and the white office worker in *The Crowd*. Vidor's operational problems were staggering, with sound techniques still in their infancy, and MGM refused to make the film until Vidor donated the money due him under his MGM contract to the production.

For his cast, Vidor went to Chicago, New York, and Memphis, visiting black churches to hire his singers. For Zeke, he first wanted Paul Robeson, who was unavailable. Instead, he hired Daniel L. Haynes, the understudy for Jules Bledsoe, who sang "Ol' Man River" in the 1927 Broadway production of *Show Boat*. Nina Mae Mc- Kinney was hired from the chorus of a Broadway show. Three child musicians were hired when Vidor saw them dancing for quarters in a Memphis hotel. Vidor approached Harry Gray, who had been born into slavery, to play the father of the family. Musician Victoria Spivey played Missy Rose, William Fountaine played the gambler Hot Shot, and Fannie Bell McKnight was cast as the mother. All were relatively unknown.

The mood of *Hallelujah* was as somber as that of *The Crowd*. Zeke, the eldest son of a hardworking farm family, goes to town with his brother and is fascinated by Chick (McKinney), who plays a tempting Eve. He is cheated by Hot Shot; in a brawl, he accidentally shoots his brother. In atonement, he becomes a preacher, but, still fascinated by Chick, he leaves the ministry. Vidor explicitly shows Zeke's religious fervor to be an unsuccessful attempt to sublimate a sexual drive that finally conquers him. Zeke and Chick flee. Zeke ultimately kills Chick's lover, Hot Shot, and Chick dies in a symbolic fall. Zeke serves time in prison, then returns to the order and stability of his father's farm, where Missy Rose, the good girl, waits for him. They return to harvesting the earth and to the cycles of the seasons.

SIGNIFICANCE

By the end of Vidor's long life, the significance of *Hallelujah* was recognized, but its immediate reception was mixed. As Vidor recalled, the film may never have shown a profit. For the actors in the film, it was virtually a dead end, and no one at the time understood that Vidor had created a new film genre. His technical accomplishment, however, was immediately apparent.

Vidor shot the film on location near Memphis, Tennessee, and in Arkansas. Sound equipment, large and difficult to move, did not arrive, so much of the film was shot as a silent and then matched with sound tracks recorded in Hollywood, a feat so difficult that it literally drove one film cutter to a nervous breakdown.

For the scenes shot as silents, Vidor used impressionistic special effects. Perhaps the most dramatic scene shows Zeke chasing Hot Shot through a swamp. In his autobiographical *A Tree Is a Tree* (1953), Vidor recalled that "when someone stepped on a broken branch, we made it sound as if bones were breaking," and that when Hot Shot drew his foot from the sticky mud, "we made the vacuum sound strong enough to pull him down into hell." Recording a group of dock workers, Vidor for the first time used synchronous sound recording in the studio. The final print had flaws, but remarkable effects were readily evident.

Controversy, however, arose about the film's content. Although accused of racism, Vidor was unquestionably sincere; he had not intended to portray the black race as a whole but simply to show the harsh lives of the black people he had known in Galveston, where his father's lumber company had employed mostly black men and where he was taken to witness river baptisms. Although reviews in the white East Coast press were generally favorable, the black press reacted against the gambling and emotionalism of the black characters depicted in the film.

Controversy even surrounded the film's showing. In New York, the film was given dual premieres, one at the Lafayette Theater in Harlem and one downtown. Black journalists were indignant, assuming this meant that white audiences were willing to see blacks on film but were unwilling to sit next to them in audiences. In Chicago, two major theaters, the Balaban and Katz, refused to book the film for fear the black audiences would drive off white patrons. Vidor had to visit Chicago, show the film to critics, and wait for the positive reviews. Once these appeared, it was possible to convince a small independent theater to book the film. Its success at that theater forced major Chicago theaters to show it. In an attempt to get southern bookings, Vidor talked a Jacksonville, Florida, theater owner into booking the film by promising him a personal check for one thousand dollars if *Hallelujah* did not bring in more profit than whatever was currently showing. It did, and the man booked it into his theaters, but there were few other southern showings.

Even in Paris, where black entertainers had received a warmer welcome than in the United States, the film's showings were restricted. In a 1932 essay in *Le Crapouillot*, Pierre Bost recalled, perhaps with some exaggeration, that he could see the film only in the early hours of the morning and in a cellar, although it was the talk of the city.

The minor actors of *Hallelujah* are virtually lost to time. Of the stars, McKinney was signed to an MGM contract, but few roles were available for black women. Her portrait of Chick, however, is said to have created the figure of the feisty vamp later acted by such stars as Dorothy Dandridge and Jean Harlow. McKinney is said to have dubbed Harlow's songs in *Reckless* (1935). She appeared in a number of major studio films and in films made by independent black companies; in England, she appeared opposite Paul Robeson in Alexander Korda's *Sanders of the River* (1935). Her final film appearance was in *Pinky* (1949). There were also few roles for black men in American films after *Hallelujah*. Haynes played in Marc Connelly's *The Green Pastures* (1930) for five years on Broadway and for almost two thousand performances on tour; he played the major figure of De Lawd in a later revival. Haynes also played secondary roles in a number of films and achieved a distinguished career as pastor of New York churches.

Vidor went on to make a series of distinguished films. *Street Scene* (1931) and *Our Daily Bread* (1934) were in many ways reminiscent of his earlier films, with their emphasis on the overlooked dramas of everyday life. Other Vidor films included *Billy the Kid* (1930), *Stella Dallas* (1937), *The Citadel* (1938), *Northwest Passage* (1940), *Duel in the Sun* (1946), *The Fountainhead* (1949), *Ruby Gentry* (1952), and the Italian-American production of *War and Peace*

(1956). He directed the "Over the Rainbow" scene and other Kansas scenes for *The Wizard of Oz* (1939) when director Victor Fleming was called away.

In 1979, Vidor received a special Academy Award for career achievement. By that time, he was, among other things, recognized to have been the originator of the American folk musical film, a genre in which stories tend to be set in a mythic American past and tend to focus on domestic and traditional values. The genre's peculiar synthesis of these elements can be traced to the stage performance of *Show Boat*, which opened on Broadway in 1927, but it was in *Hallelujah* that it came to first fruition in film. After *Hallelujah* were to come such folk musicals as *Cabin in the Sky* (1942), *Meet Me in St. Louis* (1944), and *The Harvey Girls* (1946) as well as the film versions of *Oklahoma!* (1955) and *Carousel* (1956), but Vidor's seriousness of tone and fervor of purpose in *Hallelujah* were to distinguish it from all the rest.

—*Betty Richardson*

NATION OF ISLAM IS FOUNDED

SUMMER, 1930
The Nation of Islam, a religious organization, worked to inculcate black pride and help elevate African Americans' social and economic status.

Also known as: Black Muslim movement
Locale: Detroit, Michigan
Categories: Organizations and institutions; religion, theology, and ethics

KEY FIGURES
Wallace D. Fard (c. 1877-1934), first prophet of the Nation of Islam
Malcolm X (1925-1965), Nation of Islam minister and spokesperson
Elijah Muhammad (1897-1975), founder and spiritual leader of the Nation of Islam

SUMMARY OF EVENT
The Nation of Islam (NOI), also known as the Black Muslim movement and the Lost-Found Nation of Islam in the Wilderness of North America, is a religious organization that has successfully melded orthodox

Islam, black nationalism, and a set of social and economic principles to produce a highly structured way of life for its African American membership. A religious sect founded in 1930 in Detroit, Michigan, the NOI borrowed from earlier movements as it crystallized around

Members of the Nation of Islam, San Francisco, California, 1994, by Edmunddantes

three leaders: Wallace D. Fard, Elijah Muhammad, and Malcolm X.

Orthodox Islam was started in the city of Mecca, in what is now Saudi Arabia, by the Prophet Muwammad (570-632 CE). A major world religion, Islam may have arrived in the Americas with the Spanish explorers. In 1888, Alexander Russell Webb established an Islamic community in the United States. Members of the Islamic religion are known as Muslims. To distinguish between orthodox Muslims and members of the Nation of Islam sect, theologian C. Eric Lincoln coined the term Black Muslims. Although the NOI considers itself a branch of orthodox Islam, the majority of the organization's earliest members were affiliated with Christianity.

The Nation of Islam embraces the essential teachings of orthodox Islam: prayer five times daily; belief in one God, named Allah; acceptance of the sacred Islamic book, the Qur'ān; the coming of the "guided one," known as Mahdt; and pilgrimage to the holy city of Mecca. Both groups stress cleanliness and a strict moral code, and both shun alcohol, drug abuse, and the eating of pork. Early NOI leaders, however, expanded orthodox Islam because of the historic oppression of African Americans.

The Nation of Islam is orthodox Islam customized for the African American experience, with membership solidarity and racial pride being key added features. Black Muslims are required to drop their European last names, which are associated with enslavement, and adopt the "X" until they earn an Islamic surname. Additional elements, such as advocating a separate nation for its members and teaching about the racist deeds of the "white man," were the source of much outside criticism and prevented the NOI's acceptance into the official fold of orthodox Islam.

During the first half of the twentieth century, African Americans were treated as second-class citizens in the United States. Institutionalized racism made it difficult for many African Americans to rise above poverty and oppression. In the midst of Great Depression woes and the past specter of slavery, many African Americans were disillusioned and susceptible to philosophies and leaders who promised improvements. Consequently, a number of black nationalistic and religious movements developed during this period. The Nation of Islam includes principles that were embedded in two of these movements: Noble Drew Ali's Moorish Science Temple, founded in 1913, and Marcus Garvey's Universal Negro Improvement Association.

Timothy Drew, known as Noble Drew Ali, introduced Islam to African Americans. He and his followers adopted the Qur'ān and called themselves Moors, after an ancient North African people. Ali's church had thousands of members in northern U.S. cities before his unexplained death in 1929. Subsequently, many of Ali's followers joined Wallace D. Fard's group, which emerged a year later.

The Nation of Islam espoused the political nationalism of Jamaican-born Marcus Garvey, who amassed thousands of followers in the United States from 1916 until his imprisonment in 1923 and subsequent deportation. Garvey advocated a separate African American nation, economic and political solidarity, and racial pride. When Fard appeared on the American scene during the summer of 1930, the conditions that fostered the acceptance of the ideas of Garvey and Ali were still present, although the original founders were not. Consequently, Fard soon filled a void that, after setbacks, developed into a viable religious sect. The Nation of Islam grew out of informal visits Fard paid to the homes of African Americans in Detroit, where he peddled silk products and discussed orthodox Islam, the African heritage, and the misdeeds of the "white man."

The first prophet of the Nation of Islam is shrouded in mystery. Although he is believed to be from Mecca, his national origins, his real name, and the circumstances of his 1934 disappearance are not known. In addition to being known as W. D. Fard, Wallace D. Fard, and Wallace Fard Muhammad, he is referred to as Wali Farrad, F. Mohammad, and other names. Fard's achievements, however, are well documented. In four years during the Great Depression, he established the church's basic philosophy, created a security force known as the Fruit of Islam, opened the University of Islam, built its first temple, and amassed about eight thousand followers. Many of his followers, including Elijah Muhammad, thought Fard to be Allah reincarnated as well as the promised Mahdt. After Fard's sudden disappearance, Elijah Muhammad became the group's leader.

Elijah Muhammad, born Elijah Poole in Sandersville, Georgia, was respectfully known as the Honorable Elijah Muhammad, the Messenger of Allah. His parents had been slaves and sharecroppers. His father was a Baptist minister. While a teenager, Muhammad moved to Atlanta. He married Clara Evans in 1919, and during the 1920's he and his family migrated to Detroit. It was in Detroit that Muhammad met Fard and became one of his most devoted converts. He was rewarded by being chosen as Fard's successor, and he transformed Fard's sincere project into a thriving organization.

SIGNIFICANCE

After Fard's disappearance, rivalry caused some factionalism and a sharp decrease in NOI membership. Muhammad, often the victim of harassment and death threats, was imprisoned. Consequently, Muhammad moved the NOI headquarters from Detroit to Chicago. Although still confronted with adversities, Muhammad was able to rebuild and strengthen the organization. When Muhammad died in 1975, the Nation of Islam had temples and schools from coast to coast; owned a string of restaurants, apartments, and other businesses and real estate; operated a major printing press; and had a membership of more than 100,000. Much of Muhammad's success, however, can be attributed to one of his

ministers, Malcolm X. Malcolm X was born Malcolm Little in Omaha, Nebraska. His parents, Earle and Louise Little, were organizers for Marcus Garvey's Universal Negro Improvement Association. Because of their views, the Littles were forced to move away from Omaha.

They eventually settled in East Lansing, Michigan, where Earle apparently was murdered and Louise had a breakdown. Malcolm then lived with his sister and foster families. Later, he wandered between odd jobs and engaged in petty crime. He was imprisoned from 1946 to 1952, and he married Betty Shabazz in 1958. In prison, Malcolm became self-educated and converted to Islam. After his release, he met Elijah Muhammad, received his X, and trained for the NOI ministry. He headed temples in several cities before becoming the primary spokesperson for the Nation of Islam. His frank

Who Was Wallace D. Fard?

The first prophet of the Nation of Islam is shrouded in mystery: His national origins, his real name, and the circumstances of his 1934 disappearance are not fully known, but an FBI memorandum from Special Agent Edwin O. Raudsep, dated March 8, 1965 (approximately three decades after Fard's death), rehearses the known facts about Fard at that time.

[Wallace] Dodd arrived in the United States from New Zealand in 1913, settled briefly in Portland, Oregon. He married but abandoned his wife and infant son. He lingered in the Seattle Area as Fred Dodd for a few months, then moved to Los Angeles and opened a restaurant at 803 W. Third Street as Wallace D. Ford. He was arrested for bootlegging in January, 1926; served a brief jail sentence (also as Wallace D. Ford)—identified on record as white.

On June 12, 1926, also as Ford, was sentenced to San Quentin for sale of narcotics at his restaurant; got 6-months to 6-years sentence—released from San Quentin May 27, 1929. Prison record lists him as Caucasian.

After release, went to Chicago, then to Detroit as a silk peddler. His customers were mostly Negro and he himself posed as a Negro. He prided himself as a biblical authority and mathematician. When Elijah Muhammad (Poole) met him, he was passing himself off as a savior and claiming that he was born in Mecca and had arrived in the U.S. on July 4, 1930. In 1933 there was a scandal revolving about the sect involving a "human sacrifice" which may or may not have been trumped up. At any rate, the leader was arrested May 25, 1933, under the name Fard with 8 other listed aliases (W. D. Farrad, Wallace Farad, Walt Farrad, Prof. Ford, etc.). The official report says Dodd admitted that his teachings were "strictly a racket" and he was "getting all the money out of it he could." He was ordered out of Detroit.

[In a] newspaper article which appeared in the *San Francisco Examiner* and the *Los Angeles Examiner* on July 28, 1963, reporter Ed Montgomery . . . claimed to have contacted Dodd's former common law wife. . . .According to this account, Dodd went to Chicago after leaving Detroit and became a traveling suit salesman for a mail order tailer [*sic*]. In this position he worked himself across the midwest and ultimately arrived in Los Angeles in the spring of 1934 in a new car and wearing flowing white robes. He tried to work out a reconciliation with the woman, but she would not agree to one. . . . He stayed in Los Angeles for two weeks, frequently visiting his son. Then he sold his car and boarded a ship bound for New Zealand where he said he would visit relatives.

On Sunday, February 28, 1965, Ed Montgomery wrote a rehash of the above in which he said the Muslims claim "police and San Quentin Prison records dating back to the early 1920's had been altered and that fingerprints identifying Farad as Dodd had been doctored." Elijah Mohummad [*sic*] said he would have posted $100,000 reward "for any person who could prove Farad and Dodd were one and the same person." Ten days later Muhammad's office in Chicago was advised Farad's common law wife and a blood relative were prepared to establish the truth of Farad's identity. The $100,000 never was placed in escrow and the matter was dropped forthwith.

speeches and numerous public appearances catapulted the NOI into the national forefront. Membership swelled because of Malcolm's visibility, but the number of his enemies increased as well. For unauthorized remarks he made about President John F. Kennedy's assassination, Malcolm was suspended from the NOI. Around that time, he changed his name to El-Hajj Malik el-Shabazz. He left the NOI in March, 1964, and formed two new organizations, the success of which was curtailed by his murder on February 21, 1965.

After Elijah Muhammad's death, his son, Warith, also known as Wallace, became the NOI leader. Warith's changes forced another NOI split, spearheaded by Louis Farrakhan. The NOI expanded under Farrakhan, a controversial figure in part because of his adamant and at times incendiary statements. In October, 1995, the nondenominational NOI-sponsored Million Man March in Washington, D.C., added immensely to Farrakhan's visibility and to some extent mitigated his controversial image.

—*Linda Rochell Lane*

See also: Founding of the Niagara Movement; Great Northern Migration; Universal Negro Improvement Association Establishes a U.S. Chapter; 1920's: Harlem Renaissance

SCOTTSBORO TRIALS

March 25, 1931-July, 1937

The trials of nine young African Americans on trumped-up rape charges mirrored both entrenched southern bigotry and antiliberal sentiments. The Supreme Court's decision to grant the defendants a new trial expanded the rights of the accused to adequate counsel and due process of law.

Locale: Scottsboro and Decatur, Alabama
Categories: Laws, acts, and legal history; civil rights and liberties

KEY FIGURES

Ruby Bates (1915-1976), and
Victoria Price (1911-1982), American professed rape victims
Olen Montgomery (b. 1914), *Clarence Norris* (1912-1989), *Haywood Patterson* (1913-1952), *Ozie Powell* (b. 1916), *Willie Roberson* (b. 1915), *Charlie Weems* (b. 1911), *Eugene Williams* (b. 1918), *Andy Wright* (b. 1912), and *Roy Wright* (1918-1959), African Americans accused of rape
James E. Horton (1878-1973), American judge
Thomas E. Knight, Jr. (1898-1937), attorney general of Alabama
Samuel Leibowitz (1893-1978), American defense counsel

SUMMARY OF EVENT

On March 25, 1931, nine young African Americans were pulled off a freight train in Scottsboro, Alabama, after an alleged fight with a group of white youths. As the African Americans were being rounded up by sheriff's deputies, two women passengers told onlookers that they had been raped by the entire group. Within a month, the boys had been tried in Scottsboro, and eight of them had been convicted and sentenced to death; the case of the youngest boy, only thirteen years of age, was declared a mistrial.

Because of the speed of the convictions, the questionable nature of much of the testimony, and the hostile atmosphere in which the trial had been held, the case soon attracted widespread attention. Both the International Labor Defense (ILD), an arm of the Communist Party, and the National Association for the Advancement of Colored People (NAACP) expressed concern about the possibility of injustice and launched an appeal for a new trial. The boys and their parents chose the ILD to manage their defense.

The consolidated appeals reached the U.S. Supreme Court as *Powell v. Alabama* (1932), and the Court overturned the boys' convictions and ordered that they be given new trials. The Court's seven-to-two decision was based on the fact that the defendants had had access to counsel only immediately before the trial, preventing them from mounting an adequate defense. It also involved the lack of due deliberation in the overly speedy trial and the racial makeup of the jury.

Only three of the defendants were retried immediately. Their trials took place in Decatur, Alabama, from March to December, 1933. All three received convictions and death sentences, but the U.S. Supreme Court again sustained their appeal, this time on the basis of irregularities in the selection of jurors: The apellants pointed out that Decatur's voting rolls showed no African Americans registered to vote in the county in spite of a very large population of qualified African Americans residing there. This issue was to reappear on several occasions over the course of the Scottsboro trials.

In January, 1936, a third group of trials, held in Decatur, resulted in the conviction of Haywood Patterson, who was sentenced to seventy-five years in prison. After more than a year of delay and behind-the-scenes negotiations between Alabama state officials and a group of the defendants' supporters, the remaining eight were tried in the summer of 1937. One received the death penalty, three were sentenced to long prison terms, and the other four were released without charges. Although the one death sentence was later commuted to life imprisonment, the five convicted Scottsboro boys were unable to obtain any further reversals of their convictions. One of them was paroled in 1943, two more in 1946, and a fourth in 1950. The final prisoner escaped from a work gang in 1948 and managed to reach Michigan, whose governor refused to extradite him back to Alabama. The former defendant quickly found himself in trouble, however, committing a murder and being sentenced to Michigan's worst prison. He was unable to escape the environment in which he had spent most of his days, the prison.

It was not simply the length of the Scottsboro trials that accounted for the vast amount of publicity they attracted throughout the 1930's. Most observers outside Alabama and an increasingly large number of people within the state came to believe that the defendants were innocent and were, therefore, the victims of southern racial injustice. One of their two accusers, Ruby Bates, had retracted her testimony by 1934 and admitted that she had lied in her original accusations. The other, a prostitute named Victoria Price, presented testimony so full of contradictions that one of the judges in the 1933 trials, Alabamian James E. Horton, overruled the jury's guilty verdict and declared a mistrial. At least one of the defendants was ruled physically incapable of rape, and a physician testified that a medical examination of Bates and Price, performed shortly after the presumed attack, did not support their claims. Although both women were found to have had recent sexual intercourse, there were no contusions or other injuries that would have matched their stories about brutality at the hands of the nine men.

None of this had any appreciable effect on the juries, the prosecutors, or Judge William W. Callahan, who presided after Horton was removed from the case. Even the milder sentences meted out in 1937 resulted as much from a desire to end the unfavorable publicity surrounding the trials as from any reevaluation of the evidence. That is why four of the defendants were eventually released on the same testimony that convicted the other five.

SIGNIFICANCE

Aside from serving as a symbol of southern bigotry, the Scottsboro trials attracted attention because of the efforts of the Communist Party to identify the cause of the defendants with their own. Working through the ILD, the Communist Party was one of the first groups to protest the verdicts in the 1931 trials, and it was the only group to offer direct aid at that time. For several years, the party engaged in a running battle with the NAACP and an "American Scottsboro Committee" over the right to manage the boys' defense. The effect of these struggles was to unite many Alabamians against all "reds and foreigners" and make it more difficult to revise the verdicts.

The chief defense counsel after 1931 was Samuel Leibowitz, a Jewish attorney from New York who became the target of scurrilous attacks from the prosecutors. Even he, along with Judge Callahan and part of the Alabama press, came to regard the defendants' Communist support as a liability, and Leibowitz sought to dissociate the ILD from the case. In 1935, the NAACP, the American Civil Liberties Union, and the ILD joined to form the Scottsboro Defense Committee (SDC), which was designed to coordinate support for the defendants and seek cooperation from moderate Alabamians. Although the ILD played a much smaller role in the case from that point on, there remained enough hostility toward outside interference in Alabama to frustrate the SDC's efforts.

The Scottsboro case mirrored many of the important social currents of the 1930's. Although it illustrated the extent to which white southerners would go to defend a system of white supremacy, it also marked a change from the not-too-distant era when the defendants might well have been summarily lynched. The hysterical attitude with which many Alabamians reacted to outside interest in the case underlined a regional insecurity that had been intensified by the unsettled conditions of the Great Depression.

It was common for both men and women to hop onto freight trains, which the nine men had done, as had the two alleged victims. The Scottsboro boys had gotten into a fight with several white men. In Scottsboro and Decatur, race was on trial, not nine boys and men, much to the lasting chagrin of the state of Alabama. The episode would not end until 1976, when the Alabama Board of Pardons and Paroles granted Clarence Norris a full pardon. It thus took forty-five years for justice to be served.

—*Courtney B. Ross and John Jacob*

See also: National Association for the Advancement of Colored People Is Founded; Wright's *Native Son* Depicts Racism in America.

TUSKEGEE EXPERIMENT
1932–1972

During the Tuskegee experiment, scientists charted the course of the disease in men who had contracted the disease before their participation in the study. None of the men received any treatment, and at least 254 men died from the disease or its complications. Moreover, the men were told that they were receiving medical treatment, and none of them knew that they were being observed as part of an experiment on the effects of syphilis.

Subject blood draw, c. 1953

The Event: Long-term syphilis study conducted by the U.S. Public Health Service on four hundred African American men

Place: Tuskegee, Alabama

It has been argued that the Tuskegee experiment was motivated by the assumption that African Americans were more susceptible than whites to syphilis, and therefore the Public Health Service was interested in studying whether this was the case and, if so, why. One critic of the study, Martin Levine, went so far as to argue that the origins of the experiment lay in a stereotypical view of black sexuality:

> It was widely believed [among whites] that black racial inferiority made them a notoriously syphilis-soaked race! Their smaller brains lacked mechanisms for controlling sexual desire, causing them to be highly promiscuous. They matured earlier and consequently were sexually active; and the black man's enormous penis, with its long foreskin, was prone to venereal infections. These physiological differences meant the disease must affect the races differently. . . .

Other critics of this medical study point to it as evidence of the federal government's complicity in institutionalized racism against African Americans. Comments such as those by John Heller, the director of the Department of Venereal Diseases at the Public Health Service from 1943 to 1948, are often cited as evidence of this racism. Heller, for example, is quoted as saying of the men in the Tuskegee study that their "status did not warrant ethical debate. They were subjects, not patients: clinical material, not sick people."

For many African Americans, the Tuskegee study has come to represent verifiable evidence that institutionalized racism still exists in the United States. The study is also often cited to support possibly less verifiable claims of such racism. In the early 1990's, the Tuskegee study was often cited as supporting evidence for the AIDS conspiracy theory, which posited that the U.S. government manufactured the AIDS virus and intentionally infected people in Africa through immunization programs in order to commit genocide.

During the mid-1990's, a rumor spread through the African American community reporting that the company that made Snapple, a popular brand of bottled beverages, was owned by the Ku Klux Klan. On April 19, 1996, ABC's news magazine, *20/20*, aired a segment, narrated by journalist John Stossel, that investigated this claim. Stossel interviewed a number of people from various African American communities, many of whom believed this and other rumors, such as the U.S. government's manufacturing of the AIDS virus, and cited the Tuskegee experiment as evidence that such institutional racism has existed in the past in the United States and still existed.

—*Susan Mackey-Kallis*

See also: Brownsville incident; Stereotypes

NIXON V. CONDON

May 2, 1932

In the second round of the white primary cases, the Supreme Court struck down an exclusion of African Americans from primary elections by a party's executive committee, holding that the committee was acting as an agent of the state.

The Case: U.S. Supreme Court ruling on white primaries

In *Nixon v. Herndon* (1927), the Supreme Court unanimously overturned a law that directly excluded African Americans from voting in the primaries. The Texas legislature responded by authorizing the political parties' executive committees to set qualifications for primary elections. The Democratic committee quickly limited the primaries to whites only. When A. L. Nixon, an African American physician, challenged his exclusion, the Democratic Party asserted that the equal protection clause of the Fourteenth Amendment did not apply to private organizations.

Speaking for a 5-4 majority, Justice Benjamin N. Cardozo ruled narrowly that state action was involved because a state statute had vested the executive committee with its authority to set voting qualifications. The discrimination, therefore, violated the Fourteenth Amendment. The Texas legislature responded by repealing all primary election statutes and giving full control over the primaries to the political parties. This approach to African American disfranchisement would continue until *Smith v. Allwright* (1944).

—*Thomas Tandy Lewis*

See also: Gerrymandering; *Grovey v. Townsend*; *Nixon v. Herndon*; *Smith v. Allwright*; Voting Rights Act of 1965; White primaries

POWELL V. ALABAMA

November 7, 1932

In this, the first of the Scottsboro cases, the Supreme Court overturned the death sentences of the seven African Americans unjustly convicted of rape.

The Case: U.S. Supreme Court ruling on the right to counsel

Near Scottsboro, Alabama, nine young African American men were tried on charges of raping two white women on a freight train in 1931. Eight were convicted and sentenced to death. Alabama's highest court upheld the convictions of seven of the young men. The Scottsboro cases were then appealed to the Supreme Court. Justice George Sutherland wrote the opinion of the 7-2 majority, overturning the conviction and death sentence of the Scottsboro boys for rape. Sutherland held that the Fourteenth Amendment's due process clause mandated a fair trial, which required the effective assistance of legal counsel in capital cases. Because the Fourteenth Amendment applied to the states, the Alabama conviction could not stand. Justice Pierce Butler dissented and was joined by James C. McReynolds, arguing that the defendants had had effective representation and that the Court was making an unnecessary intrusion into the functioning of state courts.

—*Richard L. Wilson*

See also: Fourteenth Amendment; *Norris v. Alabama*

BILLIE HOLIDAY BEGINS HER RECORDING CAREER

1933

Producer John Hammond's recording of Billie Holiday singing with Benny Goodman's band in 1933 brought her to the attention of jazz aficionados, and she gradually became a legendary singer.

Locale: New York, New York
Category: Music

KEY FIGURES
Billie Holiday (1915-1959), jazz and blues singer whose recordings and innovative techniques would prove widely influential
Lester Young (1909-1959), celebrated saxophonist who teamed with Holiday on many of her best recordings
Teddy Wilson (1912-1986), pianist who recorded with Holiday and helped to launch her career

Holiday at the Downbeat Club, New York, c. February 1947 by William P. Gottlieb

John Hammond (1910-1987), Columbia Records producer who signed Holiday to her first recording contract
Benny Goodman (1909-1986), renowned bandleader
with whom Holiday made her first recordings
Louis Armstrong (1901-1971), hugely influential trumpeter and jazz musician

SUMMARY OF EVENT

Billie Holiday was born Eleanora Fagan in Baltimore,
Maryland, on April 7, 1915, to Sadie Fagan and guitarist
Clarence Holiday, a guitarist in the renowned band led
by Fletcher "Smack" Henderson. Her parents were later
married, but only for a brief time. After they separated,
Holiday was left with relatives while her mother went to
New York to find work. Several stories have been told
about the origin of the name "Billie," including that she
was a tomboy, that her father called her "Bill," and that
the actress Billie Dove was her idol.

When Holiday was ten years old, she was raped by
a forty-year-old man. He went free, and she was sent to a
Catholic "correctional" home. At thirteen, she went to live
with her mother in Harlem. She smoked marijuana and
was jailed as a prostitute. She said she ran errands for a
madam so that she could hear the Bessie Smith and Louis
Armstrong records played in the parlor of the brothel.

At seventeen, she began to sing professionally in
Harlem at Monette Moore's speakeasy on 133rd Street
for ten dollars a week. She soon began working at other
Harlem clubs, and eventually Columbia Records producer
John Hammond heard her. He arranged for her to record
with Benny Goodman's band on Columbia in 1933. The
two sides were "Riffin' the Scotch" and "Your Mother's
Son-in-Law." In that same year, Teddy Wilson came to
New York and signed with Brunswick Records. He played
piano with Goodman's small group (Lionel Hampton was
on vibes) and recorded pop tunes for Brunswick in 1935.
Earlier, Wilson had been allowed to record with Goodman
for Victor Records; in return, Goodman had agreed to record as a sideman with him for Brunswick. Billie Holiday
was chosen as the vocalist, and these recordings created a
following among jazz musicians and jazz buffs.

In 1936, Count Basie's band came to New York
City. "The Count" had a Decca Records contract and
could not play on the Wilson-Holiday recordings, but
his sidemen—Buck Clayton, Freddie Greene, Walter
Page, and Lester "Prez" Young—could. Young is generally recognized as the person who gave Holiday the
nickname "Lady Day" or "The Lady." In the jazz world,
there was a Duke (Ellington), a Count, a "Prez"—short
for "president"—and now a Lady.

In addition to Holiday, the 1936 recordings featured other fine musicians, including Jonah Jones, Johnny Hodges, Harry Carney, John Kirby, Cozy Cole, Vido
Musso, Ben Webster, and of course, Teddy Wilson,
whose ability to play with his left hand was far ahead
of most other pianists. For eight months, Holiday was
Count Basie's vocalist, and three airchecks—recordings
of the Basie band live at the Savoy Ballroom in Harlem in 1937—made during this time were later released
commercially. For a short time, she was also the vocalist
for bandleader Artie Shaw, but a miserable trip on the
band bus through the segregated South helped inform
her decision to work on her own from that point.

In 1936, she began recording with her own group for
Vocalion Records. Shaw was a sideman on one session
along with Bunny Berigan and Joe Bushkin. She again
recorded for Vocalion in 1938 and 1939 and also worked
for Columbia as Wilson's vocalist and as the leader of
a group called Billie Holiday and Her Orchestra. From
1939 through 1941, she recorded with her own band for
OKeh Records and as vocalist with Teddy Wilson and his
orchestra. On a number of the OKeh recordings, Lester
Young, Walter Page, Freddie Greene, and Jo Jones joined
her. Roy "Little Jazz" Eldridge played trumpet on several of the recordings, and Charlie Shavers also played
on one. Lester Young, Eddie Heywood (on piano), and
Kenny Clarke (on drums) were among the people who
recorded "Georgia on My Mind" with Holiday in 1941.

In the late 1940's, some of the Teddy Wilson recordings were reissued by Commodore Records, including "Gloomy Sunday," which was more of a folk
song than a piece of jazz or popular music but nonetheless became identified with Holiday. The recording was
purportedly a version of a Hungarian "suicide song"
that had, it was said, been banned from radio because
some listeners had killed themselves—although a dis-
claimer toward the end of the song noted that the singer
was "only dreaming."

Another song that was neither jazz nor pop belongs
to Holiday alone. "Strange Fruit," a poem set to music, describes the contrast between the ugly violence of
lynchings and the physical beauty of the South. She recorded it in 1939, a brave act at a time when the issue
of such a racially charged song could have wrecked her
career or led to physical harm. Southern writer Lillian
Smith used the song's title as the title of a novel about
racial violence in the South.

Holiday created some other songs that would always be identified with her, including "God Bless the
Child," which has the structure of a pop tune but the

feel of a blues lament and is still recorded by vocalists in many genres. Several original blues tunes that she performed have stayed in the jazz vocalist repertoire, including "Fine and Mellow," "Billie's Bounce," "Long Gone Blues," and "Billie's Blues."

Later, Holiday made other recordings of the tunes she had first sung in the 1930's and early 1940's, but the early recordings give the listener a strong, young Holiday at home within the structure of the song. Among these often-recorded early performances were "Them There Eyes," "Love Me or Leave Me," "I Cover the Waterfront," "I Can't Get Started," "These Foolish Things," "No Regrets," and "Some Other Spring." Other later songs also identified with Holiday include "Trav'lin' Light," "Don't Explain," "Good Morning, Heartache," and "Easy Livin'." Even some songs originally identified with blues giant Bessie Smith came to be known as Holiday's, including "Gimme a Pigfoot" and "Ain't Nobody's Business."

SIGNIFICANCE

In 1938, Holiday moved from Harlem into Manhattan. She began performing at the well-known Café Society, and until the late 1940's she worked at various Manhattan jazz clubs. In 1947, she appeared, dressed as a maid, in the film *New Orleans*. In that same year, however, she was arrested for possession of heroin and sentenced to a year and a day in a federal prison in Alderson, West Virginia. Ten days after her release, she performed to a sold-out crowd at Carnegie Hall. She could not, however, work in any jazz club in New York City; an archaic law required performers in establishments that sold liquor to obtain a "cabaret card" that permitted them to work there, and cabaret cards were unavailable to musicians with drug convictions. Holiday was thus prohibited from working in her own town, the center of live jazz performance in the United States at that time.

In the early 1950's, Steve Allen, the host of an early New York television variety show that would later become *The Tonight Show*, featured a number of notable jazz performers, including Holiday, on his program. In 1957, a television special with Lester Young and others let fans see and hear her one more time; the sound track to the special was released as the album *The Sound of Jazz*.

In 1956, Holiday wrote her autobiography, *Lady Sings the Blues*, with coauthor William F. Dufty. A hit 1972 film based on the book starred Diana Ross as Holiday. Although Ross's music was very different from Holiday's, the film's sound track introduced another generation to Holiday's songs.

Holiday toured Europe in the last few years of her life and was enthusiastically received. Her last performance in New York City was a 1959 benefit performance at the Phoenix Theater. On May 31 of that year, she collapsed at her Manhattan apartment. In a coma, she was taken by a police ambulance to a private hospital, where she lay unattended for an hour. She was then taken to Metropolitan Hospital in Harlem. She lingered, under an oxygen tent, for more than two weeks, with a policeman outside her door. Authorities denied that the officer was waiting to arrest her, but rumors of Holiday's pending arrest continued, and the officer was removed by court order the day before Holiday died.

When Holiday collapsed, she had seventy cents in her bank account and $750 in cash taped to her leg. Three thousand people attended her funeral at St. Paul the Apostle Catholic Church in Harlem, and she was buried in Raymond's Cemetery in the Bronx. For some time, her grave was not marked by a headstone, a fact that resulted in an angry article in *Downbeat* magazine. (Ironically, she never won the top spot in any of *Downbeat*'s celebrated polls.)

The success of Holiday's music was entirely dependent on her much-discussed style. Despite the fact that many scholars have written about the way she altered the melodic line of a song, she did not, in fact, play around with melody very much—no more, for example, than the young Miles Davis, who played "Blue Room" almost note for note. Unlike other popular African American stars of the day such as Ella Fitzgerald, Fats Waller, the Ink Spots, and the Mills Brothers, Holiday's music was not featured on the jukeboxes in white establishments. She simply recorded the popular songs of the day, some of which became standards.

Others commented that Holiday sang "like a horn player," but this is not quite right. Holiday shared Louis Armstrong's ability to use vocals to play with the time, a skill she demonstrated on the "up" tunes on her 1930's recordings. On such songs, the last bars of the chorus that led into a musician's solo often anticipated the solo, inviting the instrumentalist into the tune. Holiday's talent, however, was not confined to the room she could make inside those four-beat rhythms. Sometimes it emerged from the spaces between the notes or in her accents on particular notes, words, or syllables. Although "percussive" is too strong a term to describe her technique, her work is almost percussive and almost syncopated. To her unique sense of timing she added bent, gliding notes in a voice that could seem both sweet and sassy. Although toward the end of her career—when both her health and breath were fading—she sometimes sounded like an imitation of herself, many people preferred her later style, which seemed to embody a universally held idea of suffering.

—*Katherine Lederer*

See also: Bessie Smith Records "Downhearted Blues"; Armstrong Records with the Hot Five; Ellington Begins Performing at the Cotton Club; Marian Anderson Is Barred from Constitution Hall; Wright's *Native Son* Depicts Racism in America.

JOSEPHINE BAKER, THE FIRST BLACK MOVIE STAR, *ZOUZOU*

1934

The French film Zouzou, *featuring Josephine Baker in the starring role, becomes the first film to feature an African American woman as the central star.*

Identification: The 1934 film *Zouzou*, makes Josephine Baker the first African American woman to star in a film.

Famed singer, dancer, fashion icon, and actress Josephine Baker, born in St. Louis, Missouri in 1906, first became famous as a dancer and vaudeville performer in New York City. However, dispirited by segregation, prejudice, and racism in the United States at the time, Baker left for Paris in 1925, where she stared in *La Revue Negre*, becoming one of the most famous performers in 1920s Europe. While Baker was often marketed using racial associations with jungles and tribal savagery, she embraced the forced connotation with "primitivism" and demonstrated female agency at a time when women, and especially women of color, were fighting for independence and recognition in male dominated societies. By 1930, Baker was not only famous in Europe, but had also become popular in the United States and some historians have speculated that she was the first African-American woman to become a global star.

Though Baker appeared in a 1927 silent film, *Siren of the Tropics*, her 1934 role in the French film *Zouzou* made her the first African American woman to star in a major studio film. The plot of the film centers around two orphans, Jean, a white boy, and Zouzou, a mixed-race girl, who grow up together in a traveling circus and develop a brother-sister relationship. In Paris, when Jean is wrongly accused of murder, Zouzou performs in a show to earn money for Jean's defense. The film, directed by French director Marc Allegret, was written to reflect Baker's talents and personality and Baker later called the film her favorite of all her film appearances. In the film, Jean eventually rejects Zouzou's affections in favor of a white woman, and thus did not interracial romance, which was still a social taboo in France at the time of the film's release. The year after the release of *ZouZou*, Baker starred in another film, *Princess Tam Tam*, which was another major success in France, though it was not widely shown in the United States due to censorship. Baker's film career largely ended during World War II, when Baker served the resistance effort by informing on soldiers in occupied France. After the war, she resumed her singing and dancing career, but did little acting. Returning to the United States to perform in the 1950s, Baker used her celebrity to become a leader in the Civil Rights Movement, giving speeches promoting racial equality and refusing to perform for racially segregated audiences. Baker was one of the speakers at the 1963 March on Washington alongside Martin Luther King Jr.

—*Micah Issitt*

BLACK CABINET

Mid-1930's

The black cabinet had no dramatic impact on federal policies but made white New Dealers more responsive to African American problems.

Identification: Informal body of African American officials in the federal government

The black cabinet was formed by more than a dozen African American men and women who had been appointed to federal positions by President Franklin D. Roosevelt by the year 1935. Known as the Federal Council on Negro Affairs after 1935, it was an informal gathering of African American advisers from various New Deal agencies led unofficially by Mary McLeod Bethune, the director of the National Youth Administration's Division of Negro Affairs. Its members included Robert Weaver, the Negro Affairs adviser in the Public Works Administration, and William Hastie, assistant solicitor in the Department of the Interior. Several other cabinet members later became nationally prominent. They usually met at the homes of Bethune and Weaver and informally had some impact on New Deal agencies. First Lady Eleanor Roosevelt often provided the impetus behind certain changes after meeting with Bethune.

The appointment of African Americans to federal positions symbolized the attempt by some New Dealers to eradicate racial injustice in the United States and influenced some African Americans to convert from the Republican to the Democratic Party. President Roosevelt, however, ultimately did not challenge the more intransigent elements of a still segregated society. Still, although the black cabinet did not dramatically alter federal government policies toward African Americans because the appointments were not at the highest levels and its membership was fluctuating, it made white New Dealers more responsive to African American problems.

—David L. Porter

See also: Politics and government; Summit Meeting of National Negro Leaders; Talented Tenth

GROVEY V. TOWNSEND
April 1, 1935

In the third round of the white primary cases, the Supreme Court accepted the right of political parties—acting as private organizations—to exclude African Americans from voting in primaries.

The Case: U.S. Supreme Court ruling on white primaries

One of the most successful devices in eliminating black voters in the South was the white primary. Since the Democratic Party dominated the solid South, whoever won the Democratic primary went on to win the general election. If African Americans could not participate in the primaries, they were denied any real choice in selecting public officials.

In *Newberry v. United States* (1921), the U.S. Supreme Court held that primary elections were not constitutionally protected. Although the *Newberry* case took place in Michigan and involved the issue of vote fraud rather than racial discrimination, the South immediately took advantage of the ruling. In 1924 the Texas legislature passed a law that barred African Americans from participation in that state's primary elections. Three years later, a unanimous Supreme Court struck down the Texas law in *Nixon v. Herndon* (1927), finding the actions of the Texas legislature a clear violation of the equal protection clause of the Fourteenth Amendment. The Texas

legislature then passed a law authorizing the executive committees of the political parties to determine eligibility for voting in primary elections. As expected, the executive committee of the Texas Democratic Party excluded African Americans from the primary. In *Nixon v. Condon* (1932), in a 5-4 decision, the U.S. Supreme Court ruled that the executive committee had acted as the agent of the state. As such, the attempt to bar black participation in the primary still violated the equal protection clause.

Texas succeeded on its third attempt to ban black voting. Immediately after the *Condon* decision, the Texas Democratic Party convention, without any authorization from the legislature, adopted a resolution restricting party membership to whites. R. R. Grovey, a black resident of Houston, brought suit against the county clerk who refused to give him a primary ballot. On April 1, 1935, a unanimous U.S. Supreme Court upheld the actions of the state party convention. According to the Court, there was no violation of the equal protection clause because there was no state action involved. The Democratic Party was a voluntary association of individuals who acted in their private capacity to exclude African Americans from primary elections.

In 1941 the U.S. Supreme Court reversed *Newberry* in *United States v. Classic* (1941). The *Classic* decision brought primary elections under constitutional protection for the first time. *Classic* also paved the way for

Smith v. Allwright (1944), the Supreme Court case banning white primaries.

—*Darryl Paulson*

See also: National Association for the Advancement of Colored People; *Newberry v. United States*; *Nixon v. Condon*; *Nixon v. Herndon*; *Smith v. Allwright*; *United States v. Classic*; White primaries

NORRIS V. ALABAMA

April 1, 1935

In its second ruling on Alabama's Scottsboro rape case, the Supreme Court held that the African American defendants had been denied a fair trial because black citizens had been systematically excluded from juries.

The Case: U.S. Supreme Court ruling on jury composition

In *Powell v. Alabama* (1932), the Supreme Court ruled that the conviction of the "Scottsboro boys," a group of young African American men, without effective assistance of counsel violated the Fourteenth Amendment's due process requirement. After defendant Clarence Norris was sentenced to death in a second trial, his lawyers presented evidence of systematic racial exclusion from both the grand jury and trial jury. Writing for a unanimous Court, Chief Justice Charles Evans Hughes reversed the conviction as inconsistent with the due process and equal protection clauses. In both *Powell* and *Norris*, the justices ruled on the basis of immutable principles of justice and declined the opportunity to make the Sixth Amendment explicitly binding on the states through the Fourteenth Amendment.

—*Thomas Tandy Lewis*

See also: *Batson v. Kentucky*; *Edmonson v. Leesville Concrete Company*; Fourteenth Amendment; *Powell v. Alabama*; *Powers v. Ohio*

NATIONAL COUNCIL OF NEGRO WOMEN

Founded in 1935

Since its founding, the National Council of Negro Women organization has advocated women's issues nationally and internationally.

Identification: Organization that seeks to promote cooperation among women

The National Council of Negro Women (NCNW) seeks to facilitate cooperation among women and act as an advocate for women's issues nationally and internationally. Founded in 1935 by Mary McLeod Bethune, an educator and presidential adviser, the organization encompasses a coalition of thirty-one national organizations. It has local chapters throughout the United States, the Women's Center for Education and Career Advancement in New York City, and offices in western and southern Africa. The NCNW maintains a clearinghouse in which information that will improve the socioeconomic status of African American women and other women of color is compiled and disseminated.

The organization also publishes *Black Woman's Voice*, a periodical, and *Sister's Magazine*, a quarterly. In addition, the council is responsible for an archive for black women's history and the Bethune Museum. One of the primary goals of the council is to assist women in developing leadership skills to be used on community, national, and international levels. One of its international projects is to improve social and economic conditions for rural women in developing countries.

—*K. Sue Jewell*

See also: Colored Women's League; Combahee River Collective; National Association of Colored Women; National Black Women's Political Leadership Caucus

MISSOURI EX REL. GAINES V. CANADA
December 12, 1938

Chipping away at the separate but equal doctrine, the Supreme Court ruled that states must provide equal opportunities for legal education within the borders of the state.

The Case: U.S. Supreme Court ruling on the separate but equal doctrine

The state of Missouri, like other southern states, had no law schools that admitted African Americans. The state claimed to provide separate but equal opportunity by offering a few scholarships to help pay expenses for African Americans to attend law schools in other states. The state also indicated that it would begin a separate law school for African Americans if there were sufficient demand. Lloyd Gaines, an African American resident of the state, sued the registrar of the University of Missouri, S. W. Canada, after being denied admission to the law school because of his race.

By a 6-2 vote, the Supreme Court held that the University of Missouri's scholarship policy fell short of the demands of the equal protection clause of the Fourteenth Amendment. Chief Justice Charles Evans Hughes, for the majority, wrote that the policy denied African Americans the equal right to obtain a legal education without leaving the state. Hughes noted that the state, if it wished, might fulfill its constitutional obligations "by furnishing equal facilities in separate schools." The *Gaines* decision suggested that the Court would henceforth disapprove of segregated schools unless they met standards of near-absolute equality.

In *Sweatt v. Painter* (1950), the Court built upon *Gaines* when it held that an all-black law school in Texas was inadequate because it did not provide "substantial equality" of educational opportunities available to white persons.

—*Thomas Tandy Lewis*

See also: Education; Segregation; Separate but equal doctrine

ANDERSON'S LINCOLN MEMORIAL CONCERT
April 9, 1939

The Daughters of the American Revolution (DAR) rejected contralto Marian Anderson for a singing engagement at Constitution Hall, but Anderson rescheduled her appearance outside the Lincoln Memorial.

The Event: Recital by contralto Marian Anderson on the steps of the Lincoln Memorial
Place: Washington, D.C.

Even with her rich, warm, evocative contralto, Marian Anderson, the first African American to perform with New York's Metropolitan Opera Company, did not arrive easily at fame and acceptance, particularly among prejudiced whites. The daughter of a poor Philadelphia widow, she got what training she could afford, then evolved an expanded vocal repertoire including material ranging from spirituals to folk songs and grand opera. She developed a significant following among classical music fans. In 1939, after requesting

Anderson in her 1939 concert at the Lincoln Memorial by U.S. Information Agency

the use of Washington's Constitution Hall from the Daughters of the American Revolution, she was humiliated by a flat rejection.

A PROMISING CAREER

Marian, the first of three daughters of John and Annie Anderson, was born at her grandmother's house in South Philadelphia on February 17, 1902. Her father, a coal and ice seller, died of brain cancer ten years later, leaving his wife, a schoolteacher, to support the family by taking in laundry and working in Wanamaker's Department Store. Anderson, who progressed from the Union Baptist Church junior choir to public performances of duets and solos, also learned to play the piano and violin. She concentrated on a business curriculum at William Penn High School, then transferred to South Philadelphia High for music training and studied privately under voice coach Mary Patterson.

Public response to Anderson's extensive range and expressive talents brought invitations to a variety of public musical forums and Negro colleges as well as membership in the Philadelphia Choral Society. White philanthropists often donated funds to assist her obviously promising future in music. Despite the beneficence of a few, laws of segregation and local custom required her to travel on separate train cars, ride service elevators, and eat in substandard dining areas maintained for nonwhite patrons. Overnight accommodations in hotels proved so difficult to obtain that she usually stayed in private residences.

In 1921, Anderson received a church-sponsored scholarship for voice lessons with Giuseppe Boghetti, who strengthened her technique and stage presence and taught her operatic roles. With the help of accompanist and manager William "Billy" King, a black pianist, she increased her fee to a hundred dollars per performance. A period of low self-esteem arising from unfavorable reviews deflated her enthusiasm temporarily. The expertise she gained from learning foreign languages to augment her vocal talent, in addition to the backing of her mother, sisters, coach, and manager, restored her to earlier levels of confidence.

In 1925, after defeating three hundred contenders in a local competition, Anderson won the privilege of appearing with the New York Philharmonic at Lewisohn Stadium under the direction of Eugene Ormandy. Good reviews bolstered her competitiveness. As a result, in 1930, on a National Association of Negro Musicians scholarship, she traveled to Europe to study. While sailing on the *Ile de France*, she sang for distinguished passengers. The experience proved beneficial to her career, encouraging her to return to Berlin to immerse herself in the German language. Back in the United States, she demonstrated her cosmopolitan training with a cross-country tour.

ORGANIZED BIGOTRY

It was in the midst of this increasing professional success that Anderson was refused permission by the Daughters of the American Revolution (DAR) to sing at Constitution Hall in Washington, D.C., in 1939. The refusal came solely on account of Anderson's race. At the time of the turndown, Anderson was on tour in California. She met with interviewers to voice her sadness and shame. In characteristic low-key, nonjudgmental style, she refused to affix blame and noted, by way of explanation, that crusading for racial equality was foreign to her nature. She did, however, alter her personal criteria for performance sites and refused to sing where non-whites were refused admittance.

The refusal to let Anderson sing proved embarrassing to the two hundred thousand members of the DAR, an elite women's historical society founded in 1890 to honor descent from patriots, encourage patriotism and activities related to teaching history, foster genealogical research, honor the American flag and Constitution, found citizenship clubs, award scholarships and medals, assist veterans with disabilities, and generally further Americanism. To save face in response to press stories about their actions, the group's leaders cited a Washington, D.C., law restricting integrated performances. They insisted that the DAR had in fact challenged bigotry by publicizing the local restrictions that forbade Anderson's performance. This story proved to be false.

Other entertainers and leaders came to Anderson's defense and protested the obvious attempt to hide racial discrimination. As a conciliatory gesture, Eleanor Roosevelt resigned from and broke all ties with the DAR and persuaded Anderson to sing a free Easter concert at the steps of the Lincoln Memorial. The Sunday performance, attended by more than seventy-five thousand people, including government dignitaries, representatives from Howard University, and the secretary of the National Association for the Advancement of Colored People (NAACP), showed Anderson's sincere response to the racist action of an elitist clique. Choked with tears at the sight of so many supporters, Anderson faltered on the words to the national anthem. She drew on her professional training and years of onstage experience to help complete her usual repertoire of hymn tunes, classical arias, and national favorites. She closed with a simple rendition of "America."

Anderson's performance at the Lincoln Memorial became the focal point of her career. To commemorate her public triumph, the Department of the Interior commissioned a mural. Fellow entertainers of all races boycotted future performances scheduled for Constitution

Hall. For her self-control and positive attitude, Anderson accepted honors from Eleanor Roosevelt and the king and queen of England. She later entertained at the White House for the inaugural galas of Dwight D. Eisenhower and John F. Kennedy. The policy at Constitution Hall changed in regard to use by nonwhites, and Anderson eventually gave her long-delayed performance.

The nationwide notoriety resulting from the Washington rejection and its triumphant aftermath brought Anderson a deluge of opportunities to travel, perform, study, and record. Reluctant to release many of her RCA recordings, she reworked studio performances until they reached her high standards. Her most popular disc, a soulful, intense rendering of "Ave Maria," marked by her characteristic vibrato and amplitude, sold a quarter of a million copies.

INTERNATIONAL SUCCESS

Twice Anderson toured Denmark, Sweden, Norway, and Finland, impressing Finns by singing in their language. Royalty, local fans, and notable musicians, especially composer Jean Sibelius, escalated her Scandinavian appearances from mere acclaim to "Marian fever." European and Asian audiences, particularly Russians and those in other nations under communist regimes, demanded encores of her spirituals, claiming "Deep River" and "Heaven, Heaven" as their favorites. Konstantin Stanislavsky carried a bouquet of lilacs to entice her to sing *Carmen*.

Returning to America in triumph, Anderson came under the management of Russian impresario Solomon Hurok. Under his direction toward new challenges, she accepted tours in Japan, Africa, and South America and gave standing-room-only concerts at New York City's Town Hall and Carnegie Hall and at the Philadelphia Forum. Far from her original rewards of fifty cents per performance, she earned hefty fees commensurate with her talents. Fans poured out their response to her compassion, which brought them comfort in times of personal crisis. Critics acknowledged her maturing grace, range, control, and musical technique. She performed more than seventy-five concerts per year and had many opportunities she could not accept without overextending her voice and sapping her energies.

Even with increased audience rapport, racism continued to crop up in correspondence, reviews, and public treatment, especially after Anderson was invited to sing before Nazis in the 1940's. Following her reply to their questions about race, Hitler's staff dropped their request for a concert. In the United States, she was presented with the key to Atlantic City, but white hotels refused her requests for a reservation. These unsettling public slurs were somewhat offset by awards and honoraria from fifty universities including Howard, Temple, Smith, Carlisle, Moravian, and Dickinson.

At the age of thirty-seven, Anderson received the Spingarn Medal, awarded annually by the NAACP to an African American achiever. A year later, in 1940, she earned the Bok Award, an annual $10,000 prize accorded a native Philadelphian. She used the money to endow the Marian Anderson Scholarship for students of the arts. To assure unprejudiced administration of the annual award, she placed her sister Alyce in charge.

In 1943, Anderson left the Philadelphia home she shared with her mother and married architect Orpheus Fisher of Wilmington, Delaware, whom she had met during her school years. The couple built Mariana Farm in a rural setting outside Danbury, Connecticut. Often absent from home on tour, she reserved the summer months for domestic pleasures, particularly sewing, cooking, and gardening. Her particular delight was the success of her strawberry patch. By choice, she had no children so that she could avoid the problem of separation from family while she devoted her life to music. To fill the gap left by voluntary childlessness, she immersed herself in the activities of her sisters' children, who were frequent visitors to her home.

LATER YEARS

In middle age, Marian Anderson continued to achieve renown. At the bidding of German fans, she returned to post-Nazi Berlin to perform. In 1955, New York impresario Rudolf Bing organized her debut as Ulrica, the aged sorceress in Giuseppe Verdi's *Un ballo in maschera* (1857–1858; *The Masked Ball*). This performance at the Metropolitan Opera House was the first ever by an African American performer. It made extra demands on her limited stage experience, which she met by practicing her acting role and deliberately subduing stage fright. She reprised her part in the opera on tour in Philadelphia, where black fans mobbed the performance. Continuing to refine the role of Ulrica in later appearances, she commented that she felt that perfection of the small character part was an essential part of her training for the operatic stage.

At the age of fifty-four, Anderson wrote her autobiography, *My Lord, What a Morning* (1956), in which she revealed personal reflections on poverty and longing in her childhood, when performing before distinguished audiences lay far outside the grasp of a black singer. Late in her career, having toured Europe and the United States once more, she was named in 1958 as an alternate delegate to the United Nations for her support of human rights. In 1959, two years before formal retirement, she accepted from President Dwight D. Eisenhower the Presidential Medal of Freedom. At the age of seventy-six, she appeared at the Kennedy Center and, as the sole woman among fellow honorees George Balanchine, Arthur Rubinstein, Richard Rodgers, and Fred Astaire, received a national award.

The famed singer returned to the spotlight long after the end of her stage career. At the age of eighty-seven, to raise scholarship funds, Anderson, still regal and gracious, presided over a concert at Danbury's Charles Ives Center. Feted by admirers including Jessye Norman, Isaac Stern, William Warfield, Cicely Tyson, Phylicia Rashad, Connecticut's governor William A. O'Neil, and President George Bush, she graciously accepted the national acclaim that well-wishers extended. She later became more reclusive but remained a symbol of African American achievement and grace under pressure.

—*Mary Ellen Snodgrass*

See also: Harlem Renaissance; Music

WRIGHT'S *NATIVE SON* DEPICTS RACISM IN AMERICA

1939

Richard Wright's Native Son *shocked white Americans with its graphic depiction of the rage and violence engendered by racism in the hearts of African Americans.*

Date: 1939
Locale: Chicago, Illinois
Categories: Literature; social issues and reform

KEY FIGURE:
Richard Wright (1908-1960), African American writer

SUMMARY OF EVENT
In 1939, Richard Wright completed work on *Native Son,* his second work of fiction and his first full-length novel. The book's publication in 1940 immediately established Wright as an important author and a spokesman on conditions facing African Americans. Earlier, Wright had published a collection of four novellas titled *Uncle Tom's Children* (1938), which gained him the attention of some literary critics and helped him to win a Guggenheim Fellowship. The fellowship enabled Wright to devote all his time to writing.

Native Son, published by Harper's, was unlike any book by an African American writer ever published up to that time. Speaking of *Uncle Tom's Children*, Wright had said, "I had written a book which even bankers' daughters could read and weep over and feel good. I swore to myself that if I ever wrote another book, no one would weep over it; that it would be so hard and deep that they would have to face it without the consolation of tears." *Native Son* was indeed such a book. To avoid

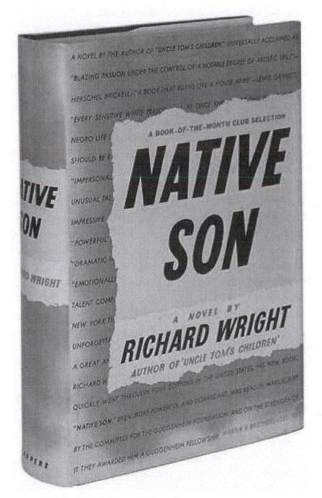

Cover of 1st edition of Wright's Native Son

the unfocused sympathy of those who wished to avoid the hard realities of life for African Americans, Wright created for his protagonist a violent young black man in Chicago, Bigger Thomas, who murders two women, one black and one white, and who is then condemned to death, which he faces unrepentantly. Bigger and all his friends are resentful, frustrated by racism, and both fearful of the white world and inclined to violence toward it.

Harper's was somewhat concerned about the graphic nature of some of the book, but the publisher insisted on only limited changes. Just before publication, however, the Book-of-the-Month Club expressed interest in including *Native Son* as one of its selections if several sexually explicit scenes were removed and if Bigger Thomas did not show such obvious sexual interest in the white character, Mary Dalton. Wright agreed to these changes.

Upon publication in 1940, *Native Son* became an immediate hit. In less than six months, a quarter of a million copies had been sold at five dollars a copy—at a time when the minimum wage in the United States was thirty-five cents an hour. The first edition sold out in only three hours. Virtually every major newspaper and magazine in the nation reviewed the book. *Native Son* was on the best seller list for nearly four months. No other African American writer had ever achieved such fame and financial success. Moreover, no other African American writer had ever focused such attention on the conditions of life in black ghettos before. In the introduction to the first edition, Dorothy Canfield wrote: "*Native Son* is the first report in fiction we have had from those who succumb to . . . crosscurrents of contradictory nerve impulses, from those whose behavior patterns give evidence of the same bewildering, senseless tangle of abnormal nerve-reactions studied in animals in laboratory experiments." For many white Americans, Bigger Thomas became a symbol of the entire black community.

Prior to the publication of *Native Son*, Wright had worked at a variety of jobs to support himself, his invalid mother, a number of relatives, and a wife. These jobs had included janitorial work, selling burial insurance, employment on the Federal Writers' Project of the Works Progress Administration, and occasional writing for leftwing and Communist Party publications. Wright had joined the Communist Party in 1935, but he resigned his membership in 1944. With the financial security brought by the success of *Native Son*, Wright could devote himself to literary pursuits, and he spent the rest of his life writing.

The first impact of *Native Son* on Wright's writing was to encourage him to produce an autobiography, *Black Boy: A Record of Childhood and Youth* (1945), which described his life growing up in the South. Wright was born near Natchez, Mississippi, in 1908, and his parents then took the family to Memphis, where Wright's father abandoned them. There followed an itinerant existence in Tennessee, Arkansas, and Mississippi that entailed rough and bruising contact with Jim Crow segregation laws and the heavy-handed demands for obsequious behavior made by the racial etiquette of the place and time. *Black Boy* ended with Wright's migration to Chicago and the vaguely expressed hope that life would be better there. This book also became a matter of national debate and helped to establish Wright as a commentator on current racial conditions, not just a writer of fiction.

More than four hundred thousand copies of the book were sold within a few weeks. The financial independence delivered by *Native Son* also allowed Wright to make some personal changes. He divorced his first wife, to whom he had been married for less than a year, and married Ellen Poplar, a Jewish woman, in 1942. The couple had one child, a daughter named Julia.

The African American community recognized the accomplishment represented by *Native Son* when the National Association for the Advancement of Colored People (NAACP) awarded Wright its prestigious Spingarn Medal in 1940. *Native Son* launched Wright's career as a writer. He went on to produce nineteen major fiction and nonfiction works, screenplays, and stage plays, and he became the first of the modern generation of African American writers.

Significance

Since its publication in 1940, Richard Wright's *Native Son* has never been out of print. Orson Welles produced a Broadway play based on the book, and film versions were released in 1950 and 1986. The book and its author have been the subject of numerous scholarly and popular investigations from literary, historical, and sociological perspectives.

Although the author was a Mississippian who set his story in Chicago and wrote it while living in New York, the plot of *Native Son* has continued to be a metaphor for much of the black experience throughout the United States. The book explores individuals, their environments, and the ways in which environments shape people.

In an essay titled "How Bigger Was Born," Wright wrote of his character:

> He is a product of a dislocated society; he is a dispossessed and disinherited man; he is all of this and he lives amid the greatest possible plenty on earth and he is looking and feeling for a way out. . . . He was an American because he was also a native son; but he was also a Negro nationalist in a vague sense because he was not allowed to live as an American. Such was his way of life and mine; neither Bigger nor I resided fully in either camp.

In 1940, most white Americans were unaware of such feelings on the part of African Americans. There was little contact between the races. In a survey taken in 1942, less than half of all white Americans approved of integrated transportation facilities, and only about one in three approved of integrated schools or neighborhoods.

Most whites, however, seemed to feel that blacks were satisfied with existing conditions. The usual white concept of African Americans was bifurcated. On one hand were the happy-go-lucky "darkies," who were obviously poor and socially unequal but who did not worry about their situation at all; on the other were the fearful, downtrodden victims of southern bigotry. *Native Son* confronted the United States with the fact that the first of these stereotypes was false and the second was a national, not a regional, problem.

The growing urban ghettos of the North and West were not lands of opportunity but instead festering wounds in which people lived and died largely without hope. On a broad scale, Wright brought into the open the hatred, fear, and violence that he saw as characterizing American race relations. After *Native Son*, literary critic Irving Howe asserted, "American culture was changed forever." Quaintness and idealized folksiness disappeared from black literature, and the way was opened for later African American writers to emphasize their own ethnic culture. Later black writers could repudiate white culture and could celebrate black identity and even militancy. Wright's message in *Native Son*, variations of which have appeared frequently since, is that African Americans may wish to destroy the symbols of white cultural dominance and control. Trickery, when directed toward the dominant culture, is acceptable, as is militancy.

These ideas have become widespread since the publication of *Native Son*. This does not mean that the influence of *Native Son* has been seen as all positive, even by blacks. James Baldwin commented that the book was "the most powerful and celebrated statement we have yet had of what it means to be a Negro in America." Baldwin, however, did not think Wright dealt adequately with the psychological and social conditions of Bigger Thomas's life, and he argued that this failure prevented Wright from conveying any sense of black life as a complex group reality. In a 1949 essay titled "Everybody's Protest Novel," Baldwin wrote that *Native Son* was in its own way as simpleminded as Harriet Beecher Stowe's *Uncle Tom's Cabin: Or, Life Among the Lowly* (1852). In "Many Thousands Gone," an essay published in 1951, Baldwin remarked that Wright wrote as if racism were a social problem that could not be cured but could be checked.

Although Wright's reputation as a writer and as a spokesman for African Americans ebbed during the 1950's, as younger black writers such as Baldwin and Ralph Ellison rejected Wright's naturalistic style of writing as well as the Marxist overtones of *Native Son,* Wright's influence was revived in the 1960's. With the growth of the militant black consciousness movement, there came a resurgence of interest in Wright's work. It is generally agreed that Wright's influence in *Native Son* is not a matter of literary style or technique. The novel's impact, rather, comes from ideas and attitudes, and Wright's work became a force in the social and intellectual history of the United States in the last half of the twentieth century. A part of this impact developed from Wright's work after *Native Son*. Wright described Bigger as "vaguely a Negro nationalist." During the years Wright spent in France, from 1947 to his death in 1960, he spent much of his time supporting nationalist movements in Africa.

Wright wrote with a mixture of fearlessness and brilliance. He said he wanted to move black writing beyond the servile depiction of stereotyped "colored people." With *Native Son* he accomplished that while at the same time showing how little black Americans and white Americans really knew about one another.

—*Michael R. Bradley*

See also: Great Northern Migration; Harlem Renaissance

NATIONAL ASSOCIATION FOR THE ADVANCEMENT OF COLORED PEOPLE LEGAL DEFENSE AND EDUCATIONAL FUND

Founded in 1939

The NAACP Legal Defense and Educational Fund has organized litigation campaigns on a variety of key equity issues, bringing suits on behalf of individuals and of major civil rights groups seeking to end legal discrimination against African Americans and other people of color.

Identification: Legal arm of the National Association for the Advancement of Colored People

The NAACP Legal Defense and Educational Fund (sometimes abbreviated as LDF, sometimes as LDEF) was established in 1939-1940 as a tax-exempt corporation by the National Association for the Advancement of Colored People. Its charter was handwritten in March, 1940, by Thurgood Marshall, who stated the new organization's dual purpose: to provide legal aid to African Americans "suffering legal injustices by reason of race or color" and to create education opportunities for African Americans that had been denied them by reason of race or color.

The LDF was founded to carry on litigation in the spirit of the social change agenda already established by the actions of NAACP attorneys in the American courts. It provides or supports legal representation on behalf of African Americans and other people of color in defending their legal and constitutional rights against discrimination in education, employment, land use, recreation, transportation, housing, voting, health care, and other areas. It has successfully argued against grandfather clauses, restrictive housing covenants in city ordinances, white primaries, white juries, capital punishment, and segregation of public facilities. Since the 1950's the LDF has operated independently from its parent organization, which maintained its own legal department, and at times the relationship between the LDF and NAACP has involved some conflict. The LDF both represents individuals and brings suit on behalf of civil rights groups. Its clients have included the Congress of Racial Equality (CORE), the Southern Christian Leadership Conference (SCLC), the Student Nonviolent Coordinating Committee (SNCC), and local branches of the NAACP. It has been based in New York City since its formation and also maintains a center in Washington, D.C.

FUNDING AND LITIGATION

Fund-raising for the Legal Defense and Educational Fund is conducted by the Committee of 100, a volunteer group. In the formative years of the 1940's, the fund-raising drives of the committee were spearheaded by Harold Oram and Anna Caples Frank; during the Civil Rights movement, they were led by Allan Knight Chambers and Paul Moore. The LDF is supported by thousands of individual donations and by sustaining grants from smaller foundations, notably the Field Foundation. The largest contributions to the LDF come from major foundations, including the Ford, Carnegie, and Rockefeller foundations, and from corporations.

The LDF has litigated many hundreds of court cases on the state level and has argued many of the key civil rights cases heard before the U.S. Supreme Court since World War II. While always pursuing cases on a variety of fronts—including, in the 1940's, victories in white primary cases, which ended the exclusion of African Americans from the Democratic Party in the South (*Smith v. Allwright*, 1944), and the restrictive covenant cases, which held unconstitutional covenants prohibiting the sale of property to people of color—the initial focus of the LDF was the desegregation of American schools. Its landmark case was *Brown v. Board of Education* (1954), argued before the U.S. Supreme Court by the LDF team of Thurgood Marshall, Jack Greenberg, Louis Redding, George E. C. Hayes, Howard Jenkins, James M. Nabrit, Jr., and Spotswood W. Robinson III.

In *Brown* the Court, under Chief Justice Earl Warren, ruled in a unanimous decision that racial segregation of public schools was inherently unequal. At its inception the LDF had begun challenging the legal precedent of the "separate but equal" doctrine established in regard to transportation by the U.S. Supreme Court in *Plessy v. Ferguson* (1896) and extended through other cases to educational institutions. In a series of cases argued by Marshall and LDF staff, the LDF chipped away at the strength of the separate but equal doctrine.

Beginning with higher education, the LDF initiated suits in several different states and won favorable rulings from the U.S. Supreme Court that opened professional and graduate schools to African American applicants. One of the key cases in this effort was *Sweatt v. Painter* (1950), in which the Court found against the University of Texas Law School, which had been refusing admission to African Americans, on the grounds that a separate black law school did not meet the criteria for equal professional education. *Brown v. Board of Education* broadened the issue of equal access to education to the more comprehensive level of elementary and secondary schools. In their ruling, the Supreme Court justices found that the black children represented by the LDF had been denied equal protection under the laws as guaranteed by the Fourteenth Amendment, thus—at long last—reversing the separate but equal mandate of *Plessy v. Ferguson*.

AFTER BROWN

In the years following *Brown*, the LDF initiated hundreds of civil rights demonstration cases in support of the public actions taken by organizers and activists of the Civil Rights movement. These included the defense of Martin Luther King, Jr., Ralph Abernathy, and other SCLC activists in their criminal contempt case arising from their defiance of a court injunction prohibiting marches during the 1963 Birmingham demonstrations (*Walker v. City of Birmingham*, 1967). In *Walker*, the U.S. Supreme Court ultimately upheld the ruling of the Alabama Supreme Court, diminishing the constitutional protection afforded protestors under the Bill of Rights. The 1957 "Little Rock Nine" action in Arkansas was one of the LDF's key school desegregation cases. In the Little Rock case, members of the local NAACP aided nine black high school students who challenged the school district and the state to admit them into a previously all-white high school. Their admittance was eventually secured under federal military guard. Another major LDF desegregation case was that of James Meredith. In that suit the U.S. Court of Appeals for the Fifth Judicial Circuit in New Orleans ordered the University of Mississippi to admit its first African American student (*Meredith v. Fair*, 1962). The Meredith case was argued by Constance Baker Motley, who had been one of the central figures on the LDF staff since the 1940's. LDF lawyers also defended the organizers of sit-ins, participants in the Freedom Rides, and those who spearheaded other public protests. Their court victories, combined with the public activism of the Civil Rights movement, led to passage of the Civil Rights Act of 1964 and the Voting Rights Act of 1965. An LDF case, for example, created the doctrinal base for Title IV of the 1964 act, which made federal funding of institutions that discriminate against members of minorities illegal.

In addition to desegregation, voting, residential discrimination, and other civil rights causes, the LDF has devoted campaigns since the late 1960's and early 1970's to overturning the death penalty and initiating prison reform. In response to the women's movement, the LDF established a program in the 1970's to promote educational and employment opportunities for black women. Key victories came in 1972, when LDF attorneys succeeded in separate cases in getting the U.S. Supreme Court to rule that the death penalty was unconstitutional as then administered and that towns with primarily white residents could not withdraw from school systems in which the student population was predominantly African American. In the post-Civil Rights movement era, the LDF expanded into poverty law and began taking the cases of Mexican Americans, Native Americans, gays and lesbians, women, and others bringing suits on discrimination grounds.

EDUCATIONAL WORK

In addition to bringing litigation, the LDF lobbies for equal rights legislation and monitors federal programs for compliance with civil rights aims. LDF staff members give advice to lawyers involved in rights cases and supply information on current legal trends and decisions affecting the status of people of color. Funds are also allocated to provide counsel and to train attorneys to do activist work. Since the late 1970's, the Herbert Lehman Education Fund, an LDF scholarship program established in 1965, has awarded African American students some two hundred scholarships per year to offset the costs of state college tuition. In 1962 the LDF began providing internships to recent law school graduates to work in the LDF offices and then to go into the field and work in integrated firms in areas of the South where there were few African American attorneys. Marian Wright Edelman (founder of the Children's Defense Fund) and Julius Chambers (later a president of the LDF, and director-counsel of the organization beginning in 1984) were among the early interns. The internship process was formalized in 1971 with the creation of the Earl Warren Legal Training Program, funded with grants from the Carnegie and Rockefeller foundations. Over time, as increasing numbers of African Americans began working in legal practices in the South, the internship aspect of the program was abandoned, but the Earl Warren Legal Training Program continues to grant fellowships to black students attending formerly all-white law schools in the South and to give financial assistance to lawyer training.

OTHER PROGRAMS

The LDF supplies community assistance through its Division of Legal Information and Community Services. The LDF also sponsors several publications, including its *Annual Report*, the *Equal Justice* quarterly, and numerous legal materials, brochures, and pamphlets. It also issues press releases on current legal and political events and prepares watchdog reports. It hosts an annual institute to encourage public awareness of current problems faced by people of color.

HEADQUARTERS AND LEADERSHIP

Thurgood Marshall headed the LDF for more than two decades, from its inception in 1939 until 1961. Jack Greenberg, who had been an LDF staff member since the 1940's, succeeded Marshall as LDF director-counsel when Marshall was appointed by President John F. Kennedy to the U.S. Court of Appeals. Like Marshall, Greenberg had a long tenure as head of the LDF. He resigned in 1984 to accept a position as a professor at the Columbia University School of Law. Greenberg, who is white, was the subject of a 1983 boycott by African American students at Harvard University who believed that the legal rights organization should be headed by a person of color. Julius Chambers succeeded Greenberg as head of the LDF. During the early 1980's, the LDF moved from

its old location at 10 Columbus Circle to new offices at 99 Hudson Street in the Tribeca area of New York, joining with the Puerto Rican Legal Defense and Education Fund, the Asian American Legal Defense and Education Fund, the NOW Legal Defense and Education Fund, and the Council of New York Law Associates to constitute the Public Interest Law Center. Elaine Jones (the first black woman graduate of the University of Virginia Law School), who, as part of her long career with the LDF, had worked closely with LDF staff lawyer Lani Guinier on voting rights issues in the 1970's, became the director of the LDF office in Washington, D.C., in 1977. She became the director-counsel of the LDF in 1993.

—*Barbara Bair*

See also: *Brown v. Board of Education*; Civil Rights Act of 1964; Civil Rights movement; Little Rock school desegregation crisis; Marshall's appointment to the Supreme Court; National Association for the Advancement of Colored People; Voting Rights Act of 1965

BLACK FLIGHT

1940s

Urban flight is often thought of as occurring primarily among whites. However, middle-class African Americans have also been leaving; cities for suburbs, often settling in primarily black suburbs.

Definition: Population shift from urban to suburban areas

In the decades following World War II, the United States became; an increasingly suburban nation as Americans left cities for suburbs. During the 1940's, the federal government began guaranteeing; mortgage loans in order to encourage Americans to become; homeowners. These mortgage guarantees went primarily; to those buying homes in the suburbs, and they frequently underwrote; home ownership in neighborhoods that intentionally excluded; African Americans. At the same time, the growing use of; private automobiles and the construction of the freeway network; encouraged movement to the suburbs.

As white Americans became more suburban, African Americans; became more urban. Early in the twentieth century, the African; American population had been primarily rural. As agriculture; became more mechanized, African Americans moved to; urban areas.

Black concentration in cities, like white concentration; in suburbs, was encouraged by the federal government. The; federal Public Housing Authority established public housing largely in central city areas and restricted residence in public; housing to the most economically disadvantaged. Because African; Americans were proportionately much more likely to be poor; than whites were, the availability of public housing in cities combined; with housing discrimination in the suburbs to bring black; Americans into urban areas.

"WHITE FLIGHT"

By the 1970's, white movement from the cities to the suburbs; had become known as "white flight." Many observers of current; events believed that whites were fleeing the cities to get away; from African Americans. The racial integration of schools, and especially; the busing of children to achieve racial integration, may; have contributed to the movement of whites out of the cities, although; social scientists continue to debate this point.

Whites, however, were not the only ones to move to the suburbs. After the 1960's, the middle-class African American population; grew rapidly, and suburban housing became more widely; available for them. During the 1970's, the African American suburban; population of the United States grew at an annual rate of 4 percent, while the white suburban population grew at a rate of; only 1.5 percent. African American movement to the suburbs, labeled "black flight" by some social scientists, continued throughout; the 1980's and 1990's. It was driven by many of the same factors; that had been driving "white flight": the concentration of the; poor in central city areas, the deteriorating condition of urban; neighborhoods and schools, and the availability of suburban; housing.

Black movement to the suburbs did not, however, lead to fully; integrated neighborhoods across the United States. Instead, as; authors Douglas S. Massey and Nancy A. Denton maintained in; their influential book, *American Apartheid* (1993), African Americans tended to move into majority black suburban neighborhoods. Thus, "black flight" further concentrated minority poverty in the inner city by removing the middle class from inner city neighborhoods, while largely failing to integrate the American suburbs.

—Carl L. Bankston III

See also: Demographic trends; Economic trends; Employment; Great Migration

UNITED STATES V. CLASSIC

May 26, 1941

Overturning its 1921 decision, the Supreme Court held that Congress has the power to regulate primaries whenever state law makes them an integral part of the process for electing candidates to federal office.

The Case: U.S. Supreme Court ruling on white primaries

Two decisions of the U.S. Supreme Court, in 1921 and 1935, gave southern states the authority to exclude African Americans from voting in primary elections. These decisions were important because the South was dominated by the Democratic Party from the end of Reconstruction until the middle of the twentieth century. If African Americans could not vote in the Democratic primary, they were denied any real choice in the selection of elected officials.

In 1921, the Supreme Court ruled in *Newberry v. United States* that Congress did not have the authority to regulate primary elections. At issue was a Michigan senatorial primary race between Henry Ford and Truman Newberry in which Newberry alleged that he was the victim of vote fraud. The *Newberry* case provided the opportunity for southern states to pass white primary laws, since the Court declared that such elections fell outside constitutional protection. In *Grovey v. Townsend* (1935), the Court ruled that state party conventions could exclude African Americans from primaries without violating the Constitution. In the battle to eliminate the white primary, the U.S. Justice Department had to persuade the Supreme Court to overturn the *Newberry* decision. *United States v. Classic* provided the opportunity to reverse *Newberry*. Although the *Classic* case did not involve racial discrimination or the white primary, it did involve the relationship of the primary to the election process.

Vote fraud was a common feature of Louisiana elections. While investigating charges of fraud by the heirs of former governor and senator Huey Long, the Justice Department discovered that Patrick Classic, an opponent of the Long faction, had engaged in altering and falsely counting votes. Classic, invoking the *Newberry* decision, argued that primaries were beyond federal control.

Reversing *Newberry*, the U.S. Supreme Court declared that the Constitution protected the right to vote in primaries as well as general elections. This was certainly true in Louisiana, the Court stated, "where the state law has made the primary an integral part of the procedure of choice, or where in fact the primary effectively controls the choice."

The reversal of *Newberry* by the *Classic* decision provided the framework for the final attack on white primaries. It was evident that in the one-party South, whoever won the Democratic primary won the general election. Only three years after the *Classic* decision, the National Association for the Advancement of Colored People (NAACP) successfully challenged the white primaries in *Smith v. Allwright*. Without the *Classic* decision, the assault on the white primaries would have been delayed for years.

See also: *Grovey v. Townsend*; National Association for the Advancement of Colored People; *Newberry v. United States*; *Smith v. Allwright*; Voting Rights Act of 1965; White primaries

DEFENSE INDUSTRY DESEGREGATION
June 25, 1941

The 1941 desegregation of the U.S. defense industry was a major step in the advancement of African American civil rights and black-white relations.

The Event: President Franklin D. Roosevelt's issuing of Executive Order 8802, which prohibited discrimination of race or color in the defense industry and armed forces

Ever since the Revolutionary War, the United States had experienced difficulty in bringing African Americans into its military. Although one of the victims of the Boston massacre, Crispus Attucks, was an African American, and black soldiers were with George Washington when he made his famous 1776 Christmas crossing of the Delaware River to attack the Hessians at Trenton and Princeton, it was not until the Civil War (1861–1865) that African American troops were recruited officially into the United States Army. Even then, however, a rigid policy of segregation was maintained. In the two wars that followed, the Spanish-American War (1898) and World War I (1914–1919), both the Army and Navy had black troops, but largely in supporting roles, and always as separate, segregated units. In addition, black troop strength was kept deliberately low, partly to avoid offending white soldiers and partly because the military establishment had a low opinion of the abilities of African American troops.

ROOSEVELT'S ROLE
During the 1930's, however, under the presidency of Franklin D. Roosevelt, these prejudiced traditions began to change. Roosevelt's New Deal, which had been put into place to fight the ravages of the Great Depression, also addressed a number of social conditions, including civil rights. Although civil rights were never at the forefront of Roosevelt's agenda, his administration was more committed to them than any previous presidency had been, and his wife, the redoubtable Eleanor Roosevelt, was an especially strong and capable advocate for racial equality and justice. In addition, the shrewdly realistic president, who foresaw the coming struggle with Nazi Germany, realized that the U.S. military needed every capable citizen, of whatever color or background. The policy of "Jim Crowism," or rigid segregation of black and white people, remained largely in place, however.

Correctly estimating the extent and depth of prejudice against African American participation in the military, especially in positions of responsibility, Roosevelt moved cautiously. He had been assistant secretary of the Navy under President Woodrow Wilson during World War I, and he now prodded and encouraged the Navy high command to enlist additional African Americans and to place them in positions of greater responsibility than stewards or mess servers.

Gradually and slowly, the Navy responded. A similar broadening took place in the Army in 1935, when the president insisted that African American medical officers and chaplains be called up from the reserves. On October 9, 1940, Roosevelt announced a revised racial policy for the armed forces; its intent was to bring more African Americans into the military and to place them in positions of trust and responsibility. At a glacial but perceptible pace, the United States military was becoming more receptive to African Americans.

SLOW PROGRESS
The progress was not sufficiently rapid for many African Americans, among them A. Philip Randolph, president of the Brotherhood of Sleeping Car Porters, one of the strongest and most effective African American unions in the country. Randolph, who well understood that black voters had become an essential part of the Democratic Party's electoral base, calculated that Roosevelt would need to respond to African American demands, especially as the 1940 presidential elections approached. Randolph's logic and timing were correct.

In 1940, Roosevelt ran for an unprecedented third term as president. Randolph, along with former Republican city councilman Grant Reynolds of New York City, began a campaign against the Jim Crow practices still prevalent in the United States military. Randolph and Reynolds also called for greater opportunities for African American workers in the rapidly growing defense industries, which had arisen as the United States rearmed against the threat from Nazi Germany and imperialist Japan. As the campaign intensified, Roosevelt faced a difficult situation that threatened his southern, conservative support at the same time that it endangered his urban, liberal allies. When Randolph announced plans for a march on Washington, scheduled for July 1, 1941, Roosevelt knew he must act. His determination was steeled by the resolve of his wife, Eleanor, who

342

had long been a champion of equal rights for African Americans, and whose contacts with the black community were strong and deep.

EXECUTIVE ORDER 8802

On June 25, 1941, Roosevelt issued Executive Order 8802, which enunciated a broad policy of racial equality in the armed forces and the defense industry. The order was clear and sweeping in its intent:

> In offering the policy of full participation in the defense program by all persons regardless of color, race, creed, or national origin, and directing certain action in furtherance of said policy . . . all departments of the government, including the Armed Forces, shall lead the way in erasing discrimination over color or race.

President Roosevelt backed up the policy by establishing the Fair Employment Practices Committee, which was charged with monitoring and enforcing compliance among civilian contractors. It is estimated that Roosevelt's executive order, combined with the work of the commission, helped to bring fifty-three thousand African American civilians into defense industry jobs they otherwise would not have held.

The timing of the policy was impeccable. Randolph and the other campaign leaders, satisfied that the Roosevelt administration was sincere in its commitment to civil rights, called off the march on Washington. Political conservatives, who otherwise might have challenged the president's order, had to admit that it would not be proper to expect African Americans to serve in the military without allowing them to hold responsible positions and achieve corresponding rank. Black voters responded enthusiastically to the Roosevelt reelection campaign, helping him to sweep to victory in the November balloting.

Inevitably, there were racial tensions and outbreaks of violence, especially in lower- and middle-class northern neighborhoods. In 1943, for example, tension between black and white workers led to open violence at a park on Belle Isle near Detroit; in the end, federal troops had to be called in to restore order, and twenty-five African Americans and nine whites had been killed. Similar, if less bloody, events took place in other cities. Still, the transition to a more equitable situation continued in both civilian and military life.

However, the traditional segregation remained. During World War II, black units still were kept separate and apart from white troops, and were generally reserved for support and logistical duties rather than combat. When the difficulties and emergencies of battle required it, African American units were brought into the fighting line; generally, they acquitted themselves well. By the end of the war, African Americans had distinguished themselves as ground soldiers, sailors, and pilots in both combat and noncombat situations. After the surrender of the Axis Powers in 1945, there was a sense of inevitable change ahead for the United States military. The question of whether it would be a peaceful, productive change remained.

AFTER WORLD WAR II

Harry S. Truman, who assumed the presidency in 1945 after the death of Franklin D. Roosevelt, was determined to make the change in a proper fashion. He assembled a special Civil Rights Committee which, on October 30, 1947, issued its report, To Secure These Rights. Clearly and unhesitatingly, the report called for the elimination of segregation in the United States military.

As the 1948 presidential elections approached, the issue of African Americans in the military affected the political atmosphere. Truman and the national Democratic Party, as heirs of the Roosevelt New Deal, had strong connections with the Civil Rights movement and its leaders; at the same time, much of the traditional Democratic strength was in the South, where civil rights issues were strongly opposed by the entrenched establishment. Southern politicians, such as Strom Thurmond of South Carolina, threatened to bolt the party if the Democrats adopted a strong civil rights platform at their convention; however, inspired by the passionate appeal of Mayor Hubert H. Humphrey of Minneapolis, the Democrats did indeed adopt a positive plank on civil rights. The southerners stormed out, nominating Thurmond to run on the "Dixiecrat" ticket, and Truman went on to win a come-from-behind victory in November.

One element of that victory was Truman's own Executive Order 9981, issued on July 26, 1948, just after the Democratic Party convention. Truman's order was similar to but stronger than Roosevelt's: It required equal opportunity in the armed forces of the United States, regardless of race, and called upon the military services to move immediately to implement the directive. The Air Force reacted promptly and soon achieved remarkable integration of black and white troops; the Navy and Marines were more hesitant in their acceptance. In the end, however, all branches of the armed forces responded, making them among the most egalitarian and equitable of U.S. institutions.

—*Michael Witkoski*

See also: Brotherhood of Sleeping Car Porters; Fair Employment Practices Committee; Integration; Military; Military desegregation; President's Committee on Civil Rights; Race riots of 1943; World War II

FAIR EMPLOYMENT PRACTICES COMMITTEE

Spring, 1941

Although the committee was somewhat successful in its endeavors it was disbanded by 1946. The federal government did not establish another organization devoted to eliminating racial discrimination in employment practices until the Civil Rights Act of 1964.

Identification: Committee formed to investigate complaints of discrimination that arose from Executive Order 8802

In the spring of 1941, as the United States prepared to enter World War II, African American leaders pressured the administration of Franklin D. Roosevelt to eliminate segregation in the armed forces and discriminatory hiring practices in the booming war industries. A. Philip Randolph, president of the Brotherhood of Sleeping Car Porters, the largest black labor union, threatened a massive march on Washington, D.C., by a hundred thousand demonstrators under the banner Democracy Not Hypocrisy—Jobs Not Alms. Roosevelt, hoping to avoid an embarrassing racial protest that might divide the Democratic Party and his administration at a time when he needed unity for his war-preparedness program, moved to head off the March on Washington movement by meeting with Randolph and Walter White, president of the National Association for the Advancement of Colored People (NAACP).

On June 25, 1941, a week before the planned march, Roosevelt issued Executive Order 8802. It prohibited discrimination by employers, unions, and government agencies involved in defense work on the basis of race, creed, color, or national origin but made no mention of desegregating the armed forces. Roosevelt established the Fair Employment Practices Committee (FEPC) to investigate complaints and redress grievances stemming from the order. Randolph and White accepted the compromise arrangement and called off the march.

Although African Americans hailed the FEPC as the greatest step forward in race relations since the Civil War, Roosevelt initially gave the agency little authority.

Underfunded and understaffed, the FEPC at first could do little more than conduct investigations into complaints received and make recommendations, relying on the powers of publicity and persuasion to achieve change. In mid-1943, however, amid mounting concern that manpower shortages were hurting the war effort, Roosevelt beefed up the agency by giving it the authority to conduct hearings, make findings, issue directives to war industries, and make recommendations to the War Manpower Commission to curb discrimination.

IMPACT

The FEPC had a mixed record of accomplishment in eliminating racial discrimination in the war industries and government agencies. It resolved less than half of the eight thousand complaints received, and employers and unions often ignored its compliance orders with impunity. Although African American employment in the war industries increased from 3 percent in 1942 to 8 percent in 1945 and the federal government more than tripled its number of black employees, such changes had more to do with wartime labor shortages than FEPC actions. Nevertheless, the FEPC scored some significant successes. In 1944, federal troops broke up a strike by white Philadelphia transit workers and enforced an FEPC directive that African Americans be upgraded to positions as streetcar operators. At war's end, despite the FEPC's shortcomings, African American leaders and white liberals hoped to transform the committee into a permanent agency. In 1946, however, southern Democrats in the Senate filibustered a bill to extend the FEPC and killed the agency. Although several northern states passed their own Fair Employment Practices acts, the Senate again blocked bills to create a permanent FEPC in 1950 and 1952. Not until the Civil Rights Act of 1964 did the federal government establish another agency devoted to eliminating racial discrimination in employment practices.

—*Richard V. Damms*

See also: Brotherhood of Sleeping Car Porters; Civil Rights Act of 1964; Defense industry desegregation; Economic trends; Employment; Equal Employment Opportunity Act of 1972; Equal Employment Opportunity Commission; Military desegregation; National Association for the Advancement of Colored People

WORLD WAR II

US entered the war December 8, 1941; Japan's surrender August 14, 1945

Despite segregation and widespread discrimination, African Americans made important contributions to the American war effort. By linking racism at home with fascism abroad, civil rights activists promoted a "Double V" strategy—a victory against oppression at home as well as abroad.

The Event: Worldwide conflict that the United States entered after Japan's attack on Pearl Harbor

The Selective Service Act of 1940, which initiated a military draft, forbade racial discrimination in the recruitment and training of men, but it continued the traditional policy of segregation. When black leaders protested, President Franklin D. Roosevelt announced a policy of seeking to use African Americans in numbers approximately equal to their proportion of the national population, which was about 10 percent. Soon thereafter, Roosevelt promoted Colonel Benjamin O. Davis, Sr., to brigadier general, making him the first African American to hold this rank. He also appointed Judge William Hastie as a civilian aid to the secretary of war.

THE HOME FRONT

As U.S. involvement in the war approached and defense industries grew, African Americans grew dismayed by their lack of employment opportunities in businesses contracting with the government. Hoping to promote change, A. Philip Randolph and other black leaders organized the March on Washington movement in early 1941, hoping to involve 150,000 protesters. Roosevelt persuaded the organizers to call off the demonstration in exchange for his issuing Executive Order 8802, which formally prohibited discrimination in defense industries because of "race, creed, color, or national origin." To implement its provisions, the order created the Fair Employment Practices Committee (FEPC), the first federal agency devoted to combating racial discrimination.

Although the FEPC lacked enforcement powers, the booming defense industries soon had such a need for labor that African Americans increasingly secured factory jobs. They constituted only 3 percent of American defense workers in 1942, but that proportion increased to 8 percent by 1945. In the automobile industry, representation of African Americans grew to about 12 percent of the United Auto Workers in Detroit. With the growth of job opportunities in the North and California, more than a half-million African Americans migrated out of the South.

Many instances of ugly racial violence occurred during the war years. Authorities reported fourteen instances of racially inspired lynchings, with two black soldiers among the victims. In 1943 alone, researchers at Fisk University recorded 242 instances of racial fighting in forty-seven cities. The most destructive conflict took place in Detroit, where a minor skirmish among teenagers escalated into bitter fighting in which twenty-five African Americans and nine white Americans were killed. A few weeks later, in Harlem, a disagreement between a black soldier and a white police officer set off a race riot that resulted in six deaths, 550 arrests, and five million dollars in property damage.

THE WAR FRONT

During the course of the nearly four years that the United States fought in the war, almost one million African Americans served in the armed services. About half of them served overseas, in the European and Pacific theaters of the war. Nevertheless, due mostly to disparities in education and health, African Americans represented less than 6 percent of the military in 1942. Denied equal opportunities for combat service, they were assigned disproportional numbers of mundane tasks in areas such as supply and support. When Walter White, the secretary of the National Association for the Advancement of Colored People, investigated the morale of black soldiers abroad, he found that one of their most common complaints was that the backbreaking work of unloading supplies was often as dangerous to soldiers as fighting on the front lines.

Despite these limitations, significant numbers of African Americans engaged in combat, often with great distinction. The most famous of them were the seven hundred pilots trained at the Tuskegee Air Force Base. These Tuskegee Airmen, as they were known, flew 15,533 sorties and destroyed 261 enemy planes. Sixty-six of the pilots were killed in action. In 1945, the 332d Fighter Group, commanded by Benjamin O. Davis, Jr., received a Presidential Unit Citation, and eighty of its pilots were awarded the Distinguished Flying Cross. This impressive record proved that African Americans, when given the chance, could become skilled pilots.

In 1942, the Army reactivated two traditionally all-African American infantry divisions: the Ninety-second (buffalo soldiers) and the Ninety-third (Blue Helmets). Soldiers of the Ninety-second Division, who were deployed in Italy, received more than 12,000 decorations. The Ninety-third Division fought in many bloody battles in the Solomon Islands, Treasury Island, and the Philippines in the South Pacific. Another unit, the highly decorated Back Panthers of the 761st Tank Battalion, engaged in some of the fiercest fighting at the Battle of the Bulge, after which they helped breech the Siegfried line and captured seven German towns. Nominated many times for a Presidential Unit Citation, the 761st finally received the award in 1978.

Late in 1944, General Dwight Eisenhower approved a limited experiment of using racially integrated units. The experiment utilized African Americans who volunteered to fight with white troops. Out of 5,000 volunteers, 2,500 men were selected and organized into 37 platoons of 40 men each, which were then attached to white units containing 200 white soldiers. The integrated units fought in the Battle of the Bulge as well as on German soil. Although white officers reported that the experiment was an unqualified success, it was quietly discontinued at the end of the war because of fears of undermining white southern support for a postwar military draft.

Many African Americans viewed a tragedy that occurred at the Navy base at Port Chicago, California, in 1944 as an illustration of the problem of unequal treatment in the military. While black sailors were loading ammunition there, the ammunition cargos of two ships exploded, killing 320 men, including 202 African Americans. When ordered to resume loading several weeks later, 258 black sailors refused to obey and called for improved safety procedures. The Navy court charged 50 of the sailors with mutiny and charged the remainder with lesser offenses. Those convicted of mutiny were sentenced to fifteen years in prison but were granted amnesty after the war. Controversy over the incident had one positive result: The loading of ammunition ceased being a "blacks only" assignment.

Frequently the efforts of African Americans to oppose discrimination and segregation led to clashes on military bases. In July, 1944, for instance, Army lieutenant Jackie Robinson, the future baseball star, disobeyed a command to sit in the back of a military bus at Fort Hood, Texas. He was court-martialed but acquitted because the court ruled that the command had violated the Army's antidiscriminatory policies in transportation. At Freeman Field, Indiana, more than a hundred black officer trainees were arrested and disciplined in 1945 for entering a club reserved for white officers. Second Lieutenant Roger Terry was court-martialed and convicted of brushing against a superior officer when entering the club—a conviction that was not overturned until 1995.

DEMOBILIZATION

Black soldiers returning home, even if wounded in action, continued to experience invidious discrimination in employment, education, and political rights. Even German prisoners of war held in the United States were treated with more respect and dignity. Conservative white southerners were ready to use violence against anyone challenging the Jim Crow system. In a highly publicized incident of 1946, Army veteran Isaac Woodward was attacked and blinded by policemen. President Harry S. Truman, incensed to learn of such events, created the President's Committee on Civil Rights, which was charged with investigating discrimination and making proposals for change. Progress would be slow, but World War II helped put the issue of equal rights on the national agenda.

—*Thomas Tandy Lewis*

See also: Defense industry desegregation; Military; Military desegregation; Tuskegee Airmen; Vietnam War

TUSKEGEE AIRMEN

1942–1946

African Americans have made important contributions to the military services in every war in which they have fought, but the achievements of the Tuskegee Airmen during World War II brought them previously unparalleled distinctions.

Identification: African American aviators who served in World War II

African Americans made noteworthy gains in the military services during World War II, particularly in the U.S. Army Air Forces. Despite opposition from southern legislators, African American recruits began training at Tuskegee, Alabama. Challenged by substandard training conditions, discrimination, and segregation, the Tuskegee Airmen responded with resolve and discipline. Between 1942 and 1946, 996 African Americans received their silver wings at Tuskegee Army Air Field. Some 450 of these pilots flew with the 99th Fighter Squadron and later, the 332d Fighter Group. They became known as the red tails" for the scarlet coloring on the tail and nose of their P-51B Mustang aircraft. After their baptism of fire in North Africa, the Tuskegee Airmen moved into Italy.

Their commanding officer was Colonel Benjamin O. Davis, Jr. Particularly notable is a daring strafing mission that Davis led in Austria. Despite intense group fire, Davis and his squadron destroyed or damaged thirty-five locomotives, six of which are credited to Davis himself. Around that same time, another pilot in the 332d destroyed a German destroyer single-handedly with machine guns. The Tuskegee Airmen were also the first U.S. pilots to down a German jet.

The 332d achieved lasting fame when it assumed escort duties for U.S. bombers striking deep into

Portrait of Tuskegee airman Edward M. Thomas by photographer Toni Frissell, March 1945

Germany. The 332d established a record for never losing a single bomber in approximately two hundred missions, a truly extraordinary accomplishment. The group's heroics in the air and dignity on the ground won them many medals and broke the color barriers of the U.S. military. By the end of World War II, one out of sixteen aviators in the U.S. Army Air Forces was an African American.

—Douglas W. Richmond

See also: Buffalo soldiers; Military; World War II

CONGRESS OF RACIAL EQUALITY FORMS

Spring, 1942

The Congress of Racial Equality, more than any other civil rights group, was responsible for the widespread use of Mahatma Gandhi's nonviolent direct-action protest techniques in the Civil Rights movement in the United States from the 1940's through the 1960's. The

group's ideology of nonviolence inspired Martin Luther King, Jr.

Also known as: CORE; Committee of Racial Equality
Locale: Chicago, Illinois

Categories: Organizations and institutions; civil rights and liberties; social issues and reform

KEY FIGURES

James L. Farmer, Jr. (1920-1999), cofounder of CORE, and later its director

Bayard Rustin (1912-1987), early Quaker member of CORE and organizer of the 1963 March on Washington

A. Philip Randolph (1889-1979), organizer of the first civil rights March on Washington planned for 1941

Mahatma Gandhi (1869-1948), Indian political leader who developed and used nonviolent direct-action protest against British rule in India

SUMMARY OF EVENT

African Americans began protesting racial discrimination in the United States before the Civil War, with the main objectives of eliminating racial discrimination and segregation and living inU.S. society on an equal footing with other citizens. Controversy within the African American community about what tactics to use and strategies to follow accompanied the protests.

At the end of the nineteenth century, the position of African Americans in U.S. society was declining. Racial prejudice flared. Disenfranchisement, lynchings, "Jim Crow" or segregation laws, and exclusion on the basis of race from the skilled trades were prevalent. The early twentieth century sawmounting oppression and discrimination and an increasing frequency of race riots in both the North and the South. In general, this spurred accommodation, rather than protest, among African Americans.

Two other strategies for dealing with racial tensions developed in the early twentieth century. Booker T. Washington and his followers advocated "separatism" as a means of overcoming racism. Another group, the National Association for the Advancement of Colored People (NAACP), began attacking racial discrimination in the courts. One of the most powerful and longest-lived civil rights groups in U.S. history, the NAACP was founded in 1909 by black radicals, white progressives, and socialists, under the leadership of W. E. B. Du Bois.

It had as its purpose the fight for black constitutional rights, particularly that of integration. As a rule, the NAACP employed legalistic methods of fighting for civil rights, that is, active propagandizing, legal activity, and lobbying for legislation against racial discrimination and segregation.

During World War I, therewas a massive migration of African Americans to the North, where there were more jobs. Living conditions, however, were extremely poor. With the end of the war came widespread unemployment and race riots. A new militancy arose among many blacks during this period. The NAACP thrived on this militancy as it fought against lynchings, disenfranchisement, and segregation, particularly in housing and schools. By the 1920's, the NAACP's legalistic approach was seen as too conservative by those who advocated physical resistance to white mob violence and those who advocated racial separatism.

During the 1930's, white American attitudes toward African Americans began to change greatly, as humanitarian interest developed in improving conditions among the underprivileged. An increasingly large black vote in northern cities also drew the attention of Anglo politicians to black welfare. This was a period when interest focused on economic problems among the black community.

The conservative NAACP continued its fights for integration, especially in the schools, and the vote for blacks. TheNAACPemphasized legal argument as a tactic. A few other black protesting groups, however, used boycotting and picketing during this decade.

During and after World War II, a new, liberal respect for non-Anglos began to grow in the United States. During the early 1940's, the NAACP continued its legal battle against discrimination and segregation. Two new movements, with a new approach, emerged alongside the NAACP—the March on Washington Movement (MOWM)and the Congress of Racial Equality (CORE).

The March on Washington Movement was born in 1941, when African American railroad workers, led by A. Philip Randolph (then president of the Brotherhood of Sleeping Car Porters) threatened to march on Washington, D.C., unless President Franklin D. Roosevelt integrated U.S. defense industries and the military. Randolph proposed that blacks from across the nation gather in Washington and march en masse to the Lincoln Monument. He also urged similar small-scale local marches.

Calling for the march in July, 1941, Randolph cautioned against violence, which he argued would be more harmful than helpful. Roosevelt issued an executive order in June, 1941, establishing a federal Fair Employment Practices Committee. Randolph called off the march.

The March on Washington Movement continued to exist for a short while. In an address to the movement in

September, 1942, Randolph advocated that nonviolent direct action, similar to that used by Mahatma Gandhi in India, be used by all-black groups to combat racial discrimination and segregation. He outlined a plan for forming small blocs of blacks ready to mobilize by the millions to march on Washington or to conduct simultaneous smaller marches across the nation. The movement was important, first, because it was an all-black organization that advocated mass action by those living in urban ghettos to solve economic problems and, second, because it laid the groundwork for the nonviolent direct action movement of the 1960's.

CORE, however, was the group that made nonviolent direct action a widespread and effective civil rights protest technique. CORE grew out of the Chicago Committee of Racial Equality, which met in Chicago in the spring of 1942. The Fellowship of Reconciliation (FOR), an almost entirely white Quaker pacifist group, had established a "cell" of about a dozen people at the University of Chicago in October, 1941. Many of the cell's members wanted to apply Gandhi's nonviolent direct action techniques to the United States' racial problems.

FOR authorized James L. Farmer, Jr., a FOR staff member, to form in 1942 what later was named the Chicago Committee of Racial Equality. The group's first six members were Farmer and George Houser (another FOR staff member), Bernice Fisher, Homer Jack, Joe Guinn, and James R. Robinson. The group contained blacks and whites as well as Protestants and Catholics, but all members were pacifists.

CORE wrote two statements in 1942 outlining its basic commitment to interracial, nonviolent direct action and setting down the principles according to which its direct action demonstrations later would proceed. Its statement of purpose proclaimed goals of eliminating segregation and racial discrimination in public accommodation, housing, and other areas, through one method only—interracial nonviolent direct action. It denounced violence as a method of opposing racial discrimination, even if the protester is physically attacked, because CORE members believed social conflicts could not be resolved by means of violence. Among acceptable forms of protest, they identified negotiation, mediation, demonstration, and picketing.

CORE's second important statement, its "Action Discipline," explained the group's belief that nonviolent direct action should be combined with goodwill toward those who discriminate. Although it underwent some revision, the "Action Discipline" remained the

group's official statement of principle and philosophy until the 1960's. CORE's protest technique was a combination of Gandhi's approach and the "sit-in," the latter of which had developed from "sit-down" strikes similar to Gandhi's that had been used in the United States in the 1930's.

During its first year, the Chicago Committee worked to eliminate racial discrimination at a Chicago roller rink and at an apartment building, as well as at the University of Chicago hospital, medical school, and barbershop. According to Farmer, the first sit-in was directed against the Jack Spratt restaurant in Chicago in May, 1942. It was successful in ending segregation of seating.

Local CORE committees formed in large cities around the country, as Farmer and another early CORE member, Bayard Rustin, lectured on race relations for FORin late 1942 and early 1943. An independent federation of local committees was formed at a planning conference organized by Bernice Fisher and the Chicago Committee. It was held in Chicago in June, 1943, under Farmer's leadership. Nine local committees sent representatives, and they decided to affiliate under the name of the Committees of Racial Equality. In 1944, the national federation adopted the name Congress of Racial Equality and appointed Farmer as its national chairman and Fisher as the national secretary-treasurer.

SIGNIFICANCE

CORE influenced the progress of the Civil Rights movement in the United States in a variety of ways. It was the black protest group that used nonviolent direct-action protest techniques, such as sit-ins, more than any other. Beginning with its first sit-in in a Chicago restaurant, CORE organized pivotal events in the history of civil rights protest. In April, 1947, CORE and FOR staged a "Journey of Reconciliation" across the upper South to test the integration of interstate bus transport. This was the first example of what was later called a "Freedom Ride," a nonviolent direct-action protest technique. In the mid-1950's, the attack on segregated public accommodations and transportation intensified. In May and June, 1961, the Freedom Rides brought CORE to national attention and made it the principal national exponent of nonviolent direct action protest and the principal national black civil rights protest group.

CORE also was involved in organizing the March on Washington on August 27, 1963. This march originally intended to call attention to increasing black unemployment, but it also took on the goal of pressuring the administration to pass the Civil Rights Act of 1964. It was at this huge, peaceful rally of 250,000 people on the steps of the Lincoln Memorial in Washington, D.C., that the Reverend Martin Luther King, Jr., gave his famous "I Have a Dream" speech.

CORE spread the message of nonviolent direct action protest to other leaders and groups. King, one of the major figures in the Montgomery, Alabama, bus boycott beginning in 1955, was greatly influenced by CORE's ideology. In the late 1950's, the use of nonviolent, direct action protest increased markedly. This was partly a result of King's personal appeal and his founding of the Southern Christian Leadership Conference in 1957, which advocated Gandhian nonviolence.

Nonviolent direct action reached its peak in the student sit-ins of 1960. These began with the February, 1960, sit-in by four North Carolina Agricultural & Technical State College students at a lunch counter in Greensboro, North Carolina. This event is regarded as the beginning of the civil rights revolution, and it was the most significant single event that encouraged and gave form to mass protest in the Civil Rights movement. These college students formed the Student

Nonviolent Coordinating Committee in 1960 and took their philosophy from King, but they called on CORE for assistance in training protesters and organizing sit-ins. As college sit-in groups multiplied in the South after 1960, direct action techniques won success and became the favored tactics among civil rights protest groups.

Justifiably remembered as one of the key groups giving rise to the Civil Rights movement, given its pioneering use of nonviolent direct-action techniques in the 1940's, CORE's influence and activity diminished during the late 1970's. It has since revived and is based in New York City.

—*Martha Ellen Webb and Charles W. Johnson*

See also: Supreme Court Rules African American Disenfranchisement Unconstitutional; Congress of Racial Equality Holds Its Journey of Reconciliation; Supreme Court Ends Public School Segregation; Montgomery Bus Boycott; SCLC Forms to Link Civil Rights Groups; Greensboro Sit-Ins; Civil Rights Protesters Attract International Attention; King Delivers His "I Have a Dream" Speech.

CHICAGO SIT-INS

May-June, 1943

These demonstrations were intended to change the attitudes of business owners and thus differed from the sit-ins of the later Civil Rights movement era; however, they set important precedents for the later sit-in movement.

The Event: Earliest sit-in demonstrations
Place: Chicago, Illinois

Still in its first year when it launched the 1943 sit-ins in Chicago, the Congress of Racial Equity (CORE) had enthusiasm for nonviolent methods developed by Mohandas K. Gandhi in India's struggle for independence but had little experience with those methods. The Chicago Committee of Racial Equality that developed into CORE was founded in 1942, chiefly by James Farmer, Bernice Fisher, Homer Jack, George M. Houser, Joe Guinn, and James R. Robinson, all students in Chicago. This biracial group was headed by Farmer, one of two African Americans among the major founders. Farmer

was a theology student whose father was a professor at Wiley College in Texas, and he was deeply interested in Christian pacifism. As a staff member of the Fellowship of Reconciliation (FOR), like Houser, Farmer wanted to apply Gandhian and Christian ideals to society with a view toward creating harmony and mutual respect among all races and classes.

This kind of social vision informed those who experimented with the sit-in technique in Chicago. In retrospect, Farmer has written, their early efforts there were idealistic. They hoped to change the minds of the restaurant owners and were "childishly literal-minded." They were not insistent that they be given access to public facilities on the basis of law but tried to convince their resisters that access would be good for business.

PREPARATIONS
The 1943 sit-ins were months in the making. CORE's earliest efforts to combat racial discrimination in Chicago were undertaken on a broad front: the university

barber shop (which refused in November, 1942, to cut Bayard Rustin's hair), the medical school and the hospital, even the roller rink. By the end of 1942, CORE's attention was increasingly focused on restaurants that refused to serve African Americans. Two such restaurants were the Jack Spratt Restaurant near CORE Fellowship House and Stoner's Restaurant, a downtown establishment in the Loop that served chiefly an upper-middle-class clientele.

CORE first learned of racial discrimination at Stoner's in October, 1942, when three of its members (one of them black) were refused service by the owner himself. During the following five months, CORE gathered information at these two restaurants, attempting to comply with the Gandhian strategy that called for careful investigation to determine whether there was undeniable evidence of discrimination before proceeding to direct action. Interracial test groups were sent both to Stoner's and to Jack Spratt's. Sometimes the groups were served, but after a long period of waiting. On some occasions, they were served food that was overly salted or laced with broken eggshells. By December, 1942, CORE was sufficiently convinced of discrimination to spend a full week distributing to customers leaflets that pointed out the evidence and asked customers to protest against it as they paid their bills.

Some Chicago residents began to question CORE's pressure on Stoner's Restaurant, and as a result Houser and other CORE leaders decided to survey dozens of other Loop restaurants to determine whether Stoner's policy was typical or an exception to prevailing practices. The study showed that virtually all Loop eating establishments operated on a nondiscriminatory basis. CORE published the results in a pamphlet entitled "50 Loop Restaurants That Do Not Discriminate." CORE distributed this pamphlet to various groups, both white and black, and sent a copy to Stoner's management. Further efforts to desegregate the restaurant by test groups failed, and by January, 1943, Houser, Farmer, and other CORE officials were debating the possibility of direct action.

In March, 1943, CORE leaders considered staging what it called a sit-down, in which participants would occupy seats until served, at Stoner's. They decided against it after considering the logistical difficulties involved in a small group's efforts to gain meaningful attention in a two-hundred-seat restaurant. The project was delayed until June to coincide with CORE's first national convention, which would bring several direct action groups into Chicago and thus provide enough

people to increase the chances of success. In May, however, CORE led a smaller sit-in operation at Jack Spratt's.

The sit-in at Jack Spratt's involved twenty-one CORE members, most of them white. The group entered the restaurant at the dinner hour on May 14, 1943, and refused to eat until the African Americans among them were served. Police officers were called, but they found they could do nothing to disperse the participants in the sit-in. Within two hours, the management of Jack Spratt's decided to serve all in the group, and in that sense the sit-in was a success. It was not clear whether such a demonstration would work at the larger Stoner's Restaurant, but the experience at Jack Spratt's encouraged CORE to follow through with the plans for a June sit-in there.

The sit-in at Stoner's Restaurant involved more than three times the number of participants. Some sixty-five people, sixteen of them African American, sat in at Stoner's during the evening meal on Saturday, June 5. Around 4:30 p.m. white demonstration participants entered the restaurant in groups of two, three, and four. They were readily seated. When the first of the two interracial groups entered shortly after 5:00 p.m., the six African Americans and two whites were ignored when they requested seats. After a half-hour wait, they were taken to a table and served. Houser reported that one of the white participants was kicked in the leg by the restaurant owner as the group passed.

As the first interracial group was seated, the second entered. Its nine African Americans and one white person were refused service and threatened, but they stood near the entrance for more than ninety minutes. The police were called three times but saw no cause for making arrests since the group was orderly. After the third call, the police officers instructed the restaurant owner not to call again unless there was a compelling reason. Encouraged by expressions of sympathy from some of the restaurant staff, the interracial group stood quietly, refusing to budge. Other customers in the restaurant expressed support, and several of the black employees threatened to quit if the group was not served. CORE members pledged to stay all night if necessary.

BREAKING THE IMPASSE

Eventually, the deadlock was broken when an elderly white woman who was not involved with CORE invited one of the black women in the group to sit at her table. The white CORE participants who were already seated followed her example and invited the unseated group to join them. When only two were left standing, one of the hostesses approached them and invited them to follow her to a small table at the center of the restaurant. With that, applause broke out across Stoner's Restaurant. For several minutes, a spontaneous demonstration of support changed the tense atmosphere to one of relief.

IMPACT

The CORE-sponsored sit-ins of May and June, 1943, in Chicago, were less dramatic and received far less press coverage than the sit-ins of the early 1960's. Their historic significance has, however, been recognized. Considered the first sit-in of the modern Civil Rights movement in the United States they served as examples for later sit-ins conducted by the National Association for the Advancement of Colored People (NAACP) and for the massive wave of sit-ins triggered by an incident at Woolworth's lunch counter in Greensboro, North Carolina, in February, 1960.

To the leaders of the 1943 sit-ins, the results were gratifying. Almost no violence resulted, and the response from white people who observed the demonstration was generally very supportive. CORE leader Houser considered it a "well executed nonviolent demonstration for racial justice." The racial discrimination of Stoner's Restaurant continued unevenly throughout the war years, but by 1946 interracial groups were served without resistance.

For CORE, the experience confirmed the viability of the Gandhian methods to which it was committed. The Gandhian model called for investigation, early efforts at negotiation, firm expression of determination, personal spiritual preparation, and, if necessary,

nonviolent direct action. CORE followed those steps meticulously in Chicago and was reinforced in its belief in the effectiveness of such an approach. James Farmer, the best known of the early CORE leaders, was convinced that the 1943 sit-ins strengthened CORE's resolve and heightened its influence. The sit-in at Stoner's coincided with CORE's first national convention, bringing groups from nine cities together; out of this convention grew the beginnings of national organizational affiliation known collectively as the Congress of Racial Equality (1944). The broadened organization's "Statement of Purpose and Action Discipline" clearly committed it to nonviolent direct action and the elimination of all racial discrimination and segregation. The Chicago experience was one of the specific examples of success to which the organization could point in future years and from which it could draw inspiration.

CORE soon began to sponsor training workshops to promulgate the principles of nonviolence and to train people in its techniques. Regional organizational subdivisions linked the national office with local affiliated committees. In that way, CORE retained a democratic structure while offering guidance and personnel for various campaigns. The Chicago experience continued to provide a point of reference demonstrating that collective nonviolent action could produce results.

—*Thomas R. Peake*

See also: Chicago riots; Civil Rights movement; Congress of Racial Equality; Greensboro sit-ins; Sit-ins

RACE RIOTS ERUPT IN DETROIT AND HARLEM

June 20-21, 1943, and August 1, 1943

The race riots in Detroit and Harlem were among the most violent of the 250 such outbreaks that occurred in 1943, as wartime America experienced growing racial and ethnic tensions on the home front. They vividly demonstrated the contradiction between the United States' fight for freedom abroad and the denial of basic freedoms to African Americans at home.

Locale: Detroit, Michigan; Harlem, New York
Categories: Wars, uprisings, and civil unrest; social issues and reform; civil rights and liberties

KEY FIGURES
Edward J. Jeffries, Jr. (1900-1950), mayor of Detroit, 1940-1948
Harry F. Kelly (1895-1971), governor of Michigan, 1943-1946
Fiorello Henry La Guardia (1882-1947), mayor of New York City, 1934-1945, and chief of the U.S. Office of Civilian Defense, 1941-1942
Franklin D. Roosevelt (1882-1945), president of the United States, 1933-1945

SUMMARY OF EVENT

The entry of the United States into World War II required the complete mobilization of the U.S. economy to produce the materials necessary to defeat the Axis Powers. One consequence of this national mobilization was the migration of millions of African Americans from the rural South to the industrial centers of the north in search of high-paying factory jobs vacated by whites inducted into the armed forces. In addition to economic betterment, African Americans hoped to escape the harsh legacy of Jim Crow relations that characterized the South, a system that effectively maintained segregation of the races and negated black political power by preventing African Americans from voting through mechanisms such as the poll tax. As they migrated northward, African Americans hoped to make better lives for themselves and their children. There was, however, little real change for African Americans upon their arrival in northern American cities. Some white workers resented their arrival and participated in "hate strikes." In addition, few cities were prepared to handle the sudden influx of tens of thousands of African Americans. With domestic production oriented primarily to the war effort, there was increased competition between blacks and whites over scarce amenities. Some blacks sought escape from the bleak conditions confronting them by enlisting in the military, only to suffer further injustices. The armed forces remained strictly segregated throughout World War II, as blacks were excluded from the Marines and the Coast Guard and were relegated to the Navy's mess section.

It is against this backdrop that the 1943 riots in Detroit and Harlem must be understood. Detroit, the reputed "Arsenal of Democracy," experienced lesser racial disturbances prior to the riot of June, 1943. The most notable such disturbance occurred when African Americans were forcibly prevented from moving into the Sojourner Housing Project in 1942 by police armed with guns and tear gas. This ongoing racial antagonism culminated in the June riot.

The immediate impetus of the riot occurred late in the evening of June 20 at the Belle Isle municipal park. Minor clashes between blacks and whites took place throughout the day. The bloody riot that would eventually leave thirty-four people dead (twenty-five of them black, seventeen of whom were killed by the police) was precipitated by two rumors. The first rumor held that an African American man had raped a white woman at the amusement park and that a group of African Americans had begun to riot. Shortly afterward, the second rumor began at a popular black nightclub. This one said that some white sailors had killed an African American woman and her baby by throwing them off of the bridge that connected Belle Isle to Detroit, and that the police had begun to beat African Americans in the city.

The actual rioting began early in the morning of June 21. Police reported stabbings, store windows being smashed, looting, and indiscriminate interracial beatings of pedestrians and passengers in cars and public transportation. At the riot's end, in addition to the thirty-four dead, more than one thousand people had been injured. Detroit suffered more than two million dollars in property losses and lost 100 million work hours in war production, according to one account. Detroit Mayor Edward J. Jeffries, Jr., conceded that much of the loss of life and property could have been prevented had federal troops been requested earlier from President Franklin D. Roosevelt, especially considering that the Detroit Police Department was understaffed by approximately one-third because of the draft. It was with the arrival of federal troops that order was finally restored in Detroit very late in the evening of June 21.

In the riot's aftermath, Michigan Governor Harry F. Kelly appointed a committee to investigate what had caused it. The committee found no evidence of foreign subversives instigating the riot; it blamed the riot on the militancy of the African American press and on African American leaders. The panel exonerated the Detroit Police Department (which was less than 1 percent black) of any wrongdoing. Jeffries's administration rejected repeated calls for a grand jury inquiry into the causes of the riot and of the actions undertaken by the police to quell the riot.

African American leaders such as James J. McClendon, president of the Detroit Chapter of the National Association for the Advancement of Colored People (NAACP), as well as the black press, disputed the committee's findings. They charged that the police had not been fair in their treatment and protection of African Americans during the riots. They also maintained that the police generally failed to protect blacks from attacks by whites, even assisting white attackers in some cases, and that police had authorized a shoot-to-kill policy for black rioters. African American leaders also accused the city administration of Detroit of failing to act on previous committee reports specifying necessary improvements for African Americans in Detroit, especially regarding housing and education. The committee pointed out the hypocrisy of the United States fighting Nazi and

Japanese racism abroad while condoning and maintaining similarly racist behavior at home.

As was true for the Detroit riot, the precipitating event of the Harlem riot of 1943 was a rumor. On Sunday night, August 1, 1943, a white New York police officer wounded an African American army private, Robert Bandy, who had intervened on behalf of an African American woman being questioned by the officer at a Harlem hotel. A rumor began to circulate that a black soldier had been shot and killed by the police.

The rumor found a receptive audience. As in Detroit, the residents of Harlem, the majority of whom were African American, faced job discrimination. For example, the aircraft industries in nearby Long Island refused to hire African Americans, even though newspaper advertisements clamored for workers needed by that industry. The complete lack of African American faculty members in permanent teaching positions at any of the city's four municipal colleges was also a sore point to the community. A critical shortage of housing confronted residents, and existing housing in Harlem was dilapidated. Even so, New York Mayor Fiorello Henry La Guardia had recently authorized a semipublic housing develop- ment for lower Manhattan that would be all white. Added to this situation were continual accounts of police brutality and verbal harassment suffered by Harlemites, especially African American servicemen. Harlem had become a tinderbox, and it needed only the Bandy incident to ignite it.

Upon hearing the rumor, a group of African Americans immediately took to the streets of Harlem. They began to destroy white property. Residents initially confined themselves to breaking the windows of white merchants; only later did looting occur. Almost none of the interracial clashes that characterized the Detroit riot occurred. When the riot ended at daybreak on August 2, the damage totaled six deaths (five African Americans and one Caucasian), five hundred injuries, five million dollars worth of property damage, 550 arrests, and 1,450 stores either damaged or destroyed. Further destruction probably was prevented by Mayor La Guardia's prompt and effective leadership at the scene of the riot, pleas for calm by recognized African American leaders who toured the area in sound trucks countering the rumor about the Bandy shooting, and the dispatching of biracial teams of military police to Harlem.

A committee was empaneled to investigate the riot. Again, no evidence was found of foreign instigation of the event. In marked contrast to the Detroit administration, La Guardia acknowledged that the black community had legitimate grievances and pledged to take steps to remedy them.

SIGNIFICANCE

The race riots in Detroit and Harlem represented the most destructive of the almost 250 racial battles that occurred in forty-seven cities throughout the United States in 1943. Such disturbances had immediate effects on the country during the war, as well as a long-term impact on race relations in the postwar era.

In New York, the City-Wide Citizens Committee on Harlem was formed to articulate black needs. It achieved limited success in obtaining jobs for blacks and in keeping black concerns before the general public. In Detroit, the findings of the governor's committee intensified the already strained relations between blacks and whites. The panel overemphasized the militancy of African American leaders and the stridency of the African American press, while minimizing the serious discrimination affecting the black community. Social, economic, and political conditions in Detroit would continue to deteriorate, ultimately setting the stage for the United States' most extensive urban riot in the summer of 1967.

On a national scale, the riots were a visible testimony and ugly reminder of the wide chasm that existed between the expressed ideals of the United States—freedom, democracy, justice, and equality—and the reality of the black experience in America. Despite the riots, however, the plight of African Americans remained largely ignored by the United States' white population through the end of the 1940's. President Roosevelt, for example, studiously avoided using the riots as a springboard to discuss racism and necessary social reforms. He sought to avoid mentioning them at all, fearing that highlighting the nation's internal strife would harm its unified war effort. The underlying problems that led to the riots of 1943 would achieve national prominence only in the following two decades, with the Supreme Court's decision desegrating schools in *Brown v. Board of Education* (1954) and the rise of the Civil Rights movement in the 1960's.

—*Craig M. Eckert*

See also: Supreme Court Ends Public School Segregation; Race Rioting Erupts in Detroit.

STORMY WEATHER OFFERS NEW FILM ROLES TO AFRICAN AMERICANS

July 21, 1943

Stormy Weather and other big-band musicals created new roles for African Americans in Hollywood films, allowing some actors the opportunity to escape older stereotypes and take on more substantive roles.

Locale: Hollywood, California
Categories: Motion pictures and video; social issues and reform

KEY FIGURES

Lena Horne (b. 1917), African American actor and singer
Walter White (1893-1955), executive secretary of the National Association for the Advancement of Colored People (NAACP)
Wendell Willkie (1892-1944), Republican presidential candidate and attorney
Louis B. Mayer (1885-1957), head of Metro-Goldwyn-Mayer studios
Hazel Scott (1920-1981), African American actor and musician
Hattie McDaniel (1895-1952), African American actor

SUMMARY OF EVENT

Prior to the 1940's, African Americans in Hollywood films were generally limited to playing a few stereotyped roles, such as the mammy, the villain, the jungle dweller, the servant, or the jester. There were a few exceptions, however, including the films of African American director Oscar Micheaux. Even in films in which black actors were cast in servant roles, some were shown to be uninhibited entertainers or jesters, as in the films *Hallelujah* (1929) and *Hearts in Dixie* (1929).

The African American as entertainer became particularly important in the musicals of the 1940's. Dustpans and mops were exchanged for zoot suits and sequined gowns. As Hollywood's African American singers, dancers, musicians, and acrobats grew in popularity, a platform evolved for them to display their talents. Unrelated song-and-dance numbers were injected into some films; African American entertainers would pop up and entertain the film audience, unhampered by a story line. Frequently, a nightclub scene would be introduced into a film so that performers would have a natural setting in which to entertain. Because such musical numbers were not integrated into the films' plots, scenes featuring African Americans could be cut from a specific print

of a film without spoiling the story should a local or Southern theater object to such scenes.

Metro-Goldwyn-Mayer (MGM), under the direction of Louis B. Mayer, offered its first long-term contract to an African American artist when it signed Lena Horne. The musical *Panama Hattie* (1942) featured Horne, sumptuously gowned and playing herself, performing a Latin song. For most of her film career, Horne found herself limited to roles as an onstage performer. The studios had not made her into a maid, but they had not made her into much of anything else, either. Horne described herself as "a butterfly pinned to a column" in her films.

All-black musicals were considered a risk, and nearly fourteen years had passed when the last one was produced when MGM decided to proceed with Arthur Freed's production of *Cabin in the Sky* (1943), directed by Vincente Minnelli. The film's depiction of African Americans resembled that of earlier films. Blacks in the film were depicted as removed from the daily routine of American life, and the film's characters were placed in remote, idealized worlds. Black stereotypes were played up, and folk culture was passed off as actual African American culture.

On July 21, 1943, Twentieth Century-Fox introduced a different kind of all-black musical: *Stormy Weather*. As in the integrated book musicals being produced on Broadway, the songs and dances of *Stormy Weather* were integral to the film's storyline, which did not revolve around the stereotypes of *Cabin in the Sky*. *Stormy Weather* was the story of an African American dancer (portrayed by Bill Robinson) who wooed Lena Horne and eventually won her over. The film was also a revue of black entertainment as seen through the eyes of Robinson.

Stormy Weather displayed the talents of such African American performers as Fats Waller, Cab Calloway, Katherine Dunham, Ada Brown, and the Nicholas Brothers. In the South, where all-black films were usually shunned, both *Stormy Weather* and *Cabin in the Sky* reached the all-black movie houses, where audiences greeted them with enthusiasm. The films also enjoyed popularity at Army camps and abroad.

The National Association for the Advancement of Colored People (NAACP) had been attempting to force change in Hollywood's degrading treatment of African Americans for twenty-five years. With the success of these 1940's musicals, the NAACP found one of its best weapons. The group's big gun was Lena Horne. NAACP Executive Secretary Walter White assumed personal control over Horne's career. White felt that, since Horne was beautiful and had not yet been typecast, she would be able to establish a different kind of Hollywood image for African American women.

Hazel Scott was another African American performer who refused to be typecast. She had been a child prodigy, reading by the age of three, learning piano at four. Scott grew into a demanding performer who never attempted to conceal her color or her fiery temperament. She refused to appear before segregated audiences or accept fictional roles in films, because she felt she would have to perpetuate stereotypes. Instead, she consistently appeared in films as herself, seated at the piano as she would have been in a nightclub. Her specialty was in blending classics and swing music in such films as *I Dood It* (1943), *Broadway Rhythm* (1944), and *Rhapsody in Blue* (1945). She invested her characters with refinement and taste by always sitting upright at the piano, professionally gowned and supremely confident. Unfortunately, her brand of militancy may have dampened her career, and many later African Americans viewed her as a woman who was simply trying to prove her worth.

Stormy Weather and the other big-band musicals of the 1940's came at a time of war abroad; it was also a time when the war for racial equality was beginning to erupt on the home front. These 1940's musicals were Hollywood's first attempts, no matter how archaic by later standards, to move beyond black stereotypes. The musicals represented the first time African Americans could be seen out of their servant, mammy, or jungle costumes; they had been elevated to the status of acceptable, even glamorous, entertainers. Except for small glimpses of real-life characterizations in *Stormy Weather*, however, African Americans were still not portrayed as everyday Americans in everyday situations.

With the release of *Stormy Weather* and the other big-band musicals of the 1940's, a new front was opening for African American artists. The social climate of the country was also beginning to change. Wendell Willkie, the 1940 Republican presidential candidate, had aligned himself with the NAACP and was representing the organization in negotiations with the Hollywood studios. Willkie was giving the NAACP campaign new clout.

In 1941, President Franklin D. Roosevelt had issued an executive order that forbade racial and religious discrimination in employment in war-related industries. Integration was being pushed by the government. Many of the more liberal studios agreed to follow new racial guidelines when depicting African American characters and to use African American extras whenever possible.

New opportunities were beginning to benefit African American entertainers while paving the way for the emergence of sympathetic African American characters. The studios also strove to integrate more African Americans into behind-the-scenes jobs. Even *Variety* announced, "Better Breaks for Negroes in H'Wood." African American artists themselves were taking different paths with their lives and careers. Lena Horne and Hazel Scott were confident in their mission, although Horne sought to manipulate the system from within more than did Scott. However, other African Americans who had already fought for their niche in the Hollywood system did not want to shake up the status quo.

Horne, especially, was feeling the heat from other African Americans who were afraid that she was beginning a large-scale campaign on the part of African American actors to raise their status, and in the process, to eliminate jobs held by African Americans who excelled at the older, stereotyped roles. One unofficial but influential group of African American Hollywood actors protested her close association with the NAACP, saying that she would make it impossible for them to get work, since soon there would be no more "jungle" or "plantation" parts left. Hattie McDaniel, who had been enormously successful playing stereotypical African American maids, sympathized with Horne's position but would not support it; McDaniel argued that Horne was not realistic in her approach to working in a white person's world.

When the Disney Studios released *Song of the South (*1946), the film seemed to signal the demise of the "African Americans" as entertainers stereotype. A throwback to the extreme stereotypes of the 1920's and 1930's, *Song of the South* took place in the pastoral old South, with Hattie McDaniel providing the voice of the family mammy. Although the film made a profit, it was panned by both the white and black press and incited protests from black audiences.

Significance *Song of the South* did not presage a return to the stereotypes of earlier films. The United States in the 1940's had confronted fascism in Europe, and the nation was reminded by civil rights groups of the bigotry and racial inequality in American industries and in the armed forces. More forcefully than ever before, The

United States was urged to right its old wrongs. Sympathetic and real-life African American characters began to emerge on the scene alongside the 1940's jazz musicals. In *The Ox-Bow Incident* (1943), Leigh Whipper portrayed a somber African American preacher who objected to the lynching of suspected cattle rustlers.

In *In This Our Life* (1942), Eric Anderson played an intelligent young law student arrested on hit-and-run charges. Anderson's character was able to maintain his dignity and innocence until the guilty party, played by Bette Davis, stepped forward. In Alfred Hitchcock's *Lifeboat* (1944), a group of Americans confined to a battered lifeboat after their freighter is torpedoed symbolized the elements of American society. An intelligent African American steward (Canada Lee) represented America's second-class citizenry. Lee's character was first greeted by Tallulah Bankhead as "Charcoal," but when it was revealed he saved a white woman and child from drowning, he became "Joe."

War films also began eschewing caricatured African American roles. *The Negro Soldier* (1944) was an Army orientation film produced by Frank Capra and directed by Stuart Heisler that was distributed to the public. Instead of a handkerchief-headed mammy, the film depicted a distinguished African American mother who was concerned about and proud of her G.I. son. The soldier, too, was not portrayed as a superstitious clown but as an intelligent African American recruit who qualified for officer training.

During this time of struggle abroad and at home, the stereotyped image of the African American began to crumble. Through the success of *Stormy Weather* and other big-band jazz musicals, Hollywood sought to elevate its servants and mammies to roles as entertainers. With their talents uncovered and with a change in the social climate, African Americans began to be offered more sympathetic, realistic, and positive roles. Following the war came further advancements, as African Americans pressed on to win other roles more in keeping with their status in and contributions to American life and culture.

—*Steven C. Kowall*

See also: Poitier Emerges as a Film Star in *The Blackboard Jungle*; *Spy* Debuts to Controversy; Carroll Becomes the First African American Woman to Star as a Nondomestic on Television

SMITH V. ALLWRIGHT

April 3, 1944

The Supreme Court held that excluding African Americans from primaries was an unconstitutional violation of the Fourteenth and Fifteenth Amendments.

The Case: U.S. Supreme Court ruling on white primaries

In 1923, the Texas legislature sought to disfranchise African American voters in the state by passing a resolution that "in no event shall a Negro be eligible to participate in a Democratic primary. . ." Since the 1890's, in Texas as in all other southern states, nomination in the Democratic primary was tantamount to election; therefore, while African Americans would be permitted to vote in the general election, they would have no meaningful role in the political process.

Almost immediately after the Texas legislature barred African Americans from participating in the Democratic primary, the National Association for the Advancement of Colored People (NAACP) secured a plaintiff, Dr. L. A. Nixon, to test the constitutionality of the legislative act. In *Nixon v. Herndon* (1927), the U.S. Supreme Court, in an opinion written by Justice Oliver Wendell Holmes, Jr., held that the Texas statute violated the equal protection clause of the Fourteenth Amendment to the U.S. Constitution by discriminating against African Americans on the basis of race. He also ruled, however, that it was unnecessary to strike down the white primary as a denial of suffrage "on account of race [or] color" repugnant to the Fifteenth Amendment.

TEXAS LEGISLATURE
The Texas legislature reacted defiantly to the Supreme Court decision. On June 7, 1927, the legislature passed a new resolution granting to the state executive committees of every political party the authority to establish the qualifications of their members and to determine who was qualified to vote or otherwise participate in

the party. In turn, the Democratic Party State Executive Committee limited participation in its primary to white voters in Texas. Once again Nixon filed suit, this time against James Condon, the election officer who refused to give him a ballot in the 1928 Democratic primary. In *Nixon v. Condon* (1932), the Supreme Court struck down this new Texas statute as a violation of the equal protection clause. The vote was five to four.

The Democratic Party State Executive Committee immediately rescinded its resolution prohibiting African Americans from voting in its primary, but the state party convention voted to limit participation in its deliberations to whites, and Nixon and the NAACP, after two Supreme Court cases and an expenditure of six thousand dollars, were once more back at the beginning. In July, 1934, Richard Randolph Grovey in Houston, Texas, was refused a ballot to vote in the Democratic primary. On April 1, 1935, in *Grovey v. Townsend*, Justice Owen J. Roberts ruled that the Democratic Party was a private organization, and that its primary, although held under state law, was a party matter paid for by the Democrats. Since Roberts could find no state action in the process by which Democrats nominated their candidates, there was, he said, no violation of the Fourteenth Amendment.

There the matter rested. The primary was held not to be part of the general election, so there was presumably no relationship to the Fifteenth Amendment's protection of suffrage. Because the Democratic Party was a private organization, it was free to establish membership qualifications, and there was not sufficient state involvement to invoke the guarantees of the Fourteenth Amendment.

A SUPREME COURT REVERSAL

It seemed there was no way to contest the validity of the Texas white primary. In 1941, however, in *United States v. Classic*, a case that ostensibly had nothing to do with African Americans or the white primary, the Supreme Court held for the first time that the right to vote was protected in a primary as well as in the general election, "where the state law has made the primary an integral part of the process of choice or where in fact the primary effectively controls the choice."

United States v. Classic dealt with a Louisiana primary in which there had been fraudulent returns, but otherwise there was no way to distinguish the Texas primary from the one held in the neighboring southern state. In Texas, as in Louisiana, in 1941 as in 1923, Democratic Party nomination in its primary was a

virtual guarantee of election, and the general election was a mere formality.

The NAACP was back in action. Lonnie Smith, a Houston dentist and NAACP member, sued a Texas election official for five thousand dollars for refusing to give him a ballot to vote in the 1940 Democratic congressional primaries. The NAACP's legal counsel, Thurgood Marshall, and William Hastie, dean of the Howard Law School, brought *Smith v. Allwright* to the U.S. Supreme Court.

In April, 1944, mindful of southern sensibilities but intent upon overruling the nine-year-old precedent in *Grovey*, the Court chose Stanley Reed, a Democrat from Kentucky, to write its opinion. Justice Reed's opinion made it clear that the Court, except for Justice Roberts (the author of the *Grovey* decision), had concluded that the primary was an integral part of a general election, particularly in the southern states. The *Classic* decision, wrote Justice Reed, raised the issue of whether excluding African Americans from participation in the Democratic Party primary in Texas violated the Fifteenth Amendment. The answer was in the affirmative, and *Grovey v. Townsend* was expressly overruled. "If the state," Reed said, "requires a certain election procedure, prescribing a general election ballot made up of party nominees so chosen, and limits the choice of the electorate in general elections for state officers . . . to those whose names appear on such a ballot, it endorses, adopts, and enforces the discrimination against Negroes practiced by a party entrusted by Texas law with the determination of the qualifications of participants in the primary. This is state action within the meaning of the Fifteenth Amendment."

The long litigative battle against the Texas white primary seemed to be over—but it was not. In Fort Bend County, Texas, the Jaybird Democratic Party, organized after the Civil War, held primaries closed to African American voters; its candidates consistently won county offices. In spite of *Smith v. Allwright*, the Jaybirds refused to open their primary to African Americans, arguing that they did not operate under state law or use state officers or funds. Nevertheless, in *Terry v. Adams* (1953), the Supreme Court held that the Jaybird primary violated the Fifteenth Amendment, because it controlled the electoral process in Fort Bend County.

AFTERMATH

It took twenty-one years for the U.S. Supreme Court to rule that the Texas white primary violated the right to vote guaranteed by the Fifteenth Amendment. It would take another twenty-one years before the Voting Rights Act of 1965 finally secured the ballot for African Americans in the South. In the interim, the fall of the white primary had the practical effect of increasing African American registrants in the southern states from approximately 250,000 in 1940 to 775,000 seven years later. African Americans were still intimidated and defrauded of their suffrage rights, but *Smith v. Allwright* was an important landmark on the road to uninhibited enfranchisement. It also was a symbol that the Supreme Court would examine the reality behind the subterfuge

and act to protect African Americans in the enjoyment of their civil rights.

—*David L. Sterling*

See also: Civil Rights Act of 1960; Disfranchisement laws in Mississippi; Fifteenth Amendment; Fourteenth Amendment; Gerrymandering; *Grovey v. Townsend*; *Newberry v. United States*; *Nixon v. Condon*; *Nixon v. Herndon*; *United States v. Classic*; Voting Rights Act of 1965; White primaries

UNITED NEGRO COLLEGE FUND

Established on April 25, 1944

Since its foundation, the United Negro College Fund has played a major role in assisting students and helping to support predominantly black colleges and universities, which produce more than 25 percent of all African American college graduates.

Identification: Privately funded education assistance organization created to help African American students attain college educations

Under the direction of Frederick D. Patterson, president of Tuskegee Institute, the United Negro College Fund (UNCF) was established in 1944, with twenty-seven member colleges and a combined enrollment of fourteen thousand students. The goal was to become one of the world's leading education assistance organizations. With a few exceptions, most UNCF member institutions had been founded by religious societies from the North after the Civil War and before the turn of the century. Located principally in the Southeast and in eastern Texas, these institutions operate with a variety of organizational structures and program offerings.

Since its inception, UNCF has grown to become the oldest and most successful African American higher-education assistance organization. In 1998, UNCF provided support for a consortium of forty-one private, accredited four-year black colleges and universities. UNCF raises operating money for its member schools so that they can maintain the highest academic standards and prepare their students for demanding professions and careers. Although these institutions constitute only about 3 percent of all colleges and universities in the United States, they graduate more than one-quarter of all African Americans who earn the baccalaureate degree and nearly 40 percent of African Americans who later earn a doctoral degree. These graduates help build a stronger nation as community leaders and educators and in numerous other vocations.

—*Alvin K. Benson*

See also: Ashmun Institute; Black colleges and universities; Education

PARKER'S PLAYING EPITOMIZES BEBOP

March 28, 1946

Charlie Parker's first 1946 recording session for Dial Records produced some of the finest jazz recordings of the bebop era and helped to define a style that would prove influential in jazz history.

Also known as: "Moose the Mooche"; "Yardbird Suite"; "A Night in Tunisia"; "Ornithology"
Locale: Los Angeles, California
Category: Music

Parker with (from left to right) Tommy Potter, Max Roach, Miles Davis, and Duke Jordan, at the Three Deuces, New York, circa 1945, by William P. Gottlieb

KEY FIGURES

Charlie Parker (Bird; 1920-1955), American alto saxophonist, composer, and bandleader

Dizzy Gillespie (1917-1993), American trumpeter, composer, and bandleader

Miles Davis (1926-1991), American trumpeter, composer, and bandleader

Billy Eckstine (1914-1993), American singer, musician, and bandleader

SUMMARY OF EVENT

There was nothing in the early life of Charlie Parker to indicate the remarkable achievements he was to make. Born in Kansas City, Kansas, he began his musical career by playing the baritone horn in high school. He gained some musical knowledge playing the horn, but he had another instrument in mind. When he was fifteen years old, he persuaded his mother to buy him an alto saxophone. From then on, Parker neglected school to concentrate on playing music. Initially, however, his efforts bore little fruit.

Parker was fortunate in being able to play professionally early on, and he gained valuable experience both on the bandstand and by asking questions of the more experienced musicians with whom he worked. After having played for only one year, he joined the band of Lawrence Keyes (bassist Gene Ramey later recalled that Parker was the worst player in the band), and later he played frequently with alto saxophonist Buster Smith, who became his mentor.

In 1937, Parker spent the summer playing with a band in the Ozarks. He spent all of his free time that summer practicing the saxophone and studying the records of the Count Basie band, a Kansas City mainstay. Lester Young (known as Prez, or the President), the featured tenor saxophonist in the Basie band, was one of Parker's favorite musicians, and he memorized all of Young's recorded solos. When Parker came back to Kansas City, he was a changed musician. He played with a new confidence, an improved technique, and a greater understanding of music than he had had only a few months earlier.

From that point on, Parker's musical ability increased rapidly and dramatically. He played in various bands, including that of Jay McShann, and traveled to Chicago and New York. All the while, he worked to increase his knowledge and understanding of music. His relentless desire to become a better musician stood him in good stead; he demonstrated in his playing a discipline that was lacking in his personal life. Like many musicians of his era, he fell victim at an early age to drug and alcohol abuse. This proclivity to indulge himself to excess ultimately contributed to his early death, but his fierce determination enabled him to achieve musical greatness despite it.

In 1943, in New York, Parker joined the band of pianist Earl Hines. He met a number of other fine young musicians who were, like him, open to experimentation. These musicians, who included trumpeter Dizzy Gillespie, trombonist Benny Harris, and singer and bandleader Billy Eckstine, were tired of playing the same old music and wanted to find a new way to play. They, and other musicians, were experimenting with new harmonies, new rhythmic patterns, and new approaches of all kinds.

Parker became particularly close to Gillespie, who was as restless an innovator as himself. In 1944, Gillespie, Parker, and a host of superb young musicians joined the newly formed Billy Eckstine band, which became a kind of incubator for the music that came to be called bebop (the word is derived from a rhythmic pattern that occurred frequently in the music).

Charlie Parker and dizzy Gillespie, along with such musicians as pianists Thelonious Monk and bud Powell, pianist and arranger Tadd Dameron, and drummer Kenny Clarke, revolutionized the world of jazz. The style that they developed featured harmonies more complex than those that had previously been heard in popular music, a tendency to rework standard songs to create entirely new musical entities, and a new approach to drumming that rejected the usual straightforward four-to-the-bar approach in favor of less regular accents. In addition, they often played this complex music at a fast tempi that intimidated all but the very best players. Within a relatively short period, these players were lionized by many young musicians. They were also reviled by many others, particularly those who could neither understand nor play their music. Both attitudes served to increase the notoriety of the music.

After he left the Eckstine band, Parker played and recorded in New York in a small band of his own that included the young trumpeter Miles Davis, who received the schooling of his life trying to keep up with Parker's blazing tempi. It was partly the experience of trying (and being unable) to play as cleanly and rapidly as the virtuosic Parker and Gillespie that led Davis to develop the style that made him famous, which involved playing only what he considered the essential notes--the fewer the better.

Parker was involved in a number of recording sessions in 1946 that yielded classic jazz recordings, but one of the finest took place in Los Angeles, where Parker had traveled with Gillespie's band. Although their music, which was quite popular in New York, was not well received in Los Angelese, and although Parker struggled financially there and had difficulty procuring the heroin and other drugs he required, he remained in Los Angeles when the rest of the Gillespie band returned to New York.

Parker's recoding date for Dial Records, a company that had just been founded by Ross Russell, previously a record-shop owner, began inauspiciously. Pianist Joe Albany and bassist Red Callender left Parker's band just before the session, which took place on March 28, 1946, included Miles Davis on trumpet, Lucky Thompson on tenor sax, Dodo Marmarosa on piano, Arv Garrison on guitar, Vic McMillan on bass, and Roy Porter on drums.

The four pieces recorded for Dial on March 28 included two tunes by Parker, "moose the Mooche" (named for Parkers' local drug dealer) and "Yardbird Suite"; one by Dizzy Gillespie, "A Night in Tunisia"; and a piece by Benny Harris, "ornithology," which was derived from a solo Parker had played with Jay McShann. Parker's playing throughout the session was superb, and all the recordings made that day are still studies and appreciated by jazz musicians and aficionados. A few of the recordings were truly remarkable. Parker's four-bar solo on the first take of "A Night in Tunisia" was an astounding example of bebop playing that jazz critic Gary Giddins has called a "break of baroque complexity and numbing speed" and Ira Gitler has described as "a miniature history of modern jazz." Unfortunately, the rest of the band had difficulty with the pieces, and the take was unsuccessful and incomplete. The solo was so remarkable, however, that Dial released it in incomplete form as "Famous Alto Break." The three recorded versions (four were made, but the second was lost) of "Ornithology" were also excellent, and the final (and fastest) version contained a solo by Parker that would stand as one of the finest of his career. The two versions of "Yardbird Suite" were notable for the "cool" style of Parker's playing (as opposed to his frequent "fiery" style), and the three takes of "Moose the Mooche" contained some fine playing by Miles Davis on trumpet, as well as excellent playing by Parker.

Parker signed over half of his proceeds from the session to Moose the Mooche to cover his drug debts. Not long after, as a result of drug abuse, lack of money and acceptance, and stress, Parker wound up in a mental institution in Camarillo, California. After six months in the hospital, however, he emerged healthy and ready to play, and he went on to make many more classic recordings before his premature death in 1955.

SIGNIFICANCE

Parker's March 28, 1946, recording session for Dial Records was significant because it produced recordings that would come to be considered essential by musicians, critics, and fans. The body of Parker's best work was important, because his music, more than that of any other artist, defined bebop. The influence of bebop changed popular music in general, and jazz in particular, forever.

One indication of the influence of bebop is the fact that certain aspects of the music that shocked at least some listeners in the 1940's sound perfectly normal to modern ears. The innovations of Parker, Gillespie, Monk, and many others are now heard commonly not only in jazz but also in rock and pop music, film and television scores, and even in Muzak.

One of the most important influences of bebop had to do with its use of harmonic structures that were more complex than those that had been used in earlier jazz. It was common practice in jazz playing to use the harmonic structure of a recognizable song as a jumping-off point for improvisation, but a bebop player would play, when a particular chord was called for, notes that were different from those that a swing player would use. For example, when a swing player was improvising over a piece of music that called for a C dominant seventh (C7) chord, he or she would be likely to play the notes that are part of that chord: C, E, G, and B-flat. A bebop player, however, would be likely to play the notes D, F-sharp, and A over the same chord, actually playing a thirteenth chord instead of a seventh chord. This practice is known as playing the extensions of the chords

that are specified. One does not need to have musical training to understand that playing completely different notes over a particular chord gives the music an entirely different sound. It was this sound that beboppers enjoyed and certain other players and listeners despised.

Another area in which bebop differed from earlier forms of jazz was that of drumming. During the swing era, it was common for drummers to play the bass drum on every beat, or every other beat, of the bar, which tended to give the music a predictable sound. Bebop drummers such as Kenny Clarke and Max Roach, however, began to keep time on the cymbals, reserving the bass drum for punctuation at irregular intervals. Using the bass drum in this way was called "dropping bombs." In addition, bebop drummers tended to play in a somewhat softer, more legato style that made it possible to use a wider range of sounds and play more flexibly. In contrast, swing drummers were required to adhere more rigidly to the specific role of keeping the beat. Although bebop drummers also kept the beat, they tended to imply it rather than to mark it explicitly.

It was not only bebop drummers who took a new approach to rhythm. Saxophonists, trumpeters, trombonists, pianists, and bassists also experimented with new ways of accenting notes and phrases, and they sought to use in their solos and compositions rhythmic patterns that had not been commonly used up to that time. Parker was a master of rhythmic phrasing, as even the most cursory exposure to his music will demonstrate. Many well known swing musicians had difficulty learning to "feel"

this new rhythmic approach. One common practice in bebop (it had also been used by earlier musicians) was that of soloists playing in such a way that they seemed to be slightly behind (slower than) the rhythm section. This practice gave the music a particular kind of swing feeling that is difficult to define but easy to hear.

Another important contribution of beboppers was that they raised the standards of musicianship. Musicians such as Parker and Dizzy Gillespie were so technically skilled that they could play music that many established musicians simply could not play. One feature of bebop was that it was frequently played at extremely fast tempi, which meant that in order to play the music effectively, a musician had to have a high level of technical ability. It often happened that when musicians who were not completely grounded in bebop attempted to play with beboppers, they found that they simply could not keep up. The high level of musicianship exhibited by the beboppers performed a tremendous service to jazz, because it provided young musicians with an extremely high level of skill to which to aspire.

Parker's Dial Records recording session of March 28, 1946, provides a superb example of the features of bebop playing. In addition, it should be noted that Parker's playing here, as elsewhere, demonstrates an extremely unusual combination of tremendous creativity, passionate emotional intensity, and remarkable technical skill.

Many musicians exhibit one or two of these qualities, but only the greatest possess all three. Charlie

Parker was certainly one of the finest musicians in the history of jazz, and his music continues to inspire players and listeners.

—Shawn Woodyard

See also: Davis Develops 1950's Cool Jazz; First Newport Jazz Festival Is Held; Berry's "Maybellene" Popularizes Rock and Roll; Brown Introduces Funk Music; Hendrix Releases Acid Rock Album *Are You Experienced?*; Davis Introduces Jazz-Rock Fusion.

MAHALIA JACKSON BEGINS HER RECORDING CAREER

October 3, 1946

Mahalia Jackson launched a influential recording career that included a contract with Columbia Records and popularity that transcended racial lines. She was one of several important African American performers to bring gospel music into the mainstream of the U.S. recording industry.

Also known as: "I Want to Rest"; "(I'm Going to) Wait Until My Change Comes"; "I'm Going to Tell God"
Locale: New York, New York
Category: Music

KEY FIGURES

Mahalia Jackson (1911-1972), American gospel singer
Thomas A. Dorsey (1899-1993), American gospel song composer
Martin Luther King, Jr. (1929-1968), American preacher and civil rights leader
Studs Terkel (b. 1912), American radio personality writer
John Hammond (1910-1987), American record producer

SUMMARY OF EVENT

On October 3, 1946, Mahalia Jackson made her first gospel recordings for the New York label Apollo. Her first singles for the label did not sell well, but in 1947 she recorded a song that went on to sell a million copies.

"Move on Up a Little Higher," recorded September 12, 1947, covered both sides of the record. It had been

written by the Reverend W. Herbert Brewster, a well-known Memphis preacher and songwriter. The song put Jackson on the path to national prominence.

Other Apollo recordings in the next eight years sold well, and Jackson became in demand nationwide as a leading exponent of the newer gospel songs. She became the official soloist of the National Baptist Convention, an African American church, and was a popular figure on Studs Terkel's radio program in Chicago, where she lived. Terkel had an ear for folk, blues, and gospel music and found Jackson to be one of the finest singers and interpreters, with her rich and strong contralto voice. Her outgoing personality and deep knowledge of African American culture and musical roots made her a local favorite when she appeared on Terkel's television show in the early 1950's. In the segregated United States of that time, her artistry was confined mainly to African American audiences. In the huge ghettos of Chicago's South Side, New York's Harlem, and Los Angeles's Watts, she began to reign supreme.

Jackson was born poor in New Orleans in 1911. She grew up listening to the blues recordings of singers such as Bessie Smith and Ma Rainey but gravitated more to the religious songs of the Baptist Church. Nevertheless, she thought that the more passionate singing in the Sanctified and Holiness churches, where instruments were allowed, matched better with the feelings she wanted to express. Hearing the local jazz musicians and their improvising bands also inspired her at an early age. After moving to Chicago's South Side ghetto in 1927, she began to sing in church choirs and joined a small gospel group committed to the newer up-tempo gospel songs she admired. Singing at storefront churches and around the Chicago area, she started to develop the ecstatic and freely embellished style of handling spirituals and hymns that became her trademark.

Through the 1930's, Jackson survived by singing and by running a series of small businesses including a florist's shop, a hairdresser's shop, and even a house-to-house homemade cosmetics sales operation. She also met Thomas A. Dorsey, a central figure in the creation of modern African American gospel songs. Dorsey had by this time turned away from his earlier blues performing, recording, and songwriting career to write gospel blues songs. These religious songs with blues tonalities soon caught on among the new migrants to Chicago from the Deep South who had grown up with the older African American religious song styles. Dorsey recaptured much of that style in his songs and slowly won over the more staid mainline church choirs and pastors—as well as their congregations—to the new impassioned singing of the good news (the gospel).

Teaming up with Jackson, Dorsey toured the Chicago area and the South, selling his songs on sheet music and playing piano behind Jackson's interpretations of his songs. Jackson and Dorsey thus helped expose Northern African Americans to their folk-derived music. They came to a parting of ways, however, over her freedom with the printed music he wrote. Jackson had developed her own style of decorating, embellishing, slowing down, or speeding up traditional spirituals and hymns, and even the new songs, so that each of her performances was different. She had brought the old oral tradition, stemming from Africa, to the North. Her singing became a testimony-in-song to joy and faith, to suffering and loss, as she shouted and moaned or pushed her contralto into falsetto. The musical assimilation of the mainline churches, with formal music reading and stolidness, was not for her.

Jackson made her very first recording—on the Decca label—on May 21, 1937, but it went nowhere. The songs were recorded with a combination of piano and organ that she came to prefer for live performances throughout her career. Undaunted by the failure of her Decca single, she kept touring, singing in whatever church wanted her, communicating with audiences through inviting them to respond with hand clapping and sung responses in the traditional call-and-response style.

Jackson's piano accompaniment was most often in the hands of Mildred Falls, who came to understand Jackson's style and simply provided backing triplets or a percussive touch to Jackson's improvisatory handling of lines and phrases. The organ, likewise, played its role by sustaining notes and chords while Jackson "worried" words and phrases and frequently sang in a free rhythm over the accompaniment. Using *melisma* (a group of notes sung to the same syllable), she freely altered melodies, repeated phrases, and marvelously reshaped old spirituals and new songs in her own style. With her style solidified and an audience clamoring for live performances, she was on her way.

SIGNIFICANCE

Jackson's success with the Apollo label from 1946 through 1954 made hers a household name among African Americans. She had a half-hour radio show in 1954 and 1955 and even broadened her repertoire to include pieces such as Brahms's *Lullaby* and *Silent Night*. Network television seemed afraid of her in this segregated era. Even on radio and local Chicago television, she found pressures that bothered her and that she would encounter for the rest of her career.

Jackson never sang a song the same way twice. As she moved into the world of recordings, radio and television broadcasts, and the mass media, she found producers, directors, and musicians who did not know black culture or religious music and who pressured her to limit the length of her performances to fit into time slots or the limits of singles recordings. Studio musicians and orchestras worked from written parts and scores; she was used to improvising and establishing her own pulse with Mildred Falls. This difference created conflicts in her recording career. Later in her career, strings, horns, guitars, drums, and large choirs were added to her recordings—sometimes overdubbed—and she thought that this sometimes compromised her music. As she became more mainstream, some of her roots in folk traditions were lost.

A major turning point in her career came in 1951, when she appeared at the Music Inn in Lenox, Massachusetts. Singing her songs and explaining their roots before an audience of jazz experts and musicologists, Jackson was surprised to find a fan in John Hammond, a famous talent scout and record producer. He soon worked to get her a contract with Columbia Records, a mainstream label that had earlier, under Hammond's guidance, recorded such important artists as Bessie Smith, Billie Holiday, Benny Goodman, and Count Basie. Hammond had organized the famous 1938 and 1939 Spirituals to Swing concerts in New York and would later in his career help get Bob Dylan and Bruce Springsteen signed to Columbia. He had a great ear for traditional and indigenous American music. In Jackson, he saw an important American talent with folk roots.

From 1954 until her death from heart failure in 1972, Jackson recorded for Columbia. She recorded many albums of spirituals, hymns, and gospel songs. Although producers urged her to appeal to pop audiences by recording pallid inspirational songs and Christmas carols, she largely resisted. Some recordings were overproduced with orchestral accompaniment, but she now had the opportunity to record her songs without restrictive time limits. Most of her recordings were albums; some featured live performances such as those at the prestigious Newport Jazz Festival and on foreign tours. Two singles reached the pop charts: "He's Got the Whole World in His Hands" in 1958 and "Silent Night, Holy Night" in 1962.

In the late 1950's and through the 1960's her fame spread across the world. She was acclaimed in Germany, France, Sweden, England, Japan, and India, among other countries. She met presidents and royalty and sang at John F. Kennedy's inaugural. Utilizing the William Morris booking agency, she appeared at better venues, from Carnegie Hall to Constitution Hall. In the 1960's, she also became a favorite guest on network television shows including those of Dinah Shore, Ed Sullivan, and Steve Allen. Church benefits and one-night stands continued, but Jackson now had a wider choice.

One of the most important aspects of her life was her deep and lasting friendship for and active support of Martin Luther King, Jr. She shared with him the Christian message of love and tolerance and a sharp sense of the injustices that they and all African Americans had to endure. After meeting King in 1955, Jackson immediately took to singing for his rallies. Risking her safety, she journeyed to Montgomery, Alabama, in 1956 to sing gospel songs for the civil rights demonstrators.

She walked with King and thousands of others through the violent streets of Chicago in 1966 in a demand for open housing. As a preacher, King shared with Jackson a love of spirituals and gospel song. For him, she sang the spiritual "I Been 'Buked and I Been Scorned" before thousands in front of the Lincoln Memorial at the great March on Washington in August, 1963, just before he delivered his famous "I Have a Dream" speech. Most poignantly, she sang his favorite gospel song at his funeral in April, 1968: Dorsey's "Take My Hand, Precious Lord."

Jackson's example of finding a mass audience for religious music ran parallel to the popularity of white singers such as Tennessee Ernie Ford, whose network television show in the 1950's and 1960's featured his singing of gospel songs. His best-selling spiritual albums also brought the old spirituals, hymns, and new gospel songs to a mainstream audience. Because a considerable overlap exists between the repertoires of white and black religious song, Ford's efforts added further to the acceptance of the gospel in song. Singers such as Elvis Presley and Johnny Cash also fostered a mass acceptance of religious songs. It was Presley who sang Dorsey's "Peace in the Valley" on Ed Sullivan's television show in January, 1957, and then saw his recording of it become a pop hit.

In 1971, Jackson sang the classic folk spiritual "Amazing Grace" on Johnny Cash's network television show. Jackson set an example of service to her music and her people. Her influence crossed racial lines and helped immeasurably to ensure the emergence of one of America's great musical forms.

—Frederick E. Danker

See also: Parker's Playing Epitomizes Bebop; Davis Develops 1950's Cool Jazz; Berry's "Maybellene" Popularizes Rock and Roll; Gordy Founds Motown Records; King Delivers His "I Have a Dream" Speech; Davis Introduces Jazz-Rock Fusion.

PRESIDENT'S COMMITTEE ON CIVIL RIGHTS

Created on December 5, 1946

The report issued by the committee was a bold and unprecedented step for the federal government to take in the field of civil rights. It led to little immediate action but would later help to bring the need for civil rights reform to the attention of the nation as a whole.

Identification: Government commission appointed by President Harry S. Truman to investigate the condition of African American civil rights and make recommendations for government action

Like many white southerners of his time, U.S. president Harry S. Truman inherited the racial attitudes of his ancestors. He attended segregated schools in Missouri and regarded segregation as normal and desirable. He used what people today consider offensive racial language and once claimed that African Americans belonged in Africa, not America. Yet when he became president in 1945, Truman rose above his racist heritage and responded to African American demands. As a successful politician, he had learned to work with African American political groups and to understand the necessity of serving all of his constituents. He disliked social mixing among people of different races, but he believed that African American people had the right to equality under the law and deserved equal opportunity.

At the end of World War II, racial tension rose as African Americans tried to cement economic and social gains they had made during the war. Racial violence increased. For example, in February, 1946, a South Carolina policeman blinded an African American veteran still in uniform, and in July, two more veterans were killed in Monroe, Georgia. In addition to domestic racial problems, the Cold War was beginning to destroy the wartime alliance between the United States and the Soviet Union. The two superpowers began to divide spheres of influence between them and to compete for the allegiance of Asian and African peoples. Truman, recognizing the negative image presented by American segregation, said, "The top dog in a world which is 90 percent colored ought to clean his own house."

On December 5, 1946, Truman issued Executive Order 9008 to create the President's Committee on Civil Rights and filled the fifteen-member committee with prominent Americans who were sympathetic to civil rights. It was a high-profile committee that included important businessmen, educators, labor leaders, and members of the African American community. On October 29, 1947, in a document entitled *To Secure These Rights*, the committee recommended establishment of a civil rights division in the Department of Justice, a commission on civil rights, and a fair employment practices committee.

The committe's report urged Congress to strengthen existing civil rights statutes, pass an antilynching law, and provide new protection for voting rights. To move toward desegregation, the committee said, the government must discontinue federal funding to private and public bodies that practiced discrimination, prohibit discrimination in private employment and in health services, and seek court action to end restrictive covenants in housing.

These recommendations established the civil rights platform for Truman and his successors. In 1948, Truman issued Executive Order 9980 to forbid discrimination in federal government employment and Executive Order 9981 to integrate the armed forces. Under Truman's direction, the Justice Department entered *amici curiae* briefs in court cases to back the National Association for the Advancement of Colored People (NAACP) and others in their assaults on the legal edifice that supported segregation. It took many years before the vision expressed in *To Secure These Rights* started to become reality, but the report moved civil rights to the forefront of the national reform agenda.

—William E. Pemberton

See also: Defense industry desegregation; Military desegregation; Politics and government; Race riots of 1943

BASEBALL'S RACIAL INTEGRATION

1947

Until Jackie Robinson established himself as a major-league player, opening the way for other African Americans, professional baseball was rigidly segregated in North America.

The Event: Jackie Robinson's breaking of the color line in Major League Baseball
Place: Brooklyn, New York

In 1945, the United States was both triumphant and troubled. The most powerful nation in the world in the aftermath of World War II, the United States measured its strength not only in military and economic terms but also in the supposed moral superiority of American democracy. In 1945, however, segregation and racial exclusion remained the norms in American society. Even the U.S. armed forces were largely segregated. In the years following the war, Americans would have to come to terms with the gap between what their democracy was supposed to be and what it was. In this context, organized baseball extended an opportunity to African Americans and, in so doing, lost its status as a racist institution.

BACKGROUND

The change did not come easily and might have been significantly delayed if not for Branch Rickey, the president of the Brooklyn Dodgers. The color line that excluded African Americans from organized baseball had its origins in the previous century and was solidly established. In 1923, it had been reinforced by an informal agreement among the major-league owners. This agreement was still very much in force in 1945, when Rickey decided to proceed with his plan to bring down baseball's color barrier.

Finding skilled African American players was not a problem. Although they were excluded from organized baseball, African Americans had not stopped playing the game. Barnstorming professional and semiprofessional teams and eventually entire "Negro" leagues arose, with the level of play comparable to that of the major and top minor leagues. Negro League teams often beat white all-star teams during the off-season. Separate, however, was not equal. African American players were paid much less and had to spend far more time traveling than white players. Nor did the Negro Leagues enjoy the stability of organized baseball. As a result, a pool of talented African American players was available to Rickey.

The integration of baseball had previously been advocated by African American sportswriters such as Sam Lacy of the *Baltimore Afro-America* and Wendell Smith of the *Pittsburgh Courier*. What Rickey brought to the issue was clout. He had the position and personality to do something about integrating baseball and to deal with any opposition that might arise. As with other civil rights advances of the 1940's, 1950's, and 1960's, there was stern opposition. Other major-league owners were opposed to Rickey's experiment. They argued that

white fans and players were not ready for integration. Rickey believed that the time was right, and he pushed ahead.

Rickey's motivation has been the subject of considerable debate. He claimed to be acting on religious and moral grounds, but he undoubtedly was aware of the growing economic success of the Negro Leagues and the wealth of talent they might offer to the Dodgers. On the other hand, Rickey did not monopolize the best African American prospects, even recommending star outfielder Monte Irvin to the rival New York Giants. While motives are complex and difficult to discern, one thing is clear: Rickey had an unshakable belief in what he was doing.

RICKEY'S CHOICE

The question of who would shoulder the burden of breaking the color line was a difficult one. Rickey and other advocates of integration knew that the honor of being that person would be at least equaled by the ordeal, and that even a very strong individual might be broken by the twofold pressure of competing on the major-league level and being a crusader for racial justice. Because of the demanding job description, Rickey saw his choice to be one of awesome importance. It was Wendell Smith who recommended Jackie Robinson. Rickey had Robinson scouted and interviewed him. All the qualifications were there. Robinson was college educated and had played his college ball (three sports) on integrated teams. At twenty-six years of age, Robinson was mature but still in his prime. He also had demonstrated his dedication to the cause of racial equality, struggling against segregation while serving in the armed forces. Rickey saw in Robinson a man with fire in his belly, great self-control, and superb baseball skills. Robinson saw both an athletic and social challenge. With the support of his wife, Rachel, he decided to accept the challenge, signing a contract to play in the Dodger organization.

One obstacle had to be overcome before the Jackie Robinson experiment could begin. Rickey wanted Robinson to acclimate himself to organized baseball in the minor leagues for one year. In order for Robinson to be optioned to the Dodgers' minor league team in Montreal, the other major-league owners would have to approve. None of them did. Into this impasse stepped the new commissioner of baseball, Happy Chandler, a former Kentucky politician and veteran of public life. The previous commissioner, Judge Kenesaw Mountain Landis, had been an uncompromising opponent of integration. Indeed, it was Landis more than anyone who had engineered and maintained the 1923 agreement out-lawing interracial play. Chandler had inherited Landis's autocratic power but not his attitude on the color line. Despite considerable pressure from the owners, Chandler overruled their fifteen-to-one vote against Rickey, allowing Robinson to begin his career in organized baseball in the spring of 1946. Later, Chandler claimed he made his decision because he did not wish to explain to his Creator that he had denied a fellow human being a chance to play baseball because of the color of his skin. Chandler's political sense was also astute. He correctly surveyed the political winds and realized that the criticism he took for allowing Robinson to play would have been dwarfed by the damage to his image if he had championed the cause of segregation. Americans were changing, not entirely or all at once, but enough to shift the tide on matters of race.

Then it was up to Robinson. He came through in every respect. He led Montreal to a league championship, winning the respect of International League players and fans alike. He proved that he could keep his mind on the game of baseball while putting up with verbal abuse and physical intimidation in the form of brushback pitches and high spikes. Playing half of his games in Montreal, a multicultural Canadian city, probably helped, but Robinson had clearly proved his mettle.

The following spring, Robinson made the Dodgers' roster, playing his first regular-season major-league game on April 15, 1947. Although Robinson got off to a slow start, he believed that his teammates were behind him. (This might not have been the case had Rickey not traded several Dodger players who refused to play with an African American.) Opposing teams were another matter. They rode Robinson unmercifully, as was the custom of the time with all rookies, often making race the focus of their comments. In living up to his agreement with Rickey, Robinson turned the other cheek to such comments to avoid jeopardizing his cause by touching off a feud or a brawl. Sympathetic reporters such as Walter Winchell tried to ease Robinson's burden by criticizing the worst offenders in their publications, a gesture for which Robinson later expressed gratitude. Soon Robinson began to play well, proving himself to be an excellent hitter and base runner as well as a versatile fielder.

ROBINSON ON THE FIELD

By the end of the year, Robinson had batted .297, won Rookie of the Year honors, and, quite literally, revolutionized baseball. The Dodgers won the National League pennant. With Robinson and many other African American players, they would win five more pennants in the next nine years, becoming a convincing testament to the possibilities of interracial cooperation. The other owners had been proved wrong. White players and fans overwhelmingly accepted integration, rejecting a past which most Americans were more than willing to forget.

The cost to Robinson was significant. His hair turned prematurely gray, and he spent many years recovering from the trauma of his groundbreaking achievement. He had made himself a target in order to rub out baseball's color line. For this Robinson suffered, but he never expressed regret.

IMPACT

The initial and most obvious impact of Jackie Robinson's triumph over the color line in baseball was to open up career opportunities for other African American players in organized baseball. Moved primarily by the need to stay competitive (the Dodgers dominated the National League for a decade with the help of African American players such as Robinson, Roy Campanella, Joe Black, Don Newcombe, and Jim Gilliam), and in the absence of the dire consequences they had predicted, other owners began to scout and sign talented African American players. There was still hesitancy on the part of some franchises, most notably the New York Yankees and Boston Red Sox, but by 1959 every major-league team had been integrated. Baseball had been successfully transformed into a symbol of racial equality and harmony rather than one of hypocrisy and frustrated dreams.

The indirect benefits of baseball's integration were also substantial. Understood not as a first cause, but as an important link in the chain of events, it facilitated later gains such as *Brown v. Board of Education* (1954), which desegregated schools, and the Civil Rights Acts of 1957, 1964, and 1965, which addressed other forms of segregation, job discrimination, and voting rights. The integration of baseball had rendered absurd the contention that the races were incapable of interacting fruitfully for common ends. Clearly, if athletes of different races could play together, people of different races could work and live together. Equal opportunity in baseball was clearly analogous to that throughout American society. Finally, baseball's integration fostered bonds between white fans and African American players. This made it less likely that white northerners would accept segregation and other forms of racial injustice passively, as they had in the past.

It is a mistake, however, to see Jackie Robinson's triumph over baseball's color line as a signal that racial justice and equality are no longer problematic issues in American society. While the player rosters of organized baseball teams became thoroughly integrated, African Americans remain clearly underrepresented in managerial, coaching, and front-office positions. There have, in addition, been charges of remaining discrimination on the field. Specifically, it has been alleged that players of marginal ability have better chances to make big-league rosters if they are white. Similarly, pockets of racial prejudice continued to exist among fans. Moreover, the existence of a pool of well-paid African American athletes is a misleading indicator of economic distribution according to race. African Americans continue to make up a disproportionate number of America's poor. Equality of opportunity and education remain goals of American society rather than accomplishments.

It has also been alleged that there were negative consequences to the integration of baseball. Obviously damaged by organized baseball's integration were the Negro Leagues, which had enjoyed their greatest success during the war years. While much of the profit from the Negro Leagues went into the hands of white promoters and agents, they still can be seen as an early enterprise in black capitalism, one for which Branch Rickey and Jackie Robinson did no good at all. It has also been argued that the integration of baseball hindered the development of alternative, separatist routes to true racial equality. Finally, because of the way he turned his cheek in response to various kinds of abuse from white players, Jackie Robinson has been seen as too passive a role model.

None of these limitations, allegations, or problems should diminish appreciation of Jackie Robinson. They simply encourage the acceptance of his character and accomplishments for what they were rather than the distortion of them for one purpose or another. Jackie Robinson did not manage to strike down racism with a single blow. Nor was he an "Uncle Tom" by any means. He was a fine athlete with highly developed social values and the courage to back them up. Perhaps most impressive was Robinson's refusal to become rigid in his thinking. As the terrain of race relations in the United States changed toward the end of his life, Robinson changed his political affiliation, citing the Republican Party's lack of commitment to the cause of racial equality. Recognizing the need for new initiatives rather than worship of the past, Robinson never presented his own experience as a reason for complacency. He saw clearly that the quest for racial justice was an ongoing struggle.

—*Ira Smolensky*

See also: Journey of Reconciliation; Military desegregation; Segregation; Sports

JOURNEY OF RECONCILIATION

April 9-23, 1947

The Journey of Reconciliation attracted national attention to the Congress of Racial Equality, helping to strengthen the organization at a time when its resources were scarce, and also established nonviolent direct action as the organization's identifying mark and served as a model for the Freedom Rides of the early 1960's.

The Event: Direct-action campaign organized by the Congress of Racial Equality
Place: Washington, D.C., Virginia, North Carolina, Tennessee, and Kentucky

Three forces converged to bring about the 1947 Journey of Reconciliation, which was sponsored jointly by the Congress of Racial Equality (CORE) and the Fellowship of Reconciliation (FOR). The first and most basic was CORE's desire to launch a direct action campaign that would attract national attention and thus strengthen the organization at a time when its resources were meager and its activities limited. Since its founding in 1942 by a biracial group in Chicago, CORE had been committed to nonviolent direct action on the model of Mohandas K. Gandhi in India and had sponsored sit-ins and other forms of nonviolent protest. Its budget was barely $100 per month in 1945-1946, however, and its public visibility was low. When George M. Houser became the executive secretary of CORE in 1945, a successful national campaign was one of his chief goals. A white activist in FOR when he was chosen for the new position,

Houser had been involved with James Farmer and others in founding CORE and was concerned that its first three years of efforts had fallen short of his dream of making CORE a major force for nonviolent reform in the United States.

The second major impetus for the journey was the U.S. Supreme Court decision in the *Morgan v. Virginia* case (1946) that declared Virginia's policy of racial segregation on interstate motor carriers unconstitutional. When several bus companies refused to comply with the decision, Houser saw their resistance as the opportunity he had looked for. Nonviolent direct action, he believed, might help the cause of desegregated transportation while strengthening CORE's impact. Bayard Rustin, a longtime activist who had served causes such as Gandhi's liberation efforts in India and several antiwar campaigns, agreed.

A founder of CORE's New York branch, Rustin was quite familiar with the organization's goals and needs. At CORE's fall, 1946, executive committee meeting, he and Houser argued that the recent *Morgan v. Virginia* decision provided a promising setting for demonstrating the potential of nonviolent direct action. Both men at the time were secretaries in FOR's Racial Industrial Department and had the support of A. J. Muste, a widely known pacifist and FOR executive.

Throughout the fall and winter of 1946-1947, Rustin and Houser gained other supporters both within and outside their organizations. By January, 1947, they were ready to take a preliminary trip along the proposed route both to gain additional partners and to finalize the details. Their original plan to extend the trip into the Deep South all the way to New Orleans was abandoned because of the possibility of violent resistance. The Journey of Reconciliation, as they called it after discussions with FOR staffers, would be confined to the upper southern states from Virginia to North and South Carolina.

The third contributing factor to the journey was interorganizational cooperation among civil rights groups, augmented by local individuals and churches. During their planning trip in January, 1947, Houser and Rustin enlisted a significant number of college students and African American church members to provide housing and food for the journey participants. The National Association for the Advancement of Colored People (NAACP) had serious misgivings about the journey and refrained from active support, but it did offer its local contacts in several communities along the route. The NAACP's reluctance was caused by its fear of violent backlash if the travelers went into the Deep South or possibly even the border states. CORE's decision to confine the trip to the Virginia and Carolina areas helped ameliorate this concern, but not sufficiently to convince the NAACP executive secretary, Walter White, to provide funds or active assistance.

In late March and early April, 1947, the sixteen participants in the journey engaged in intense training in Washington, D.C. Anticipating the training techniques of the 1960's, such as role-playing, lectures and discussions, and learning ways to protect oneself in case of violent resistance, they prepared.

THE JOURNEY BEGINS

On April 9, the group of eight whites and eight African Americans left the nation's capital and headed southward through northern Virginia. Ideologically, the biracial group shared much. All the white members were pacifists—James Peck of the Peck and Peck clothing business family, George M. Houser, Homer Jack of the Chicago Council Against Racial and Religious Discrimination, New York horticulturalist Igal Roodenko, and four others of varied professional backgrounds. Two of them, Joseph Felmet of Asheville, North Carolina, and James Peck, were socialists affiliated with the Workers Defense League. Peck was editor of the league's news bulletin. The other three white participants were two North Carolina Methodist pastors, Ernest Bromley and Louis Adams, and Worth Randle, a Cincinnati biologist. Four of the black participants in the Journey of Reconciliation were also pacifists, among them Bayard Rustin, whose activist career included support for Gandhi's liberation efforts in India. Rustin was particularly controversial because of his earlier affiliation with communism, an unusual association among black leaders, but he had abandoned communism by the early 1940's. In addition to Rustin and Homer Jack, the black participants were freelance lecturer Wallace Nelson; Conrad Lynn, a New York attorney; Andrew Johnson, a student from Cincinnati; Chicago musician Dennis Banks; William Worthy of the New York Council for a Permanent FEPC (Fair Employment Practices Commission); and Eugene Stanley of A. and T. College in North Carolina.

From Washington, the group traveled to Richmond, Virginia, where the first overnight stop was scheduled. Half the group traveled on a Greyhound bus, the other half on the Trailways line. Each ticket listed every planned stopover in cities where the riders would address meetings in churches, but the planners had determined that the ultimate destination on each ticket required crossing a state line, since their specific goal was to implement the *Morgan* decision of 1946. The plan was to travel across Virginia, into North Carolina, Tennessee, and Kentucky, and then back across Virginia.

The entire journey took two weeks. Meetings were arranged chiefly by the NAACP in cooperation with local churches. Peck reported that it was exciting to begin the journey after months of anticipation and to be actually "on stage," trying to challenge resistance to the recent court decision. The underlying hope of the participants was not only to enforce a law but also to change attitudes. If idealistic, this goal was basic to those who set out on the potentially dangerous trip, usually regarded as the first Freedom Ride.

Although the journey elicited no major violent response, there were several arrests. The first was on a Trailways carrier as the group left Petersburg, Virginia. James Peck was arrested in Durham, North Carolina, along with Rustin and Andrew Johnson, during a rally in a church. Durham was a small but prosperous city with better paving, housing, and other facilities in the white sections than in the black; Peck was bothered by this and spoke out against it. He and the others were detained only briefly and then taken by car to Chapel Hill, the nearby site of the University of North Carolina. Interestingly, the Chapel Hill area was the only stop on the journey that witnessed real violence. In Cargill, a small town just outside Chapel Hill's city limits, Peck was hit by a group of taxi drivers as he stood outside his bus. Inside four of the journey group were arrested when they tried to integrate the front seats. Released on bail, they were taken by a local white Presbyterian minister to his home for protection, but cabs full of hostile resisters wielded rocks and sticks and warned the minister that they would burn his home if he did not get the group out of town.

Other arrests occurred in Asheville, North Carolina, as the group traveled westward toward Tennessee after stopping in Greensboro. Again, Peck was arrested. The issue was the same in Asheville as in Chapel Hill—trouble over the effort to integrate the whites only seats. Asheville happened to be the home of one of the white participants Joe Felmet, and some of the group stayed overnight in his home. In the trial the next day, Peck and his codefendant, a black participant from Chicago named Dennis Banks, were found guilty and sentenced to thirty days on a road gang. The state's attorney and the judge who presided did not know about the *Morgan* decision and borrowed a copy of the decision from Curtis Todd, a black attorney who represented the riders.

As it turned out, Banks and Peck remained in jail only a few hours and were released, but during that time, the other prisoners vented their anger at Peck, a white man supporting African Americans. Eventually, the state dropped the case when its officials learned more about the 1946 Court decision.

From Asheville, the Journey of Reconciliation continued into Knoxville, Tennessee, then northward into Kentucky and back across Virginia before ending in Washington on April 23. Of the five arrest cases during the two-week trip, all but one were dropped. The Chapel Hill case was pursued by prosecutors, and Rustin, Joe Felmet, and Igal Roodenko served thirty days at hard labor on a road gang. Nevertheless, there were no reporters waiting to interview the participants and nothing like the intense journalistic enthusiasm that would mark the Freedom Rides fourteen years later. The Journey of Reconciliation was a pioneering effort that at the time attracted a disappointingly slight response from the press and the public.

IMPACT OF THE JOURNEY

The significance of the Journey of Reconciliation lay, in the short run, in the heightened publicity it elicited and the inspiration it gave to advocates of social change by means of nonviolent direct action. Although no reporters were waiting to interview the participants when they returned, press coverage of the various incidents during the trip was fair and rather extensive. Both Houser and Rustin were pleased with the details of press accounts and considered them positive. For the participants themselves, newspaper articles were important for their later efforts to gain support and recruit new activists. Indeed, many years later, CORE leaders used stories of the journey to teach nonviolent theory and encourage participation. James Peck was particularly encouraged by the response of people in general to the effort and noted that drivers, other passengers, and observers were sympathetic toward desegregation but were ignorant of various laws. Seeing the journey activists demonstrate nonviolent techniques, he felt, contributed to greater understanding and support.

At a deeper level, the Journey of Reconciliation was a truly paradigmatic event. Strictly speaking, it was the first Freedom Ride. What is usually termed the first Freedom Ride in popular parlance was actually modeled after the 1947 precedent in key respects. Peck, who was active in both the 1947 journey and the 1961 Freedom Rides, saw the earlier event as supremely significant in the longer process of rides by desegregationist activists, describing it as "perhaps the most unique and outstanding undertaking CORE has ever made." CORE trainers used both the concept of the journey and the methodology of nonviolent protest in preparing for the 1961 rides into the Deep South.

As a factor in the history of racial and ethnic rights, the Journey of Reconciliation is somewhat analogous to the 1962 desegregation efforts in Albany, Georgia. In both cases, the immediate goals were not achieved quickly. The specific objective of the journey was to intensify grassroots efforts to achieve a greater degree of desegregation in public transportation. That did not happen quickly, but the effort did increase public awareness of the problem and did encourage many other efforts to desegregate interstate buses, trains, and other conveyances. In doing that, the 1947 journey into the upper South also demonstrated that nonviolence had much more potential than many people realized to augment legal efforts to bring about racial equality. Spiritually and intellectually, the leaders were encouraged to perpetuate the nonviolent method. Like Albany, the Journey of Reconciliation was a source of inspiration to challenge racial segregation and discrimination by concerted group action. That aspect of the journey's impact continued to have influence throughout the 1950's and into the following decade.

CORE

The judicial proceedings that occurred during and after the Journey of Reconciliation were also significant for CORE's later development. The several cases that grew

out of the trip were pursued by attorneys who supported CORE's objectives and provided useful experience in using the details of local and state laws to show contradictions with Supreme Court decisions and thus to bring to bear on local problems the larger influence of federal law. This was a rather slowly developing process since bus companies often cited state law as their guide and delayed implementing federal mandates until the courts made it clear that they applied.

CORE's finances and public visibility remained rather low even after the journey, but it was the first of several undertakings that would gradually propel the organization to higher public recognition and larger membership. FOR assisted CORE in pursuing some of the cases, including the Chapel Hill litigation in the months immediately following the journey. By the 1950's, CORE was beginning to grow in several of its chapters and to equip it self for a larger role in racial desegregation litigation. Above all, the trip was a favorite topic of conversation and sparked training programs that led eventually to the 1960's Freedom Rides, an event that elicited widespread media coverage and support by youth across the nation. The Journey of Reconciliation was clearly a high point in CORE's history, as well as a model for the potential efficacy of nonviolent direct action.

—*Thomas R. Peake*

See also: Baseball's integration; Freedom Rides; President's Committee on Civil Rights

MILITARY DESEGREGATION

July 26, 1948

The official desegregation of the armed forces continued a process of granting equal civil rights in American life and acted as an important impetus for the desegregation of public facilities.

The Event: Formal abolition of racial segregation in the organization of the U.S. military services by an executive order
Place: Washington, D.C.

At the beginning of World War II, the American armed services, reflecting larger patterns in American society, were almost completely segregated. Although African

Americans had participated in every war, their numbers were small, their roles were limited, and their units were almost always segregated.

HISTORY OF SEGREGATION
Few African American units engaged in combat in the Spanish-American War or in World War I. Their uneven levels of performance allowed many white Army officers to retain their prejudices, thus limiting African American troop deployment and obstructing the services' willingness to desegregate. American success in both those wars allowed for the maintenance of a racial status quo in the military. Change effected by World

War I and the industrialization of America created conditions allowing for movement toward a more egalitarian civilian life. Many African Americans moved from the rural South to the industrialized North, where their incomes and education rose dramatically. Racial relations began to change.

World War II provided the spark to ignite the Civil Rights movement. In addition to the underlying internal demographic changes, the war provided specific conditions enabling progress in civil rights. First, America went to war with the avowed intention of defeating the racism and aggression of both Nazi Germany and Imperial Japan. The main reason for American involvement in the war was protection of human rights. Second, the large African American emigration to the North created a new voting bloc, historically Republican but newly Democratic because of the economic and political policies of the New Deal. Moreover, African Americans were concentrated in industrial states with large electoral college slates, especially important for presidential elections. Third, World War II was a protracted war in which American human resources were taxed. At the end of the war replacement personnel became harder to come by. Any policy of under-enlisting or under-training any sizable segment of the population, such as a policy segregating African Americans, led to problems of inefficiency and shortages.

The armed services remained largely segregated throughout the war, although some desegregation occurred toward the end of the war. Units from the Army's four black regiments—overstaffed with draftees—were merged with larger white ones suffering manpower shortages. In some cases, the same training facilities were made available to black and white units.

POST-WORLD WAR II CHANGES

Immediately after the war, the direction bifurcated: internal armed services developments hindered significant change in the racial balance, while societal developments encouraged more rapid desegregation. Internally, as occurred after each previous war, pressures on the armed services to desegregate abated. The numbers of African Americans declined so drastically that African Americans could easily be accommodated in segregated units. Externally, the African American emigration from the rural South accelerated during and after World War II. African American voters increased in number.

Civil rights organizations also grew in number and in political power: Over a period of six years, membership in the National Association for the Advancement of Colored People (NAACP) exploded nine-fold to 450,000. Moreover, non-southern whites grew more sympathetic to the demands for greater equality, although there were periodic race riots in the North revolving especially around the issue of jobs and the fear that African Americans would dispossess whites.

During the war, President Franklin D. Roosevelt took a few small steps to address the question of segregation. He recommended that African Americans be given more options in the Navy; he revived a 1937 War Department program to increase the numbers of African American soldiers to their proportion in society; and, most important, in 1941, via Executive Order 8802, he established the Fair Employment Practices Commission (FEPC). Roosevelt, much less committed to civil rights than his wife, Eleanor, was concerned primarily with winning the war and pleasing the southern component of his political coalition.

Little was known about the civil rights orientation of Roosevelt's successor, Harry S. Truman. As a senator from Missouri, Truman had been able to win essential African American votes by supporting the few pieces of civil rights legislation and by supporting New Deal economics. Truman, a centrist with humanitarian leanings and a respect for the Constitution, was a sharp politician but also a man moved by personal experiences. One national incident which shocked him and touched the hearts of many Americans involved a returning African American veteran. While still in uniform, literally on his return, Sergeant Isaac Woodard was removed from a bus by a local South Carolina sheriff and beaten with a nightstick so badly that he was blinded.

A series of vicious attacks against and murders of African Americans in the South in 1946 led to public protests. Truman was quoted by Walter White as responding, "My God! I had no idea that it was as terrible as that. We have to do something." Reacting to these incidents, to the changing demography, to a changing world environment, and to a new world of domestic politics, Truman set out on a course that would dramatically change human rights.

Immediately after the war, Truman spoke out periodically about human rights, including statements in his State of the Union addresses in 1946 and 1948. He helped commission several internal studies of the armed forces which looked specifically at the status of African Americans. The most comprehensive study was made by the Gillem Board. In April, 1946, the board came up with a plan to expand the role of African Americans in the Army and to provide more equal facilities and opportunities. One key item was a quota of 10 percent in each large unit. The board did not, however, push for integration within the smaller units. Thus, the report, reflecting the military's reluctance to change radically, was largely rejected by civil rights organizations, which favored desegregation of all facilities.

By 1947, two important conditions had changed. The Cold War was beginning in earnest, leading both the military and Truman to push for stronger, larger armed forces. Moreover, the United States began an ideological war of propaganda against the Soviet Union focusing in part on basic human rights. The international audience for this campaign was largely nonwhite. Second, the Republicans controlled both houses of Congress and Truman's chances for a presidential victory in 1948 looked bleak. He knew that he could not win without a substantial proportion of the African American vote.

MOUNTING PRESSURES

The African American leadership pushed for more desegregation. On October 23, 1947, W. E. B. Du Bois and other radical African Americans embarrassed the administration by bringing charges against the American government before the newly formed United Nations Commission on Human Rights. Six months later, in a more mainstream development, A. Philip Randolph's Committee Against Jim Crow in Military Service threatened an African American boycott of a new conscription law if it contained no antisegregation clause.

In response to all these pressures and frustrated by Congress's refusal to extend the FEPC, Truman took a major step when he commissioned the President's Committee on Civil Rights, a fifteen-member board composed of leading figures from the worlds of business, academia, government, and religion.

On October 29, 1947, this committee published its findings in *To Secure These Rights*, a monograph that received widespread public attention. The committee argued strongly on behalf of racial equality and prescribed deep-seated societal changes, including specific recommendations for desegregating all branches of the armed services. Truman took the report seriously, although he chose to implement it according to his own political calendar. That calendar became crowded in 1948, a presidential year that promised what looked like a certain victory for the Republicans.

Frustrated with the Republican Congress, liberal Democrats pressured Truman to push for a liberal agenda. Some even joined a committee to draft Dwight

D. Eisenhower. Part of that frustration led to a third-party, strongly pro-civil rights Progressive candidacy of Henry Wallace, Roosevelt's former vice president. To make election matters even more complicated for Truman, some of the southern wing of the party bolted and nominated Strom Thurmond for president.

Truman obliged the liberals, knowing that he needed the industrial states for victory. A Republican convention that made a strong statement on race—specifically, the desegregation of the armed services—and the surprising success of the liberal forces led by Hubert Humphrey on the Democratic Convention floor prompted Truman to release two key executive orders on July 26, 1948.

Order 9980 called for a Fair Employment Board to provide redress for racial discrimination in federal employment. Executive Order 9981 announced the policy of "equality of treatment for all persons in the armed services without regard to race, color, religion, or national origin." A second provision called for an advisory committee to oversee that policy of equality, constituted in September, 1948, as the Fahy Committee.

IMPACT

Exactly what did Executive Order 9981 entail? Was it another rhetorical promise, was it a plan to implement the *Plessy v. Ferguson (*1896) principle of "separate but equal," or was it a plan to desegregate? In answer to a reporter's public question, Truman made clear that it was indeed a plan to desegregate.

In reality, the armed services did not desegregate immediately. Rather, there was uneven compliance both in time and in depth. Entrenched forces in the services resisted the orders and put up barriers to implementation.

Nevertheless, desegregation progressed, supervised by the Fahy Committee and with the prodding of African American defense organizations. Wartime Secretary of War Henry Stimson, who opposed the idea, had been replaced by the first secretary of defense, James Forrestal, who was committed to the idea but unwilling to force it upon the service leadership. His successor, Louis Johnson, was more willing to go along with Truman in imposing it from the top.

In part, the decisions were hindered or expedited by individuals along the chain of command. The most resistant force was Kenneth Royall, secretary of the same army which had previously been the service most open to African Americans. Eventually, Truman intervened personally with Royall's successor, Gordon Gray. In the Far East, Douglas MacArthur managed to delay the policy, but it was accelerated when Truman replaced MacArthur with a more cooperative Matthew Ridgway.

Change was more forthcoming from the Air Force, largely because of the strong support of Stuart Symington, later a Democratic senator from Missouri. The Marines, which had long been lily-white, also fell into place in short time. The Navy earlier had been more accommodating to African Americans in terms of numbers, but the overwhelming percentage of those were in the food service. Slowly, the Navy began to give more equal training to African Americans in other jobs and upgraded the ranks of some of the stewards.

The war in Korea provided the final thrust for desegregation, again supported by the need for more troops to engage in combat. The remaining pockets of segregation were systematically eliminated, even under President Eisenhower, who was less committed to civil rights than was Truman. By the end of the Korean War, virtually all the armed services were desegregated at the most basic level.

Segregation practices, however, still faced African American soldiers and their dependents, especially in the southern towns where many were stationed. Because local policy involved states' rights, it took longer to overcome that discrimination. These practices were not legally resolved until the Supreme Court decisions that grew out of Executive Order 9981.

The desegregation of the armed forces served as a reference point for the further desegregation of the rest of society. Under Truman, the Justice Department argued a number of cases before the Supreme Court which systematically eroded segregation as a legal policy. The Court issued decisions making restrictive housing covenants illegal (*Shelley v. Kraemer*, 1948); banning segregation in interstate busing (*Henderson v. the U.S.*, 1950); giving rights to education (*Sweatt v. Painter* and *McLaurin v. Oklahoma*, 1950); and eventually, a year after the Korean War ended, banning segregation in public schools (*Brown v. Board of Education*, 1954).

Beyond the legal cases, an important human dynamic arose from the consequences of Executive Order 9981. Those African Americans who were integrated in the armed forces found it difficult to return to a segregated civilian lifestyle. Their experiences in the military acted as an impetus for them to reject the segregation of civilian life. For whites who served with African Americans on the front lines, it also became more difficult to return to a completely segregated life. Moreover, especially after World War II and then Korea, it became increasingly difficult to accept the war contributions made by African American soldiers but then to deny them basic civilian rights afterward.

Desegregating the armed services allowed for much greater contact between whites and African Americans, as well as among whites and significant numbers of Puerto Ricans and Filipinos, many of the latter also formerly in segregated units.

In retrospect, the conditions allowing for successful interracial contact as a means of breaking down prejudice were more propitious in the military than they were in the school systems. Not only was there more regimentation in the military, but the soldiers also had both a common goal and a common enemy, conditions supporting the effectiveness of contact in dissolving differences. Although contact often has surprisingly little effect in diminishing prejudice, a study on soldiers conducted at Johns Hopkins University found that contact in the armed forces did contribute to a lessening of prejudice and discrimination.

President Truman later remarked of Executive Order 9981, "It's the greatest thing that ever happened to America." A less effusive but similar evaluation was proffered by eminent legal and political historian Milton Konvitz: "[I]n the history of civil rights in the United States, this order ranks among the most important steps to end racial discrimination."

—Alan M. Fisher

See also: Buffalo soldiers; Defense industry desegregation; Fair Employment Practices Committee; Integration; Military; President's Committee on Civil Rights; Vietnam War; World War II

MILES DAVIS DEVELOPS 1950'S COOL JAZZ
1950s

A jazz trumpeter, composer, bandleader, and painter, Davis played a vital role in the history of modern jazz. During a career that spanned more than fifty years, Davis developed an original, lyrical soloing style and emerged as a pioneering leader of several jazz idioms, including cool jazz, hard bop, modal jazz, jazz-rock, and jazz-funk fusion.

Born: May 26, 1926; Alton, Illinois
Died: September 28, 1991; Santa Monica, California
Also known as: Miles Dewey Davis III
Areas of achievement: Art and photography; Music: bandleading; Music: composition; Music: funk; Music: jazz

EARLY LIFE
Miles Dewey Davis III was born in Alton, Illinois, to an affluent, middle-class African American family. Davis's father was a dental surgeon who moved his family to an all-white neighborhood in East St. Louis within a year of his son's birth. Although Davis's mother, Cleota Henry Davis, wanted him to learn how to play the violin or piano, his father gave him a trumpet on his thirteenth birthday. He began taking lessons with Elwood Buchanan, who encouraged Davis not to play his trumpet with vibrato. Davis also began to spend time with the trumpeter Clark Terry, who became one of his early mentors. Within two years, he was performing professionally with Eddie Randall's Blue Devils.

In 1944, the Billy Eckstine band came to St. Louis to perform at the Club Riviera for two weeks. One of Eckstine's trumpeters was sick, and Davis had the opportunity to substitute for him. The band included bebop innovators Charlie Parker and Dizzy Gillespie, who both left a profound impression on the young musician. In September, 1944, Davis moved to New York to attend the Juilliard School of Music with the additional motive of spending time with Parker. He spent a year at Juilliard and soon joined Parker in live appearances and recording sessions.

In 1948, Davis began his influential collaboration with the Canadian arranger Gil Evans. Their associations with Gerry Mulligan and John Lewis resulted in a series of nonet recordings for Capitol Records that became known as *Birth of the Cool* (1957). In 1949, Davis traveled to Paris with Tadd Dameron; when he returned,

he became addicted to heroin for four years. In 1953, Davis returned to his father's home in East St. Louis and quit heroin cold turkey. By the beginning of 1954, he was free of his addiction and focused on reigniting his career.

LIFE'S WORK
In 1955, Davis appeared at the Newport Jazz Festival, where his remarkable soloing—particularly his improvisations on "'Round Midnight"—brought him widespread notoriety. The publicity allowed him to obtain sufficient engagements to establish the first of his great quintets, which featured bassist Paul Chambers, pianist Red Garland, drummer Philly Joe Jones, and saxophonist John Coltrane, who was eventually replaced by Sonny Rollins in 1956. He also met producer George Avakian, who persuaded him to sign a contract with Columbia Records. To rapidly fulfill his unfinished obligations to his previous label, Prestige, Davis assembled a quintet for several historically significant recordings that would be released in 1956 as *Steamin'*, *Cookin'*, *Workin'*, and *Relaxin'*. The albums include popular bebop songs, jazz standards, and pre-bop era songs. Each record was well received by musicians and fans. In 1957, the original quintet was dismantled by Davis as a result of personal issues among some of the band members.

In 1957, Davis revived his association with arranger Evans and recorded a series of albums. This time they assembled new works with Davis as the primary soloist, backed by a large band. *Miles Ahead*, recorded in 1957, showcases Davis on flugelhorn, an uncommon instrument in jazz at the time. Although Shorty Rogers and Clark Terry had played flugelhorn before 1957, Davis's recordings provoked a new popularity for the instrument.

In 1958, Davis recorded selections from George Gershwin's opera *Porgy and Bess*. *Sketches of Spain* was recorded in November, 1959, and March, 1960, and features songs by contemporary Spanish composer Joaquin Rodrigo, Manuel de Falla, and Evans. In 1958, Davis turned his quintet into a sextet by adding Cannonball Adderley and recorded the landmark album *Milestones* for Columbia. Davis's composition "Milestones" broke from the tradition of solo improvisation that relies on frequently changing chord progressions. Instead, it allowed for a modal approach to melodic improvisation in which the soloist uses one mode or scale as inspiration for solo development. The popularity of the new modal style increased with the release of *Kind of Blue* in 1959. *Kind of Blue* is one of the best selling and most influential recordings in jazz history and featured Adderley, Coltrane, pianist Bill Evans, bassist Paul Chambers, and drummer Jimmy Cobb. Pianist Wynton Kelly also appears on "Freddie Freeloader." Many of the compositions were modal, including the popular "So What." After the release of this album, many jazz musicians began to use its song formats instead of popular or bebop song forms.

From 1959 to 1963, Davis used a rhythm section that consisted of Chambers, Kelly, and Cobb. Their work is featured on the albums *Someday My Prince Will Come*, *Miles Davis at Carnegie Hall*, *Saturday Night at the Blackhawk*, and *Friday Night at the Blackhawk*.

Their relaxed, even swinging sound distinguished them from other groups of the time, and many modern musicians identified the rhythm section as one of the most sought-after in jazz. In 1963, Davis hired a new rhythm section that stayed together until 1968. The section included pianist Herbie Hancock, bassist Ron Carter, and drummer Tony Williams. In 1964 tenor saxophonist Wayne Shorter joined Davis and became the quintet's primary composer. This ensemble is often considered to be Davis's "second great quintet," and itwas one of the most significant and progressive ensembles in jazz during the 1960's.

Important recordings produced by this group include *Miles Smiles*, *E.S.P.*, *Nefertiti*, and *The Sorcerer*. In albums *Miles in the Sky* and *Filles de Kilimanjaro* (1968), Davis began to seriously incorporate rock influences. He also began to experiment with open-ended compositions based on rock-oriented grooves, short melodic fragments, and driving bass patterns. In 1969, Davis recorded *Bitches Brew*, which became a best-selling album and a pioneering jazz-rock fusion recording. Many of the musicians who performed on this album would go on to lead the major pioneering jazz-rock fusion groups, including Weather Report, Tony Williams Lifetime, Mahavishnu Orchestra, and Return to Forever.

In the 1970's, Davis turned from rock toward funk. Bassist Michael Henderson was a mainstay of these groups. In the 1980's, Davis's music became more influenced by popular music and commercial calculations. *You're Under Arrest* (1985), *Tutu* (1986), and *Music from Siesta* (1988) were all recorded through layered overdubbing, similar to pop albums of the time.

Miles Davis and Cool Jazz

The term "cool jazz" applies to the modern jazz idiom from the late 1940's that derives largely from bebop. Unlike its parent style, it is characterized by the use of smooth timbres, soft dynamics, the avoidance of vibrato, and restrained emotional content. In 1949 and 1950, trumpeter Miles Davis and arranger Gil Evans collaborated to create a set of recordings that would become exceedingly influential in the spread of this new style. The nine-piece band originally comprised Davis, trombonist Mike Zwerin, tuba player Bill Barber, French horn player Junior Collins, baritone saxophonist Gerry Mulligan, alto saxophonist Lee Konitz, pianist John Lewis, bassist Al McKibbon, and drummer Max Roach. The group had several brief engagements that were not financially successful.

In 1949, Davis was under contract with Capitol Records to record several singles. To fulfill his obligation, he revived the ensemble to record for three additional sessions. Although the instrumental lineup remained unchanged, Davis, Barber, Mulligan, and Konitz were the only musicians who performed in all of the sessions. The tracks were originally released as singles until eight of them were compiled in 1953 as a part of Capitol's Classics in Jazz series. In 1957, a twelveinch LP titled Birth of the Cool was released. Although some of the musicians, including Konitz, did not like the connotations of the term "cool," the style profoundly influenced many musicians, particularly in California. The musical movement became known as "West Coast jazz," and Davis's sound and musical concept influenced many of its leaders, including Chet Baker, Shorty Rogers, and Paul Desmond.

Toward the end of his life Davis appeared in two films: *Scrooged* (1988) with Bill Murray and *Dingo* (1991). Davis died on September 28, 1991, of a stroke and respiratory failure in Santa Monica, California. He was buried at Woodlawn Cemetery in the Bronx, with one of his trumpets.

SIGNIFICANCE

Because of his musical innovations, profound influence, sustained leadership, and creativity from the 1940's to the early 1990's, Miles Davis occupies a position in jazz analogous to that of Louis Armstrong, Duke Ellington, and Charlie Parker. He played a crucial role in every major development in jazz during his lifetime and became a major cultural icon, outspoken social critic, and painter.

In 2009, the United States House of Representatives passed a resolution honoring Davis's landmark album *Kind of Blue* as a national treasure.

—N. Michael Goecke

RALPH BUNCHE RECEIVES NOBEL PRIZE
1950

During his distinguished career, Bunche promoted the Civil Rights movement, helped to organize the United Nations, worked as a mediator in numerous conflicts, and was awarded the Nobel Peace Prize.

Born: August 7, 1903; Detroit, Michigan
Died: December 9, 1971; New York, New York
Also known as: Ralph Johnson Bunche; Ralph Johnson Bunch (birth name)
Areas of achievement: Civil rights; Diplomacy; Education; Government and politics

EARLY LIFE
Ralph Johnson Bunche was born into a poor family in Detroit, Michigan, in 1903. His father, Fred Bunch, a barber, was frequently unemployed, and his mother, Olive Johnson Bunch, who contracted tuberculosis around 1912, was a member of a large extended family. In 1915, the family moved to Albuquerque, New Mexico, where they lived with Bunche's light-skinned grandmother, Lucy Johnson. In 1916, Fred left his wife and two children in search of work, promising to call for them when he found work, but Bunche never saw him again. In 1917, his mother died from tuberculosis. The night she died, he later recalled, "she had asked for milk and there was none in the house because I had drunk it up." Lucy Johnson assumed responsibility for raising the two children.

They moved to South Central Los Angeles at a time when the region was beginning its economic decline.

Bunche always was an excellent student. At Jefferson High School, he was on the debate team, played basketball, worked as a paperboy, and was valedictorian of the class of 1922. His graduation address was titled "Our New Responsibility." He later attributed his "spirit of competition" to his grandmother's constant insistence "to let them, especially white folks, know that you can do anything they can do." Despite the economic challenges of the family, his grandmother insisted that he attend college.

Bunche at the 1963 March on Washington for Jobs and Freedom, by U.S. Information Agency.

He enrolled at the University of California at Los Angeles (UCLA), where he was president of the debating society, a writer for the school newspaper, and a star basketball player. In 1927, he was awarded a B.A. with a major in political science, graduating summa cum laude and as class valedictorian. The next year, Bunche started work toward a master's degree in political science at Harvard University. He had a tuition scholarship and earned his living expenses by working at a secondhand bookstore. His determination to outperform

RALPH BUNCHE RECEIVES NOBEL PRIZE

the other students created much stress, and he became addicted to cigarettes. Although offered a scholarship to pursue a Ph.D., Bunche declined in order to teach and organize a political science department at Howard University, the nation's premier black institution of higher learning. His colleagues at Howard included philosopher Alain Locke, sociologist E. Franklin Frazier, and the first black president of the school, Mordecai Wyatt Johnson. In 1929, Bunche took a leave of absence to earn a doctorate at Harvard, and while there he married Ruth Ethel Harris, one of his Howard students.

In 1934, he was awarded a Ph.D. for his dissertation on the decolonization of the French empire in Africa, which won the Toppan Prize for the year's best dissertation in the field of government. During the next two years, a scholarship allowed Bunche to do postgraduate study in African anthropology at the London School of Economics and the University of Cape Town in South Africa.

LIFE'S WORK

In 1936, Bunche returned to his teaching and administrative activities at Howard University. During this period, he was committed to a quasi-Marxist ideology and was a contributing editor of *Science and Society: A Marxian Quarterly*. His first book, *World View of Race* (1936), predicted that the future would see many class-based wars between the haves and have-nots. In 1938, he began working with Swedish economist Gunnar Myrdal, who had funding from the Carnegie Corporation to study the status of African Americans. Bunche was responsible for substantial parts of the monumental work *An American Dilemma: The Negro Problem and Modern Democracy (*1944), which would later make a significant contribution toward the Civil Rights movement. In doing field research for the study, Bunche spent considerable time in the South. One of the valuable fruits of the research was his long monograph *The Political Status of the Negro in the Age of FDR*, which was published in 1973.

When the United States entered World War II in 1941, Bunche left academia to do research on African colonial affairs for the Office of Strategic Services (OSS). Among other tasks at OSS, Bunche wrote the manual used by U.S. troops for fighting in North Africa. In early 1944, he was transferred to the U.S. Department of State, and he was soon promoted to the Office of Political Affairs as head of the division concerned with trusteeships. In this capacity, he actively participated in many of the high-level meetings responsible for negotiating the charter of the United Nations (U.N.),

and he was the first African American to serve on the U.S. delegation to the General Assembly. By this time, his ideological commitment had changed from Marxist socialism to democratic liberalism, and he disagreed with many of his earlier writings.

In 1946, the Secretary General of the United Nations, Trygve Lie, appointed Bunche as director of the Trusteeship Division, a position Bunche held for the next nine years. His greatest achievement during this period was negotiating the 1949 truce that ended the first Arab-Israeli War, for which he was awarded the Nobel Peace Prize. Bunche was promoted to undersecretary general of the United Nations in 1955; his title was changed to undersecretary general for special political affairs in 1957.

In 1956, Bunche's mediation during the Suez Canal Crisis helped secure an agreement on the stationing of U.N. emergency forces to supervise the Egypt-Israeli border. Shortly thereafter, he was actively involved in negotiations to end the violent civil war in the former Belgian Congo (now known as the Democratic Republic of the Congo) and helped to prevent the dissolution of the fragile new country. During this complex conflict, some militant African Americans attacked him as an "Uncle Tom" because of his refusal to give unqualified support to the popular nationalist leader, Patrice Lumumba, and some people blamed him for Lumumba's tragic death. In subsequent years, Bunche was frequently the U.N.'s primary troubleshooter in attempts to mediate peace settlements in places such as Cyprus, Yemen, and Kashmir.

Throughout his busy career, Bunche was a strong supporter of the Civil Rights movement. In August, 1963, he was one of the speakers at the momentous March on Washington, although his address was overshadowed by Martin Luther King, Jr.'s "I Have a Dream" speech. In March, 1965, despite suffering from chronic phlebitis, Bunche joined King and Ralph Abernathy to lead the Alabama march between Selma and Montgomery. When the group arrived at Montgomery, Bunche gave a speech denouncing the flying of the Confederate flag over the state capitol and declared that "peace in the world can be built only upon the principle and practice of equal rights and status for all peoples, respect and dignity for all men." After this speech, he received a considerable amount of hate mail.

Bunche's schedule at the United Nations kept him away from home on many occasions, and he often expressed guilt for not spending more time with his family. On October 6, 1966, his thirty-three-year-old daughter Jane died, almost certainly by suicide, and Bunche apparently felt that he was partly to blame for the tragedy. The shock of her death probably promoted the rapid deterioration of his own health. In addition to struggling with diabetes since 1958, Bunche increasingly suffered from phlebitis, diminished eyesight, and kidney failure.

When he tried to resign for health reasons in 1967, Secretary General U Thant persuaded him that his continued presence was essential. By May, 1971, Bunche's many illnesses had made it impossible for him to attend meetings, although he continued to hold his position until that summer. He died in New York Hospital on December 9 at the age of sixty-eight.

SIGNIFICANCE

Many monuments and buildings honor Bunche's career and achievements. In 1980, the park across from the United Nations headquarters was renamed the Ralph Bunche Park, and a fifty-foot-high stainless-steel obelisk, *Peace Form One*, designed by Daniel Larue Johnson, was installed to celebrate his efforts for peace. In 1982, the U.S. Postal Service issued a postage stamp in his memory. In 1997, the library of the U.S. Department of State, the federal government's oldest library, was named the Ralph J. Bunche Library.

Although Bunche's name was not well known in the early twenty-first century, he was one of the most accomplished diplomats in history. His most important achievement was helping to bring about the armistice of the Arab-Israeli War in 1949, but he also was instrumental in promoting settlements in numerous other disputes throughout the world. His part in the creation of the United Nations was substantial. By setting an example of courage, moderation, and reason, Bunche also made a positive contribution to the Civil Rights movement. Finally, his research and writings, particularly his study

---

Bunche's Nobel Peace Prize

Ralph Bunche was awarded the Nobel Peace Prize in 1950 for his central role in mediating the truce that ended the Arab-Israeli War of 1949. His involvement in the conflict began in 1946, when the secretary-general of the United Nations, Trygve Lie, commissioned him to assist the committee that recommended Palestine be portioned between Arabs and Jews. Soon after fighting broke out in 1948, Bunche served as assistant to U.N. mediator Folke Bernadotte, and after Bernadotte's assassination, Bunche replaced him. The negotiations dragged on for eleven months, taking place mostly on the island of Rhodes. Bunche became an expert on the conflict and exercised a combination of persuasion, determination, and patience. After negotiating Israeli agreements with Egypt, Lebanon, and Jordan, he announced on June 24, 1949, that Israel and Syria had accepted his compromise proposals. Representatives signed an armistice near Mishmar Ha Yarden, Israel, on July 20. Bunche later said that his success was partially attributable to a "coolness of temper and attitude of objectivity when dealing with human sensitivities and irrationalities." When informed that he had won the Nobel Peace Prize, he at first wanted to decline the honor, saying he should not be given an award for doing a job for which he had been paid, but U.N. officials insisted that the award would help to publicize the organization's contributions to peace. Bunche devoted his Nobel address to the importance of U.N. efforts to preserve world peace. He was the first person of African ancestry to receive the prestigious award.

---

of African Americans during the New Deal era, remain valuable works of scholarship.

—*Thomas Tandy Lewis*

RALPH ELLISON'S *INVISIBLE MAN* IS PUBLISHED
1952

Best known for his novel Invisible Man, *which is frequently hailed as a masterpiece of world literature, Ellison also became known for his opposition to black nationalism and radicalism and for connecting African American culture to the larger Western culture.*

Born: March 1, 1914; Oklahoma City, Oklahoma
Died: April 16, 1994; New York, New York
Also known as: Ralph Waldo Ellison
Area of achievement: Literature

EARLY LIFE

Ralph Waldo Ellison was born in Oklahoma City in 1914. His father, Lewis, the son of a former slave in South Carolina, died when Ralph was three, leaving him to be raised in poverty by his mother, Ida. Named for the nineteenth century writer Ralph Waldo Emerson, Ellison was interested in the arts from an early age. At first, his focus was on music. He played the trumpet and thought of becoming a composer. Attending the Tuskegee Institute in Alabama beginning in 1933, he initially specialized in music and played in the school band, Only later did he become interested in literature. He also developed interests in sculpture, drawing, and photography.

After leaving Tuskegee in 1936 without earning a degree, Ellison traveled to New York City, where he met the noted African American writers Langston Hughes and Richard Wright, both of whom encouraged his writing and also influenced him to become active in left-wing politics. He became associated with the Communist Party and wrote reviews and essays for its journal, *New Masses*. He also tried his hand at fiction and published his first story, an excerpt from a never-completed novel, in 1939.

During World War II, Ellison wrote several short stories and essays, served in the Merchant Marines, and drifted away from the Communist Party. In 1945, while vacationing in New England, he first got the idea for what became his masterpiece, *Invisible Man*. In 1946, having divorced his first wife, Rose Poindexter, he married Fanny McConnell Buford, who helped support him until his eventual literary success gave him a secure income.

LIFE'S WORK

Even before beginning work on *Invisible Man*, Ellison had received offers to publish a novel. His stories and essays had won him praise, and he began to carve out a niche for himself on matters related to the situation of African Americans. From the time he dissociated himself from the Communist Party until the end of his life, Ellison promoted the view that despite the oppression they had suffered, African Americans were not mere victims. Moreover, he said African American writers should not restrict themselves to writing protest literature full of anger and should certainly not separate themselves from the larger American culture, but should integrate into it, draw on it and the larger European heritage, and celebrate the African American contribution to it in all its forms, including jazz, blues, and folklore.

Ellison's approach earned him some criticism from African Americans, especially during the Black Power era of the 1960's and 1970's, but he held to his views, avoided overt political commentary, and insisted that he was a writer first and an African American second. When *Invisible Man* appeared in 1952, after the publication of some excerpts in magazines as early as 1947, he found himself much in demand, especially in white literary circles, as someone who could comment on race relations, though he preferred discussing literature.

In 1953, *Invisible Man* won the prestigious National Book Award, and over the succeeding years it was frequently hailed as a masterpiece and as the most

Invisible Man

On one level, *Invisible Man* (1952) is the story of the coming of age of its nameless black protagonist, who now lives underground, hibernating, while waiting to emerge and enter the next phase of his life. After presenting a jazz-influenced introduction to his current situation, the Invisible Man (who is invisible only metaphorically) produces an extended flashback to explain how he got to that point. He leads the reader through a sometimes nightmarish but simultaneously exuberant account of a bloody battle with fellow African Americans, a riot in Harlem, involvement in "the Brotherhood" (which echoes the Communist Party), expulsion from college, betrayal by his respected college principal, a visit in the company of a white trustee of his college to an incestuous black family and a bar full of crazed war veterans, and electric shock treatment in a factory hospital after an explosion in the factory.

There is also a black nationalist leader named Ras the Destroyer, who dresses like an Abyssinian chief and who throws a spear at the Invisible Man, who throws it back at him. There also is Rinehart, the man of multiple identities, and various women who throw themselves at the Invisible Man as part of their sexual fantasies. It is a wild phantasmagoria of a novel, mildly experimental in its style, which veers from realism into surrealism in a Modernist way influenced by James Joyce. The story addresses the oppression of African Americans but also examines the more general problems of the human condition, including issues of identity, alienation, learning to think for oneself, freeing oneself from others' plans, and finding one's path in life.

important novel in the postwar period. The acclaim led to speaking engagements at college campuses around the country, a European lecture tour, and a Prix de Rome fellowship, which Ellison held for two years, beginning in 1955, during which time he worked on a new novel.

The new novel occupied Ellison for the rest of his life, but although he published eight excerpts from it over two decades and wrote thousands of pages of manuscript, he never finished it. An edited version was published posthumously in 1999 under the title *Juneteenth*. Ellison did publish two nonfiction books in the decades after *Invisible Man*: the essay collections *Shadow and Act* (1964) and *Going to the Territory* (1986). In producing these essays, he established himself as a respected commentator on literature and culture and the role of African Americans.

In his later years, Ellison continued to accumulate honors, including several honorary degrees, and held teaching positions at various American colleges, including Bard, Yale, and New York University. He served on many governmental bodies and commissions, including the commission that led to the creation of public television, often as the only African American among white notables. He lived to see *Invisible Man* become an assigned text at universities, and after the conflicts of the 1960's it came to be seen as an inspiration to a new generation of African American writers and intellectuals.

Even after his death from pancreatic cancer in 1994, Ellison continued to attract attention. Several new collections of academic articles and two major biographies appeared over the next fifteen years, and the criticisms of him made by radicals and Black Nationalists in the 1960's came under scrutiny, with some commentators arguing that Ellison was more truly political and more reflective of the African American community than his critics had been.

SIGNIFICANCE

Ellison is known above all for his novel *Invisible Man*, an expression of the African American experience and a depiction of universal themes that has been hailed as an important work of world literature. He also is known for resisting black nationalism and for being an important representative of the view that African American culture made a complex and important contribution to American culture as a whole. His literary and cultural essays established him as a leading cultural critic on par with T. S. Eliot.

—*Sheldon Goldfarb*

TERRY V. ADAMS
May 4, 1953

In this case, the Supreme Court clearly declared the white primary unconstitutional.

The Case: U.S. Supreme Court ruling on white primaries

Beginning in 1889, the Jaybird Democratic Association in Texas started the practice of holding a primary election to select candidates for the Democratic Party in order to circumvent the Fifteenth Amendment. These candidates, often uncontested, usually were elected to office. Although white voters could participate in this process, black voters were excluded. The Supreme Court, by a vote of eight to one, declared the white primaries unconstitutional. Justice Hugo L. Black announced the decision for the 8–1 majority in this case, but there was no majority opinion. Instead, there were a series of opinions issued by various justices. Black emphasized that the government could not exclude African Americans from primaries, which were the only significant elections in most southern jurisdictions. Justice Felix Frankfurter criticized the complicity of southern election officials in excluding African Americans from the process. Justice Tom C. Clark focused on the fact that the white primary was an adjunct of the state-regulated Democratic Party. In general, eight justices believed that in some way, the white primary was a public institution in violation of the Fifteenth Amendment. Only Justice Sherman Minton dissented, finding that the white primary acted simply as an interest group.

—*Richard L. Wilson*

See also: Fifteenth Amendment; Gerrymandering; Voting Rights Act of 1965; White primaries

BROWN V. BOARD OF EDUCATION
May 17, 1954

The Supreme Court unanimously held that de jure (legally mandated) segregation of the public schools was prohibited by the equal protection clause of the Fourteenth Amendment.

The Case: *Landmark U.S. Supreme Court ruling on school desegregation*

Following the Civil War (1861–1865), racial segregation in public accommodations and education—through so-called "Jim Crow" laws—was one of the major tools of the southern states for maintaining a social system of white supremacy. In *Plessy v. Ferguson* (1896), the Supreme Court allowed state-mandated racial segregation based on the separate but equal doctrine. In *Cumming v. Richmond County Board of Education* (1899), the Court simply ignored the equal part of the doctrine when it allowed a community to maintain a public high school for white students without any similar institution for African Americans. In *Gong Lum v. Rice* (1927), the Court explicitly recognized the "right and power" of the states to require segregation in the public schools.

THE CHALLENGE BEGINS
In the 1930's the Legal Defense and Educational Fund of the National Association for the Advancement of Colored People (NAACP) began to mount a serious challenge to the constitutionality of Jim Crow laws in education. Rather than confronting *Plessy* directly, the NAACP first concentrated on equality of opportunity at publicly funded law schools. Decisions such as *Missouri ex rel. Gaines v. Canada* (1938) and *Sweatt v. Painter* (1950) indicated that the Court would insist on substantial equality of educational opportunity. In *McLaurin v. Oklahoma State Regents for Higher Education* (1950), the Court recognized that the policy of required separation was sometimes relevant to educational equality. With these victories, Thurgood Marshall and other NAACP lawyers decided that the time was ripe to question the constitutionality of segregation in elementary and secondary education.

Linda Carol Brown, an eight-year-old African American girl, was not allowed to attend the all-white school in her neighborhood of Topeka, Kansas. Her parents did not want her to be bused to the all-black school, which was far from home, and they filed a suit charging

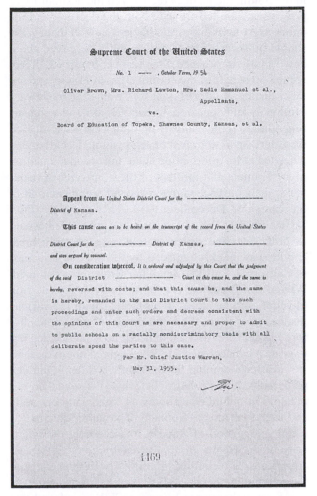

Judgment in the Supreme Court Decision for Brown et al. v. Board of Education of Topeka et al., *by The U.S. National Archives*

a violation of the Fourteenth Amendment. When the case was appealed to the Supreme Court, it was consolidated with similar cases from South Carolina, Virginia, Delaware, and Washington, D.C. The cases were listed in alphabetical order, so that the name *Brown v. Board of Education* appeared first. The cases were first argued in December, 1952. Marshall and other NAACP lawyers emphasized the psychological and sociological evidence of negative effects from mandated segregation. In defense of segregation, the school districts invoked *Plessy* and claimed that their all-black schools either had or would soon have equal funding for facilities and teachers' salaries.

THE COURT'S RESPONSE

Because of the great opposition to school integration in the South, the justices recognized the desirability of presenting a united front in both the decision and the opinion. At least six of the justices agreed that *Plessy* should be reversed, but they strongly disagreed about how rapidly to proceed. One justice, Stanley F. Reed, argued on behalf of the continuation of *Plessy*, and another justice, Robert H. Jackson, wanted to move very cautiously and appeared determined to write a concurring opinion if the majority opinion were too critical of the Court's past approval of segregation. Deciding that it needed more information about the original intention of the framers and ratifiers of the Fourteenth Amendment, the Court scheduled a second argumentation of the cases for December, 1953. That summer, Chief Justice Fred M. Vinson, a moderate who was hesitant to order massive desegregation, unexpectedly died, and he was quickly replaced by the popular governor of California, Earl Warren. After Brown was reargued, Warren convinced his colleagues to defer the question of relief, and he skillfully consulted with the various justices in order to get a consensus. About a week before the decision was announced, Jackson decided not to issue a concurrence and Reed agreed not to dissent.

Warren's opinion for the Court, written in thirteen paragraphs of nontechnical language, declared that segregation in public education was "inherently unequal" and therefore unconstitutional. The public interpreted racial segregation of students "as denoting the inferiority of the Negro group," generating among African Americans "a feeling of inferiority as to their status in the community that may affect their hearts and minds in a way unlikely ever to be undone." Warren found that the historical evidence about the original intent of the Fourteenth Amendment was "inconclusive." Even if the framers and ratifiers had not intended to prohibit segregation in education, they had wanted to provide equal rights for public services, and the experiences of the twentieth century demonstrated that segregated schools were incompatible with the goal of equality. Formal education in the twentieth century, moreover, was much more important for a person's life chances than it had been when the Fourteenth Amendment was written.

IMPLEMENTING DESEGREGATION

The following year, in a decision commonly called *Brown II,* the Court addressed the issue of implementing desegregation. The NAACP wanted to proceed rapidly with firm deadlines, and the states warned that rapid desegregation would lead to withdrawal from the public schools and acts of violence. The Court settled on a cautious and ambiguous formula, requiring that segregation end "with all deliberate speed." The implementation of *Brown II*, which left much discretion to federal district judges, proceeded somewhat slowly for the first ten years. In *Alexander v. Holmes County* (1969), the Court abandoned the deliberate speed formula and ordered an immediate end to all remaining de jure segregation.

Brown is probably the most momentous and influential civil rights case of the twentieth century. In effect, the decision meant the eventual elimination of all state-sanctioned segregation. When *Brown* was announced, its implications were unclear in regard to the constitutionality of freedom of choice plans and de facto segregated schools based on housing patterns. The Court began to move beyond the issue of de jure segregation in *Green v. County School Board of New Kent County* (1968), ruling that previously segregated school districts had an "affirmative duty" to take the steps necessary to promote racially integrated schools.

—*Thomas Tandy Lewis*

See also: *Bolling v. Sharpe*; Civil Rights movement and children; *Cooper v. Aaron; Cumming v. Richmond County Board of Education*; Education; Fourteenth Amendment; Little Rock school desegregation crisis; *McLaurin v. Oklahoma State Regents for Higher Education*; *Milliken v. Bradley*; National Association for the Advancement of Colored People; *Plessy v. Ferguson*; School desegregation; Separate but equal doctrine; Southern Manifesto; *Swann v. Charlotte-Mecklenberg Board of Education*; *Sweatt v. Painter*; White Citizens' Councils

KENNETH CLARK'S DOLL STUDY CITED BY SUPREME COURT IN *BROWN V. BOARD OF EDUCATION*

1954

Clark was one of the most influential social scientists of the twentieth century. He is best known for his contribution to the historic Brown v. Board of Education *decision, which declared separate-but-equal education unconstitutional. His scholarship on the social construct of race made him a prominent voice during a time of transition and turmoil in the United States.*

Born: July 24, 1914; Panama Canal Zone
Died: May 1, 2005; Hastings-on-Hudson, New York
Also known as: Kenneth Bancroft Clark
Areas of achievement: Law; Social sciences

EARLY LIFE

Kenneth Bancroft Clark was born in 1914 in the Panama Canal Zone to Miriam Clark, a native of Jamaica, and Arthur Bancroft Clark, a native of the West Indies. Arthur was employed as a superintendent of cargo for the United Fruit Company. The family lived a comfortable life in Panama, but Miriam was sure the United States would provide Clark and his sister, Beulah, with better educational and professional opportunities. Arthur was wary of migrating to the United States because of the volatile racial climate; he feared his race would be an impediment to employment, which would prevent him from supporting his family. Miriam was undeterred, so she moved with the children to New York in 1918, when Clark was about four years old.

Clark began his formal education in the Harlem public school system. Later, he was accepted to Howard University in Washington, D.C., where he studied political science under Professor Ralph Bunche; he completed his undergraduate degree in 1935 and graduate degree in 1936. While a student at Howard, Clark met a psychology student named Mamie Phipps, whom he later married.

The couple later jointly created and implemented innovative studies and scholarship on the pathology of racism and the effects of racism on the identity and self-worth of African American students. Clark continued his education at Columbia University; as a student there, he worked as research associate for Gunnar Myrdal. He earned a Ph.D. in psychology in 1940 from Columbia University, becoming the first African American to accomplish this goal.

LIFE'S WORK

Clark was committed to solving problems arising from the social construction of race. Therefore, much of his life's work stemmed from observations of how race affected the identity and educational experiences of African Americans. He is best known for his groundbreaking doll study, which found that segregation had dire effects on African American children's self-esteem. The study was cited by the U.S. Supreme Court in the historic 1954 *Brown v. Board of Education* decision, which declared segregated schools unconstitutional. A vocal supporter of school integration, Clark was called to testify in at least three cases that led to *Brown*. His work on the psychological impact race had on students was highly regarded and positioned Clark as one of the most influential social scientists of his generation.

Clark taught at Hampton Institute from 1940 to 1941 and City College of the City University of New

Dr. Kenneth B. Clark by Chicago Urban League

York from 1941 to 1975. Clark cofounded the North Side Center for Research and Child Development in 1946; was a member of a commission created to investigate issues of integration for New York City's Board of Education from 1954 to 1958; served as president of the Society for Psychological Studies on Social Issues from 1959 to 1960; created Harlem Youth Opportunities Unlimited in 1962; and was the first African American president of the American Psychological Association from 1970 to, Clark also wrote books such as *Desegregation: An Appraisal of the Evidence* (1953), *Prejudice and Your Child* (1955), *Dark Ghetto (*1965), *Pathos of Power* (1974), and *King, Malcolm, Baldwin: Three Interviews* (1985).

When Clark retired from college instruction in 1975, he was a distinguished professor of psychology emeritus of the City University of New York. Soon after, he, his wife, and their two children (Kate Miriam and Hilton Bancroft) founded a consulting firm called Clark, Phipps, Clark, and Harris, which designed professional training programs to address inequities faced

by people of color in the corporate environment. Even though Clark began his career as a staunch integrationist and did not succumb to the deluge of separatist ideologies popular during the 1960's and 1970's, in the early 1980's he reluctantly admitted the educational outlook was extremely poor for children of color; he also began to doubt the possibility of racial harmony through integration. Clark died May 1, 2005, in Hastings-on-Hudson, New York.

SIGNIFICANCE

Clark's examinations of the effects of segregation on self-esteem helped provide the basis for the Supreme Court's decision in the landmark *Brown v. Board of Education* case. He was a longtime advocate of integration and equality in education who played an active role in increasing opportunities for African American children.

—*Kidogo A. Kennedy*

BOLLING V. SHARPE

May 17, 1954

This case had major theoretical implications, for it indicated that the Supreme Court continued to interpret the due process clauses as protecting substantive rights as well as procedures.

The Case: U.S. Supreme Court ruling on school desegregation

In *Bolling v. Sharpe*, a companion case to *Brown v. Board of Education*, the issue of segregated public schools in the nation's capital, a matter of congressional jurisdiction, was treated in an opinion separate from *Brown* because the Fourteenth Amendment did not apply to the federal government and because the applicable Fifth Amendment did not include an equal protection clause. From the perspective of practical politics, it would have been highly embarrassing for the Court to allow segregated schools in Washington, D.C., while ruling them unconstitutional in the rest of the country.

Speaking for a unanimous Supreme Court, Chief Justice Earl Warren first noted that the petitioners were

African American minors who had been refused admission to a public school "solely because of their race." He then declared that the Court had long recognized that certain forms of governmental discrimination violated the constitutional mandate for due process of law. For precedents, he looked to an 1896 dictum by Joseph M. Harlan and to *Buchanan v. Warley*, a 1917 decision that had defended the equal right of citizens to own property based on a substantive due process reading of the Fourteenth Amendment. Also, Warren referred to obiter dicta in the Japanese American cases that acknowledged that racial classifications were inherently suspect, requiring that they be "scrutinized with particular care."

Warren gave an expansive interpretation of the "liberty" protected by the Fifth Amendment, explaining that it extended to the "full range of conduct which the individual is free to pursue."

The government could restrict liberty only when justified by a "proper governmental objective," and racial segregation in education was not related to such an objective. Thus, theWashington, D.C., schools were imposing an "arbitrary deprivation" on the liberty of black children. In addition, Warren noted that it was "unthinkable" that the federal government might practice the kind of discrimination prohibited in the states.

Bolling v. Sharpe had major theoretical implications, for the case indicated that the Supreme Court continued to interpret the due process clauses as protecting substantive rights as well as procedures, although the substantive focus had shifted from property interests to liberty interests. Also, the decision affirmed that the ideas of liberty and equality are often overlapping and that constitutional due process of law prohibits government from practicing invidious discrimination.

—*Thomas Tandy Lewis*

See also: *Brown v. Board of Education*; *Buchanan v. Warley*; Little Rock school desegregation crisis; School desegregation; Segregation

WHITE CITIZENS' COUNCILS

Summer of 1954

The highly popular White Citizens' Councils led the fight to prevent integration throughout the South during the mid-1950's.

Identification: Prosegregation bodies that arose in the American South following the U.S. Supreme Court's 1954 decree that public schools must be racially integrated

On May 17, 1954, the U.S. Supreme Court ruled in *Brown v. Board of Education* that racial segregation of public schools was unconstitutional. This decision held special significance in the South, where African American students traditionally attended separate, poorly funded schools. Many southern communities were outraged at this threat to what they regarded as white privilege. In response, white citizens quickly organized to impede attempts at integration. The White Citizens' Councils became a prominent force in this resistance movement.

The inspiration for organized white resistance came from a strident speech delivered by Tom Brady, a Mississippi circuit court judge, shortly after the Supreme Court's decision. Later expanded into a ninety-page tract titled *Black Monday*, Brady's speech was distributed widely and served as a rallying cry for concerned white citizens. Robert B. Patterson, a plantation manager, responded by organizing influential citizens of Indianola, Mississippi, into the first chapter of the White Citizens' Council. Other chapters quickly sprung up, predominantly in communities that possessed small white populations and where civil rights organizations were active.

The councils' memberships largely consisted of middle-class whites who possessed influence in their communities, such as business owners, lawyers, judges, bankers, politicians, and doctors. The councils were viewed as the "respectable" alternative to violent segregationist groups such as the Ku Klux Klan. Determined to present their members as responsible, upstanding citizens, they publicly encouraged legal acts of resistance. Often they used propaganda to educate the public. The propaganda typically attempted to unify white communities into fighting integration by linking it to communism, depicting African Americans as inferior, and disparaging leading civil rights organizations. Nevertheless, some councils used more disturbing and underhanded means of achieving their ends. For example, in his book *The Fiery Cross* (1987), Wyn Wade reported that a council in Mississippi retaliated against a group of African Americans who supported integration by prominently publishing their names and addresses in a local newspaper. As a result, some of the African Americans lost their jobs; others were intimidated into moving from the town.

By 1956, membership in the councils reached a peak of between 250,000 and 300,000 southerners. At this time, a sufficient number of council chapters had been established to prompt the creation of a national organization called the Citizens' Councils of America.

Despite the grassroots attempts of middle-class southerners to defend their racist traditions, their efforts ultimately failed. By the early 1960's, the influence of the White Citizens' Councils had dwindled in the face of the gains made by the Civil Rights movement and by the rising popularity of the Ku Klux Klan. Nonetheless, the councils did demonstrate that appeals to racial division could resonate powerfully in the political arena. Thus, they served as forerunners to later neo-Confederate organizations such as the Council of Conservative Citizens.

—*Beth A. Messner*

See also: *Brown v. Board of Education*; Civil Rights movement; Ku Klux Klan; Little Rock school desegregation crisis; Montgomery bus boycott; School desegregation; Southern Manifesto

FIRST NEWPORT JAZZ FESTIVAL IS HELD

July 17-18, 1954

The 1954 Newport Jazz Festival symbolized jazz's popular and commercial revival and marked another stage in its curious and exciting evolution.

Locale: Newport, Rhode Island
Category: Music

KEY FIGURES

Charlie Christian (1916-1942), pioneering American jazz guitarist

Lester Young (1909-1959), American saxophonist

Roy Eldridge (1911-1989), American trumpeter and bass player

Jimmy Blanton (1918-1942), American bass player

Charlie Parker (1920-1955), American alto saxophonist, composer, and bandleader

Dizzy Gillespie (1917-1993), American trumpeter, composer, and bandleader

Lennie Tristano (1919-1978), blind American pianist

Gerry Mulligan (1927-1996), American saxophonist

Oscar Peterson (b. 1925), American pianist and leader of a jazz trio

Miles Davis (1926-1991), American trumpeter, composer, and bandleader

SUMMARY OF EVENT

The fortunes and visibility of jazz's varied styles and players, and public acceptance of them, have swung almost cyclically since the 1890's. Jazz began in parochial obscurity as an apparent musical and cultural eccentricity endemic to groups of musicians in New Orleans, St. Louis, Memphis, Kansas City, Oklahoma City, San Francisco, and New York City from the 1880's through the early 1900's. It emerged into national prominence as ragtime, blues, and Dixieland music, and the various styles had become widely known as "jazz" by 1917. While purists and some music historians exclude all such styles but Dixieland from classification as early jazz, performers in each instance knew that it was still jazz that they were singing or playing.

Intended as a "four-letter" word, always intentionally shocking to the non-jazz musical world, jazz derived from and thrived upon dispute and divisions among its own devotees as well as upon a measure of social disrepute. Consequently, its varied temporal currents—including ragtime, Dixieland, blues, Chicago jazz, swing, boogie-woogie, Kansas City jazz, bop, hard bop, and cool jazz—have enjoyed their greatest popularity when the general public has undergone significant social and generational changes (among them altered racial attitudes), when dominant musical styles become stale, or when public taste overtakes the products of jazz musicians' ingenuity. Jazz historians and musicians can therefore conveniently trace the evolution of jazz by charting its preeminent styles—with a due reckoning of subtle, long-term developments—almost decade by decade.

The late 1940's and 1950's were marked by the partial consummation of a jazz revolution, notable for its stylistic diversity but more particularly for the early dominance of the styles of bop and cool jazz—as well as for the novel commercial attraction of large audiences through live and recorded performances. Such was the broad context into which the Newport Jazz Festival of July, 1954, fit. Sponsored by the Newport Chamber of Commerce, by town residents such as Louis and Elaine Lorillard, and by Boston impresario George Wein, the festival was an outgrowth of the tremendous successes of Norman Granz. A serious jazz fan, Granz had in the 1940's and early 1950's introduced the jazz concert, often in conjunction with philharmonic orchestras, to various parts of the country. His self-described motives were to improve race relations—contractually, all audiences had to be unsegregated—to offer great jazz, and to turn a profit. He realized something of all three objectives, in the process becoming a multimillionaire.

When musicians and performers gathered on the Newport Casino's tennis courts on the evening of July 17, 1954, jazz was in the midst of another of its transitions, in this instance away from its roots and toward bop music (a rapid, complex style of jazz variously known as "bebop" and "rebop") and its many distinctive substyles. Bop, of course, had not sprung full-blown from jazz musicians' instruments; it had sunk roots of its own decades earlier in the unique or experimental playing of Charlie Christian, Lester Young, Jimmy Blanton, Roy Eldridge, and Bix Beiderbecke. These experiences were passed to or absorbed by Lennie Tristano, Miles Davis, Lee Konitz, Gil Evans, Dizzy Gillespie, and, among still others, Stan Getz, Gerry Mulligan, Charlie Mingus, and Thelonious Monk.

The playing of all these men departed rhythmically from the solid beat of hot jazz and swing; harmonically, chords were more ambitious, forming new progressions away from familiar sequences; and, accordingly, melody often was shifted away from singable or even recognizable tunes, and the focus was typically on a series of short-duration notes. Such jazz was more complex and required more abstract comprehension from its listeners than did earlier styles; indeed, the new approach alienated many audiences, just as its counterparts in fine arts, classical music, and architecture had done as those disciplines, too, were revolutionized during the first half of the twentieth century.

At Newport's inaugural jazz festival, the billing made a propitiatory bow toward various styles of jazz. Stan Kenton, the former leader of the first great West Coast jazz band, acted as master of ceremonies and recited a history of jazz. Trumpeter Bobby Hackett, bandleader Eddie Condon, clarinetist Pee Wee Russell, and the magnificent—and versatile—singer Ella Fitzgerald were on hand to symbolize the fading "swing" era. However, it was the modern—particularly the "cool"—jazz musicians who dominated the two evenings of performances.

The already popular Modern Jazz Quartet, which had sprung from Dizzy Gillespie's orchestra in 1952, with vibraharpist Milt Jackson, pianist John Lewis, drummer Connie Kay, and bassist Percy Heath, performed to acclaim. So too did famed Canadian pianist Oscar Peterson, Chicago saxophonist Lee Konitz (who had worked with Claude Thornhill's and Kenton's bands as well as with Miles Davis and Lennie Tristano), and Gerry Mulligan, a baritone saxophonist, composer, and arranger of cool West Coast jazz. Nearly fourteen thousand people attended the festival, and the profits reportedly exceeded twenty-five thousand dollars—a measure of acceptance adequate to drive forward plans for further festivals.

In addition to Norman Granz's managerial abilities, several other factors accounted for the first festival's success.

Certainly, a wartime ban on recordings and audience boredom with reiterations of swing-band music from the 1930's and the World War II years created an immense demand for novel musical styles. The new forms of jazz grew enormously in popularity; nightclubs featuring jazz proliferated. Newspapers and magazines began treating jazz seriously, hiring specialists to review its evolution. Bookstores offered comprehensive encyclopedias and specialized studies on jazz and its personalities.

In addition, a number of radio stations—notably FM stations—accorded jazz an accepted place alongside mainstream music, while recording companies produced spates of jazz records. These developments were paralleled by the emergence of a new generation of highly trained jazz musicians who were eager in their own right to experiment freely and break with old routines. At least equally important, as concerts and the Newport festival confirmed, jazz at last appealed to a mass paying audience.

SIGNIFICANCE

Despite popular impressions to the contrary in the United States, the Newport Festivals were not the first jazz shows of their kind, even in America. Trying to make jazz respectable, for example, bandleader Paul Whiteman had attempted something similar in New York City's Aeolian Hall in 1924 with his introduction of George Gershwin's *Rhapsody in Blue*; and overseas, as jazz became a special American export, jazz shows were familiar events. There had been festival-like shows in Australia in 1946, in Nice, France, in 1948 (a show that had featured Louis Armstrong, Earl Hines, Baby Dodds, Pops Foster, Barney Bigard, and Jack Teagarden, among others), and in Paris—a show featuring Miles Davis, Sidney Bechet, and Charlie Parker—in 1949. Relative to the Newport festivals and other later shows, however, these were modest affairs.

In this regard, there is no question that the context in which the first Newport festival occurred was a unique one. Indeed, it was amid a veritable popular jazz revival, evidenced by newspaper, magazine, book, and radio coverage and promotion, that Newport sponsors organized their initial presentation. The success of the first festival encouraged more. In 1955, a three-day event held in a Newport football stadium that accommodated fifteen thousand people reported profits in excess of fifty thousand dollars. By 1956, when saxophonist Paul Gonsalves, under the direction of the enduring and remarkable Duke Ellington, performed successive choruses of "Diminuendo and Crescendo in Blue," the crowd danced in the aisles—and profits rose above the previous year's.

The 1957 festival, not surprisingly, thus became a four-day affair, and for added interest even featured nonjazz performances by the New York City Ballet and popular singer and dancer Eartha Kitt. Again, profits soared. Regardless of the performers—the 1958 and 1959 festivals, for instance, included international jazz talents as well as the Stockholm Opera Company—the commercial success continued, not only at Newport, but also elsewhere in the United States and Canada, where appetites of audiences and promoters alike had been whetted. Nationally, by the end of the 1950's, nine festivals were reported having grossed nearly one million dollars.

Profits notwithstanding, by 1960, disillusionment with Newport's festivals—and with some imitative gatherings elsewhere—became increasingly apparent, chiefly for two reasons. First, as festival promoters catered to larger audiences, they drew in constituencies of people to whom the event itself was more important than the music presented. Rowdyism broke out in 1959, and alcohol-fueled riots disrupted the third night of a five-day festival in 1960. Newport's city council, previously lax in its enforcement of liquor laws, closed the festival, causing its organizers losses of more than $100,000. Reopened under stricter law enforcement, the festival still encountered the same difficulties, largely because of the fans drawn to the event. Riots occurred again in 1961, 1969, and 1970, with the result that operations were transferred to New York City in 1972. Newport's experience through the decade had a dampening effect on festivals and concerts elsewhere.

Mass-audience jazz events at New York City's Randall's Island, at the Hollywood Bowl in Los Angeles, and at Quaker City, Philadelphia, all thereafter caused significant financial losses for their sponsors. Meanwhile, smaller jazz concerts that attracted fewer but more devoted fans to such places as Monterey, California, and Long Island continued to prosper. Yet the steam had gone out of Newport-style festivals by the close of the 1960's.

There was further disillusionment with large festivals among jazz musicians themselves. Many, like Miles Davis, found "jazz supermarkets" offensive. Others complained, as did Oscar Peterson, about redundant programming and about the modest—often exceedingly brief—playing time allotted to even headline performers. Moreover, despite accrued experience with festivals, organizers often did little to improve basic facilities such as sound, lighting, staging, and timing. Similarly, Newport and other "festivals" scarcely lived up to their names as such, concentrating instead almost exclusively on jazz numbers and not upon other jazz-related festivities.

There were exceptions; though the music was roundly criticized, the President's Music Committee's so-called International Jazz Festival of 1962 did sponsor an event in Washington, D.C., that was notable for the scope of its jazz entertainments, which ranged from films to ballet. In other areas, however, the impetus lent to jazz by Newport and by comparable festivals continued. Hundreds of thousands of people had listened to live jazz concerts, and nearly eighty million dollars in jazz recordings had been sold by the end of the 1960's. Moreover, jazz poetry had gained a foothold on the West Coast and in New York, and jazz playing was welcomed into the services and other activities of many churches eager to take advantage of the revival. Jazz musicians, who were often more comfortable playing for themselves, for one another, or for small but devoted audiences, remained divided between traditionalists—who played "hot" music—and those whose training and interpretations of tradition kept them experimenting with cooler, freer, and more esoteric forms.

—*Clifton K. Yearley*

See also: Parker's Playing Epitomizes Bebop; Davis Develops 1950's Cool Jazz; Brown Introduces Funk Music

POITIER EMERGES AS A FILM STAR IN *THE BLACKBOARD JUNGLE*

March 19, 1955

In The Blackboard Jungle *and succeeding films, Sidney Poitier became a true Hollywood leading man, helping redefine the on-screen image of African Americans and paving the way for generations of later actors.*

Locale: United States
Categories: Motion pictures and video; social issues and reform

KEY FIGURES

Sidney Poitier (b. 1924), African American actor
Richard Brooks (1912-1992), American director
Glenn Ford (b. 1916), American actor

SUMMARY OF EVENT

As late as 1954, success as an actor still eluded the young Sidney Poitier, who had to take nonacting jobs to make ends meet. True, he had come far, considering his lack of formal education. Born in the United States in 1924, he had spent his childhood in the Bahamas before returning to the United States as a teenager. Starting out in New York City as a dishwasher, he had begun taking acting lessons after answering an advertisement by the American Negro Theatre in a Harlem newspaper; with great effort, he had eliminated his West Indian accent. Stage roles were followed by an appearance in an Army Signal Corps film, *From Whence Cometh My Help* (1949).

In 1949, Poitier, despite his meager film experience, was chosen by director Joseph L. Mankiewicz to appear in *No Way Out* (1950). In the film, Dr. Luther Brooks (Poitier), an African American intern in a Northern city hospital, is accused by white racist Ray Biddle (Richard Widmark) of murder after Biddle's brother dies while under Brooks's care. A race riot erupts and, ultimately, Brooks is cleared of all wrongdoing; when Biddle is injured, Brooks cares for him. Though *No Way Out* was a break for Poitier, the film was a financial failure.

Poitier's next film, *Cry the Beloved Country* (1952), explored South Africa's racial problems at the family level and was a critical but not a box-office success. Between 1951 and 1954, Poitier played in only two other films: *Red Ball Express* (1952), a story about African American U.S. Army soldiers in World War II; and *Go, Man, Go!* (1954), about the Harlem Globetrotters basketball team. Neither film reaped the critical and popular acclaim Poitier sought.

In 1954, Poitier was offered a role in a film about a young teacher's ordeal in a New York City high school. The director, Richard Brooks, a nonconformist by nature, wanted Poitier despite Poitier's rumored association with left-wing entertainers, a disadvantage in the anticommunist climate of the times. Glenn Ford played Richard Dadier, who teaches rebellious older teenagers too young to join the Army or get full-time jobs. Playing Gregory Miller, an intelligent but troubled youngster, Poitier, the only African American member of the cast, skillfully makes viewers feel Miller's alienation and anger. As in later films, he projects passion without seeming menacing. Although Miller at first joins the other pupils in harassing Dadier, he is ultimately won over by Dadier's arguments and example; when the school bully attacks Dadier with a knife, Miller steps in to defend Dadier.

The scenes of student violence in *The Blackboard Jungle* shocked audiences when the film was released on March 19, 1955. In the relatively prosperous and tranquil 1950's, many film viewers could not believe that such chaotic schools actually existed. The film's vision of bigcity schools, educators insisted, was exaggerated. The American ambassador to Italy pressured judges into dropping the film from the Venice Film Festival. Censors in the South objected not merely to the film's depiction of violence but also to the racial integration of Dadier's classroom.

The Blackboard Jungle was a hit, not only because of Poitier's fine acting but also because it was released when juvenile delinquency was attracting nationwide attention. The confused and angry teenager was appearing in other films of the day, most notably the 1955 James Dean classic *Rebel Without a Cause*. Poitier played a character with whom millions of young Americans, black and white, could identify. The pulsating rhythms of Bill Haley and His Comets' version of "Rock Around the Clock," included as background music, made the film unforgettable.

The furor over *The Blackboard Jungle* made agents and directors aware of Poitier. An aggressive new agent found Poitier a role in the television play *A Man Is Ten Feet Tall*. In this play, and in the film version, *Edge of the City* (1957), a black dockworker dies defending a white coworker against a bullying white foreman. In *The Defiant Ones*, a big hit of 1958, Poitier played one of two escaped convicts—one black, the other (played

391

by Tony Curtis) white—who come to depend on each other during their flight from the law. At the film's end, the black prisoner forgoes a chance to avoid recapture when his white partner cannot join him. After 1958, Poitier played in at least one film a year for an entire decade.

Later films included *A Raisin in the Sun* (1961), about a struggling Chicago African American family; the Oscar-winning movie *Lilies of the Field* (1963), in which a wandering African American handyman helps German nuns in the Southwest to build a chapel; and *A Patch of Blue* (1965), in which an African American journalist befriends a poor, blind white girl. In 1967, Poitier was in three hits. *In the Heat of the Night* showed a bigoted Southern white sheriff coming to respect the Northern African American detective who helps him to crack a murder case; in *Guess Who's Coming to Dinner*, a wealthy white newspaper publisher is shocked to learn that his daughter plans to marry an African American man but eventually approves the match; and in *To Sir, with Love*, an African American London schoolteacher wins his white pupils' respect. From 1968 on, Poitier's near-monopoly was broken, as more African American actors (some playing in violence-filled "blaxploitation" films) made their way in films. As these actors learned how to become leading men, they continued to look to Poitier as an exemplar both on and off the screen.

SIGNIFICANCE

As late as the 1930's, most Hollywood films portrayed African Americans as buffoons, servants, athletes, dancers, or musicians. World War II made white filmmakers more sensitive to racial injustice; some began to produce films treating racial issues more openly and giving African Americans a more dignified screen image. Stanley Kramer, who brought out *Home of the Brave* (1949), about a troubled African American war veteran, directed Poitier in the racial "message" movies *The Defiant Ones, Pressure Point* (1962), and *Guess Who's Coming to Dinner.*

From the appearance of *The Blackboard Jungle* in 1955 onward, Poitier benefited from this trend toward fairer treatment of African Americans on the screen; he also did much himself to promote the trend. In only one post-1955 film, a 1959 remake of *Porgy and Bess*, did Poitier play an obviously stereotypical role. In most films, Poitier's screen persona was that of a competent, likable man who channels whatever racial resentments he has into productive activity, helping whites who are

either no smarter than he is or are his intellectual or moral inferiors. In *No Way Out*, the African American intern played by Poitier is almost saintly; his white accuser (and later patient) is a small-time crook. Although the racial issue is muted in *Lilies of the Field*, its hero's efficiency is a clear refutation of stereotypes of African American incompetence. In *In the Heat of the Night*, the intellectual superiority of Poitier's character to the redneck sheriff played by Rod Steiger is obvious. Even in *The Blackboard Jungle*, the troubled youth played by Poitier is intelligent and salvageable; the incorrigible school bully who attacks Dadier with a knife is played by white actor Vic Morrow.

In many films (although not in *The Blackboard Jungle*), Poitier presents an image of a well-trained, professional African American who is articulate in standard English; this was new for the time. In *No Way Out*, he plays a medical intern; in *All the Young Men* (1960), an officer commanding white troops in the Korean War; in the suspense drama *The Slender Thread* (1965), a suicide hotline worker; in *Pressure Point*, a prison psychiatrist who interrogates a Nazi; in *A Patch of Blue* and *The Bedford Incident* (1965), a journalist; and in *To Sir, with Love*, a teacher. Poitier's character in *Guess Who's Coming to Dinner*, a young white woman's fiancé, is a world-famous physician.

In two films, Poitier crossed a barrier by playing roles originally designed for whites. In *The Bedford Incident,* he is a journalist trapped in a submarine with a trigger-happy anti-Soviet zealot of a commander (Richard Widmark). In *Duel at Diablo* (1966), Poitier portrays a cowboy gunfighter.

One barrier was hard to break: that of portraying an African American man, on the screen, as both sexual and romantic. In *No Way Out*, Poitier's character is happily married; in his other films up to 1965, including *The Blackboard Jungle*, Poitier's characters have no love interest at all. In *A Patch of Blue*, Poitier's character ends a budding love interest by having the blind white girl sent away to a special school. In *Guess Who's Coming to Dinner*, viewers catch only a brief glimpse, through the rearview mirror of a taxicab, of a kiss exchanged between Poitier's character and his white fiancée; the couple leaves the country shortly after their marriage. The man upon whom Poitier's character in *To Sir, with Love* was based had had an interracial romance with a fellow teacher, but the romance was omitted from the film. A frank interracial love scene occurs in *The Lost Man* (1969), but that film failed. *For Love of Ivy* (1968) was the first film in which Poitier had a frankly sexual romance (with bedroom scene) with an African American woman.

As Poitier's star currency declined during the 1970's wave of "blaxploitation" films, he began to shift his attention to directing. He directed the comic Western *Buck and the Preacher* (1972), in which he also costarred, and a series of comedies with all-black casts—*Uptown Saturday Night* (1974), *Let's Do It Again* (1975), and *A Piece of the Action* (1977). These films, as well as the Richard Pryor/Gene Wilder buddy comedy *Stir Crazy* (1980), enabled Poitier to display a brand of slapstick humor that had not been evident in his more serious roles.

After abandoning acting for much of the 1980's, Poitier returned to the screen intermittently in his later years. He played a driven cop in *Shoot to Kill* (1988), National Association for the Advancement of Colored People (NAACP) attorney and future Supreme Court Justice Thurgood Marshall in *Separate but Equal* (1991), and South African president Nelson Mandela in *Mandela and de Klerk* (1997). Poitier married the actor Joanna Shimkus in 1976 and had two more daughters, Anika and Sydney. He has received numerous lifetime achievement awards, including an honorary Oscar in 2002 and the Presidential Medal of Freedom in 2009 from President Barack Obama. In 1997, he was appointed Bahamian ambassador to Japan.

SIGNIFICANCE

As one of the most important black actors in the history of American cinema, Poitier represents both the promise and the pitfalls of African American participation in Hollywood. At a time when African Americans were lobbying for civil rights, Poitier helped to usher in a new era of "positive" black screen portrayals that broke decisively from a racist Hollywood past in which African Americans had largely been caricatured as servants, buffoons, or carefree singers and dancers. However, Poitier's buttoned-up screen persona—righteously angry but often mild-mannered, sexually restrained, and always willing to work within the confines of an existing white social order—made him both a target of frustration and a symbol of the limits of white liberal goodwill. After his acting heyday, Poitier became a respected elder statesman whose principled life and dignified manner have enabled him to outlast many of the political and cultural fashions of the late 1960's and early 1970's. He came to be widely regarded as a racial pioneer and humanitarian whose

career helped to pave the way for such late twentieth and early twentyfirst century black film stars as Denzel Washington and Will Smith.

As Poitier's star currency declined during the 1970's wave of "blaxploitation" films, he began to shift his attention to directing. He directed the comic Western *Buck and the Preacher* (1972), in which he also costarred, and a series of comedies with all-black casts—*Uptown Saturday Night* (1974), *Let's Do It Again* (1975), and *A*

Blackboard Jungle and *To Sir, With Love*

Two Hollywood films that attempted to dramatize the social problem of high school juvenile delinquency, *Blackboard Jungle* (1955) and *To Sir, with Love* (1967), offer a revealing picture of the evolution of Sidney Poitier's screen persona as he shifted from supporting player to superstar. In *Blackboard Jungle*, set in an inner-city American high school, Poitier plays a small but pivotal role as Greg Miller, a classroom rebel who smokes cigarettes in the restroom and talks back to novice teacher Richard Dadier (Glenn Ford) with cool insouciance. Although Miller is ultimately redeemed by his teacher's sincere efforts to reach out to him, Poitier brings authenticity and a hint of danger to the part that transcends the film's somewhat stagey melodramatics. *Blackboard Jungle*, which memorably opens with Bill Haley and His Comets' "Rock Around the Clock," gave Poitier his biggest hit to that point in his career.

In contrast, *To Sir, with Love* finds Poitier playing a teacher instead of a student. As Mark Thackeray, an unemployed engineer from British Guyana who somewhat improbably inspires a class of unruly ne'er-do-wells at a high school in London's rough East End, Poitier is dignified, commanding, and buttoned up to a fault. As with so many of Poitier's films, the premise of *To Sir, with Love* straitjackets its star in the role of the "Noble Negro" whose primary purpose is to uplift the white characters around him. Although Poitier alternately gets to box, dance, and lose his temper, the film devotes more attention to capturing the era's Carnaby Street youth culture than to giving his character any meaningful backstory or personal motivation. Nonetheless, the film was the third-highest-grossing box-office attraction of 1967, and Poitier reprised his role as Thackeray for a made-for-TV sequel in 1996.

Piece of the Action (1977). These films, as well as the Richard Pryor/Gene Wilder buddy comedy *Stir Crazy* (1980), enabled Poitier to display a brand of slapstick humor that had not been evident in his more serious roles.

After abandoning acting for much of the 1980's, Poitier returned to the screen intermittently in his later years. He played a driven cop in *Shoot to Kill* (1988), National Association for the Advancement of Colored People (NAACP) attorney and future Supreme Court Justice Thurgood Marshall in *Separate but Equal* (1991), and South African president Nelson Mandela in *Mandela and de Klerk* (1997). Poitier married the actor Joanna Shimkus in 1976 and had two more daughters, Anika and Sydney. He has received numerous lifetime achievement awards, including an honorary Oscar in 2002 and the Presidential Medal of Freedom in 2009 from President Barack Obama. In 1997, he was appointed Bahamian ambassador to Japan.

SIGNIFICANCE

As one of the most important black actors in the history of American cinema, Poitier represents both the promise and the pitfalls of African American participation in Hollywood. At a time when African Americans were lobbying for civil rights, Poitier helped to usher in a new era of "positive" black screen portrayals that broke decisively from a racist Hollywood past in which African Americans had largely been caricatured as servants, buffoons, or carefree singers and dancers. However, Poitier's buttoned-up screen persona—righteously angry but often mild-mannered, sexually restrained, and always willing to work within the confines of an existing white social order—made him both a target of frustration and a symbol of the limits of white liberal goodwill. After his acting heyday, Poitier became a respected elder statesman whose principled life and dignified manner have enabled him to outlast many of the political and cultural fashions of the late 1960's and early 1970's. He came to be widely regarded as a racial pioneer and humanitarian whose career helped to pave the way for such late twentieth and early twenty-first century black film stars as Denzel Washington and Will Smith.

—*Andrew Sargent*

See also: *Stormy Weather* Offers New Film Roles to African Americans

BERRY'S "MAYBELLENE" POPULARIZES ROCK AND ROLL

Spring, 1955

Chuck Berry's song "Maybellene" unexpectedly rocketed to the top of the music charts and set the stage for the rock-and-roll era, demonstrating the potential mainstream popularity of what was then perceived as "racial" music.

Locale: Chicago, Illinois
Category: Music

KEY FIGURES

Chuck Berry (b. 1926), American singer, songwriter, and guitarist
Leonard Chess (1917-1969), Chicago-based independent record producer
Alan Freed (1922-1965), American pioneering rock-and-roll radio disc jockey
Bill Haley (1925-1981), American singer, guitarist, and bandleader

SUMMARY OF EVENT

"Maybellene" (1955) was Chuck Berry's first hit and arguably, despite Elvis Presley's considerable fame, the most important initial reference point in the history of rock and roll. Berry melded rhythm and blues and country-western music with his special brand of guitar playing to fashion witty, defiant songs that have influenced virtually every rock musician. In his best work—including "Sweet Little Sixteen," "Carol," "Brown Eyed Handsome Man," "Roll Over Beethoven," "Living in the USA," and "Little Queenie"—Berry successfully melded resonant teen concerns with a blues base and country rhythms to fashion the basis of rock and roll.

Berry grew up in legally segregated St. Louis, Missouri. His teen years were troubled, and he spent time in a reform school; as a young adult, he tried working as a beautician and on a General Motors assembly line. Making music, though, was his real love. By the early

1950's, he and pianist Johnny Johnson were leading a blues trio in clubs in and around St. Louis. In the process, Berry struggled to find a sound that appealed to both black and white audiences.

In this period, Berry melded a wide range of influences. Among guitarists, he favored the works of technical innovator Les Paul and jazz virtuoso Charlie Christian. Above all, though, T-Bone Walker's improvisational guitar stylings provided the source for Berry's highly danceable, insistent rhythms. Berry's vocal style owed much to Nat "King" Cole and Louis Jordan.

Berry's break came in the spring of 1955, when he traveled to Chicago to see his idol Muddy Waters perform. After the show, Berry asked Waters for help in becoming a professional musician. Recognizing the young man's talent, Waters promptly referred him to Leonard and Phil Chess, owners of Chicago's biggest blues label, the nationally distributed Chess Records. The Chess brothers were so impressed by Berry's vivacious, original sound that they insisted on recording him right away. Soon Chess Records released Berry's first hit, "Maybellene," which rocketed up both the R&B and pop charts. A string of other seminal recordings followed. By 1961, Berry had amassed ten more top-ten hits and had become one of the most popular and influential musicians in rock and roll.

Just when Berry was reaching the peak of his popularity, he ran into more legal trouble. Convicted in 1962 of taking an underage girl across state lines for immoral purposes under a 1910 federal statute known as the Mann Act, Berry spent the better part of 1962 and 1963 in prison in Springfield, Missouri. Because the incarceration was not widely publicized, Berry publicly denied it for several years. He later acknowledged the conviction in his autobiography, and he also claimed that while behind bars in Springfield he wrote several of his most memorable hits, including "Nadine" and "No Particular Place to Go." Once he was released from prison and had resumed recording and performing, Berry was both pleased and amused to find that many younger artists were recording successful covers of his songs. Several American acts released Berry compositions in the early 1960's, earning him enormous respect as a songwriter, not to mention lucrative royalties. During the British Invasion of 1964 through 1967, major English artists such as the Rolling Stones and the Beatles covered many of Berry's hits. Early Beatles albums included remakes of "Johnny B. Goode" and "Rock and Roll Music," while memorable Rolling Stones covers include "Oh, Carol" and "Come On." Berry continued to perform regularly throughout the 1960's, 1970's, and 1980's. He had several hit albums during this period and his last number-one single, "My Ding-a-Ling," appeared in 1972. In 1986, Berry was fittingly one of the first musicians inducted into the Rock and Roll Hall of Fame. The film *Hail! Hail! Rock 'n'Roll,* a documentary about his life and legacy, was released to wide acclaim in 1987.

SIGNIFICANCE

The unique shuffle rhythm and universally recognizable guitar hooks Berry brought to classic recordings like "Johnny B. Goode" and "Sweet Little Sixteen" have made them some of the best-known songs in rock and roll. Berry's innovative musicianship, lighthearted but incisive lyrics, and irresistible showmanship combine to make him one of the true giants not only of rock and roll but also of twentieth century popular culture.

One would be hard pressed to find a fan of modern music unfamiliar with his work. Although Berry's disdain for authority led him to run-ins with the law throughout his career, that same rebelliousness is what makes his music so reflective of the spirit of rock and roll.

Berry's distinctive musical style has in someway influenced the music of practically every rock performer to follow him. Echoes of his guitar style can be heard in the work of Eric Clapton, George Thorogood, Albert Lee, and scores of other guitarists. The carefree spirit evoked by his lyrics is present in the songs of artists as diverse as the Beach Boys, the Beatles, and even punk rockers like the Clash, the Sex Pistols, and Green Day. Few artists besides Elvis Presley, John Lennon, or Paul McCartney have had more influence on modern popular music than Berry. His ability to bring what had previously been considered "race music" to a mainstream white audience secures his place as one of the founding fathers of modern rock and rhythm and blues. Without Berry, rhythm and blues might never have been embraced by a mass audience.

One can forget how revolutionary Berry's approach was. In 1954, sanitized pop music was the rage. Patti Page was breaking "Young at Heart" on television's popular *The Colgate Comedy Hour.* Bing Crosby was a major star. It was only four years earlier that *Billboard* had dropped the term "race records" in favor of "rhythm and blues." Bill Haley's "Rock Around the Clock" was considered scandalous when it was introduced in the 1955 teen film *The Blackboard Jungle,* and Elvis Presley was still considered a country-western music star trying to sound like Dean Martin.

—Douglas Gomery

TILL LYNCHING

August 28, 1955

Emmett Till's widely publicized murder helped make Americans more aware of the depth of racism that still existed in the United States.

The Event: Murder of an African American youth who merely whistled at a white woman
Place: Money, Mississippi

An African American youth, Emmett Till was born in Chicago in 1941. Shortly after he turned fourteen, his mother sent him to visit relatives in the small town of Money, Mississippi. On the afternoon of August 24, 1955, Till and a group of other teenagers went to a grocery store to buy candy and soft drinks. Till reportedly whistled at Carolyn Bryant, the wife of Roy Bryant, the store's white owner.

Early in the morning of August 28, Roy Bryant and his brother, J.W. Milam, kidnapped Till from his great uncle's home. The men beat him and shot him in the head and dumped his body in the Tallahatchie River. Till's mutilated and badly decomposed body was found three days later by a fisherman. Bryant and Milam were tried for Till's kidnapping and murder. After deliberating for only one hour, the all-white jury acquitted them. Later, Milam sold his story to *Look* magazine; in the

article, he confessed to the killing. Neither Bryant nor Milam was ever convicted for Till's murder.

Till's remains were shipped to Chicago, where his mother insisted on an open-casket funeral. An estimated fifty thousand people came to see his body. Photographs of his corpse were also published in *Jet* magazine, and the murder was covered by magazines and newspapers all over the world. The murder case, and the subsequent lack of justice, is considered a major catalyst to the Civil Rights movement.

In May, 2004, the U.S. Justice Department announced that it was reopening its investigation into Till's murder. The two men tried for Till's murder decades earlier had been acquitted of all charges and had since died. However, evidence remained implicating other, still living, men in Till's lynching. The five-year federal statute of limitations had long since lapsed, but anyone charged with the murder could still be tried in a state court.

—Phyllis B. Gerstenfeld

See also: Civil Rights movement; Civil rights worker murders; Dyer antilynching bill; King assassination

CIVIL RIGHTS MOVEMENT

Mid-1950's to late 1960's

The modern Civil Rights movement broke down many racial barriers, forced legislative changes, and transformed American politics and society.

The Event: Mass movement led by African Americans during the mid-twentieth century

Although the modern Civil Rights movement began with the Montgomery bus boycott in 1955, the struggle for civil rights has been an ongoing battle. The founding of the National Association for the Advancement of Colored People (NAACP) in 1909 was one of the first attempts to organize in the pursuit of civil rights. With the exception of some legal victories under the leadership of the NAACP, there was little progress in the field of civil rights until the end of World War II.

VOTING RIGHTS AND A LEGACY OF DISCRIMINATION
With the end of Reconstruction after the Civil War, all the southern states developed devices to eliminate black voters. Each of the southern states adopted new state constitutions between 1890 and 1910 and employed devices such as the grandfather clause, the white primary, the poll tax, and the literacy test to strip African Americans of their right to vote. These devices were enormously successful. There were more than 130,000 black voters in Louisiana in 1896. By 1900, only two years after Louisiana adopted a new constitution containing many discriminating features, there were only 5,320 black voters left on the rolls.

For several reasons, African Americans made securing the right to vote their number-one objective. First, the U.S. Constitution, particularly the Fifteenth

Amendment, contains specific guarantees against voter discrimination. Second, African Americans believed there was less social stigma involved in granting the right to vote than in integration. Integration meant race mixing, which was feared by white southerners. Giving African Americans the right to vote did not mean that whites would have to intermingle with African Americans. Finally, African Americans believed that securing the right to vote would bring about other changes. Black voting would result in the election of black politicians, and it would force white politicians to moderate their racial views.

The grandfather clause was the first major barrier to fall. Grandfather clauses said that if a person had a relative who voted before the Civil War (before 1861), then the person was exempt from other voter qualifications. Because African Americans were not allowed to vote before the Civil War, they had to meet voter qualifications such as poll taxes and literacy tests. The U.S. Supreme Court unanimously struck down grandfather clauses in *Guinn v. United States* (1915).

The next major barrier to fall was the white primary election. As the term implies, only whites were permitted to vote in primaries. Since southern politics was dominated by the Democratic Party, whoever won the Democratic primary would win the general election. If African Americans could not participate in the primary selection process, then they had no real input into the selection of political candidates.

In 1923, the Texas legislature passed a law prohibiting African Americans from participating in that state's primary election. A unanimous U.S. Supreme Court struck down the Texas law in *Nixon v. Herndon* (1927). Immediately, the Texas legislature passed another law delegating authority to the executive committee of each party to determine who could participate in the primaries. As expected, they excluded African Americans from participation. In a 5–4 decision, the U.S. Supreme Court once again threw out Texas's white primary in *Nixon v. Condon* (1932). Undaunted, Texas made a third effort to ban African Americans from the primaries. In 1932, the state convention of the Texas Democratic Party, without any authorization from the state legislature, limited primaries to white voters. A unanimous U.S. Supreme Court, in *Grovey v. Townsend* (1935), upheld the action of the state convention, concluding that there was no state discrimination involved. Political parties were voluntary associations that had the right to determine their membership. It was not until *Smith v. Allwright* (1944), some twenty years after the

first Texas white primary law was passed, that the U.S. Supreme Court finally declared white primaries to be unconstitutional. The NAACP had brought most of the white primary cases, including the Smith case, to the U.S. Supreme Court.

The third major voting barrier to fall was the poll tax, which was the payment of a fee in order to vote. African Americans were less able to afford the tax, and poor whites could always find someone to pay or waive their tax. Opponents of the poll tax tried to get Congress to abolish the fee. Five times the House of Representatives passed legislation to ban poll taxes, but each time the legislation was filibustered by southern senators. In 1964, the Twenty-fourth Amendment, which eliminated poll taxes in federal elections, was approved. Two years later, in *Harper v. Virginia Board of Elections*, the U.S. Supreme Court abolished poll taxes in state and local elections.

The last barrier to fall was also the most significant barrier in keeping African Americans from voting: the literacy test. Most literacy tests required the voter to be able to read, write, and understand sections of the state or federal constitution. Although many African Americans could pass the reading and writing portion of the test, almost all failed the understanding portion, primarily because white voter registrars had the sole authority to determine if a person understood a section of the constitution.

Attempts to get the courts to ban literacy tests were unsuccessful. The U.S. Congress passed the Voting Rights Act of 1965, which prohibited literacy tests in areas that were covered by the law. In 1970, an amendment to the Voting Rights Act banned literacy tests in all fifty states, and another amendment in 1975 permanently banned literacy tests.

SCHOOL DESEGREGATION

Before the Civil War, most states prohibited African Americans from getting an education. After the Civil War, schools were established for black education, but on a segregated basis. In many areas, education for African Americans ended at the sixth grade. High schools, vocational schools, and colleges and universities were often unavailable for black students.

In 1890, the Louisiana legislature passed a Jim Crow law requiring "separate but equal" accommodations for white and black passengers on the railroads. The railroads backed a challenge to the law because of the additional expense they would encounter. Homer Plessy, one-eighth black, was selected to test the law; he sat in the whites-only coach and was arrested. In *Plessy v. Ferguson* (1896), in a 7–1 decision, the U.S. Supreme Court upheld the Louisiana law. The Court found no violation of the "equal protection clause" of the Fourteenth Amendment because whites were as separated from blacks as blacks were from whites. Although the *Plessy* decision had nothing to do with education, the doctrine of "separate but equal" was quickly adopted to justify segregated schools.

The NAACP led the legal attack against segregated schools. The first strategy of the organization was not to seek to overturn *Plessy* but, on the contrary, to seek enforcement of *Plessy*. African American schools were indeed "separate," but were they "equal"? Black schools received far fewer dollars per student to operate, and black teachers were paid a fraction of what white teachers received. Black schools had a limited curriculum, few textbooks, no transportation for students, and often the buildings were no more than one-room shacks. In a series of Supreme Court cases involving higher education in the South, the NAACP time and again demonstrated that black schools were not equal. In fact, in many of the cases, there were no law schools or professional schools available to African Americans. The Supreme Court consistently ordered the enrollment of black students where "separate but equal" was not being met.

CHALLENGING "SEPARATE BUT EQUAL"

By the late 1940's, the NAACP was ready to mount a direct challenge to *Plessy v. Ferguson*. Cases were brought in South Carolina, Delaware, Virginia, Kansas, and the District of Columbia. In 1954 the U.S. Supreme Court overturned *Plessy* and the "separate but equal" doctrine in *Brown v. Board of Education*. Chief Justice Earl Warren, speaking for a unanimous Court, wrote: "We conclude that in the field of public education the doctrine of 'separate but equal' has no place. Separate educational facilities are inherently unequal."

Many southern states invoked the doctrine of states' rights and argued that the federal government was usurping the power of states to control education. Massive resistance to the court's decision became the standard policy throughout the South. Some school districts closed their schools rather than integrate, while other communities exploded in violence. When a large, unruly mob prevented the integration of Little Rock Central High School in Little Rock, Arkansas, President Dwight D. Eisenhower was forced to send in federal troops to protect the nine black students.

Token integration was the policy during the 1960's, but in 1969 the U.S. Supreme Court finally declared that the time for delay was over. Fifteen years after Brown, the Court declared that school districts were ordered to comply "at once" with the Brown decision. School districts increasingly relied upon busing as the means to desegregate the schools, and opponents of busing in both the North and South argued that it was leading to the destruction of neighborhood schools.

DIRECT ACTION

On December 1, 1955, a racial incident in Montgomery, Alabama, transformed the face of the Civil Rights movement. On that day, Rosa Parks, a black seamstress, refused to give up her seat on a Montgomery bus to a white passenger. Parks was arrested, and her arrest ushered in the Civil Rights movement. African Americans, led by a new resident to the community, the Reverend Martin Luther King, Jr., organized one of the most effective mass movements and boycotts in the nation's history, a boycott of the city's bus system. Almost a year after the boycott began, Montgomery officials reluctantly desegregated the bus system after a decision from the Supreme Court.

King emerged from the bus boycott as a national political figure, and in 1957, he and his supporters established the Southern Christian Leadership Conference (SCLC). Combining his Christian beliefs with the precepts of nonviolent resistance, King led several mass protest movements against what he perceived to be the moral injustices of a segregated society. In 1963, King wrote his famous "Letter from Birmingham Jail," in which he outlined his views on just and unjust laws. That same year, King led more than 200,000 civil rights supporters on a March on Washington, D.C. In 1965, King led one of the last major protests of the Civil Rights movement when he and his supporters marched from Selma to Montgomery, Alabama, to pressure Congress to pass a voting rights bill.

Another significant phase of the Civil Rights movement was characterized by "sit-ins." Triggered by four black college students seeking service at the "white" lunch counter of the local Woolworth's in Greensboro, North Carolina, within days similar sit-ins took place in more than sixty communities. Two months after the sit-in started in Greensboro, the lunch counters were integrated.

Many of the student leaders in the sit-in movement came together in 1960 and established the Student Nonviolent Coordinating Committee (SNCC). SNCC played a major role in voter registration drives throughout the South. By the mid-1960's, tired of the violence against them and the slow pace of change, SNCC became one of the most militant of the civil rights organizations and a key exponent of "black power."

In 1961, the Congress of Racial Equality (CORE) initiated the "Freedom Rides." Thirteen riders—some white, some black—boarded buses in Washington, D.C., on a trip through the heart of the deep South. Attacked and viciously beaten by white mobs outside Anniston, Alabama, and in Birmingham, the Freedom Riders focused the attention of the nation on the failure of southern states to protect passengers in interstate travel.

Realizing the difficulties African Americans experienced in seeking service in public accommodations such as hotels, restaurants, and theaters, Congress passed the landmark Civil Rights Act of 1964, which made it illegal to discriminate in public accommodations on grounds of "race, color, religion or national origin." Another section of the law banned discrimination in employment and established the Equal Employment Opportunity Commission (EEOC) to enforce the law. The section on employment discrimination established "affirmative action," an approach that has been blamed by some for eroding white support for the Civil Rights movement.

CIVIL RIGHTS MOVEMENT AND CHILDREN

In the course of the struggle to obtain civil rights, African American children were beaten, clubbed, gassed, threatened by lynch mobs, attacked by police dogs, blasted by high-power water hoses, arrested, jailed, and even killed. Many African American children—from the very young to teenagers—were involved in the Civil Rights movement of the 1950's and 1960's in the United States. They participated in marches, demonstrations, boycotts, pickets, sit-ins, desegregation of schools, voter registration campaigns, and freedom rides. Some children accompanied their activist parents to organizing meetings, which were often held in black churches and conducted by members of the National Association for the Advancement of Colored People (NAACP), the Student Nonviolent Coordinating Committee (SNCC), the Southern Christian Leadership Conference (SCLC), the Council of Federated Organizations (COFO), and other civil rights organizations.

The children were primarily involved in the movement in the South, especially Mississippi, Alabama, Georgia, Tennessee, Arkansas, and Florida,

where both de jure (by law) and de facto (by custom) segregation existed. Although the movement was non-violent, it elicited violent acts from angry white mobs who gathered around protests, local authorities trying to break up demonstrations and arrest protesters, and racist groups who bombed churches and attacked African Americans in an effort to intimidate them. In the course of the struggle to obtain civil rights, African American children were beaten, clubbed, gassed, threatened by lynch mobs, attacked by police dogs, blasted by high-power water hoses, arrested, jailed, and even killed.

In May of 1963, in Birmingham, Alabama, thousands of children marched for civil rights as part of the Children's Crusade. Reverend James Bevel organized the controversial initiative over the objections of his advisors and Dr. Martin Luther King Jr.. Malcolm X in particular believed that "real men don't put their children on the firing line." But Bevel argued that if a child is old enough to accept Christ, he or she is old enough to live out their faith.

Birmingham police commissioner Eugene "Bull" Connor, a staunch segregationist, gave the order for police to attack the children with nightsticks, police dogs, and high-power water hoses. The police arrested the children, filling the city jails and then imprisoning children in a makeshift jail at the fairgrounds. In September, 1963, a bomb exploded in the Sixteenth Street Baptist Church in Birmingham, killing four young girls who had been attending Sunday school. The church had been selected as a target because civil rights activists gathered there and organized protests.

Children also played an important, and difficult, role in school desegregation. Their parents filed lawsuits on their behalf, but it was the children who attended these schools who bore the brunt of racially motivated attacks, verbal and physical abuse, and social isolation. Two of the nationally publicized cases occurred in Topeka, Kansas, and Little Rock, Arkansas. Topeka operated eighteen public elementary schools for white children only and four schools for black children. Oliver Brown—pastor of St. Mark's AME Church—on behalf of his daughter Linda Carol Brown, and twelve other black plaintiffs, on behalf of their children, filed a lawsuit to protest this segregation. After much expert testimony, the U.S. Supreme Court on May 17,1954 issued a landmark decision that ended segregation of children in public schools solely on the basis of race, because segregation deprived minority children of equal educational opportunities. In 1957, nine black youths (known as "the Little Rock Nine"), led by Daisy Bates were the first black students to attend the formerly segregated Little Rock Central High School after the historic *Brown v. Board of Education* ruling. President Dwight D. Eisenhower had to use state troopers to protect the children from physical violence by armed white adults opposed to desegregation.

THE COLLAPSE OF THE CIVIL RIGHTS MOVEMENT

After 1965, the Civil Rights movement fell into disarray and decline. There were numerous reasons for the decline of the movement. To begin with, the broad base of public support for civil rights began to erode. Many Americans believed that Congress had passed enough legislation to deal with the problem of discrimination (most notably the sweeping 1964 Civil Rights Act) and that now it was time to let those laws work. Another factor was the nationalization of the push for civil rights. Until the mid-1960's the civil rights issue was widely viewed as a southern problem. When the movement moved northward, some white northerners withdrew their support. With the institution of busing for school desegregation and the attempt to integrate housing, many white Americans in the North felt threatened.

The controversy over affirmative action policies also divided support for the movement. To many Americans, affirmative action meant quotas and programs that unfairly threatened their own job security. Another factor was the diffusion of the movement as it was broadened to include discrimination based on age, gender, physical disability, and sexual orientation. Fewer Americans were willing to support what they viewed as special privileges for women, people with disabilities, and homosexuals than to support civil rights, particularly voting rights, for African Americans.

The urban riots of the 1960's shattered white support for civil rights. White voters and politicians—President Lyndon B. Johnson among them—felt betrayed by the riots. They thought that the nation was trying to deal with the problems of racism and discrimination. Congress had passed three civil rights laws and one voting rights law within an eight-year period. When the Watts riot in Los Angeles broke out within a week after passage of the Voting Rights Act of 1965, the "white backlash" against civil rights essentially brought the movement to a halt. The riots represented the chasm that still existed between black and white, and they frightened many whites into thinking of "law and order" first and civil rights gains second. On the national scene, the escalating war in Vietnam drew attention away from the

Civil Rights movement. When Martin Luther King, Jr., openly opposed the war, he was widely criticized by many civil rights leaders, as well as by President Johnson. In the late 1960's, the Vietnam War displaced the issue of civil rights.

Ideological disputes among black leaders of the movement also led to its collapse. Major disputes arose among civil rights organizations such as the NAACP, SCLC, CORE, and SNCC with respect to tactics and objectives. Younger African Americans, particularly those in SNCC, were dismayed by the slow pace of change and, as a result, favored more militant tactics. The emergence of the Black Power movement in 1966, led by young leaders such as Stokely Carmichael of SNCC, was a direct assault on the approach of King and other moderates.

ACCOMPLISHMENTS

The Civil Rights movement forever altered the political landscape of the United States. Perhaps the greatest accomplishment of the movement can be seen in the thousands of African Americans who hold elective office. The number of black members of Congress was at a record high in the mid-1990's. African Americans have been elected to virtually every political office in all areas of the country. The Civil Rights movement also ended the humiliating practice of segregation and abolished the laws that attempted to create two classes of citizens. Finally, the Civil Rights movement created a sense of pride and self-esteem among those who participated in the movement.

—Darryl Paulson

See also: Birmingham March; Black church; Black Power movement; Chicago sit-ins; Church bombings; Civil Rights movement and children; Civil rights worker murders; Congress of Racial Equality; Freedom Rides; Greensboro sit-ins; "I Have a Dream" speech; Jews and African Americans; King assassination; Little Rock school desegregation crisis; Mississippi Freedom Democratic Party; Montgomery bus boycott; National Association for the Advancement of Colored People; National Urban League; Rainbow Coalition; School desegregation; Sit-ins; Southern Christian Leadership Conference; Southern Manifesto; Student Nonviolent Coordinating Committee; Summit Meeting of National Negro Leaders; United States Commission on Civil Rights; University of Mississippi desegregation; Voting Rights Act of 1965; White Citizens' Councils

MONTGOMERY BUS BOYCOTT

December 5, 1955-December 21, 1956

African Americans in Montgomery, Alabama, fought entrenched racial discrimination in the public transportation system by refusing to use it, demonstrating the inability of the system to sustain itself without the patronage of the group against which it discriminated.

Locale: Montgomery, Alabama

Categories: Civil rights and liberties; social issues and reform; trade and commerce

KEY FIGURES

Rosa Parks (1913-2005), African American seamstress

Martin Luther King, Jr. (1929-1968), African American civil rights leader and pastor of Dexter Avenue Baptist Church

E. D. Nixon (1899-1987), head of the sleeping-car porters' union and president of Alabama's National Association for the Advancement of Colored People

Jo Ann Robinson (1912-1992), African American civil rights activist and educator

Ralph David Abernathy (1926-1990), pastor of the First Baptist Church of Montgomery

Clifford Durr (1899-1975), liberal white attorney *Fred Gray* (b. 1930), African American attorney

SUMMARY OF EVENT

When the Supreme Court issued its decision in *Brown v. Board of Education* in May, 1954, ruling that racial segregation in public schools was unconstitutional, it marked the beginning of a period of dramatic change in the relationships between African Americans and whites. Until the mid-1960's, that change was hastened by the organized nonviolent resistance by many African Americans to laws and conditions that they regarded as discriminatory. The first occasion in which such tactics proved successful was a boycott of public buses in Montgomery, Alabama.

Although African Americans had achieved some hardfought successes before 1954—most notably the desegregation of the armed forces—in many respects they remained a separate community, enjoying fewer rights and opportunities and less legal protection than whites. This was especially true in the Deep South, where the doctrine of "separate but equal" was held to apply to most areas of daily life and was used to justify a decidedly unequal segregation. Hundreds of laws, many of them passed in the late nineteenth century, restricted the rights of black Southerners to eat, travel, study, or worship with whites.

The school desegregation ruling brought no immediate change to race relations in Montgomery. Once the capital of the Confederacy, this city of about 130,000 people—50,000 of whom were African American—continued resolutely in the old pattern of racial separation. The African American community of Montgomery had undertaken initial steps to challenge certain local segregation practices that were particularly offensive. E. D. Nixon of Montgomery headed the National Association for the Advancement of Colored People (NAACP) in Alabama.

Because he worked as a sleeping-car porter, he was less susceptible to attempts by the white establishment to control his behavior by threatening his job. Jo Ann Robinson helped lead the African American clubwomen in Montgomery, who provided a powerful organizational backbone among the small African Americans middle class in Montgomery. This nascent movement still lacked both a unified structure and a single issue to mobilize the African American community to push for civil rights.

The issue came to a head on December 1, 1955, when Rosa Parks, a seamstress at a Montgomery department store and formerly the secretary of the local NAACP chapter, refused to give up her seat to maintain a row of vacant seats between white and black riders on a public bus system in Montgomery, as required by

Rosa Parks being fingerprinted by Deputy Sheriff D.H. Lackey after her arrest for boycotting public transportation by Associated Press

401

law. She was arrested and charged with violating the segregation ordinance. Parks's action was in part spontaneous—she had not boarded the bus with the intent to violate any segregation ordinance. She had, however, attended the Highlander Folk School in Tennessee, where members of the community learned to become more effective, and a lifetime of enduring racial indignities had made her acutely aware of the evils of segregation.

Immediately, Montgomery's African American community sprang into action. Fred Gray, one of but four black lawyers in Alabama, contacted Clifford Durr, a liberal white attorney, to post bail for Parks. Nixon brought together two ministers, Ralph David Abernathy and Martin Luther King, Jr., with Jo Ann Robinson to plan for a massive boycott of Montgomery public buses, a majority of whose riders were African Americans. It would be necessary to arrange for transportation for scores of African Americans who did not own cars. To coordinate the massive undertaking, Montgomery's African American leaders created the Montgomery Improvement Association (MIA), presided over by King, the twenty-six-year-old pastor of Dexter Avenue Baptist Church. The boycott began on December 5, 1955. At first, whites reacted with indifference or amusement, until the bus company's revenues dropped by 75 percent. A series of meetings between the city commissioners, representatives of the bus company, and the MIA failed to produce any agreement on the African Americans' demands—courteous treatment by bus drivers; a first-come, first-served seating arrangement, with blacks filling the rear and whites the front of the bus; and the employment of African American drivers on routes that served predominantly African American neighborhoods of Montgomery. Instead, the city police department began to harass the carpools that had been set up by the MIA to provide alternative transportation and arrested some of the drivers. Police officers arrested King himself for speeding, and on January 30, persons unknown blasted King's house with dynamite. The houses of two other boycott leaders met a similar fate.

These acts of violence and intimidation affected the course of events in several ways. First, they united the African Americans in Montgomery, inspiring them to continue the boycott for more than a year. The violence also attracted national attention to Montgomery and led to substantial outside support for the boycott, assistance vital to its success. Finally, the violence served as a foil for the rhetoric of nonviolent resistance that King so eloquently articulated. In one mass meeting after another, he urged his followers to ignore hostile provocations, to confront their persecutors passively, and to refuse to fight back, relying on the moral authority of their actions to sway the hearts and minds of their antagonists.

While the boycott continued, the legal issues it raised were argued in federal courts. On February 1, 1956, five Montgomery women filed suit to have the Supreme Court strike down the city bus seating ordinance. The case was heard on May 11, by which time eighty-nine MIA members faced local charges for conspiracy to interfere with normal business. In November, city officials obtained an injunction against the MIA officials for running a carpool, which nearly brought the boycott to a halt. Nevertheless, the federal suit received a favorable hearing and was affirmed by the Supreme Court in *Browder v. Gayle* in November, and the court ordered the seating on Montgomery buses desegregated on December 17, 1956. Four days later, King, Abernathy, and Nixon rode the bus downtown and were able to sit wherever they wanted.

Until Montgomery, the only effective tactic challenging segregation had been the legal approach used by the NAACP. After Montgomery, it was clear that boycotts, mass meetings, and demonstrations could be used along with court challenges. There was some bickering between the MIA and the NAACP over which approach worked best. The court ruling forced the Montgomery bus company to end segregation at a time when it might have held out longer against economic pressure, but without the organization of the black community, there would have been no roused national conscience to encourage legal and legislative action.

It is difficult to think of the Civil Rights movement without thinking of King. On December 1, 1955, King was a young, unknown minister of a black Baptist church in the Deep South. By December 20, 1956, he was an internationally recognized black leader. If Rosa Parks had not refused to give up her seat, the world might never have heard of King.

Integration of the city buses was not the last act of the drama of race relations in Montgomery. There would be violence and blood would be shed at later dates, but an irreversible step had been taken. One of the major streets in Montgomery was renamed Rosa Parks Boulevard. Appropriately, city buses traveling this thoroughfare carry the destination sign "Rosa Parks." Her death on October 24, 2005, unleashed a flood of encomium for her achievement. Her casket was placed in the Capitol Rotunda in Washington, D.C., for two days so that thousands of mourners and dignitaries could pay their last respects to this person of immense character and courage.

—Courtney B. Ross, Edward R. Crowther, and
Michael R. Bradley

See also: Supreme Court Ends Public School Segregation; SCLC Forms to Link Civil Rights Groups; Greensboro Sit-Ins; Council of Federated Organizations Registers African Americans to Vote; Civil Rights Protesters Attract International Attention; King Delivers His "I Have a Dream" Speech; Supreme Court Prohibits Racial Discrimination in Public Accommodations; Selma- Montgomery March; Fair Housing Act Outlaws Discrimination in Housing.

SOUTHERN MANIFESTO

Presented to Congress on March 12, 1956

The Southern Manifesto dramatically illustrated the opposition of southern politicians to the Supreme Court's decision declaring segregation in public schools unconstitutional.

Identification: Document signed by southern legislators renouncing the U.S. Supreme Court's 1954 *Brown v. Board of Education* decision

Following the 1954 U.S. Supreme Court decision *Brown v. Board of Education*, Senate Majority Leader Lyndon B. Johnson and House Speaker Sam Rayburn, both from Texas, managed to get southern and northern Democrats to restrain themselves in response to the *Brown* decision. In 1956, however, some southern congressmen and senators were worried about being reelected if they did not oppose the decision. Southern senators, led by Strom Thurmond of South Carolina, met and drafted a resolution criticizing the Supreme Court's decision. The final draft of the resolution was presented to the U.S. Senate on March 12, 1956, by Walter George of Georgia.

Officially called the "Declaration of Constitutional Principles," the document stated that the U.S. Supreme Court had no legal basis for its decision and substituted its personal and political ideas for established law. It also criticized the Supreme Court's abuse of judicial powers and commended states that had declared their intention to resist integration by any lawful means.

The final document was signed by nineteen of the twenty-two southern senators and eighty-one southern House members. The three southern senators who did not sign the manifesto were Tennessee's Estes Kefauver and Albert Gore, Sr., and Texas's Lyndon B. Johnson.

The Southern Manifesto symbolized the open defiance of the overwhelming majority of southern congressional leaders to desegregation and gave southern segregationists hope that they could successfully resist desegregation efforts.

—William V. Moore

See also: *Brown v. Board of Education*; Civil Rights movement; Education; Little Rock school desegregation crisis; School desegregation; White Citizens' Councils

SOUTHERN CHRISTIAN LEADERSHIP CONFERENCE

Founded in 1957

The formation of the Southern Christian Leadership Conference (SCLC) in 1957 was the first Southwide grassroots movement dedicated to racial desegregation in the United States.

Identification: Civil rights organization

Place: Atlanta, Georgia; New Orleans, Louisiana; and Montgomery, Alabama

When the Southern Christian Leadership Conference was formed in 1957, black Americans faced many obstacles to economic and political equality despite decades of piecemeal reforms. The National Association for the Advancement of Colored People (NAACP), the National Urban League, the Congress of Racial Equality (CORE), and other advocacy organizations had achieved significant gains, but black Americans in many parts of the country were prohibited from voting and blocked by lack of education and segregationist barriers from advancing economically and socially. Particularly in the southern states, black Americans faced formidable barriers that had stood firmly and even intensified in spite of significant legal victories against segregation in interstate transportation and education. The major advocacy organizations began and operated chiefly in the North and had comparatively little impact on black southerners, who lived in perennial poverty and social ostracism.

THE SCLC AND THE CIVIL RIGHTS MOVEMENT

The SCLC was the first large regional civil rights organization. Its distinctive role as the political arm of many black churches gave it the ability to lead direct action campaigns with the kind of massive grassroots support that had eluded the NAACP and other older advocacy organizations. Under the leadership of Dr. Martin Luther King, Jr., from 1957 to 1968, the SCLC worked with other organizations in many desegregation campaigns. Its nonviolent direct action efforts were on a scale unparalleled in previous campaigns.

By 1957, numerous local desegregation campaigns had been launched without the benefit of a connecting framework. "Movement centers," as Aldon D. Morris called them, included Tallahassee, Mobile, Nashville, Birmingham, Baton Rouge, and several other cities where local leaders applied interorganizational cooperation to effect changes, usually desegregation of public transit systems. What they lacked was an organizational framework to link their efforts with those in other cities and thus achieve a broader impact on behalf of integration and racial equality. Several black leaders, notably the Reverend T. J. Jemison of Baton Rouge, the Reverend Charles Kenzie Steele of Tallahassee, and the Reverend Fred Shuttlesworth of Birmingham, expressed the need for such a larger connecting framework, especially after the important bus boycott in Montgomery, Alabama, during 1955 and 1956.

The 381-day Montgomery boycott, triggered by the bold defiance of segregated seating by a black seamstress, Rosa Parks, was the catalyst in bringing these various reform centers together. The "Montgomery way," as many termed it, had demonstrated the effectiveness

of mass direct action without violence. Furthermore, it underscored the value of pooling ideas and resources to challenge laws and traditions that supported segregated public facilities such as restaurants, movie theaters, and hotels. Transportation was a particularly significant area needing attention, because many African Americans depended upon public transit to get to their jobs.

EXPANDING THE STRUGGLE

Several informal groups began in late 1956 to plan a broad organization for enlarging the civil rights struggle. One of these groups included Ella Jo Baker, a perennial supporter of direct action reform, white attorney Stanley David Levison, and civil rights advocate Bayard Rustin. In New York, they formed a small group known as "In Friendship" and began to contact civil rights leaders across the South. Meanwhile, Martin Luther King, Jr., and the Reverend Ralph David Abernathy, along with others such as Joseph E. Lowery, Steele, and Jemison, met periodically in Montgomery to brainstorm on a possible southern direct action organization.

It would be a mistake to attribute this interest entirely to the Montgomery campaign or to contextual factors such as urbanization and its related tensions. The historical setting of the origins of the SCLC included these things as well as the impact of the *Brown v. Board of Education* case of May, 1954, that declared unconstitutional "separate but equal" schools, based on the 1896 *Plessy v. Ferguson* decision. The *Brown* case was a particularly encouraging factor because it showed that the Supreme Court could be a valuable ally of black reform leaders.

In early 1956, Rustin suggested to King in Montgomery the concept of a broad organization to link the various reform centers. By the end of the year, the discussions had advanced sufficiently to attempt an organization meeting. Rustin contacted Steele and others, and round-robin invitations went out from Steele, King, and Shuttlesworth to dozens of southern activists. The foundational meeting took place at the Ebenezer Baptist Church in Atlanta on January 10 and 11, 1957, with approximately sixty people, mostly black pastors, attending.

The discussions covered a wide range of topics, mostly from working papers provided by Rustin. It was agreed that the movement would be nonviolent in method and outlook and that all Americans' rights under the Constitution would be supported in order "to redeem the soul of America." The fact that many participants were ministers added to the emphasis upon faith and ethics. This basic reality of the Atlanta meeting was important in shaping the ethos of the emergent SCLC. The conference also cabled President Dwight D. Eisenhower, requesting that he or Vice President Richard Nixon travel to the South and take a strong stand in favor of civil rights. Eisenhower had already sent a civil rights package to Congress in 1956, but the administration's proposals fell short of the Atlanta delegates' expectations.

COMPLETING THE ORGANIZATION

Later meetings in New Orleans on February 14, 1957, and in Montgomery in August of the same year completed the organizational process. After experimenting with various names, the new conference arrived at its permanent name, the Southern Christian Leadership Conference, during the Montgomery meeting. Some SCLC leaders feared that adding the word "Christian" might alienate Jews such as Stanley Levison, but King supported the new name, believing that it reflected the true nature of the organization. Levison agreed. Some of the organizers thought that the word "Christian" would lessen the likelihood that the organization would be considered radical or communist.

The Southern Christian Leadership Conference focused chiefly on basic rights for members of minorities and poor people. Its first major undertaking was a Crusade for Citizenship. Its goal was to at least double the number of registered black voters in the South. Voting rights thus became one of the major emphases of the new organization. Working in conjunction with the NAACP and other organizations, the SCLC added thousands of black voters to the voting rolls in several states. It also continued to work on behalf of ending segregated transportation, desegregating schools, and gaining broader access by African Americans to public facilities such as hotel and lunch counters.

The SCLC's loose organization was important to its distinctive role in the Civil Rights movement. Without formal individual membership, it was based on affiliates, such as local churches and activist groups like Fred Shuttlesworth's Alabama Christian Movement for Human Rights (ACMHR). Operating at first in eleven states, it linked hundreds of such entities in a way that facilitated guidance from the central headquarters while maintaining considerable local autonomy. The SCLC came into cities and towns for campaigns when invited by local leaders. As the SCLC became more experienced and efficient, these invitations were carefully planned. The Birmingham campaign of 1963, which

was a highpoint of the SCLC's history, began on the basis of an invitation from Shuttlesworth's organization.

PRIORITIES

The SCLC's focus was primarily on securing rights that were based on the U.S. Constitution. It was also interested, from the beginning, in economic advancement of members of minorities and perennially poor people. This aspect of the SCLC's history had not been recognized adequately. The fact that its focus on social and economic gains increased after the Selma campaign and the Voting Rights Act of 1965 should not be taken as an indication that the SCLC came to this emphasis only in the middle 1960's. Poverty was viewed by the SCLC as a seminal cause of the political powerlessness of many black Americans, and from the beginning the organization was interested in the elimination of poverty. At the same time, King and his associates recognized that the right to vote would bring the ability to help determine political leaders and hold them accountable for such needs as jobs and housing. King sounded this note as early as the Prayer Pilgrimage of May, 1957, marking the third anniversary of the *Brown* decision. In his speech, which propelled him higher in public visibility, he gave rhythmic repetitions of the phrase "Give us the ballot," noting that if African Americans had the vote they could nonviolently eliminate many barriers to progress.

IMPACT

Thus began an important new organization dedicated to racial justice and advancement in the United States. It was quite different in key ways from the older NAACP and CORE, both of which began in the North and historically operated chiefly outside the South. The NAACP did have a strong presence in the South in 1957, but it was under attack by various groups and governments. Its distinguishing feature had always been litigation through the court system. The SCLC provided a framework for mass direct action, which many felt was urgently needed in the South. Furthermore, the SCLC was not a membership organization. It was structured around loosely linked "affiliates," such as the ACMHR, rather than individual membership.

The advent of the SCLC marked a new chapter in the history of racial and ethnic rights in the United States. Strongly grounded in local churches, it sought to bring their moral strength and organizational resources to bear upon the problems of members of minorities. With King as its president, it had an articulate spokesman who was increasingly drawing media interest. This was both an asset and a liability. King's visibility helped the young SCLC but at the same time hindered the organization's achievement of an identity apart from him. On balance, the SCLC was very significant in the continuance of the momentum gained in Montgomery and other cities in the early and middle 1950's. For more than a decade under King, it would be a major force in massive campaigns in Birmingham, Selma, and other cities, and after 1965 would venture into the northern United States.

Nonviolence was the most characteristic mark of the SCLC's campaigns. At times it had remarkable results, not only for public policy but also for individual experiences of both black and white people. During the Birmingham campaign of 1963, for example, a group of marchers who were walking to a prayer vigil were confronted by Eugene "Bull" Connor's police and firefighters, who were wielding water hoses to stop marchers. Despite Connor's orders, those in charge of the hoses would not turn them on the unarmed and nonviolent group. They were, as Coretta Scott King later observed, disarmed by the nonviolent spirit of the demonstrators. Not hitting back, not hating, and not giving cause for increased violence were the salient features of the SCLC's new mass-based direct action.

—Thomas R. Peake

See also: Birmingham March; Black Christian Nationalist Movement; Black Power movement; Church bombings; Civil Rights Act of 1964; Civil Rights movement; Congress of Racial Equality; Freedom Summer; "I Have a Dream" speech; King assassination; Montgomery bus boycott; National Association for the Advancement of Colored People; Founding of the Niagara Movement; Poor People's March on Washington; Student Nonviolent Coordinating Committee; University of Mississippi desegregation

CIVIL RIGHTS ACT OF 1957

1957

The law created the U.S. Commission on Civil Rights, to investigate complaints of violations of civil rights, along with other measures.

The Law: First federal civil rights legislation since 1875

During the mid-1950's, the Civil Rights movement gathered momentum as it challenged racial segregation and discrimination in many areas of southern life. One area where progress proved slow was voting rights. Intimidation and irregular registration procedures limited electoral participation by African Americans. By 1957, support for legislation to protect voting rights was growing among northern Republicans and Democrats in Congress. Yet Congress had not passed a civil rights bill since 1875, and there was strong southern opposition to any change in the status quo. It was, however, Senator Lyndon B. Johnson of Texas, the Senate majority leader, who took the lead. Not known at this point in his career as an advocate of civil rights, Johnson used his considerable legislative ability to shepherd the new bill through Congress. It passed just as the Little Rock school desegregation crisis was breaking.

The bill had several major provisions. It created a new body, the Civil Rights Commission, to investigate complaints of violations of civil rights. It raised the Civil Rights Section of the Department of Justice to the status of a division, to be headed by an assistant attorney general. It also made it a federal crime to harass those attempting to vote and allowed the attorney general to initiate proceedings against those violating the law.

The law's short-term effects were modest. Though the number of African American voters did grow, many impediments to voting remained, especially in the rural South. Many criticized the act's weak enforcement procedures: The Civil Rights Commission could gather information and investigate complaints, but it could take no action to protect those trying to vote. Not until the Voting Rights Act of 1965 would effective machinery for ensuring voting rights be established.

On the other hand, in the early 1960's, the administration of President John F. Kennedy did use the act's provisions (which were strengthened by the 1960 Civil Rights Act) to proceed against some of the worst cases of harassment. Also the act broke a psychological barrier by putting the first national civil rights law in eighty-two years on the books. It also highlighted the importance of voting rights to the overall civil rights struggle.

—William C. Lowe

LITTLE ROCK SCHOOL DESEGREGATION CRISIS

1957-1959

The widely publicized events in Little Rock made school desegregation a nationally recognized issue and gave momentum to the early Civil Rights movement.

The Event: Crisis in federal-state relations arising from the refusal of Arkansas state officials to comply with a court order to allow African American students to enroll in Little Rock's Central High School

Place: Little Rock, Arkansas

On May 17, 1954, in the case of *Brown v. Board of Education*, the U.S. Supreme Court ruled that racially segregated public schools were illegal. The court issued a second ruling on the case one year later, ordering local school boards to desegregate "with all deliberate speed." One of the first and most widely publicized tests of the new federal position on school segregation came in Little Rock, Arkansas.

At first, it appeared as if Little Rock schools would quietly follow the orders of the Supreme Court. On May 22, 1954, the Little Rock school board announced that it would comply with the Supreme Court order as soon as the Court established a method and a schedule for desegregation. In May 1955, the school board voted to adopt a policy of gradual desegregation to start in 1957. Under the plan devised by School Superintendent Virgil Blossom, the city would first integrate its Central High School and then gradually integrate lower grades.

THE CRISIS ERUPTS

The crisis broke out in 1957, the year that the school board had hoped to manage the quiet enrollment of a few African American pupils in white schools. Seventeen students were selected to be the first to break down the racial lines, but only nine of them decided to pursue enrollment. Shortly before the beginning of the school year, on August 27, The Mother's League of Little Rock Central High School sought an injunction to halt integration. The injunction was granted by Pulaski County chancellor Murray Reed, but it was rejected three days later by federal district judge Ronald Davies.

The enrollment of the African American students might have proceeded in a relatively peaceful manner if Arkansas governor Orval Faubus had not used the event for political advantage. Faubus was searching for political support to win a third term in office, and he decided to appeal to white constituents who were eager to preserve segregation. Governor Faubus declared that he would not be able to maintain order if Central High School were integrated, and on September 2, he ordered the state's National Guard to surround the school. His stand drew public attention to the situation and attracted white segregationist mobs to the streets. The next day, Judge Davies ordered that the integration of Central High should continue.

The National Association for the Advancement of Colored People (NAACP), under the local leadership of Daisy Bates, organized the nine African American students to arrive in a group. They were met by National Guardsmen who turned them away with bayonets. One of the students arrived after the others and was confronted by screaming segregationists. Television, which occupied a central place in most American homes by 1957, broadcast the scenes from Little Rock around the nation. On September 20, Judge Davies ruled that Governor Faubus had used the National Guard to prevent integration and forbade the guard's employment in this way. Faubus then replaced the guard with local police. The nine black students entered Central High School through a side door on September 23. As they made their way into the school, an unruly mob of more than one thousand people massed on the streets outside.

FEDERAL INTERVENTION

President Dwight D. Eisenhower met with Governor Faubus on September 14. The president believed that the governor had agreed to allow school integration to continue. It soon became evident that Governor Faubus had no such intention.

Alarmed by the developments in his city, on September 24, Little Rock mayor Woodrow Mann asked President Eisenhower for federal troops to maintain order. Eisenhower responded by sending one thousand troops of the 101st Airborne Division and placing the Arkansas National Guard under federal control. The troops then escorted the nine students to the school each day. Some Americans were shocked to see that military protection was needed to protect the basic rights of citizens. Others were disturbed at what they believed was a federal military occupation of a state, reviving historical memories of the military occupation of the South during the era of Reconstruction in the years following the Civil War.

YEARS OF STRUGGLE

The struggle continued even after the mobs in front of Central High returned to their homes and jobs. On February 8, 1958, after several angry confrontations with white students, one of the nine, Minnijean Brown, was suspended for the rest of the year and eventually expelled. Shortly after, the school board asked the federal court for a delay of the integration order until the concept of "all deliberate speed" was defined. The delay was granted in June and reversed in August. In the meantime, the first African American student graduated from Central High in May.

Upon the opening of the 1958-1959 school year, Governor Faubus ordered Little Rock public schools closed, and white students enrolled in private schools and in other districts. On September 27, 1958, Little Rock residents voted on school integration and overwhelmingly rejected it. However, on June 18, 1959, a federal court declared that Little Rock's public school closing was unconstitutional. Little Rock schools opened one month early for the 1959-1960 school year and enrolled both African American and white students.

The Little Rock crisis was the first major test of the federal government's determination to enforce the Supreme Court's *Brown* decision. President Eisenhower's willingness to use troops for school desegregation was controversial, but it marked the beginning of the U.S. government's commitment to desegregated schools. Little Rock was also the beginning of a series of struggles over school desegregation that continued for several decades across the nation. The event proved to be one of the defining events during the early Civil Rights movement.

—*Carl L. Bankston III*

See also: *Bolling v. Sharpe*; *Brown v. Board of Education*; Civil Rights Act of 1957; Civil Rights movement; Civil Rights movement and children; Congress of Racial Equality; *Cooper v. Aaron*; "I Have a Dream" speech; Montgomery bus boycott; National Association for the Advancement of Colored People; School desegregation; Southern Manifesto; *Swann v. Charlotte-Mecklenberg Board of Education*; University of Mississippi desegregation; White Citizens' Councils

UNITED STATES COMMISSION ON CIVIL RIGHTS

Created in 1957

The reports and studies of the Commission on Civil Rights have been an important factor in the passage of major civil rights legislation.

Identification: Federal commission created by the
    Civil Rights Act of 1957
Place: Washington, D.C.

The U.S. Commission on Civil Rights was created in 1957 by Congress as part of the Civil Rights Act of 1957. It consisted of six members, appointed by the president and approved by Congress. The original purpose of the agency was to monitor civil rights (particularly violations of voting rights in the South), issue reports, and then disband, but Congress has continuously renewed its mandate. The Commission on Civil Rights (abbreviated as CRC, for Civil Rights Commission) was created in the wake of the 1954 Supreme Court decision in *Brown v. Board of Education*. In this case, the Court decided that separate facilities for black and white students in public education were unconstitutional. A year later, in *Brown II*, the Court ruled that schools must integrate with "all deliberate speed." No specific timetable was given, however, for fear of further alienating southern whites.

The CRC helped lay the foundation for the civil rights legislation of the 1960's. The commission's mandate involved investigating voting rights violations, collecting and studying voting data related to denials of equal protection under the law, and appraising federal laws and policies as they related to equal protection. In addition to creating the CRC, the 1957 Civil Rights Act made the civil rights component in the Justice Department a division, and empowered the U.S. attorney general to initiate civil court proceedings to enforce voting rights. The 1957 statute gave the attorney general the power to intervene only on a case-by-case basis, which was tedious, as there were thousands of cases of voting rights violations.

CIVIL RIGHTS LEGISLATION

During Dwight D. Eisenhower's administration, the Commission on Civil Rights investigated voting rights violations in eight southern states and found no fewer than a hundred counties using discriminatory measures against African Americans. The Civil Rights Act of 1960 was passed as a result of the CRC's 1959 report. Although the CRC had recommended that Congress pass legislation authorizing federal registrars in obstructionist districts, the act provided only court-appointed referees to oversee and resolve alleged voting rights abuses. Continuing studies by the CRC would assist in more powerful legislation in 1964 and 1965.

The 1964 Civil Rights Act was instrumental in the desegregation of public facilities in a still-segregated South. Based on ongoing concerns and studies by the CRC in education, voting, and employment, and influenced by the intensifying Civil Rights movement and the March on Washington in 1963, the 1964 act forbade racial discrimination in public facilities, voting registration procedures, and employment. The act empowered the attorney general to intervene and take civil action in cases of racial discrimination in public accommodations. It also cut federal funds to school districts that discriminated and created the Equal Employment Opportunity Commission to oversee discrimination complaints in the workplace.

The 1965 Voting Rights Act is the most powerful legislation in the area of suffrage, and it eliminated virtually all remaining loopholes. The act effectively took the process of voter registration out of the hands of states and localities, providing federal machinery for this process. The legislation also forbade literacy tests in most instances. In addition, a preclearance mechanism (often called Section 5) was put in place that required political districts to submit proposed changes in elections or districts to the federal government for approval. A "clean record" provision was instituted, allowing political districts to be removed from coverage of the preclearance provision if no discrimination or voting irregularities have been found for the previous ten years.

The CRC has played a vital role in the extension of the 1965 Voting Rights Act and thus in continued suffrage among African Americans in the Deep South. One of the most controversial areas of the act, the preclearance provision, was challenged by southerners. Testimony by the CRC revealed that southern states, and particularly Mississippi, were seeking to subvert the intent of the act and dilute the black vote and black political victories. Legislatures did this by racial gerrymandering of political districts, going to at-large systems of municipal elections, developing multimember districts, and consolidating black and white counties. The CRC was instrumental in the extension of Section 5 and the drafting of other provisions of the 1970 Voting Rights Act. Reports by the commission would play an important role in the 1975 and 1982 extensions of the act as well.

CHALLENGES AND IMPACT

A major challenge to the commission came in the early 1980's, after it issued a 1981 statement entitled *Affirmative Action in the 1980's*, which advocated quotas to ensure the hiring of members of minorities. President Ronald Reagan strongly opposed the recommendations and removed three of the CRC's commissioners, appointing more conservative commissioners. A lawsuit ensued, and in 1983 Reagan was ordered by the courts to reinstate the commissioners he had fired. Also in 1983, the commission was reorganized by a compromise congressional act (Reagan had vowed to veto an act routinely renewing the commission) to consist of eight members chosen by the president and Congress. The commission was criticized from many quarters in the 1980's, partly for appearing to succumb to various political pressures, and many of its leaders, including Clarence Pendleton, were controversial. In the early 1990's, it began to resume the more active role it had played in the past.

Originally intended as a watchdog agency, the Commission on Civil Rights has been essential as a bipartisan fact-finding body and a resource for both Congress and the president in developing legislation. While its early charge was in the area of voting rights, it has conducted numerous studies and provided congressional testimony in education, housing, racial segregation, employment discrimination, and denial of civil rights on the basis of race, creed, color, religion, national origin, sex, age, or disability.

—Mfanya D. Tryman

See also: *Brown v. Board of Education*; Civil Rights Act of 1957; Civil Rights Act of 1960; Civil Rights Act of 1964; Civil Rights Act of 1968; Civil Rights Act of

1991; Civil Rights Acts of 1866–1875; Civil Rights movement; Voting Rights Act of 1965

AILEY FOUNDS HIS DANCE COMPANY

March 30, 1958

Alvin Ailey presented his first modern dance concert, strengthening the cultural diversity of American modern dance and integrating ballet, jazz, and modern dance forms.

Also known as: Alvin Ailey American Dance Theater
Locale: New York, New York
    Category: Dance

KEY FIGURES

Alvin Ailey (1931-1989), African American modern dancer and choreographer

Lester Horton (1906-1953), West Coast choreographer who served as Ailey's teacher and mentor

Talley Beatty (1923-1995), African American modern dancer and choreographer

Carmen De Lavallade (b. 1931), an original member of the Horton Dance Theater who frequently danced with Ailey

Judith Jamison (b. 1943), a soloist with the Ailey dance company who succeeded Ailey as artistic director

SUMMARY OF EVENT

Billed simply as "Alvin Ailey and Company," an ensemble of six black dancers that included Charles Moore, Claude Thompson, Jacqueline Walcott, Clarence Cooper, Nancy Reddy, and Alvin Ailey were joined by guest artist Talley Beatty at the Ninety-second Street Young Men's Hebrew Association (YMHA) in New York City.

This premiere concert performance by the Ailey dance company, on March 30, 1958, broadened the scope of American dance through the debut of works that reflected multicultural influences. As would be the case in future performances, the Ailey company's debut included pieces that portrayed aspects of the African American experience.

In addition to the development of multicultural thematic material, Ailey's personal movement style burgeoned in his first concert appearance. Ailey had teamed up with Ernest Parham to recruit dancers from the cast of the Broadway show *Jamaica* (1957) in order to present the concert. *Dance Magazine* critic Doris Hering commented on the energy, technical prowess, and versatility of the dancers, with particular mention of guest artist Talley Beatty.

Alvin Ailey, Jr., was born and reared in Rogers, Texas. His parents separated when he was very young, and in 1942 Ailey moved with his mother to Los Angeles. Although Ailey previously had studied tap dance and some ethnic forms, he began professional dance training in 1949 with West Coast choreographer Lester Horton. By 1953, Ailey was performing with the Horton company and made his debut in a revue titled *Bal*

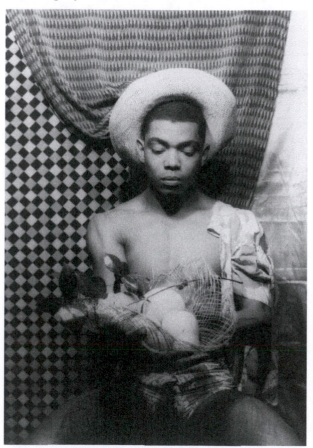

Portrait of Alvin Ailey in 1955 by Carl Van Vechten

Caribe. Horton died in 1953, and soon thereafter Ailey took over much of the responsibility of company direction. Original members of the Lester Horton Dance Theatre who later danced with the Ailey company include Carmen De Lavallade, Joyce Trisler, and James Truitte.

Ailey's most famous work, *Revelations*, premiered on January 31, 1960, at the Ninety-second Street YMHA. This signature piece of the Alvin Ailey American Dance Theater, which many maintain is a masterpiece of modern dance, premiered less than two years after the Ailey company's concert debut.

Dance critic Selma Jeanne Cohen reviewed the work favorably in *Dance Magazine* and specifically noted the vivid theatrical characterizations created by Ailey. On November 27, 1960, the Ailey company performed *Revelations* at the Clark Center of the West Side Young Women's Christian Association (YWCA) in New York City. In her review, Cohen noted the enthusiastic audience response.

According to the program notes, *Revelations* explores the "motivations and emotions of American Negro religious music." The suite is set to a series of American spirituals and reflects universal themes of deliverance and joy. *Revelations* contains images that depict much of the Southern life of the nineteenth century. The dance can be viewed as Ailey's interpretation of American spirituals. *Revelations* quickly became a signature piece for the Ailey company and it was included in nearly every concert for many years. James Haskins noted that in December, 1988, the dance continued to elicit rave reviews from critics, twenty-nine years after its premiere.

During the fall of 1960, several months after the premiere of *Revelations*, Ailey based his company at the Clark Center. During this period, Ailey augmented the company's repertory with the works of other choreographers. It was unusual at this time for a choreographer to include other artists' dances in a company repertoire, but Ailey viewed the Alvin Ailey American Dance Theater as a purveyor of all types and styles of modern dance, including works that represented a broad spectrum of cultural differences Ailey integrated his dance company at a time when black nationalism and separatism were becoming popular.

Ailey kept his company integrated even though he received some negative criticism. By maintaining integration within the Alvin Ailey American Dance Theater, Ailey helped eliminate stereotypes; he showed that dance movement is culturally based rather than racially intrinsic. Within Ailey's dance theater, white dancers perform the blues, black dancers perform classical ballet, and Asian dancers execute jazz combinations.

Six years after the premiere of *Revelations*, Ailey's vision was to maintain a company of twelve to sixteen dancers who would perform a varied repertory of modern dance works. He also envisioned a school in which to train dancers. By the beginning of the next decade, he would find those visions fulfilled: In 1971, the choreographer established the Alvin Ailey American Dance Center. Twenty years after it was founded, the company school enrolled more than twenty-five hundred students each year and sponsored a junior company, the Alvin Ailey Repertory Ensemble.

SIGNIFICANCE

Perhaps the greatest impact Ailey had on the field of modern dance was his propensity to bring black traditions and black artists into the mainstream of American dance. Since its inception, the Alvin Ailey American Dance Theater has served as a means to present works by black choreographers. In addition to several of Talley Beatty's dances, the company presented pieces by modern dance pioneers Katherine Dunham and Pearl Primus. Also included on the company roster have been works by Ulysses Dove, George Faison, Louis Johnson, Bill T. Jones, Donald McKayle, and Billy Wilson.

Ailey also created one of the first successful modern dance repertory companies to perform the works of many different choreographers. The dance movement originally created by Ailey has become part of the vocabulary of contemporary dance; the images he choreographed have become an irrevocable part of American culture.

Ailey's choreography maintains universal appeal and developed from many sources. The African American experience served as source material for many of Ailey's works, including *Revelations*; however, scholars and critics agree that his choreography cannot be simplistically categorized. Rather than only representing black dance, the works exist as part of the total multicultural American experience. Just as American culture is syncretistic, the repertory of the Alvin Ailey American Dance Theater represents a spectrum of diversity.

Like the pioneering efforts of Katherine Dunham, who fused concert dance forms with Caribbean movements and steps, Ailey's style was a fusion of modern dance, ballet, and black dance forms. Ailey's choreography has enjoyed much popularity, and many of his signature movements have become standard dance vocabulary. The Ailey style is inextricably woven into the fabric of modern dance. Ailey has commented that his particular fusion of dance genres includes aspects of ballet, modern, folk, jazz, music visualization, and both Asian and Spanish forms.

Dance scholar Brenda Dixon states that only certain sections of specific Ailey dances can be classified as black dance. She further emphasizes that it is important to view certain Ailey works within an appropriate frame of reference. Dances by Ailey that do reflect certain black aesthetic and cultural principles should be viewed within the appropriate cultural context. For example, *Love Songs*, choreographed in 1972, is a solo song cycle based in the tradition of the vocalized black ballad. *Love Songs* illustrates the black tradition of song-as-survival.

In 1962, Ailey decided to integrate his company, expanding the cultural roster of his dancers as he had expanded the troupe's repertory with the inclusion of many styles of modern dance. The company began to represent not only black dance but also the entire field of modern dance, which included much cultural diversity.

Just as his choreography and style were distinctly American, Ailey added the word "American" to the name of his company, and the troupe became known officially as the Alvin Ailey American Dance Theater in the mid-1960's. The company continued to represent the United States on many national and international tours.

In 1964, the troupe embarked on its first European tour and received enthusiastic responses, especially in Hamburg, Germany, where one performance elicited sixty-one curtain calls. After that tour, Ailey retired from dancing and focused his energy on choreography and artistic direction of the company.

From 1969 until 1971, the Alvin Ailey American Dance Theater was based at the Brooklyn Academy of Music. During this time, Ailey created fewer than ten new works, including *Mary Lou's Mass* and his famous tribute to the African American woman, *Cry*. This solo was created for company member Judith Jamison, who later would direct the Alvin Ailey American Dance Theater after Ailey's death in 1989. *Cry* was representative of the black woman's life in white society. Moreover, the dance was representative of the oppressed everywhere. Jamison became renowned for her performance of the solo, and the piece continues to have universal appeal.

The City Center in Manhattan became the home for the company in 1971. Around this time, Ailey began to revive modern dance classics for inclusion in the company repertory. Dances by prominent black choreographers such as Donald McKayle, Katherine Dunham, Pearl Primus, and Talley Beatty appeared on concert programs.

Ailey's intent was to maintain older works for future generations rather than lose classics of modern dance. These pieces also reflected the roots of the African American experience and significant contributions of black choreographers and dancers. In addition, Ailey presented choreography by Mexican-born José Limon and modern dance pioneer Ted Shawn.

Two years before his death, Ailey received the Scripps Dance Award at the American Dance Festival. Upon receipt of the award, Ailey reaffirmed his role as a conduit for American modern dance. He stated, "I am part of Isadora Duncan. I am part of Martha Graham. I am part of Doris Humphrey. I am part of Asadata Dafora. And I am part of Lester Horton, who made a boy, an eighteen-year-old athlete in sweat pants, feel important."

—*John R. Crawford*

See also: Mitchell and Shook Found the Dance Theatre of Harlem.

SUMMIT MEETING OF NATIONAL NEGRO LEADERS

June, 1958

This meeting between President Dwight D. Eisenhower and national African American leaders was the first and last White House conference with black leaders during the Eisenhower administration; later requests for meetings were denied.

The Event: Meeting between major African American leaders and President Dwight D. Eisenhower
Place: Washington, D.C.

After five years in office and repeated requests from civil rights activists for an audience, U.S. president Dwight

D. Eisenhower held a "summit meeting" in June, 1958, with four African American leaders: Dr. Martin Luther King, Jr.; A. Philip Randolph; Roy Wilkins of the National Association for the Advancement of Colored People; and Lester B. Granger of the National Urban League. The purpose of the summit was to address strategies for dealing with the approaching wave of school integration and to express concerns over the reluctance of the Eisenhower administration to support civil rights and enforce court orders mandating desegregated public schools; yet the significance of the summit lay in the fact that it was Eisenhower's first such meeting with black leaders.

The meeting itself was by all accounts brief and uneventful. The leaders presented Eisenhower with a carefully worded statement calling for increased federal visibility and involvement in advancing civil rights causes and tactfully criticized the president for his previous statement urging them to "be patient" about civil rights. Eisenhower promised the leaders that he would take their statement under consideration but responded evasively to their requests for a national conference on civil rights.

—*Michael H. Burchett*

See also: Black cabinet; Civil Rights movement; Congressional Black Caucus

NATIONAL ASSOCIATION FOR THE ADVANCEMENT OF COLORED PEOPLE V. ALABAMA
June 30, 1958

The U.S. Supreme Court explicitly recognized that freedom of association was implied in the First Amendment's guarantee of free expression and free assembly and was an "inseparable aspect" of the liberty guaranteed by the Fourteenth Amendment.

The Case: U.S. Supreme Court ruling on freedom of association

The case originated when the National Association for the Advancement of Colored People (NAACP) appealed a contempt order after the association refused to provide the state of Alabama with a state-law-mandated list of NAACP members. The U.S. Supreme Court ruled that requiring disclosure of membership in an advocacy organization would effectively deny the constitutional rights of the members to free speech. The Court held that there was a "close nexus" between the freedoms of speech and assembly. It also noted that revealing membership in a controversial organization had resulted in economic and social reprisals so hostile as to effectively interfere with the rights to free speech and assembly.

This Court decision was the first to link a right to privacy to the right to free association. The Court held for the first time that a constitutional right to associate freely with others was a basic liberty guaranteed under the due process clause of the Fourteenth Amendment.

—*Lisa M. Sardinia*

See also: Montgomery bus boycott; National Association for the Advancement of Colored People

COOPER V. AARON
September 12, 1958

The Supreme Court held that fear of violence did not provide justification for postponing school desegregation, and it also affirmed that its constitutional interpretations were legally binding on governors and state legislators.

The Case: U.S. Supreme Court ruling on school desegregation

In *Brown v. Board of Education* (1954) the Supreme Court ordered an end to segregated schools and overturned the "separate but equal" doctrine established in *Plessy v. Ferguson* (1896). The ambiguity about how to implement school desegregation, however, created the opportunity for school boards to delay and defy the Court's order.

After the *Brown* decision, the Little Rock, Arkansas, school board approved a plan calling for the desegregation of grades ten through twelve in 1957, to be followed by the desegregation of junior high schools and, finally, the elementary schools. The plan was to be completed by the 1963 school year.

Nine black students, carefully selected by the National Association for the Advancement of Colored People (NAACP), were to begin integration of Central High School on September 3, 1957. The day before desegregation was to begin, Governor Orval Faubus ordered the Arkansas National Guard to prevent the black students from enrolling. Governor Faubus claimed that he acted to prevent violence from occurring. After three weeks, a federal court injunction forced the National Guard to withdraw. On September 23, the nine black students entered Central High School and were met by an unruly mob. President Dwight D. Eisenhower was forced to dispatch federal troops to Little Rock to enforce the Court's desegregation order. In the face of the civil unrest, the school board asked for and received a two-and-a-half-year delay in their desegregation plan. The NAACP appealed the delay in *Cooper v. Aaron*.

BASIC ISSUES

Two primary issues confronted the U.S. Supreme Court. First, could the desegregation plan be postponed because of the fear of civil unrest? On September 12, 1958, a unanimous Supreme Court emphatically said no: "The law and order are not here to be preserved by depriving the Negro children of their constitutional rights." Second, were the governor and legislature bound by decisions of the federal Court? Invoking the supremacy clause of the Constitution, the Court said: "No state legislative, executive or judicial officer can War against the Constitution without violating his undertaking to support it."

Although Governor Faubus lost the legal battle, he became a political folk hero in Arkansas and was elected to six consecutive terms (1955–1967). President Eisenhower was both praised and condemned for his actions. He was praised for sending in federal troops to enforce the Court's decision and condemned for failing to endorse personally the Brown decision and lend the weight and prestige of the White House to the Court's ruling. The Cooper case was the first legal confrontation over the enforcement of *Brown v. Board of Education*. The courts stood alone in this enforcement effort until Congress passed the 1964 Civil Rights Act. The Civil Rights Act endorsed the Brown decision and cut off federal funds to school districts refusing to comply with the Court's desegregation decision.

—*Darryl Paulson*

See also: *Brown v. Board of Education*; Civil Rights Act of 1964; Little Rock school desegregation crisis; *Plessy v. Ferguson*; Segregation

GORDY FOUNDS MOTOWN RECORDS

January, 1959

Berry Gordy, Jr., founded Motown Records, which would go on to produce hundreds of recordings that crossed over from rhythm and blues to pop and would come to define popular urban music.

Locale: Detroit, Michigan
Categories: Music; business and labor

KEY FIGURES

Berry Gordy, Jr. (b. 1929), African American founder of Motown Records

Eddie Holland (b. 1939), *Lamont Dozier* (b. 1941), and *Brian Holland* (b. 1941), a songwriting and producing team who were among the premier creative forces at Motown in the 1960's
Norman Whitfield (b. 1943), African American songwriter and producer
Smokey Robinson (b. 1940), African American songwriter and lead singer of the Miracles
Diana Ross (b. 1944), African American lead singer of the Supremes
Marvin Gaye (1939-1984), African American songwriter, musician, producer, and singer

Stevie Wonder (b. 1950), African American singer and musician

Michael Jackson (b. 1958), African American lead singer for the Jackson Five, and later a solo performer

SUMMARY OF EVENT

After years of writing songs for such singers as Detroit's Jackie Wilson and dabbling in record production for others, Berry Gordy, Jr., decided in January of 1959 to open his own company. Born in Detroit into a stable, determined, and ambitious family, Gordy had tried boxing and work on an automobile assembly line before he found his true vocation as the builder of the largest and most successful black-owned independent record company in American history.

After leasing his recordings to major labels for pressing and distribution, Gordy decided to set up his own labels (Tamla, Motown, and Gordy) and soon scored with hits on the rhythm-and-blues and pop charts. One of the keys to his success was his knowledge of the local Detroit music scene, which was rich in amateur singing groups in the doo-wop and rhythm-and-blues vein and in jazz musicians.

By using the talent of Detroit's black ghettos and housing projects, Gordy had the dream of making such music palatable to young white people as well as to black youth. It was from the start a crossover dream, and it succeeded beyond Gordy's greatest expectations.

From 1961 into the 1970's, the carefully trained artists and neatly crafted and produced records from Motown would be the biggest sellers in rhythm and blues and would cross over to the mainstream market as black music had never done before. Gordy nurtured a stable of in-house songwriters, musicians, and producers who redefined black popular music and then went on to change mainstream music-making permanently. The soul music of Motown, Atlantic Records in New York City, and Stax Records in Memphis met the British Invasion head-on and offered a native challenge.

Gordy initially worked closely with his friend Smokey Robinson in writing and producing. Robinson became one of the most creative songwriters and singers with Motown, first as lead singer with the Miracles and then as a superstar solo singer. The Motown labels focused on romantic love ballads and up-tempo dance numbers that were aimed at a young audience and a crossover pop market. A song such as the Miracles' "Shop Around" of 1960 (the company's first big pop hit) was typical of the kind of material Gordy wanted: an upbeat, lighthearted song about a young man and his

search for a girlfriend. The Miracles continued to make both the rhythm-and-blues and pop charts with similar songs and slow ballads featuring Robinson's delicate high tenor. Groups such as the Four Tops, the Temptations, the Marvelettes, Martha and the Vandellas, and Gladys Knight and the Pips helped Motown to turn out hits throughout the 1960's and beyond.

Some acts were already experienced when they signed with Gordy; others, such as the Supremes, Stevie Wonder, and later the Jacksons, had to be carefully trained and directed. Motown was a comprehensive enterprise that dealt with every aspect of making and selling music, including songwriting, recording, manufacturing, distribution, touring, publishing, and grooming.

In the studio, Gordy made sure his teams of songwriters, musicians, singers, and producers worked together to craft songs that would attract both blacks and whites. Older rhythm-and-blues styles, with their raw energy, were smoothed over and polished with the use of the new technology of multi-track recording and overdubbing.

Gordy demanded quality control and each week organized executive sessions to preview intended releases. His in-house production system reminded some of the Detroit automobile companies' production-line method, but it worked wonderfully for a decade and more. Songwriters and producers Eddie Holland, Lamont Dozier, and Brian Holland were originally at Motown's center and became known simply as "H-D-H." Later, Norman Whitfield effectively took the team's place as a force in the studio.

Gordy was determined that his acts could play any venue, from the older "chitlin' circuit" houses such as New York's Apollo or Chicago's Regal to supper clubs, the best concert halls and auditoriums, and television. For this purpose, he had an artists' development department that functioned as a sort of finishing school for singers who had to learn stage deportment and dancing. Choreographer Cholly Atkins trained dozens of performers relentlessly. Again, the system worked: Motown's singing acts built upon traditions of black dance to produce some of the finest and most dynamic routines of the time.

Many of Gordy's artists later complained about his tough standards, and many eventually left Motown for better financial terms and more creative freedom on other labels. Most admitted at least grudgingly, however, that Gordy got them on their feet and prepared them for survival in the harsh world of the music business.

SIGNIFICANCE

By 1966, 75 percent of Motown's single releases reached the pop charts. *Billboard* magazine, the leading music trade journal, even dropped its separate rhythm-and-blues chart between November, 1963, and January, 1965, because there seemed no difference at the time between black popular music and mainstream pop. By late 1968, *Billboard* had changed the name of its black music chart to "Soul." Along with the British rock groups, Motown acts dominated the market. The Supremes (with Diana Ross), the Miracles (with Smokey Robinson), the Temptations, the Four Tops, Stevie Wonder, and Marvin Gaye were leading the roster with hit after hit. By the start of the 1970's, the Jackson Five (with Michael Jackson as lead) had begun a second generation of Motown headliners.

The "Motown sound" shows its roots in gospel, featuring tambourines, hand-clapping, and call-and-response vocals. The groups did not feature group harmonies but rather lead vocals over backing voices. With responses and interjections by other group members and sometimes extra voices added to enrich the sound, Diana Ross, Levi Stubbs with the Four Tops, and David Ruffin and Eddie Kendricks (often as dual leads, one medium, one higher into falsetto) with the Temptations were the outstanding voices to emerge from the Detroit scene.

The studio musicians, carefully nurtured by Gordy, varied in number and changed over two decades, but there was a solid core group in the 1960's that helped define the sound. A group led by pianist Eddie Van Dyke and featuring drummer Benny Benjamin and bassist James Jamerson formed the core of the studio band. Jamerson, in particular, became famous for his busy and percolating bass figures and riffs, which gave Motown its distinctive "bottom" sound. His inventive playing used jazz-influenced syncopated phrases in eighth- and sixteenth-note configurations with frequent harmonic changes.

Benjamin's thudding and kicking drumming pulse and the chopping and staccato rhythm chords of electric guitars combined with Jamerson's bass to create the rhythmic base upon which other musicians, with the guidance of producers such as H-D-H and Whitfield, garnished the songs. Members of the Detroit Symphony added swirling strings; flutes and vibes softened the harsher tones, and ethereal backing voices often finished the mix. Varieties of this formula applied to nearly all recordings. Funk was sweetened and decorated, saxes and horns mellow. The hits flowed.

In spite of the sense of a production-line mentality, diversity flourished at Motown. At the same time that there was plenty of mellow crooning that would sit well in intimate club settings or on television, there was still the harder-edged tradition of rhythm-and-blues shouting and rasping vocals. Lightweight teen love songs and lyrically sparse up-tempo dance pieces alternated with more mature songs that reflected pain and loss.

Singer Marvin Gaye epitomized the conflicting directions Motown's music took. Always aspiring to be a pop singer of slow ballads, he was directed by Berry Gordy to work on harsher vocal styles and more hard-driving songs reflective of black roots. He recorded both with consummate artistry. In 1971, he recorded *What's Goin' On*, an album of mostly his own songs focused on social issues. Such songs as "What's Going On," "Mercy Mercy Me," and "Inner City Blues" were in the line of message songs Motown artists started to write and record in the late 1960's and early 1970's. For a time, the real world of black poverty was reflected directly in Motown's music.

Smokey Robinson, on the other hand, always sang with a high tenor that easily soared into a falsetto. As a central songwriter at Motown and as first a member of the Miracles and then a solo singer, Robinson favored romantic love songs with an almost ethereal quality. Similarly, Diana Ross while with the Supremes had a light, sweet voice with a slight breathiness that worked well for crossing over into mainstream pop. Later, as a solo artist, she broadened her repertoire; her voice deepened and grew stronger, allowing her to handle songs of mature love and almost any sort of popular music. Stevie Wonder grew from a novelty instrumental act into a strong singer with a versatile repertoire made up largely of his own searching compositions, many of them in a socially conscious vein.

In 1971, Gordy moved the center of Motown's operation to Los Angeles and became more deeply involved in the solo career of Diana Ross, who soon became a film actor. By this time, many of the pioneer artists and producers had departed Motown, so Gordy focused more on a second generation of acts, notably the Jacksons. From 1971 through 1975, they had innumerable hits, both as the Jackson Five and with Michael Jackson as a solo performer.

The 1983 twenty-fifth anniversary television show that celebrated Motown's dominance of popular music demonstrated that even after many acts had left the company, the skills they had learned there had made them stars in mainstream pop music, black and white. Worldwide record sellers and international stars, they had taken the sound of Detroit and forever altered American music.

The Jacksons, reunited for that show, were the highlight; they sang a medley of their old hits and let Michael, now twenty-five and recording for another label, reveal how great a dancer and performer he had become. Berry Gordy's dream had come true.

—*Frederick E. Danker*

See also: Parker's Playing Epitomizes Bebop; Mahalia Jackson Begins Her Recording Career; Davis Develops 1950's Cool Jazz; Berry's

"Maybellene" Popularizes Rock and Roll; Brown Introduces Funk Music; Hendrix Releases Acid Rock Album *Are You Experienced?*

HANSBERRY'S *A RAISIN IN THE SUN* DEBUTS ON BROADWAY
March 11, 1959

Lorraine Hansberry's A Raisin in the Sun *portrayed the impact of racism on African Americans and became one of the first plays by an African American woman to achieve artistic and commercial success.*

Locale: New York, New York
Category: Theater

KEY FIGURES
Lorraine Hansberry (1930-1965), African American playwright
Lloyd Richards (1922-2006), African American director
Robert Nemiroff (1936-1991), African American writer and songwriter who was Hansberry's husband and literary executor
Sidney Poitier (b. 1924), African American actor
Claudia McNeil (1917-1993), African American actor
Ruby Dee (b. 1924), African American actor
Diana Sands (1934-1973), African American actor

SUMMARY OF EVENT
On March 11, 1959, after playing in Chicago, Philadelphia, and New Haven, Connecticut, Lorraine Hansberry's *A Raisin in the Sun* (pr., pb. 1959) opened at the Ethel Barrymore Theatre in New York City. The play instantly met with rave reviews from both black and white critics and became a quick financial success. It ran for 530 performances, setting a new record for the longest-running Broadway play written by a black American. It was also the first play written by a black woman to be performed on Broadway.

A Raisin in the Sun won the prestigious New York Drama Critics Circle Award for the year's best play over Tennessee Williams's *Sweet Bird of Youth*, Eugene O'Neill's *A Touch of the Poet*, and Archibald Mac-

Leish's *J. B.* At age twenty-eight, Hansberry was the youngest playwright to receive the award. *A Raisin in the Sun* was also instrumental in furthering the careers of the play's actors and its director, Lloyd Richards. Moreover, the play's commercial success enabled other black playwrights to get their work produced and gave Hansberry a visibility that made her an important voice in the theater. She spoke and wrote prolifically about theater and the arts, society and politics, and equal rights for blacks, women, and gays and lesbians.

A "living-room drama," the play focuses on the financial and emotional struggles of three generations of a black family in late 1950's Chicago. The play's central conflict begins when Lena Younger receives a ten thousand dollar check from her deceased husband's insurance company. Walter Lee, her son, who works as a chauffeur, wants to use the money to finance a liquor store, while Beneatha, Lena's daughter, wants to go to medical school.

After Lena takes some of the money and puts a down payment on a house in an all-white neighborhood—an emotional and economic decision, not a political one—she gives the rest to Walter, entrusting him to deposit half of it in the bank for Beneatha's education and to use the rest for his business. Walter, though, gives the money to a con artist, who absconds with it. Meanwhile, a white representative from Clybourne Park, the neighborhood where the family's new house is located, attempts to bribe the family not to move there through the rhetoric of good-neighborliness and thinly veiled threats. In the play's final scene, as Walter understands the significance of his family's pride, he refuses the white man's offer, and the family prepares to move.

Critics in 1959 discussed a number of reasons for the success of *A Raisin in the Sun*. Many praised the believability of the characters, and some even suggested that they were universal and not necessarily specifically African American. Some critics saw the play as supporting assimilation, and others noted its focus on Africa and its complex and sympathetic portrayal of Pan-Africanism. Certainly, the critics agreed on the play's emotional impact and on the significance of a Broadway theater filled with racially mixed audiences. In addition to providing a concrete example of the Broadway success of an African American drama, Hansberry's play articulates many significant political issues.

Her representations of African Americans are complex and varied. In terms of class, for example, she portrays George, an upper-middle-class black man who will inherit his father's business and who thinks that school is merely a means to an end; Beneatha, a young woman who wants to go to medical school to save people but who is also exploring her identity through various artistic expressions; Lena, the matriarch, who is concerned with providing a home for her family; and Walter Lee, the son who wants to make quick money and who harbors romantic dreams of success.

The various characters also have different relationships to their racial identity. George is portrayed as supporting assimilation, while Asagai, Beneatha's Nigerian beau, finds black Americans apolitical. Asagai's clothing and values are foreign to Lena, who identifies with black American culture. Never before had such a range of black characters been portrayed on the American stage.

While much of the plot of *A Raisin in the Sun* revolves around Walter Lee and his growth, Hansberry's female characters are strong and complex and do not merely function as sexual objects. Rather, George, Asagai, and Walter Lee are overt chauvinists. In this way, *A Raisin in the Sun* is an excellent example of the complicated intersections of oppressions of gender, race, and class.

Hansberry grew up in Chicago, the daughter of a prominent real estate broker and the niece of a Harvard University professor of African history. Her parents were intellectuals and activists, and her father won an antisegregation case before the Illinois Supreme Court, upon which the events in the play were loosely based. Although her family was middle class, she attended segregated schools. She went to the University of Wisconsin for two years, then moved to New York in 1950. She met and married Robert Nemiroff, an aspiring writer, in 1953. Several years later, Hansberry showed a draft of *A Raisin in the Sun* to Nemiroff, who suggested that

she read it to a producer friend of his, Philip Rose. Rose wanted to produce the play and immediately started to raise money. Because it seemed like a risky proposition to many New York producers, though, *A Raisin in the Sun* opened out of town, without a New York booking.

Hansberry completed one other play, *The Sign in Sidney Brustein's Window (*1964), a philosophical play about a white man in Greenwich Village. It opened before her death from cancer at age thirty-five but was neither a financial nor critical success. Later critics commented that the play was misunderstood. Nemiroff continued Hansberry's legacy by compiling various letters and notes, which he edited and published as *To Be Young, Gifted and Black: A Portrait of Lorraine Hansberry in Her Own Words* (1969). He also arranged for the television production of *The Drinking Gourd* (1972), completed Hansberry's unfinished manuscript of *Les Blancs (*1970), and published another play, *What Use Are Flowers?* (1972).

SIGNIFICANCE

Since its first production in 1959, *A Raisin in the Sun* has served as an artistic, literary, and political touchstone for African American theater. The play influenced the black theater movement of the 1960's by showing black artists that success on Broadway was attainable, and it opened a place for black realism as a dramatic genre. The play's visibility positioned Hansberry as a spokesperson for issues about race, gender, politics, and the arts.

The play effectively launched the careers of many of the people involved. *A Raisin in the Sun* was the first Broadway directing job for director Lloyd Richards, who had worked previously as an actor and a director; he was the first black man to direct on Broadway. Richards went on to direct many plays on and off Broadway, including many of the plays of Pulitzer Prize-winning dramatist August Wilson. He has also served as the director for the prestigious O'Neill Playwrights' Center, as the dean of the Yale School of Drama, and as the artistic director of the Yale Repertory Theatre.

Before the opening of *A Raisin in the Sun*, only Sidney Poitier and Claudia McNeil were well known among the play's cast. Poitier began acting with the American Negro Theatre in 1945, and McNeil worked as a nightclub and vaudeville singer before performing on Broadway in Arthur Miller's *The Crucible* in 1953. Poitier subsequently acted in many plays, films, and television shows, and he won an Academy Award for his performance in 1963's *Lilies of the Field*. Ruby

Dee, who worked with the American Negro Theatre in Harlem before *A Raisin in the Sun*, went on to establish herself on the stage, in films, and on television. Other well-known African American actors who performed in *A Raisin in the Sun* include Lonne Elder III, Glynn Turman, and Diana Sands, who died of cancer at age thirty-nine.

Numerous African American black playwrights, actors, directors, and producers have cited *A Raisin in the Sun* as having influenced their work and their ambitions. Hansberry preceded the Black Arts movement and affected Amiri Bakara, James Baldwin, and Charles Fuller. August Wilson's plays, each of which, in realist form, focuses on an African American family, are probably the best illustration of Hansberry's artistic legacy. Hansberry's work has also been important to the work of black women playwrights, including Adrienne Kennedy and Ntozake Shange.

There have been many critical debates about the meaning and significance of *A Raisin in the Sun*. Particularly during the Black Arts movement of the 1960's, many African American artists objected to the realist form of Hansberry's play, which they saw as artistically conservative. They also saw success on Broadway as a political compromise. Some thought Hansberry sacrificed her integrity to make her message palatable to a white audience. Similarly, many critics have argued over the play's meaning and about whether or not the play is assimilationist. Some have criticized the fact that many white audiences seem to have been able to identify with the characters, disregarding their own racism.

Some critics have quoted Hansberry as saying that *A Raisin in the Sun* is a play about people who happen to be black, but Nemiroff has commented on this frequent misquotation, which does imply that the play has an assimilationist meaning. In actuality, Hansberry said that *A Raisin in the Sun*, is, first and foremost, a black play.

In *A Raisin in the Sun*, Hansberry anticipated many aspects of the Civil Rights and women's movements. For example, Beneatha wears an Afro hairstyle, which was uncommon in 1959 but which emerged a few years later as a significant political statement of black pride; Beneatha, who clearly represents Hansberry in the play, also discusses the political implications of her choice of hairstyle. Ruth struggles over whether or not to have an abortion, and, of course, the central issue of the play is whether or not the family should move to a white neighborhood.

Since 1959, there have been countless productions of *A Raisin in the Sun* in both professional and

A New Neighborhood

Lorraine Hansberry's play A Raisin in the Sun *(1959) tells the story of an African American family's quest to buy their own home, one that happens to be in a "white" neighborhood. In the following final scene from the play, the family receives a visitor: a "Mr. Lindner" from the new neighborhood's "improvement association." Lindner, however, is anything but welcoming:*

Lindner: Well, I don't know how much you folks know about our organization. It is one of these community organizations set up to look after—oh, you know, things like block upkeep and special projects—as we also have what we call our New Neighbors Orientation Committee.

Beneatha: Yes—and what do they do?

Lindner: Well—it's what you might call a sort of welcoming committee, I guess. I mean they—we—I'm the chairman of the committee—go around and see the new people who move into the neighborhood and sort of give them the lowdown on the way we do things out in Clybourne Park. . . . And we also have the category of what the association calls—uh—special community problems.

Beneatha: Yes—and what are some of those? . . .

Lindner: I am sure you people must be aware of some of the incidents which have happened in various parts of the city when colored people have moved into certain areas. . . . Anybody can see that you are a nice family of folks, hardworking and honest, I'm sure.

Lindner then drops the following "advice" on the family:

Lindner: It is a matter of the people of Clybourne Park believing, rightly or wrongly, as I say, that for the happiness of all concerned that our Negro families are happier when they live in their *own* communities.

Beneatha: This, friends, is the Welcoming Committee!

Walter: Is this what you came marching all the way over here to tell us?

Lindner: Well now, we've been having a fine conversation. I hope you'll hear me all the way through.

Walter: Go ahead, man.

Lindner: You see—in the face of all the things I have said, we are prepared to make your family a generous offer . . . to buy the house from you at a financial gain to your family.

Ruth: Lord have mercy, ain't this the living gall!

nonprofessional theaters. A film version was made in 1961, and a revival was produced for television's *American Playhouse* in 1989.

—*Stacy Wolf*

See also: Ellison's *Invisible Man* Is Published; Baldwin Voices Black Rage in *The Fire Next Time*; *Dutchman* Dramatizes Racial Hatred; *The Autobiography of Malcolm X* Is Published.

CHURCH BOMBINGS

1960s

The bombings of African American churches in the South generated international interest. White segregationists in the 1960's expressed their rage at civil rights groups by destroying the churches that served as a focal point for African American activities.

The Events: Racially motivated hate crimes directed against African American churches
Places: Southern states

In the 1950's, the slow desegregation of public facilities began in the United States. The era was symbolized by the Montgomery, Alabama, bus boycott led by ministers of African American churches including Martin Luther King, Jr. Activists, often initially African American college students, challenged public places that required separate facilities such as transportation agencies, retail outlets, and medical centers. As the Civil Rights movement developed, a broader spectrum of the African American populace and some whites participated.

Congress of Racial Equality and members of the All Souls Church march in memory of the 16th Street Baptist Church bombing victims on September 22, 1963, By Thomas J. O'Halloran, photographer

As more African Americans demonstrated resistance to segregation, the reaction to that resistance increased. Although the protesters were largely peaceful, the reaction to them was often violent.

Bombings of African American buildings—churches, private homes, businesses, and schools—was fairly widespread by the early 1960's. By 1963, racially motivated bombings had been reported in Alabama, Arkansas, Florida, Georgia, Louisiana, Mississippi, South Carolina, and Virginia. However, some incidents went unreported because some victims were too afraid; other incidents were not publicized by local law-enforcement personnel who were often suspected of having condoned or having taken part in the bombings. The exact numbers of bombings of African American structures in the 1960's cannot be calculated, but it certainly far exceeds the few widely publicized incidents that eventually drew national and international attention.

HOMES AND CHURCHES

Besides churches, the homes of civil rights activists were a prime target. In Birmingham, Alabama, the home of the brother of Martin Luther King, Jr., was nearly demolished by a bomb. A firebomb was used to partially destroy the home of an African American congressman in Clarksdale, Mississippi, and in Jackson, Mississippi, a bomb exploded in the carport of Medgar Evers, the state's leader of the National Association for the Advancement of Colored People, who was later murdered. Bombs exploded at the University of Alabama at Tuscaloosa, where an African American woman was enrolled, and at the integrated University of Mississippi at Oxford. Black-owned businesses in Birmingham, the Mississippi towns of Greenwood and Gulfport, and Charleston, South Carolina, were also targeted. In many cases, the homeowners or business employees and clientele inside the structures were injured. In most cases, the targeted people and institutions were somehow associated with desegregation events. Often, the bombings were not fully investigated, no one was charged, and perpetrators, if identified, were unrestrained. In cases where indictments were sought, penalties were sometimes modest.

African American churches became a focal point of the bombings. White segregationists correctly understood how significant the churches were in the 1960's struggles for civil rights. First, the church was the most important community organization among African American people. A majority of African Americans were either members of a church or viewed it as a center of black life in the towns and cities in which they resided; no other institution was as widespread or as symbolic of African American values. Second, the churches had historically produced communal leadership. Ministers were not only spiritual leaders, they helped educate people, provided social services to the needy, and became important political leaders. Third, civil rights activists held their major meetings as well as strategy sessions in African American churches. Often, the churches were the only sites where African Americans could gather under black leadership without interruption by whites. The churches encouraged the development of leadership that was not dependent on the larger community, and this group of ministerial and lay leaders was interpreted as a threat by whites attempting to preserve segregation.

African American churches in the South had been vandalized and terrorized before the 1960's, sometimes by individual whites and sometimes by groups of whites expressing racist feelings. The bombings of the 1960's differed in that far more organization was behind the acts. Often the major white supremacist organizations, such as the Ku Klux Klan and the White Citizens Councils, planned and executed these events. Giving covert support to these organizations were white community leaders who would explicitly state their segregationist views but would not personally commit any violent acts, preferring to let the members of the supremacist organizations act on their behalf. These community leaders included governors and congressmen.

ARKANSAS AND BIRMINGHAM

The most-publicized African American church bombings that took place in the 1960's occurred in Pine Bluff and Gillet, Arkansas, and in Birmingham. In Gillet, no reason was ever given for the dynamiting of a rural African American church. In Pine Bluff, the bomb that set an African Methodist Episcopal church on fire was perceived to be a reaction to the pastor's activities: He had been an adviser to African American students who were attempting to desegregate lunch counters in the city.

The bombings of churches in Birmingham were part of forthright resistance to segregation in the 1950's and 1960's that included the use of fire hoses and police dogs against unarmed, peaceful civil rights protesters. By 1963, Bethel Baptist Church, an African American congregation, had been bombed twice, with devices strong enough to damage homes in the area. In the latter part of 1963, the Sixteenth Street Baptist Church was shattered by a bomb, and that event became an international symbol of the danger for African Americans struggling to desegregate the South. The church, a centrally located, large, and prestigious edifice, was the main meeting place for activists, until September 15, 1963, when a bomb not only injured worshipers but also killed four young girls aged ten to fourteen. They died in their Sunday school classrooms, and their bodies were mutilated by the force of the blast.

Photos of the destruction accompanied by pictures of the victims when they were alive appeared in newspapers and on television screens around the world. For many, Birmingham symbolized the depth of racism in the United States, and the four dead girls and twenty-three wounded parishioners were martyrs in a struggle for social justice. The Sixteenth Street Baptist Church was no longer safe to use for further rallies; the bombers had accomplished their immediate goal in destroying the facility. King wired Alabama governor George Wallace that the blood of the victims was on Wallace's hands. The governor disclaimed any association with the bombers and any responsibility for establishing a social climate that would lead to such acts.

IMPACT

The response to the church bombings varied. White southern politicians who favored segregation did not admit any responsibility for the bombings, and very few clearly stated their opposition to the violence and the groups believed responsible for it. Some politicians made no comment, and others claimed that civil rights activists associated with the churches had indirectly encouraged the violence. Northern and western politicians and the international press evidenced concern and some alarm, especially following the bombing of the Sixteenth Street Baptist Church in Birmingham. This concern, along with other factors, later resulted in some national policy changes: The passage of the Civil

Rights Act of 1964 was clearly influenced by the overt violence against religious organizations and especially by the deaths of the four children attending Sunday school in Birmingham. The image of innocent girls dying in a house of worship evoked both an emotional response and a practical one on a national and international level. However, although northern and western politicians decried the bombings, they did not relate these events to the more subtle racism that existed in their own districts.

The impact of the church bombings on the African American community was quite different from the intimidation that the bombers had intended. Some researchers think that the bombings and the resulting injuries and deaths were a major factor in causing many African Americans to turn away from nonviolent protest and become more attracted to organizations that emphasized self-defense and separation of the races. Integration became less attractive; black power became more inviting. Nonviolent protest organizations such as King's Southern Christian Leadership Conference (SCLC) were considered by some to be ineffectual in such circumstances, while the relatively militant Black Panther Party and the Nation of Islam, with its spokesperson Malcolm X, grew increasingly influential. The bombers of African American churches may have achieved their immediate goals, but they did not prevent desegregation or the empowering of African Americans. Rather, they further discredited the segregationist cause and encouraged many African Americans to move toward a more militant ideology.

—William Osborne and Max C. E. Orezzoli

See also: Black Christian Nationalist Movement; Black church; Church burnings; Civil Rights movement; Ku Klux Klan; *R.A.V. v. City of St. Paul*; Southern Christian Leadership Conference

LASSITER V. NORTHAMPTON COUNTY BOARD OF ELECTIONS
June 8, 1959

In this ruling, the Supreme Court upheld the right of the individual states to impose literacy tests for voting.

The Case: U.S. Supreme Court ruling on the right to vote

An African American challenged a state literacy test that applied to voters of all races. The Supreme Court did not infer that the test was being used to discriminate against members of minorities and unanimously upheld the state law. In his opinion for the Court, Justice William

O. Douglas wrote that states had wide latitude in passing laws establishing conditions for suffrage. This decision would seem to have stood in the way of the 1965 Civil Rights Act, which dispatched federal registrars to southern states that often had used literacy tests as a way to prevent African Americans from voting. The Court avoided that problem by asserting in *South Carolina v.* *Katzenbach* (1966) that the pattern of segregation justified special measures under the Fifteenth Amendment.

—Richard L. Wilson

See also: Fifteenth Amendment; Fourteenth Amendment; Politics and government; Understanding tests

GREENSBORO SIT-INS

February 1-July 25, 1960

Sit-ins by African American college students in Greensboro, North Carolina, led to the integration of variety-store lunch counters and inspired similar direct-action tactics across the South. The struggle for civil rights became a mass movement after the sit-ins in Greensboro and other cities.

Locale: Greensboro, North Carolina

Categories: Civil rights and liberties; social issues and reform

KEY FIGURES

Ezell Blair, Jr. (b. 1942), *Franklin McCain* (b. 1943), *Joseph McNeil* (b. 1942), and

David Richmond (1942-1990), the so-called Greensboro Four, freshmen students at North Carolina A&T who started the sit-in

Edward R. Zane (b. 1899-1991), Greensboro city council member who chaired the committee seeking a negotiated settlement

Ralph Johns (b. 1916), white clothing store owner who urged the black college students to act against segregation

SUMMARY OF EVENT

Despite court decisions, limited integration of public schools, and events such as the Montgomery bus boycott, much of American life remained racially segregated as the United States entered the 1960's. This was especially true in the southern and border states, where the Jim Crow system of legally imposed racial separation remained largely intact. One symbol of the discrimination suffered by southerners of African descent was the fact that while they could shop in variety stores, they were not allowed to sit down and eat at the lunch counters often found in such establishments.

In 1960, Greensboro, North Carolina, was a rapidly growing city of 120,000 that prided itself on the progressive nature of its race relations. Segregated conditions were as characteristic of Greensboro, however, as they were of cities with reputations for racial violence and intimidation.

Despite the fact that Greensboro had been one of the few southern cities to accept publicly the Supreme Court's 1954 decision in *Brown v. Board of Education* overturning the doctrine of "separate but equal" in public education, the city had permitted only token integration of its schools. Its lunch counters would serve African Americans only if they stood, and the color line was effectively maintained in most areas of the city's life.

The prevailing order was unexpectedly challenged on February 1, 1960, when four college students from the all-black North Carolina Agricultural and Technical College (A&T) entered the Woolworth's variety store in downtown Greensboro. To illustrate the illogical nature of the system, the four first bought toothpaste and school supplies, carefully collecting their receipts as proof that the store would sell them merchandise. They then took seats at the lunch counter, to the amazement of store employees and other patrons. They were refused service and, after asking why Woolworth's would sell them toothpaste but not coffee, they left the lunch counter. There was no confrontation with the police, although a reporter did arrive and news of the sit-in was reported by the local press.

The four freshmen who would come to be known as the Greensboro Four—Ezell Blair, Jr., Franklin McCain, Joseph McNeil, and David Richmond—had not launched their protest as part of an orchestrated campaign. Rather, they were encouraged to undertake a public act of protest against segregation by Ralph Johns, the white owner of a clothing store who employed A&T students. Johns provided the students with the money for the items they purchased at Woolworth's and was also responsible for tipping off the newspaper. The students, however, acted on their own initiative and decided to challenge the Jim Crow system the night before the sit-in. During an animated discussion that night, triggered by McCain's recent experience with segregated bus travel, they dared one another to act. The four later acknowledged the influence of Mahatma Gandhi's example of nonviolence but stressed that their primary motivation derived from their own Christian convictions and sense of justice. Although all four had been youth members of the National Association for the Advancement of Colored People (NAACP), neither it nor any other civil rights organization was involved in the initial sit-in.

News of the protest by the four freshmen spread rapidly over the A&T campus and throughout the city. The Student Executive Committee for Justice was quickly formed, with the four at the center. The next day, February 2, twenty-three additional students accompanied the original quartet to Woolworth's. What had begun as a small protest began to grow, eventually becoming a mass movement. Soon the demonstrators were working in shifts, and the sit-in spread to Kress's, the other downtown variety store. The demonstrators invariably were well dressed and emphasized their commitment to nonviolence. The stores refused to serve them but did not ask the local police to arrest them. White hecklers, one of whom tried to set the coat of a demonstrator on fire, created some tension.

By the end of the week, the sit-ins had grown through the support of students from Bennett College, a black women's college in town, as well as through some participation by students from Greensboro's white colleges.

Tensions ran high, however, and on February 6, a bomb scare prompted the closing of both Woolworth's and Kress's. By this time, a well-organized student protest movement was in place, one that enjoyed wide support from Greensboro's black community, as well as national assistance from the Congress of Racial Equality (CORE), which began to organize boycotts of Woolworth's and Kress's in some northern cities. On February 8, sit-ins began in the neighboring city of Winston-Salem, and from there the phenomenon quickly spread.

In the wake of the bomb scare, the students agreed to a two-week truce, which was subsequently extended as efforts began to negotiate an end to the protests. Edward R.

Zane, a city council member who had strong ties to the local business community, pressed for action from Greensboro's mayor, George Roach. The latter eventually agreed to create a committee to seek a negotiated settlement and named Zane to head it.

The mayor's committee was appointed at the end of February and spent all of March gathering information and attempting to mediate between the students and the stores. The committee's mail showed that many in the community sympathized with the students' position. Managers of the two stores, however, believed that they were being singled out unfairly and were unwilling to desegregate without other eating establishments doing the same. The city's restaurants were unsympathetic to the variety stores' plight, however. At the end of the month, the committee announced that it had failed to achieve a settlement.

The sit-ins resumed on April 1. The next day, the two stores closed their lunch counters. Greensboro's black community responded with an economic boycott and street demonstrations that demanded an end to segregated eating facilities. The picketing soon attracted counter-pickets organized by the Ku Klux Klan, and the generally peaceful confrontations between the two groups became a feature of life in downtown Greensboro.

Kress's reopened its lunch counter later in the month but roped it off to allow store personnel to control access. When students peacefully moved into the restricted area, some forty-five of them were arrested, including three of the Greensboro Four. This was the only mass arrest during the sit-in campaign. The students were released without bail.

As the stand-off continued, downtown stores found that their business was falling off; Woolworth's sales fell by 20 percent. The economic boycott was directly effective, and in addition many whites stayed away to avoid whatever trouble might occur downtown. In these circumstances, pressure for a settlement mounted. The local newspapers had for some time been sympathetic to the demonstrators' aims, if not always with their methods.

Civic leaders and businesspeople not only worried about lost revenue but also feared the loss of Greensboro's progressive image. In June, Zane's committee undertook further negotiations. Finally, the stores agreed to the committee's recommendation that they desegregate their lunch counters, although they waited until school was out in order to avoid the appearance of giving in to the students. Without public announcement, the lunch counters desegregated on July 25, 1960. The first black patrons served were the stores' own employees.

SIGNIFICANCE

The Greensboro sit-ins marked the opening of a major new phase in the Civil Rights movement, one characterized by large-scale, grassroots protests against segregated conditions in public accommodations. Such direct action tactics, rather than protracted legal battles in the courts, would mark the Civil Rights movement of the first half of the 1960's. The sit-ins in Greensboro were neither the first sit-ins nor the first protests against segregated lunch counters.

Facilities in Oklahoma City and Wichita had been desegregated by similar tactics in 1958. It was the Greensboro sit-ins, however, that touched off the tidal wave of direct, confrontational protest that marked the early 1960's. Sit-in protests spread from Greensboro to other cities in North Carolina, then to Nashville and on to dozens of other southern cities as well as a number in the North. By the end of 1960, approximately one hundred southern cities had experienced sit-ins and roughly one-third of them had desegregated their lunch counters. More would follow in subsequent years. Approximately seventy thousand people participated in the sit-ins, making the movement the most massive expression of discontent with the racial status quo that the country had yet seen.

Blacks and sympathetic whites were inspired to confront other forms of segregation, and it became increasingly difficult for other whites to maintain that southern blacks were basically content and were only being stirred up by outside agitators. In cities where lunch counters were desegregated, white patrons quickly adjusted, casting further doubt on the proposition that southern race relations were impervious to change. For Greensboro, the sit-ins marked the beginning of a decade of periodic protests and change. The spring of 1963 would see more than one thousand arrests as demonstrators sought to desegregate a range of public accommodations. Out of this later round of protests would emerge Jesse Jackson, then a student at A&T. In 1969,

another period of demonstrations resulted in violence in which an A&T student was killed and several police officers injured.

The Greensboro sit-ins also marked something of a generational shift in the Civil Rights movement. Although they had received endorsement by the local NAACP chapter and some organizational support from CORE, the sit-ins had not been initiated by any of the major civil rights organizations but by four college students. In part, the sit-ins grew out of the impatience of the younger generation of southern blacks with the pace of change in race relations. It was largely the young who answered the call, first in Greensboro and later in other cities.

While the sit-ins were still going on in Greensboro, Ella Jo Baker of the Southern Christian Leadership Conference organized a meeting of black student leaders from throughout the South at Shaw University in Raleigh, North Carolina (April 15-17, 1960). Martin Luther King, Jr., and other civil rights leaders addressed the students, who decided to set up their own organization. Out of their efforts was born the Student Nonviolent Coordinating Committee (SNCC). It quickly became one of the most active and militant civil rights organizations of the 1960's and was involved in most of the major civil rights campaigns of the decade. In a broader context, the student activism embodied in the sit-ins and SNCC helped inspire the organization of the Students for a Democratic Society later in 1960, as well as contributing to the more general campus unrest of the decade.

Nationally, the sit-in movement that spread from Greensboro helped push civil rights onto the nation's political agenda. Ultimately, the campaign against segregated facilities that began in Greensboro would help secure passage of the Civil Rights Act of 1964, a measure that outlawed racial segregation in eating places and other public accommodations.

—William C. Lowe

See also: Chicago sit-ins; Civil Rights movement; Greensboro sit-ins

STUDENT NONVIOLENT COORDINATING COMMITTEE

Founded in April, 1960

As tensions mounted during in the mid-1960's, the Student Nonviolent Coordinating Committee became increasingly aggressive and eventually dropped its nonviolent stance.

Identification: National civil rights organization also known by its acronym, SNCC (pronounced "snick")
Place: Raleigh, North Carolina

In early 1960, amid a growing number of student civil rights demonstrations, the Southern Christian Leadership Conference (SCLC), led by Martin Luther King, Jr., encouraged students to convene their own organization. In response to the call, a group of student leaders, under the guidance of Ella Baker, a former administrative head of SCLC, formed the Student Nonviolent Coordinating Committee.

Committed at the outset to nonviolence, SNCC was designed to be thoroughly democratic and to function independently from mainstream groups, including the SCLC. It also became a biracial organization although initially there was some concern that allowing white students to join SNCC might compromise the organization.

DIRECT ACTION

Despite its nonviolent philosophy, SNCC was often very aggressive and confrontational in attacking segregation. The organization took on several of the more dangerous civil rights battles including voter registration campaigns in Alabama and Mississippi. Numerous times SNCC activists were badly beaten, and in the summer of 1964, three activists who had joined the SNCC campaign—Michael Schwerner, Andrew Goodman, and James Chaney—were brutally murdered by southern segregationists including members of the Ku Klux Klan. Nevertheless, SNCC continued its confrontational strategy.

By 1964, frustrated by the slow pace of change and apparent lack of support from the federal government, SNCC members began to splinter into two factions. One group sought to maintain the organization's original principles, and the other chose to reconsider the group's nonviolent approach. Racial tensions within the organization further divided SNCC. African American volunteers were concerned that their white counterparts were

taking control of the organization, and white members were growing more critical of SNCC leadership. Amid the internal tensions, many SNCC members became increasingly radical.

During the mid-1960's, SNCC members, under the charismatic leadership of Stokely Carmichael, embraced a new creed of black power. The slogan became a call for economic self-determination and political activism as well as a symbol of black militancy. Carmichael believed that change would come only through dramatic, confrontational appeals. The evolving SNCC philosophy advocated responding to violence with violence. The increasingly strident rhetoric led some members to abandon the organization, but at the same time, it attracted new membership, particularly radical, northern, urban African Americans. Further demonstrating its new direction, SNCC shifted its activities from voting rights and educational issues in the rural South to conditions in urban ghettos.

DECLINE

SNCC, plagued by ineffective leadership and constant internal divisions, saw its membership dwindle to a handful of activists by 1968. The organization was further undermined by its entering into a formal alliance with the Black Panthers and by concern that the organization associated with other paramilitary groups. The last two SNCC chapters, Atlanta and New York, ceased operation in early 1970.

SNCC activists helped to focus the nation on the problem of institutionalized racism by taking a leading role in several major civil rights demonstrations during the 1960's. In 1961, SNCC members helped the Congress of Racial Equality (CORE) operate Freedom Rides that challenged the constitutionality of segregated interstate busing laws in the South. The rides attracted much media coverage, which brought the Civil Rights movement into middle-class white suburban homes for the first time and helped pressure President John F. Kennedy into paying more attention to civil rights issues. The rides were immediately followed by the Albany, Georgia, demonstrations, in which SNCC members sat in whites-only sections of local bus stations to test interstate transportation laws that made segregated facilities illegal.

In 1964, SNCC organized a voter registration and educational campaign in Mississippi. A biracial effort carried out by college student volunteers, the second phase of the campaign, in which young workers were to educate voters, became known as Freedom Summer. This campaign further enlightened Americans about the plight of African Americans in the South. The student volunteers who participated in the campaign were able to register more than seventeen thousand African American voters and provided more than three thousand children with educational instruction. The efforts, however, came at a price. During the summer, at least sixty-seven bombings and arson fires were directed at the volunteers. In one incident, three activists, Schwerner, Goodman, and Chaney, were killed. That same summer, SNCC helped organize the forming of the Mississippi Freedom Democratic Party, which challenged the credentials of the Mississippi delegation to the 1964 Democratic National Convention when it met to nominate Lyndon B. Johnson. SNCC members were also among the organizers and participants in most of the civil rights marches during the mid-1960's, including the March on Washington in 1963 and the march from Selma to Montgomery in 1965.

Though SNCC disbanded early in the 1970's, several of the organization's leaders and former members remained activists on both the local and national levels well into the 1970's. Among the more notable former SNCC members are James Forman, who became involved in African American economic development; John Lewis, who in 1988 won election to the House of Representatives; Charles Sherrod, who was elected mayor of Albany, Georgia; and Robert Moses, who became director of a nationwide literacy program. Other former members became involved in protesting the Vietnam War and in the women's rights movement.

—*Paul E. Doutrich*

See also: Birmingham March; "Black Manifesto"; Black Panther Party; Black Power movement; Chicago riots; Civil Rights movement; Civil rights worker murders; Congress of Racial Equality; Freedom Rides; Freedom Summer; Mississippi Freedom Democratic Party; Southern Christian Leadership Conference

CIVIL RIGHTS ACT OF 1960

May 6, 1960

The passage of the relatively weak Civil Rights Act of 1960 demonstrated the resistence to significant civil rights reform in the United States, but it also presaged the additional protections for voting rights that would be contained in the stronger Voting Rights Act, passed five years later.

Also known as: Public Law 449, 86th Congress; U.S. Code Title 42, section 1971 (amended)
Locale: Washington, D.C.
Categories: Civil rights and liberties; laws, acts, and legal history; social issues and reform

KEY FIGURES

Everett Dirksen (1896-1969), U.S. senator from Illinois, 1951-1969, and minority leader, 1959-1969
James Eastland (1904-1986), U.S. senator from Mississippi, 1941 and 1943-1978, and chair of the Senate Judiciary Committee, 1955-1978
Dwight D. Eisenhower (1890-1969), president of the United States, 1953-1961

Lyndon B. Johnson (1908-1973), U.S. senator from Texas, 1949-1961, majority leader, 1955-1961, vice president of the United States, 1961-1963, and president, 1963-1969
Richard Russell, Jr. (1897-1971), U.S. senator from Georgia, 1933-1971
Howard W. Smith (1883-1976), U.S. representative from Virginia, 1931-1967, and chair of the House Rules Committee, 1955-1966

SUMMARY OF EVENT

The Fifteenth Amendment to the Constitution, passed in 1870, was designed to protect the right of African Americans to vote. The amendment simply says: "The right of citizens of the United States to vote shall not be denied or abridged by the United States or by any State on account of race, color, or previous condition of servitude." Officials in the Southern states, however, found numerous ways to disfranchise black voters without violating the Fifteenth Amendment, such as the literacy test, poll tax, grandfather clause, and white primary. As a result of these voting barriers, most African

Americans were eliminated as voters, in spite of what the Fifteenth Amendment was designed to do. The civil rights bills of the late 1950's and the 1960's were designed to make the Fifteenth Amendment enforceable.

Since the end of Reconstruction, Congress had passed only one civil rights bill, in 1957. The 1957 law sought to empower the federal government to protect voting rights by seeking injunctions against voting rights violations. In reality, the 1957 law was so weak that only a few suits were brought by the Department of Justice against the illegal practices of voting officials. The 1957 Civil Rights Act established the U.S. Commission on Civil Rights, which was given the authority to investigate civil rights abuses. The commission could draw national attention to civil rights problems and recommend legislation to Congress, but it had no enforcement powers. African Americans and civil rights supporters realized that something substantial was needed to protect black voting rights.

In 1959, President Dwight D. Eisenhower introduced a seven-point civil rights program. Three parts of the bill dealt with education and school desegregation, the most significant provision being the attempt to make it a crime to interfere with court-ordered desegregation. The bill requested a two-year extension of the Civil Rights Commission and contained several other provisions to combat economic discrimination. The only section of the law that involved voting rights was the provision that states must preserve voting records for three years. This provision was needed to prove whether there was a pattern or practice of discrimination in voting.

Conspicuously missing from the Eisenhower bill was a request that Congress authorize the attorney general to bring civil proceedings to protect voting rights. This provision, known as Title III, had been the heart of the administration's 1957 Civil Rights Act. Title III would have allowed the federal government to prevent interference with civil rights instead of only being able to punish such interference after the fact. Intense Southern opposition to Title III forced the administration to abandon the provision in the 1957 Civil Rights Act, as Eisenhower believed that Congress was not ready to incorporate Title III in the administration's new bill.

A subcommittee of the House Committee on the Judiciary, comprising mostly Northern civil rights supporters, strengthened the Eisenhower bill and restored Title III. The full Judiciary Committee, containing many Southern opponents of civil rights, quickly gutted most of the stronger sections passed by the subcommittee. The weakened bill was passed by the Judiciary

Committee and forwarded to the important House Committee on Rules. The Rules Committee, chaired by Howard W. Smith, a Virginia segregationist, did not act on the bill until civil rights supporters threatened to discharge the bill from the Rules Committee's jurisdiction. The Democratic Study Group, a newly formed organization consisting of liberal Democrats, led the movement to free the bill from the Rules Committee. The Rules Committee finally sent the civil rights bill to the floor of the House for consideration by the entire House.

Southern Democrats led much of the opposition to the bill. Opponents contended that the bill went too far in protecting voting rights and encroached on the rights of states to control the election process. Representative William Colmer, a Democrat from Mississippi, said that "even in the darkest days of Reconstruction, the Congress never went as far as the proponents of this legislation, in this 1960 election year, propose to go." After defeating numerous Southern amendments to weaken an already weak bill, the House voted 311 to 109 to approve the civil rights bill and send it to the Senate.

The United States Senate has often been the burial ground of civil rights laws, especially during the 1940's, 1950's, and 1960's. This was primarily the result of two factors. First, Southern Democrats, by virtue of their seniority, controlled many key committees, including the Committee on the Judiciary, to which civil rights legislation, by jurisdiction, must be referred. Second, Southern senators were skillful in the use of legislative tactics, such as the filibuster, to kill legislation.

The Eisenhower bill was sent to the Senate Judiciary Committee, chaired by Democratic senator James Eastland of Mississippi. Eastland, a staunch segregationist, refused to act on the bill. Only as a result of a parliamentary maneuver undertaken by Majority Leader Lyndon B. Johnson and Minority Leader Everett Dirksen was the bill brought to the floor of the Senate for debate.

Southern senators, led by Democrat Richard Russell, Jr., of Georgia, organized a filibuster. All Southern senators participated in the filibuster, with the exception of the two senators from Tennessee and the two senators from Texas. Supporters of the civil rights bill attempted to end the lengthy filibuster by invoking cloture, which required two-thirds of the Senate to vote to stop the filibuster. When the cloture vote took place, only forty-two of the one hundred senators voted to stop the filibuster. The civil rights supporters not only failed to get the two-thirds vote required but also failed to muster a simple majority.

The defeat of cloture meant that the Southern Democratic senators had won and could dictate the terms of the final bill. The final, watered-down version of the bill contained little that would protect the voting rights of African Americans. The most significant provision authorized federal judges to appoint federal referees to assist African Americans in registering and voting if a pattern or practice of discrimination was found. The Senate passed the weakened bill by seventy-one to eighteen, and President Eisenhower signed the bill into law on May 6, 1960. The fact that only two other individuals were present when Eisenhower signed the bill into law testifies to its legislative insignificance.

SIGNIFICANCE

Perhaps the weakness of the 1960 Civil Rights Act was its main legacy. The law proved to be unable to cope with many problems confronting African Americans in the South. Many African Americans who attempted to register or vote lost their jobs, were subjected to violence, or were victimized by double standards or outright fraud on the part of voting officials. The impotence of the 1960 Civil Rights Act to deal with these issues, combined with the lack of progress in increasing the number of African American voters in the South, forced Congress to pass the powerful Voting Rights Act in 1965. This legislation would forever transform the political landscape of the South, and its consequences have continued to be felt.

—*Darryl Paulson*

See also: Supreme Court Rules African American Disenfranchisement Unconstitutional; Supreme Court Ends Public School Segregation; Montgomery Bus Boycott; Congress Creates the Commission on Civil Rights; Greensboro Sit-Ins; Civil Rights Protesters Attract International Attention; Poll Taxes Are Outlawed; Congress Passes the Civil Rights Act of 1964; Congress Passes the Voting Rights Act.

LEE'S *TO KILL A MOCKINGBIRD* CALLS FOR SOCIAL JUSTICE

July 11, 1960

Harper Lee's novel To Kill a Mockingbird, *a moving plea for social justice, was a popular and critical success, winning a Pulitzer Prize for the author and an Academy Award for the star of the film version of the book. The book remains in print and is considered one of the best American novels of the twentieth century.*

Locale: United States
Categories: Literature; civil rights and liberties; human rights; social issues and reform; women's issues

KEY FIGURES

Harper Lee (b. 1926), American novelist
Truman Capote (Truman Streckfus Persons; 1924-1984), American writer and Lee's lifelong friend
Gregory Peck (1916-2003), American actor who portrayed Atticus Finch in the film adapted from the novel

SUMMARY OF EVENT

Harper Lee's novel of social injustice, *To Kill a Mockingbird,* exposed the racism and prejudices of a fictional small southern town much like the one in which Lee grew up. Lee, however, did not intend the book to be a complete rejection of her southern heritage. Her mother, Frances Finch Lee, came from a distinguished Virginia family that founded the town of Finchburg, Alabama. Harper paid tribute to that side of her family by calling her fictional hero "Atticus Finch." Atticus was modeled on Harper's father Amasa Coleman (A. C.) Lee, a principled individual like his ancestor Robert E. Lee, the revered Confederate general.

A. C. was a community leader, a lawyer, a member of the state legislature, and part owner and editor of the local newspaper. Lee's independence of mind is reflected not only in her father's willingness to take unpopular cases but also in the fact that, at a time when women were not expected to enter the professions, he sent two daughters to law school. One of them, Alice, eventually became her father's partner. However, Harper chose her own way to influence others; in 1950, six months before she would have received her law degree, she left the University of Alabama and went to New York City to become a writer.

Lee had been writing since she was seven, and later some of her work appeared in campus publications. In New York City, however, she was just another would-be author, supporting herself by working as an airline reservations clerk. After completing two essays and three short stories, Lee took the manuscripts to a literary agent, who suggested that she develop one of the stories into a novel. At that point, a group of friends offered Lee enough money so that she could quit her job and spend all her time writing. Even after her father's illness made it necessary for her to divide her time between New York and Monroeville, Lee kept working on the novel, and, in 1957, she submitted the manuscript to an editor at J. B. Lippincott, only to be told to revise her work to make it more unified. *To Kill a Mockingbird* was finally published on July 11, 1960. Harper was soon to become part of a group of southern writers who were becoming increasingly important in the literary world.

To Kill a Mockingbird is set in the middle 1930's, long before the Civil Rights movement. It recaptures the Monroeville of the author's own childhood, when she was a tomboy like the character of Jean Louise "Scout" Finch. Lee had spent much of her time growing up with a boy named Truman Streckfus Persons (Truman Capote), who would become Charles Baker "Dill" Harris in the novel.

Scout, the novel's narrator, is a young person who, along with her brother Jem and her friend Dill, learn from Scout's father that no matter what others say, every human being has value. In addition to being a book about racial injustice, in which an innocent African American man, Tom Robinson, is accused of and found guilty of raping a white girl, the novel also tells the story of Arthur "Boo" Radley, branded a monster by the community. Boo is befriended by the children and proves his worth by saving Jem's life. Jem learns just how deceptive appearances can be when, forced by his father to read to an ill-tempered old lady, he discovers that she is bravely battling addiction to morphine.

Scout emulates her father's courage by facing down a lynch mob. Throughout the novel, she also emulates his independence of mind by refusing to adopt the mannerisms of a southern lady, thus defying the gender role her aunt is determined to force on her. Eventually, Scout learns to differentiate between consideration for others—of the kind her father practices—and mindless affectation.

After the book appeared, A. C. Lee voiced pride in his daughter's work. He saw in the novel his own life story, that of a southern liberal who for years had spoken out for social justice, like many southern liberals of the time. Though A. C. had never defended an African American man in a rape case, he rightly saw himself in the character of Atticus Finch.

Defending Tom Robinson

Atticus Finch tells Scout why he is defending Tom Robinson at trial in this excerpt from Harper Lee's To Kill a Mockingbird *(1960).*

Atticus sighed. "I'm simply defending a Negro—his name's Tom Robinson. He lives in that little settlement beyond the town dump. He's a member of Calpurnia's church, and Cal knows his family well. She says they're clean-living folks. Scout, you aren't old enough to understand some things yet, but there's been some high talk around town to the effect that I shouldn't do much about defending this man. It's a peculiar case. . . .

"If you shouldn't be defendin' him, then why are you doin' it?"

"For a number of reasons," said Atticus. "The main one is, if I didn't I couldn't hold up my head in town, I couldn't represent this country in the legislature, I couldn't even tell you or Jem not to do something"

"You mean if you didn't defend that man, Jem and me wouldn't have to mind you anymore?"

"That's about right."

"Why?"

"Because I could never ask you to mind me again. Scout, simply by the nature of the work, every lawyer gets at least one case in his lifetime that affects him personally.

This one's mine, I guess. You might hear some ugly talk about it at school, but do one thing for me if you will: you just hold your head high and keep those fists down. No matter what anybody says to you, don't you let 'em get your goat. Try fighting with your head for a change . . . it's a good one, even if it does resist learning."

Initially, *To Kill a Mockingbird*'s critical reception was mixed. Though some found the novel deeply moving, others objected to what they called sermonizing and a melodramatic ending. Nevertheless, in 1961, the book won the Pulitzer Prize for fiction, and it sold 2.5 million copies in its first year. It became a Literary Guild selection, a Book-of-the-Month Club alternate, and a *Reader's Digest* condensed book. The film *To Kill a Mockingbird* (1962) won an Academy Award for Horton Foote's adapted screenplay and a Best Actor Oscar for Gregory Peck, who played Atticus Finch. Peck had his own production company make the film, because the major studios rejected it as too controversial.

SIGNIFICANCE

Although at one time Harper Lee said that she was working on another novel with a southern setting, it evidently was not completed. Lee continued to divide her time between New York City and Monroeville. She lived quietly, rarely making public appearances or giving interviews.

In 1983, she presented a paper, "Romance and High Adventure," for the Alabama History and Heritage Festival. The paper appeared two years later in a collected work edited by Jerry E. Brown called *Clearings in the Thicket: An Alabama Humanities Reader*. Lee's reputation, though, rests on her one and only novel.

By the 1970's, unfavorable criticism of *To Kill a Mockingbird* had virtually vanished. The novel was no longer considered too preachy or too melodramatic. In fact, during the Civil Rights era, the novel was studied as a classic example of race prejudice in the South. By the 1990's, however, scholars revisiting the book began to see it in a broader perspective. Although the novel was clearly a work against racism, gender was a major theme as well.

Critical reinterpretations of Lee's novel, along with its enduring appeal to general readers, have made *To Kill A Mockingbird* a classic work in American literature. It remains in print, has been translated into many foreign languages, and is a standard text in American high schools and colleges. With its plea for tolerance and understanding, *To Kill a Mockingbird* has undoubtedly left its mark on a changing culture. Indeed, in 2003, the American Film Institute named Atticus Finch, as portrayed by Peck, the greatest hero in the history of American cinema.

—*Rosemary M. Canfield Reisman*

See also: Ellison's *Invisible Man* Is Published; 1963: Baldwin Voices Black Rage in *The Fire Next Time*.

WILMA RUDOLPH BECOMES THE FASTEST WOMAN IN THE WORLD

September 7, 1960

Wilma Rudolph became the first American female athlete to win three gold medals during a single Olympic Games, setting a record as the fastest woman in the world. Her wins marked the first time any American woman had accomplished such a feat, and the wins were especially notable because she lived with polio as a child.

Also known as: 1960 Olympic gold medals in 100-meter dash, 200-meter dash, and 4 × 100-meter relay race
Locale: Rome, Italy
Category: Sports

KEY FIGURES

Wilma Rudolph (1940-1994), Olympic track athlete
Ed Temple (b. 1927), Tennessee State University track coach and longtime trainer of Rudolph
Clinton Gray (fl. mid-twentieth century), Tennessee's Burt High School track coach
Blanche Rudolph (fl. mid-twentieth century), Rudolph's mother, whose determination was instrumental in restoring her daughter's ability to walk after living with polio

SUMMARY OF EVENT

At the 1960 Summer Olympic Games in Rome, African American sprinter Wilma Rudolph became the fastest woman in the world after winning the 100-meter and 200-meter races, tying and breaking previous records. She then anchored the American women's 4 x 100-meter relay race to a win. In all, she won three gold medals, becoming the first American woman to do so in a single Olympics. Called "The Black Pearl" and "The Black Gazelle" in newspapers worldwide, Rudolph, at twenty years old, won the admiration and adulation of fans both at home and abroad.

Rudolph was well prepared and trained for her Olympic feat in 1960. She had already won a bronze medal for the 4 × 400 relay at the age of sixteen at the Melbourne Olympics of 1956, and was still in high school at the time. Even before she went to college at Tennessee State University, she was mentored and coached by the college women's track coach Ed Temple. Her high school track coach, Clinton Gray, recognizing her potential, personally drove her to the college campus every day so she could train. Suffering several health setbacks between 1956 and 1960, including pulled muscles and a tonsillectomy, she was

431

Rudolph wins the women's 100 meter dash at the 1960 Summer Olympics in Rome.

ready for the Olympic Games in 1960. Five feet eleven inches in height, and slender at about 130 pounds, Rudolph was one of the calmest of athletes when she was about to perform. Described as relaxed and nerveless, she was even known to drift off to sleep lying on the massage table getting a rubdown for an upcoming meet.

At the Rome Olympics, Rudolph had good starts in all her races, running with arms pumping and legs moving in a flowing stride. In the 100-meter semifinal she tied the record, set at 11.3 seconds, and in the finals won the race three yards ahead of her nearest competitor. Her time for this race would have been a world record except that the race's judges determined there had been a tail wind of 2.752 meters per second, which was 0.752 meters per second more than the maximum accepted. Nevertheless, she won her first gold medal of the meet. She then went on to win the 200-meter race in 24 seconds (she had run this race in the trials at a world record 22.9 seconds), winning her second gold. The relay race might have been lost except for

her exceptional effort. The German team's runner had been leading, and Rudolph had been initially hampered in the run-up when a teammate made a faulty baton pass, but Rudolph, running the anchor position, soon overtook the German sprinter. The American team won the race in 44.5 seconds. In the semifinals, the team had set a world record for its event at 44.4 seconds.

Rudolph's wins at the 1960 Games opened the floodgates to other outstanding achievements. In 1961, she was invited to compete in the Millrose Games in New York's Madison Square Garden, the first time in thirty years a woman was invited to compete in the indoor track meet. She won the 60-yard dash in 6.9 seconds. Later that year she won the 60-yard dash in 6.8 seconds in the New York Athletic Club Games. She competed in a Louisville, Kentucky, meet and broke a world record for the 70-yard dash, and in a meet in West Germany she set a women's world record in the 100-meter dash.

Rudolph's achievements as the first American woman to win three Olympic gold medals could not have been more unexpected. Her ability to run so fast is itself phenomenal, under any circumstances. However, when she was born on June 23, 1940, in the small town of St. Bethlehem, Tennessee, about 50 miles from Nashville, she weighed only 4.5 pounds. She was feared to be too small and sickly to survive. Even after surviving her premature birth, she suffered through other health problems, including measles, mumps, chicken pox, scarlet fever, and double pneumonia. At age of four, she developed polio, losing the use of her left leg; she had to wear a metal brace.

Her parents, Ed and Blanche Rudolph, were not wealthy. Ed had fathered twenty-two children in two marriages—Wilma was number twenty—and he was a retired porter. Blanche worked as a domestic. The couple had to stretch their money, so the girls in the family had to wear homemade dresses made from flour sacks. When Wilma lost the use of her leg and doctors declared she would never be able to walk, Blanche took her to doctors at the all-black Meharry Medical College of Fisk University in Nashville, where Wilma was given physical therapy.

The 100-mile-round-trip drive to Nashville became a weekly routine for Blanche and Wilma. At home Blanche and some of the older siblings took turns massaging Wilma's leg several times each day until Wilma was eight years old, when she could walk without the metal brace. By age twelve, she was learning to play basketball in the backyard with her brothers.

Rudolph's athletic prowess was first noticed when she became an outstanding high school basketball player. In her sophomore year at Burt High School in Clarksville, she scored 803 points in twenty-five games, a record for high school girls' basketball in Tennessee.

Her athletic abilities quickly came to the attention of Temple, who agreed to train and mentor her. Gray ensured that she got to the college's summer sports camp every day to practice under Temple's guidance. She graduated from high school in 1957 and received a full scholarship to attend Tennessee State. Her athletic performance gained her so much celebrity that she took off a year from her college studies to compete in international track meets and for personal appearances around the United States. She graduated from college in 1963 with a degree in education.

SIGNIFICANCE

Although her accomplishments as an athlete are outstanding, Wilma Rudolph's work continued. She was concerned with other issues, such as racial segregation in her home state. When she was to be honored after her Olympic victories with a parade in her hometown, she insisted that the celebrations be open to everyone. For the first time in the town's history, a parade and celebratory banquet were integrated. Rudolph participated in later civil rights protests in Clarksville, leading the town to strike down its segregation laws.

When Rudolph started teaching, first in a Clarksville elementary school and later in Maine and Indiana, she also coached girls' track; wrote an autobiography, *Wilma (*1977); and saw it made into a television movie. Her awards and accolades over the years include the 1960

United Press Athlete of the Year award, the James E. Sullivan amateur athlete award in 1961, the 1962 Babe Zaharias Award, and the Women's Sports Foundation Award of 1984. She was inducted into the Black Sports Hall of Fame in 1980, the United States Olympic Hall of Fame in 1983, and the National Women's Hall of Fame in 1994. She also established the Wilma Rudolph Foundation, a community-based sports program. When she died of brain cancer at age fifty-four on November 12, 1994, she was almost universally acknowledged as a woman of grace, dignity, and extraordinary accomplishment.

Rudolph's outstanding performance in the 1960 Olympic Games reverberated throughout the sports world, as she set a high standard for female athletes in the most prestigious of international sports events; her athletic accomplishments gave her a listening audience for African American civil rights as well. She served as a United States goodwill ambassador to French West Africa, and she inspired girls and women everywhere to surmount any obstacles to reach their goals.

—Jane L. Ball

433

GOMILLION V. LIGHTFOOT
November 14, 1960

The Supreme Court struck down racial gerrymandering in Tuskegee, Alabama, opening the door for a reconsideration of the justiciability of redistricting cases.

The Case: U.S. Supreme Court ruling on gerrymandering

Justice Felix Frankfurter wrote the unanimous opinion of the Court overturning the arbitrary redrawing of the city limit lines in Tuskegee, Alabama, in such a way as to eliminate all but four or five African American voters while eliminating no white voters.

In doing so, Frankfurter had to get around his own opinion in *Colegrove v. Green* (1946) in which he had concluded that legislative redistricting was a political question best left to the legislature. He did not drop his opposition to general judicial review of legislative districts, using the Fifteenth Amendment's voting rights principle rather than the Fourteenth Amendment in his reasoning in *Gomillion*. He defended his *Colegrove* opinion in his dissent in *Baker v. Carr* (1962). Justices William O. Douglas and Charles E. Whittaker concurred but said they would have struck down the gerrymandering on Fourteenth Amendment grounds, foreshadowing the overturning of *Colegrove* by *Baker*.

—*Richard L. Wilson*

See also: Fifteenth Amendment; Gerrymandering; Voting Rights Act of 1965

VIETNAM WAR
1960's-1973

American involvement in the war in Vietnam yielded disparate results for African Americans who served there. On one hand, it was the first time that African Americans were fully integrated into the armed services. On the other, African American casualties were disproportionately greater than those suffered by white soldiers and were a significantly higher percentage than that of African Americans in the United States population. These discrepancies were mirrored at home in the conflicting attitudes of leaders of the Civil Rights movement and the African American population in general.

The Event: U.S. military involvement in Vietnam's civil war
Date:
Place: Southeast Asia

African Americans have fought in all the foreign wars in which the United States has been involved. Before the Vietnam War, most served in the Army, and all had been segregated into separate units. Not until World War II were African Americans allowed to join the Marines. Even after the services were integrated by Executive Order 9981 in 1948, the officer corps remained almost entirely white, and African Americans had few opportunities for promotion. Nevertheless, some African Americans stayed in the military services and advanced in the ranks. By the 1960's, the armed forces were among the few truly integrated institutions in American society, and many African Americans found more opportunities in the military services than in civilian life.

During the Vietnam War, the draft system helped to increase the number of African Americans in military service. College students were eligible for deferments from the draft; because fewer African Americans than whites were college students, a disproportionate number of them were drafted. Sixteen percent of draftees during the war were African Americans, although African Americans represented only 12 percent of the total U.S. population. Most African American servicemen during the war served in Army and Marine combat units, often on the front lines.

Some critics have charged that during the Vietnam War, African American soldiers were given the most dangerous combat assignments. Although fewer than 13 percent of the U.S. soldiers in Vietnam were African Americans, they constituted 20 percent of the Army's fatalities between 1961 and 1966. However, these figures may be misleading, as many African American soldiers volunteered to join the elite combat units, which offered higher pay, greater chances for promotion, and greater respect of others in the military, while also being involved in some of the most dangerous missions. At the time of the Vietnam War, women could not serve in combat roles. However, African Americans joined other women as army and air force nurses, as military personnel in noncombat positions, and in such civilian jobs as teachers, aid workers, and in government offices in Vietnam.

AFRICAN AMERICAN LEADERS SPEAK OUT

African American leaders have historically generally supported service in the military. However, as awareness and anger regarding discrimination throughout the United States grew, more leaders and soldiers questioned why citizens who were denied their rights at home should be sent to fight for the rights of citizens of other countries. The more radical factions of the Civil Rights movement further argued that members of an oppressed minority in the United States should not agree to kill members of an oppressed minority in a nation such as Vietnam.

In 1964, African Americans backed Lyndon B. Johnson for president overwhelmingly. Many initially refrained from criticizing his conduct of the Vietnam War because he had supported civil rights and voting rights legislation, and his Great Society program promised to lift the economically disadvantaged from poverty and other social ills. Critics noted, however, that Johnson's war policies drained away the money that could have been used to support these programs.

Radicals such as Eldridge Cleaver, Stokely Carmichael, and Malcolm X urged African Americans to refuse to serve in the Vietnam War. The moderate civil rights leader and winner of the Nobel Peace Prize, Martin Luther King, Jr., at first shied away from criticizing the Vietnam War. However, in April, 1967, he delivered his "Beyond War" speech, adding a highly respected voice to the growing criticism of the war. Another prominent African American critic was heavyweight boxing champion Muhammad Ali, who refused induction into the Army because of his religious beliefs. He was not granted conscientious objector status; instead, he was convicted of draft evasion, sentenced to prison, and stripped of his boxing title. However, his title was later restored.

During the early years of the Vietnam War, racial tensions in the military were muted, but as the Civil Rights movement and antiwar protests converged to increase polarity in the United States, divisions in the armed services mirrored societal chasms. At the start of American involvement in the war, many of the African Americans in the military had been career soldiers who had had little contact with the Civil Rights movement at home. As the war lengthened, more young African American soldiers arrived from the ghettos and housing projects of the cities in which civil rights protests were growing. African American soldiers began to band together, studying black history and culture, using special signs and handshakes, and calling themselves blood brothers, or "bloods."

DISTINGUISHED AFRICAN AMERICAN SERVICEMEN

The Army's 173rd Airborne Brigade, paratroopers known as the "Sky Soldiers," comprised mainly African Americans, and was considered by many to be one of the best units in Vietnam for its bravery in ferocious battles. Milton Olive and Lawrence Joel, both Sky Soldiers, were two of the twenty African Americans who received the U.S. Medal of Honor, the highest U.S. military award for bravery in battle. Colin Powell, who served two tours in Vietnam with the infantry, went on to become a general, chairman of the Joint Chiefs of Staff, and U.S. secretary of state.

—*Irene Struthers Rush*

See also: Civil Rights movement; Civil War; Military; Military desegregation; World War II

ALBANY MOVEMENT

1961-62

The Albany Movement in Albany, Georgia, was one of the first mass movements of the Civil Rights Era. Beginning in the fall of 1961, with local civil rights activists working alongside members of the Student

Nonviolent Coordinating Committee (SNCC) and Martin Luther King Jr., the Albany movement became a testing ground for tactics that King would later use in desegregation movements elsewhere in the nation.

Identification: Desegregation movement formed in Albany, Georgia, in 1961.

The Albany Movement, one of the first mass movements of the Civil Rights Era, came about largely through the work of the Albany chapter of the National Association for the Advancement of Colored People (NAACP), established in 1919 by WWI veteran C. W. King after he returned from abroad. The Albany NAACP was active in promoting African American voter registration and, in the late 1950s, advocated repealing the city's segregation laws. In 1961, Cordell Reagon, Charles Jones, and Charles Sherrod, three members of the Student Nonviolent Coordinating Committee (SNCC), an activist organization prominent in the early-1960s desegregation movement, came to Albany to help organize a voter registration drive and decided to remain, realizing that the city's large African American population and active NAACP chapter made Albany, Georgia an excellent candidate for a local desegregation movement. The SNCC encouraged more radical action, including violating laws by staging occupations of segregated establishments, while other local desegregation supporters favored a conservative approach. After debate and deliberation, the SNCC, NAACP, and other local activist organizations came together on November 17th, 1961 to found the Albany Movement, with the explicit goal of ending segregation in Albany.

With William G. Anderson, a local black physician, serving as president, the Albany Movement held mass marches and demonstrations across the community. More than 500 members of the movement were arrested in December for taking part in occupying segregated bus stations, restaurants, and libraries, and engaging in mass protests at the Albany City Hall. As the movement grew, some of the leaders contacted Martin Luther King Jr., already a famous advocate of desegregation, and asked King to come and lead the movement. King arrived in mid-December and was arrested on December 14, 1961 as part of a mass arrest of protestors.

To that point in the burgeoning Civil Rights Movement, police around the nation had reacted violently to desegregation and civil rights protests, and this violent police response helped the movement by generating negative press for the police. Police Chief Laurie Pritchett, who had studied Martin Luther King Jr.'s tactics, instructed to avoid any violent or racially-charged confrontation with protestors, at least while in view of media, and thus created a non-violent counter to King's strategies. As a result, media praised Pritchett and the local police force's restraint and handling of the situation. After his first arrest, King and fellow civil rights leader Ralph Abernathy refused to pay their fines, choosing to be imprisoned in hopes of attracting national attention to the movement. However, Prittchard and a local white attorney arranged to discretely pay King and Abernathy's fines, thus preventing them from being imprisoned and limiting press coverage.

After his release, King continued trying to lead the movement forward and he was arrested two more times, but released each time without imprisonment. By late July, the movement was running out of momentum as so many of the participants had been imprisoned and, with press coverage largely supporting Pritchard's non-violent defense of local laws, few new arrivals were coming to the city to join the movement. The movement ended in late summer, with King moving on to stage his far more successful desegregation movement in Birmingham, Alabama. Historians have noted that for King and others who took part in the Albany Movement, many of the innovations that came out of the movement, such as the use of activist gospel or spiritualist music to motivate participants, became common features of the Civil Rights Movement. King also learned from his experience with Pritchard, and, in the future, chose communities where widespread prejudice within the police guaranteed a more violent response that helped to generate sympathy in the press and, ultimately, from white voters around the nation.

Though King and many historians described the Albany Movement as a defeat, in the wake of King's departure, voter registration among the city's African Americans increased markedly, ultimately shifting the balance of political power in the community. The Spring after King Jr. left Albany, the city removed segregation statutes. The city maintained a thriving Civil Rights community throughout the 60s and 70s, later fighting for school integration and the revitalization of the city's African American neighborhoods.

—Micah Issitt

BURTON V. WILMINGTON PARKING AUTHORITY

April 17, 1961

The Supreme Court held that a state agency may not lease public property to a private restaurant on terms inconsistent with the equal protection clause of the Fourteenth Amendment.

The Case: U.S. Supreme Court ruling on public accommodations

In this case, the Supreme Court was asked to decide on the constitutionality of a segregated private restaurant located within a parking garage owned and operated by the city. William Burton, an African American, sued the city agency after he was denied service in the restaurant. By a 6–3 vote, the Court found that the city's association with the restaurant was sufficient to make it a party to the discrimination in violation of the Fourteenth Amendment. Burton illustrates the willingness of the Court under Chief Justice Earl Warren to expand the definition of state action in support of the Civil Rights movement. The public/private distinction became much less important after the Civil Rights Law of 1964 prohibited racial discrimination in private businesses open to the public. The doctrine of state action, nevertheless, continues to have significance in cases involving private clubs, as in *Moose Lodge v. Irvis* (1972).

—*Thomas Tandy Lewis*

See also: *Moose Lodge v. Irvis*; Segregation; *Shelley v. Kraemer*

COUNCIL OF FEDERATED ORGANIZATIONS

1962–1965

Through its massive Mississippi voter-registration project, the Council of Federated Organizations (COFO) played an important role in the struggle of Mississippi's African American population to achieve voting rights.

Identification: Unique coalition of the major civil rights groups operating in Mississippi
Place: Mississippi

During the 1960's Civil Rights movement, Mississippi was perhaps the most difficult and dangerous arena in which activists worked. Essentially a closed society on racial issues, white Mississippi fought tenaciously, often violently, to maintain a way of life based on white supremacy. While some civil rights groups sought to eliminate the state's dual society by pushing to desegregate schools and public accommodations, others worked to open up Mississippi through black political enfranchisement. One organization that played an important role in this effort was the Council of Federated Organizations (COFO).

MAKEUP OF COFO

COFO was a unique coalition of the major civil rights groups operating in Mississippi. The council included the Student Nonviolent Coordinating Committee (SNCC), the Congress of Racial Equality (CORE), the National Association for the Advancement of Colored People (NAACP), and the Southern Christian Leadership Conference (SCLC). Initially formed in 1961 to assist jailed freedom riders in Jackson, COFO was revitalized in 1962 to increase the number of black registered voters. An additional purpose was to eliminate interorganizational competition over the distribution of foundation funds administered through the Voter Education Project (VEP).

Neither the NAACP nor the SCLC played significant roles in COFO, although Mississippi NAACP head Aaron Henry served as its president. SNCC, which supplied COFO with most of its staff and much of its operating funds, dominated the coalition. Robert Moses, a soft-spoken Harvard graduate student and able veteran SNCC community organizer, served as voter project director; he was assisted by CORE's David Dennis, another activist skilled in grassroots voter-registration projects.

Few informed COFO staffers were unaware of Mississippi's history on black voting issues. This history had clearly indicated little white support for black political involvement. The first southern state to disfranchise its black electorate constitutionally, Mississippi had bolstered its legal impediments with extralegal efforts whenever it felt the status quo sufficiently threatened. Years of disfranchisement had combined with economic dependence, grinding poverty, rigid segregation, and educational deprivation to trap black Mississippians in an oppressive condition that often worked against direct challenges to white domination.

Significant challenges occurred. Influenced by the landmark *Brown v. Board of Education* Supreme Court decision (1954), in 1955 black Mississippians launched a major voter-registration drive. It ended in failure. Economic reprisals took their toll on many applicants, but the physical violence targeted against the leadership proved more effective. The year 1955 was especially bloody. Black Mississippi was convulsed by the murder of the city of Belzoni's NAACP president and voting-rights champion, George Lee, the near-assassination of his activist friend Gus Court, and the daylight murder of Brookhaven farmer and civil rights supporter Lamar Smith. Operating in such a repressive atmosphere, COFO's task would be difficult at best.

VOTER REGISTRATION

In 1960, African Americans constituted 42 percent of Mississippi's population; when COFO began its registration campaign, however, only 5.3 percent of the eligible black population had surmounted the discriminatory laws to qualify as voters. Primarily involved in registering rural African Americans, particularly in the share-cropping delta counties, the organization encountered stiff white resistance and considerable black apprehension. Election officials devised ingenious harassment and delaying tactics against applicants. When such maneuvers or economic intimidation failed to dissuade black interest, violence again came into play. It raged in 1963 in key locations in the delta registration drive. Moses himself barely escaped being assassinated in Greenwood; however, he remained undaunted in his efforts.

Coalition leaders believed that only with federal intervention could any reasonable amount of success be expected, but little help or encouragement came from Washington. COFO did achieve greater success in disproving white myths about black voting indifference. The highlight of the organization's 1963 activities was its registration of black voters for its so-called Freedom Election. Eighty mostly white college students from Yale and Stanford Universities were recruited by veteran activist Allard Lowenstein to assist COFO staffers in the campaign. They helped to register eighty-two thousand persons for a mock election that coincided with the regularly scheduled gubernatorial election. Voters could cast ballots for the official candidates or the representatives of a "freedom slate," consisting of gubernatorial candidate Aaron Henry and his running mate, the Reverend Edwin King, a white Tougaloo College clergyman. Mississippi officials took little interest in the symbolic Henry/King victory, but the election demonstrated that black Mississippians were clearly interested in acquiring equal political rights and representation.

FREEDOM SUMMER

Moses and COFO organizers were encouraged by the Freedom Election. Its outcome added importance to a campaign announced by Dennis for a massive 1964 voter-organizing project dubbed "Freedom Summer." The project called for a large influx of mostly white college students to assist COFO staffers in registering black voters, establishing community centers, and organizing freedom schools to teach educationally deprived youths basic subjects and to teach adults voting techniques. Project plans also included the establishment of a new political organization, the Mississippi Freedom Democratic Party (MFDP). The party was to serve as an effective alternative to the all-white state Democratic Party and to challenge its delegation in the 1964 national convention.

Freedom Summer clearly bore the influence of Moses, who insisted that whites not be excluded from participating. Dennis agreed. The two leaders reasoned that exposing the children of prominent and affluent whites to the daily terror experienced by African Americans would dramatize effectively the need for federal protection and intervention in the Mississippi movement. It was a calculated motive upon which many SNCC staffers frowned, but one which later circumstances partially justified.

After a week of orientation and training in an Oxford, Ohio, women's college, hundreds of idealistic youth came to Mississippi to work in the summer project. Mississippi hastily mobilized to combat this "invasion," increasing the size of the highway patrol and enacting legislation designed to curb the project. Jackson's enlarged police force heavily armed itself and even purchased an armored tank. The Ku Klux Klan and similar extremist groups grew in numbers and influence.

The reality of conducting civil rights activity in the South's most racially oppressive state quickly confronted the volunteers. Numerous workers were falsely arrested, assaulted, or shot at; the homes and churches of many COFO partisans were bombed and burned; and election officials redoubled their efforts not to make concessions in administering Mississippi's discriminatory registration laws. The reign of terror struck fear in the hearts of workers and prospective black registrants.

Clearly, the greatest disruptive event of the summer project was the tragic disappearance of COFO workers James Chaney, Andrew Goodman, and Michael Schwerner. An intensive manhunt uncovered their bodies in Neshoba County on August 5, six weeks after the search began, in an earthen dam on a remote farm. Their kidnapping and assassination by Klansmen shocked the nation, partially bringing to reality COFO leaders' cynical prediction of government intervention if white youths became murder victims.

That intervention did not occur to the extent desired or expected by COFO workers. Still generally unprotected, the volunteers persisted in their activities, although their registration efforts remained largely ineffective. Throughout the rest of 1964, COFO's energies centered primarily on MFDP affairs, particularly on seeking the party's recognition as a vital political force. By the beginning of 1965, the coalition and the registration drive had essentially ended; COFO officially disbanded in 1966.

CONFRONTING VIOLENCE

Nothing affected COFO's registration activities as much as the increased violence they provoked. The repercussions were widespread, affecting staff members and registrants, Mississippians and non-Mississippians alike. Violence had always been used by racial extremists against those who sought to undermine Mississippi's white supremacy, but at the height of the registration campaign its usage became more tenacious and its results more deadly. During Freedom Summer alone, in addition to the well-publicized Neshoba County lynchings, at least four other deaths occurred that were related to the state's accelerated civil rights activities. Slightly less grave were the more than one thousand arrests, thirty-five shootings, and eighty beatings, and the bombing or burning of sixty-five homes, churches, and other buildings.

The ever-present terror and the reluctance of the federal government to protect project workers and black registrants influenced the effectiveness of COFO in achieving its objectives. For working-class African Americans, the fear of physical reprisal often interacted with the reality of economic reprisal, creating a high price to pay for registering to vote. When added to the force of the state's discriminatory registration procedures, the results were discouraging. In the two years from 1962 to 1964, when COFO was functioning at its highest level, black voter registration increased by only 1.4 percent. Mississippi's 1964 registration rate of 6.7 percent for African Americans was the lowest in the nation. This lack of significant progress in Mississippi caused the Voter Education Project in late 1963 to divert its financial contributions from COFO to more promising voter projects.

Still, COFO persisted. The various campaign obstacles had a sobering effect on all involved, but the project also produced positive signs. The 1963 Freedom Election was convincing evidence of black voting aspirations, and it helped to stimulate interest across the state. This expanded interest continued into the summer project. Despite the summer's terrorism, some seventeen thousand African Americans were convinced to seek registration in their county courthouses, although only sixteen hundred actually succeeded. Additionally, the motivation translated into real grassroots political action in the form of the MFDP. The party did not gain recognition as the legitimate representative of Mississippi Democrats. Through the efforts of such personable and magnetic individuals as Fannie Lou Hamer, however, black Mississippians' political plight received further national exposure.

LEGACY

Perhaps COFO's greatest contribution in the voting-rights struggle was its role in dramatizing the inhumanity of Mississippi's resistance to black political involvement. In so doing, it aided immeasurably the national call for a greater federal role in southern voting practices. COFO's project eventually thus achieved one of its deeper aims. Martin Luther King, Jr.'s Selma voting-rights campaign clearly influenced congressional passage of the 1965 Voting Rights Act, but COFO's Mississippi project was also significant.

Ultimately, COFO aided in opening Mississippi society and shaping its participatory political culture. In 1991, Mississippi had more black elected officials than any other state in the nation. With the country's largest percentage of African Americans in its population, Mississippi had achieved the meaningful political empowerment that many COFO idealists envisioned.

—Robert L. Jenkins

See also: Disfranchisement laws in Mississippi; Gerrymandering; Mississippi Freedom Democratic Party; University of Mississippi desegregation; *Williams v. Mississippi*

MEREDITH REGISTERS AT THE UNIVERSITY OF MISSISSIPPI

October 1, 1962

Following a fifteen-month legal battle, James Meredith, under the protection of federal troops, became the first African American to attend a white university in Mississippi.

Locale: Oxford, Mississippi
Categories: Education; civil rights and liberties; social issues and reform

KEY FIGURES

James Meredith (b. 1933), African American Air Force veteran and student

Ross Robert Barnett (1898-1987), governor of Mississippi, 1960-1964

John F. Kennedy (1917-1963), president of the United States, 1961-1963

Robert F. Kennedy (1925-1968), attorney general of the United States, 1961-1964

Hugo L. Black (1886-1971), associate justice of the United States, 1937-1971

Constance Baker Motley (1921-2005), an attorney for the NAACP Legal Defense Fund

SUMMARY OF EVENT

School desegregation became a national imperative after the 1954 United States Supreme Court decision in *Brown v. Board of Education*. In its decision, the Supreme Court declared that racial segregation was a violation of the Fourteenth Amendment's requirement of "equal protection of the law." The court's decision, however, had an immediate effect only on those districts that were parties to the cases decided in *Brown*. When other schools or universities did not voluntarily desegregate, individual court suits were required. Noncompliance was the norm throughout the South.

In January, 1961, James Meredith, an African American, applied for admission to the all-white University of Mississippi, challenging the state to comply with the seven-year-old court ruling. Claiming state sovereignty in matters of public education, Barnett directed university officials to defy the orders of the Supreme Court. Eager to find another means of stopping Meredith, the state of Mississippi charged him with the crime of moral turpitude. Calling a special session of the legislature, the governor obtained passage of a bill on September 20, 1962, the very day Meredith was to register, denying admission to institutions of higher

learning to anyone charged with such a crime. The governor was then declared registrar of the University of Mississippi, and Meredith was warned that he would be arrested when he appeared to register.

The actions of the governor did little to calm those opposed to integration. In Oxford, home of the university, several thousand angry people awaited the arrival of Meredith. Newspapers across the state had encouraged citizens to support the governor as Mississippians literally prepared to fight another Civil War.

In Washington, D.C., President Kennedy had been closely monitoring events. Although reluctant to use federal troops, Kennedy was nevertheless prepared to do so if the situation worsened. The attorney general, Robert F. Kennedy, was no less determined than the president: Meredith would be admitted to the university. Hearing of the unrest and plans to arrest Meredith, Robert Kennedy telephoned Barnett. The governor agreed not to arrest Meredith but refused to allow him to register.

The scenario of Meredith appearing to register and being turned away was repeated three times. Before Meredith reached the university on September 27, his fourth attempt, a nervous Barnett asked the federal government to call it off. The crowds gathered at the university had become uncontrollable. Meredith and his federal escorts returned to Memphis, their temporary base.

A show of force by the federal government appeared to be the only solution. On September 30, President Kennedy issued an executive order authorizing the secretary of defense to call in the military in order to enforce justice in Mississippi. That same evening, hundreds of United States marshals, Mississippi National Guards, and members of the regular military lined the front of the administration building. As crowds began to gather, James Meredith was quietly installed, unseen, in a dormitory.

As Meredith studied and slept, a riot that left two dead and hundreds injured raged on the university campus. At 8:00 a.m. the following day, October 1, 1962, Meredith was registered as a student at the University of Mississippi. At 9:00 a.m., with tear gas still hanging in the air, he attended his first class.

SIGNIFICANCE

James Meredith had been victorious, but the costs were great. More than twenty-five thousand federal troops had been needed to allow his enrollment. As a student at the University of Mississippi, Meredith was constantly accompanied by federal escorts. Five hundred troops were maintained at the university to ensure his safety. The university suffered as well. In the aftermath of the riot, forty professors resigned, and many students left to pursue degrees elsewhere.

In June, 1963, Cleve McDowell became the first black to be admitted to the law school at the university. McDowell was intimidated by the fact that the troops on campus to protect Meredith would be leaving in August and asked permission to carry a gun. His request denied, McDowell nevertheless carried the weapon. Late for class one day, he dropped the gun and was summarily dismissed from the university.

When Meredith graduated in August, 1963, two lives had been lost, and the federal government had spent nearly $5 million. The fall of 1964, however, saw two black students enroll at the University of Mississippi

with little fanfare. The Civil Rights Act of 1964 further encouraged integration.

Under Title VI of this act, federal aid would be denied to any public institution discriminating against students on the basis of race. By January, 1966, all but one of the public institutions of higher learning in Mississippi had signed an agreement to comply with the stipulations of Title VI. Desegregation formally had become accepted.

—Laurie Voice and Robert E. Biles

See also: Race Riots Erupt in Detroit and Harlem; Supreme Court Ends Public School Segregation; Eisenhower Sends Troops to Little Rock, Arkansas; Greensboro Sit-Ins; Civil Rights Protesters Attract International Attention; Three Civil Rights Workers Are Murdered; Supreme Court Prohibits Racial Discrimination in Public Accommodations; Congress Passes the Voting Rights Act.

WASHINGTON, D.C., RIOTS

November 22, 1962; August 1–3, 1967

The events were short-lived but had a profound impact on the country as a whole during the Civil Rights movement.

The Event: Racial unrest that erupted in the nation's capital
Place: Washington, D.C.

Although much of the attention during the Civil Rights movement in the 1960's focused on the South, racial tension also existed in the North, especially in urban areas such as Washington, D.C. The 1962 riot broke out at a football game between two longtime rival high schools, one white and the other African American, and spilled over into the streets. In 1967, other seemingly minor incidents set off a riot.

On November 22, 1962, two high school football rivals met for a fifth consecutive annual Washington, D.C., championship game. These schools were St. John's, a mostly white Catholic high school, and Eastern, a mainly African American public school. During the game, a player ejected for roughness returned to the field and began fighting. His own teammates subdued

him, but his actions began a chain reaction. The fighting spread quickly from the field into the crowd, the parking lots, and surrounding streets. A total of thirty-four people were injured before the police brought it under control.

In 1967, a citywide riot occurred. Earlier that summer, many civil rights leaders, including Martin Luther King, Jr., had warned of possible disorders in several cities including Washington, D.C., but their warnings were largely ignored. Although some accused these leaders of giving people reasons to riot, Federal Bureau of Investigation director J. Edgar Hoover acknowledged there was no direct evidence supporting this belief. The violence broke out on August 1. The riot started with sporadic fires set mainly in African American neighborhoods. This was followed by rioters throwing rocks and bottles at police officers and firefighters responding to the blaze. In one area, two roaming gangs shot at police. The turmoil subsided on August 3.

After the 1967 racial unrest in Washington and other cities, President Lyndon B. Johnson appointed Illinois governor Otto Kerner head of the National Advisory Commission on Civil Disorders, known as the

Kerner Commission, to study the reasons for the riots and growing racial tension in the nation. The commission eventually concluded that the United States was being divided into two societies, one white and the other black. The commission concluded that the urban areas of the nation faced a downward trend unless action was taken to relieve discriminatory conditions. This gave rise to a new attitude that brought about new government legislation.

—*Robert Sullivan*

See also: Chicago riots; Chisholm's election to Congress; New York riots; Newark riot; Watts riot

BALDWIN VOICES BLACK RAGE IN *THE FIRE NEXT TIME*

1963

Reflecting on his youth and the growing popularity of the Black Muslim movement, James Baldwin wrote a thoughtful, prophetic statement on race in America.

Locale: New York, New York
Categories: Literature; social issues and reform

KEY FIGURES

James Baldwin (1924-1987), African American writer
Elijah Muhammad (1897-1975), African American activist and leader of the Black Muslims
Malcolm X (Malcolm Little; 1925-1965), Elijah Muhammad's chosen successor
Norman Podhoretz (b. 1930), editor of *Commentary* magazine
Robert F. Kennedy (1925-1968), attorney general of the United States, 1961-1964

SUMMARY OF EVENT

James Baldwin's *The Fire Next Time* (1963) created a stir even before the book was published. By 1962, Baldwin had delayed for three years writing an article on Africa that *The New Yorker*, perhaps the most influential popular literary magazine in the United States, had commissioned.

Baldwin received an advance from the magazine and did in fact travel to Africa, but he never finished the series of articles that he had promised. He did, however, finish an article suggested by Norman Podhoretz, then the new editor of *Commentary*, called "Down at the Cross," based on Baldwin's meeting with Elijah Muhammad, leader of the Black Muslims.

With William Shawn, the editor of *The New Yorker,* growing impatient to receive a finished article, Baldwin sent him the article that had originally been intended for *Commentary* but that had grown in scope well beyond its original conception. Undismayed that the article

Baldwin was submitting was quite unlike the article *The New Yorker* had commissioned, William Shawn retitled the essay "Letter from a Region of My Mind" and published it in the November 17, 1962, issue of *The New Yorker*. The essay caused an immediate stir and formed the bulk of *The Fire Next Time*, which was published in 1963.

The Fire Next Time actually begins with a short piece entitled "My Dungeon Shook: Letter to My Nephew on the One Hundredth Anniversary of the Emancipation," written to Baldwin's fourteen-year-old namesake, his brother's son, whom Baldwin at one point refers to affectionately as "Big James." The piece was originally published in *The Progressive* in December, 1962; in *The Fire Next Time*, it serves largely as a prologue to the themes that the longer essay treats in greater length.

As an essay, "My Dungeon Shook" suffers from some of the cumbersome demands of the form of the

Baldwin in 1969 by Allan Warren

public epistle, particularly the need to focus on an audience of one while addressing a much larger audience. Thus, when Baldwin tells his nephew that he—Big James—was born in conditions similar to those of Charles Dickens's London, he interrupts himself to say, a bit too coyly, "I hear the chorus . . . screaming, 'No! This is not true!'. . .—but I am writing this letter to *you*." Clearly, Baldwin is not, in fact, writing this letter to his nephew.

The essay, however, is not without the characteristic insight and rhetorical zest of much of Baldwin's work. Such lines from the essay's final paragraph as "You know, and I know, that the country is celebrating one hundred years of freedom one hundred years too soon. We cannot be free until they are free" neatly introduce some of the major ideas discussed in his longer essay: that freedom has not been achieved for either blacks or whites and that, for people of one race to live free, people of all races must live free.

It is the longer piece, later restored to Baldwin's original title, "Down at the Cross" (with *The New Yorker*'s title for the essay retained as a subtitle), that constitutes the bulk of *The Fire Next Time*. The essay begins with Baldwin's recollection of a religious crisis of his own that began when he was fourteen, when he began to be afraid of the world of Harlem around him because it seemed that he himself could conceivably become one of the "whores and pimps and racketeers on the avenue." He sought refuge in the safety of church, becoming a preacher while still a teenager. It was not long, however, before he found himself disappointed by the hypocrisy of the church.

The command to love everybody, he found, was supposed to apply "only to those who believed as we did, and it did not apply to white people at all"—and it certainly did not apply to such people as Baldwin's Jewish school friends. These autobiographical reflections constitute the first third of the essay and are compelling in their own right. In addition, they provide the basis for Baldwin's understanding of both the attractions and limitations of a religion, such as that of the Black Muslims, that preaches racial separation, the main topic of the second section.

By the time *The Fire Next Time* was published, Baldwin had already established himself as an important novelist, having published *Go Tell It on the Mountain* (1953), *Giovanni's Room* (1956), and *Another Country* (1962). After *The Fire Next Time*, however, he was often treated by the press as a celebrity intellectual. For example, in its January 4, 1963, issue, *Time*

magazine ran a short article about the importance of Baldwin's *The New Yorker* piece as a news story under the headline "Races," rather than reviewing the essay as a literary event.

Similarly, for its May 17, 1963, issue, shortly after the release of *The Fire Next Time*, *Time* used Baldwin's face on its cover; again, though, the magazine discussed the publication of his most recent book as a political event rather than a literary one. Similarly, the May 24, 1963, issue of *Life* magazine ran a feature on Baldwin that treated him as a celebrity and proclaimed that "in today's literary circles it is a sign of considerable chic to know James Baldwin well enough to refer to him as Jimmy."

Baldwin tried his best to use his newfound celebrity to promote the cause of racial integration. He traveled the South, meeting James Meredith, the first black student to be enrolled at the University of Mississippi, and Medgar Evers, the chief legal counsel for the National Association for the Advancement of Colored People (NAACP) in Mississippi, among other civil rights leaders. He also set up a series of meetings with Robert F. Kennedy, then the attorney general of the United States, to discuss the problems of racial segregation in the urban North.

By most accounts, the meetings with Robert Kennedy ended disastrously. Baldwin had assembled a group of friends, including playwright Lorraine Hansberry, singer and actor Lena Horne, singer Harry Belafonte, and many others. Kennedy arrived apparently expecting a businesslike discussion of proposals and priorities to ease the racial unrest brewing in America's cities. What Baldwin wanted to offer was a crash course in understanding what it felt like to be black in America. The two camps quickly grew impatient with each other, and the meeting ended in frustration and exhaustion, leaving Baldwin feeling bitter toward both Robert Kennedy and his brother, President John F. Kennedy. This bitterness lasted even beyond President Kennedy's assassination and was recorded in Federal Bureau of Investigation (FBI) files, as Baldwin was now suspected of being a revolutionary.

If Baldwin's emotional relationship to ideas compromised his ability to be a cool political leader, his relatively moderate integrationist views, as well as his homosexuality, made him a favorite target of younger, more revolutionary blacks such as Eldridge Cleaver, who attacked Baldwin in *Soul on Ice* (1968). Though personally wounded by such attacks, Baldwin refused to engage in tabloid squabbling. In fact, he remained something of an apologist for black revolutionaries, even those who had attacked him in public. Seven years after the publication of *The Fire Next Time*, in an open letter to Angela Davis printed in the *Manchester Guardian* on December 12, 1970, he seemed on the verge of despairing that white America would ever come to the awakening that in *The Fire Next Time* he had insisted was necessary.

The long-term impact of *The Fire Next Time* on Baldwin's literary reputation was to convince many readers and reviewers that Baldwin's foremost gift as a writer was his talent as an essayist. Baldwin found this perception frustrating, but he unwillingly contributed to it during the 1960's by publishing works of fiction that many readers found disappointing while at the same time continuing to publish much top-quality nonfiction.

This is not to suggest that *The Fire Next Time* was universally well received, either; F. W. Dupee, for example, though applauding the autobiographical section of "Down at the Cross," wondered why Baldwin had not done more research into the Black Muslim movement before publishing. Hannah Arendt, in a letter to Baldwin, wondered if love could ever serve as a panacea for society's ills. The consensus that has emerged over the course of time, however, is that Baldwin's nonfiction certainly demands a permanent place in American literature, and that *The Fire Next Time* is one of his most powerfully written and most comprehensive statements on race in America.

—*Thomas J. Cassidy*

See also: Ellison's *Invisible Man* Is Published; Lee's *To Kill a Mockingbird* Calls for Social Justice

Self-Identity Through Struggle

In this passage from The Fire Next Time *(1963), James Baldwin discusses the ultimate good that can be realized from living a life of "endless struggle": autonomy, certainty, and a knowingness "that is unshakable."*

It is entirely unacceptable that I should have no voice in the political affairs of my own country, for I am not a ward of America; I am one of the first Americans to arrive on these shores.

This past, the Negro's past, of rope, fire, torture, castration, infanticide, rape; death and humiliation; fear by day and night, fear as deep as the marrow of the bone; doubt that he was worthy of life, since everyone around him denied it; sorrow for his women, for his kinfolk, for his children, who needed his protection, and whom he could not protect; rage, hatred, and murder, hatred for white men so deep that it often turned against him and his own, and made all love, all trust, all joy impossible—this past, this endless struggle to achieve and reveal and confirm a human identity, human authority, yet contains, for all its horror, something very beautiful. I do not mean to be sentimental about suffering—enough is certainly as good as a feast—but people who cannot suffer can never grow up, can never discover who they are.

That man who is forced each day to snatch his manhood, his identity, out of the fire of human cruelty that rages to destroy it knows, if he survives his effort, and even if he does not survive it, something about himself and human life that no school on earth—and, indeed, no church—can teach. He achieves his own authority, and that is unshakable.

EDWARDS V. SOUTH CAROLINA
February 5, 1963

In this incorporation case, the Supreme Court held that local officials could not block an otherwise lawful demonstration because they disliked the demonstrators' political views.

The Case: U.S. Supreme Court ruling on freedom of assembly

About two hundred African American students marched peacefully in small groups from a church to the South Carolina state capitol, an obviously public forum, to protest the state's racially discriminatory laws. A few dozen police officers initially told them they could march peacefully but about an hour later ordered them to disperse under threat of arrest. A crowd had gathered to watch the demonstrators but did not seem threatening, and the police presence was ample. The demonstrators responded by singing patriotic and religious songs until some two hundred demonstrators were arrested and convicted of breach of the peace.

Their conviction was upheld by the South Carolina supreme court.

The Supreme Court, by an 8–1 vote, reversed the convictions of the civil rights demonstrators. Justice Potter Stewart, in the majority opinion, applied the First Amendment right to freedom of assembly to the states, refusing to let the states bar demonstrations of unpopular views in traditional forums. In line with other time, place, and manner decisions, the Court used the Fourteenth Amendment's due process clause to incorporate the peaceable assembly portion of the First Amendment and to apply it to the states. Justice Tom C. Clark dissented, defending the state's action.

—Richard L. Wilson

BIRMINGHAM MARCH

April 4-May 7, 1963

A series of demonstrations in Birmingham, Alabama, sponsored by the Southern Christian Leadership Conference (SCLC), were designed to draw attention to the violent racism that underlay white southerners' defense of segregation.

The Event: Protest march against segregation
Place: Birmingham, Alabama

A disappointing campaign in Albany, Georgia, in 1962, prompted the Southern Christian Leadership Conference to select Birmingham, Alabama, as its subsequent target for nonviolent demonstrations. Protests against segregation had failed in Albany because the city's chief of police, Laurie Pritchett, had held white mobs at bay and prevented the violent confrontations between police and protesters that would produce media coverage. Martin Luther King, Jr., and other SCLC leaders met in Savannah, Georgia, at the end of 1962 to plan a series of demonstrations in Birmingham, a city noted for its racial violence and uncompromising stand against the Civil Rights movement. The strategists hoped to gain national attention by provoking Birmingham officials into explicit displays of racial antagonism, thereby revealing the true face of southern segregation.

THE MARCH

Project C, the SCLC's code name for its assault on segregation in Birmingham, proceeded in three stages. First, on the morning of April 4, 1963, an economic boycott of downtown businesses went into effect, and small groups began staging sit-ins at downtown lunch counters. After Police Chief Eugene "Bull" Conner ordered arrests, the protest caught the attention of the media and the administration of President John F. Kennedy. Stage two began on April 6 with daily marches on city hall. As the protest leaders had expected, the Birmingham police arrested all of the demonstrators while flashbulbs popped and television cameras whirred.

King himself was arrested and during his incarceration penned his "Letter from Birmingham Jail," an eloquent statement of the motivations that guided the Civil Rights movement. Police began to respond to the daily marches with less and less restraint, and African Americans began turning out for the marches in ever-larger numbers and tightened the economic boycott. The sit-ins, protest marches, and police violence had riveted a national audience to their television sets by the time the third stage began on May 2.

That morning, more than one thousand African American children exited the Sixteenth Avenue Baptist Church as adult spectators cheered them on. The "children's crusade" sang and danced its way into the paddywagons waiting to take them to jail. Extensive criticism of the decision to use children rained down from both sides of the struggle, but King and the other leaders had little choice. Adults had become reluctant to march and serve jail time. More important, the protest leaders recognized that the sight of children being arrested would stir the heart of the nation. The police actions—beating and turning fire hoses on protesters—and their continued brutality were captured by the media as the marches and arrests continued until May 7.

The Senior Citizen's Committee, which had been organized by the Birmingham Chamber of Commerce to handle racial matters, feared that continued racial violence would drive away business and permanently damage the city's reputation. On the afternoon of May 7, they met in secret session and ordered their negotiators to open talks with the SCLC. After three days of negotiations, the two sides reached an agreement that called for the desegregation of public accommodations, nondiscrimination in the hiring and promoting of African American workers in Birmingham industries, and the formation of a biracial committee. Even though the SCLC compromised and allowed gradual rather than immediate implementation of these measures, the demonstrations in Birmingham were considered a significant victory for the movement.

IMPACT

Public reaction to the events in Birmingham, along with the easing of Cold War tensions, convinced President Kennedy that the time had come for federal action in defense of civil rights, and he asked Congress for civil rights legislation. The Civil Rights Act of 1964 was signed into law on July 2 by President Lyndon B. Johnson, Kennedy's successor. The act prohibited segregation of public accommodations,

made discrimination by employers and unions illegal, and created the Equal Employment Opportunity Commission. The broader impact of the march was to change the tone of the Civil Rights movement from gradualism to immediacy; the African American community was no longer willing to wait for decent jobs, adequate housing, and a quality education. The march also marked the entry of poor and unemployed African Americans into the struggle.

—*Robert E. McFarland*

See also: Civil Rights Act of 1964; Civil Rights movement; Million Man March; Million Woman March; Poor People's March on Washington; Selma-Montgomery march; Southern Christian Leadership Conference; Student Nonviolent Coordinating Committee

AFRICAN LIBERATION DAY

May 25, 1963

African Liberation Day is a date honored throughout the African world, as a day on which to unite and denounce racism, capitalism, and Zionism.

The Event: Internationally recognized anniversary commemorating the freeing of Africa from European colonization
Place: Worldwide

In 1963, thirty-one African heads of state convened in Ethiopia for the Summit Conference of the Independent African States, with the overall goal of freeing African people from the yoke of European domination and white supremacy. On May 25, 1963, the Charter of the Organization of African Unity was signed, and it was decided to celebrate African Liberation Day every year on May 25. Sponsored by the All African People's Revolutionary Party, African Liberation Day has led to the concerted action of the member states of the Organization of African Unity to pool financial aid to

revive, strengthen, and intensify liberation movements throughout Africa. As much as possible, the goal is to end exploitation and oppression of Africans at home and abroad by finding peaceful solutions through deliberations and frank exchange of views among the nations that are involved.

African Liberation Day has become an institution throughout the African world, being a day when all African people rally for unity and denounce racism, capitalism, and Zionism. On African Liberation Day, African people focus on what they share—their common past, set of problems, and future—as they pause to think about the plight of their African brothers who are under foreign rule and who are seeking to win their freedom and fundamental human rights.

—*Alvin K. Benson*

See also: Black Is Beautiful movement; Black nationalism; Black Power movement; Pan-Africanism

ORGANIZATION OF AFRICAN UNITY IS FOUNDED

May 25, 1963

The Organization of African Unity aimed to eradicate European political power in Africa but accepted European-imposed boundaries on African states and avoided discussion of infringements on human rights by African states.

Locale: Addis Ababa, Ethiopia
Categories: Organizations and institutions; diplomacy and international relations; colonialism and occupation; indigenous peoples' rights

KEY FIGURES

Kwame Nkrumah (1909-1972), president of Ghana, 1960-1966

Abubakar Tafawa Balewa (1912-1966), first prime minister of Nigeria, 1960-1966

Gamal Abdel Nasser (1918-1970), leader of the United Arab Republic, 1954-1970

Haile Selassie I (1892-1975), emperor of Ethiopia, 1930-1974

Léopold Senghor (1906-2001), president of Senegal, 1960-1980

Ahmed Sékou Touré (1922-1984), president of Guinea, 1958-1984

Jomo Kenyatta (1884-1978), president of Kenya, 1964- 1978

Julius Nyerere (1922-1999), president of Tanganyika, 1962-1964, 1964-1975

William V. S. Tubman (1895-1971), president of Liberia, 1943-1971

Diallo Telli (1925-1977), administrative secretarygeneral of the Organization of African Unity, 1964- 1972

SUMMARY OF EVENT

The Organization of African Unity (OAU) was founded as an attempt by African countries to achieve harmony and cooperation on the African continent. The group's 1963 charter exudes idealism. Pragmatism, however, restricts that idealism. The OAU evolved from African hostility to the European seizure of the so-called Dark Continent. This opposition sprang not only from the soil of Africa itself but also, interestingly, from the African diaspora.

The Egyptian revolution in 1952 propelled Gamal Abdel Nasser into a leading role in pan-Africanism. The Bandung Conference in 1955, with its insistence on fundamental human rights, also influenced pan-African thinking. April, 1958, marked the formal launching of pan-Africanism by individual states. Except for South Africa, all the independent states—Egypt, Ethiopia, Ghana, Liberia, Libya, Morocco, Sudan, and Tunisia—sent representatives to Accra, Ghana. The conference condemned colonialism, South Africa's racism, and France's occupation of Algeria. The conference favored a "fundamental unity" between African states on foreign questions.

Pan-Africanism received impetus from three All African Peoples Conferences. The first, a nongovernmental conference of political parties at Accra in December, 1958, proposed a commonwealth of free African states. It also favored Africa's independence and the principle of equal representation of citizens in government.

The movement for African unity received a severe setback in 1960-1961. Meeting at Abidjan, Ivory Coast, in 1960, twelve states—Cameroon, the Central African Republic, Chad, Congo (Brazzaville), Dahomey, Gabon, Ivory Coast, Madagascar, Mauritania, Niger, Senegal, and Upper Volta—formed the Brazzaville Group. It favored Mauritania's independence, mediation in the Congo (Kinshasa), and peace in Algeria by 1961. In January, 1961, eight states—the Algerian Provisional Government, Ceylon, Ghana, Guinea, Libya, Mali, Morocco, and the United Arab Republic—established the Casablanca Powers. They favored Morocco's acquisition of Mauritania, recognition of Antoine Gizinga's government in the Congo (Kinshasa), and immediate independence for Algeria.

In May, 1961, the twelve Brazzaville states joined Ethiopia, Liberia, Libya, Nigeria, Sierra Leone, Somalia, Togo, and Tunisia in the Monrovia States. This organization carried on the Brazzaville Group's program. Neither the Monrovia States nor the Casablanca Powers called for political union in Africa.

On May 25, 1963, the OAU debuted. It was a merger of the Monrovia and Casablanca blocs (minus Ceylon) and Burundi, Congo (Kinshasa), Rwanda, Sudan, Tanganyika, and Uganda. Hosted by Emperor Haile Selassie I, the meeting at Addis Ababa featured Kwame Nkrumah, Abubakar Tafawa Balewa, Gamal Abdel Nasser, Ahmed Sákou Tourá, Julius K. Nyerere, and William V. S. Tubman. A long debate occurred over the institution's name, but Malagasy's insistence on inclusion of its name failed. Arguments ensued over the frequency of holding the summit assembly; the majority vote for an assembly decision; the rules for the general secretariat and for the Commission of Mediation, Conciliation, and Arbitration; the working languages of the OAU; ratification of the charter; and admittance and withdrawal of states from the OAU.

The charter of the OAU consists of a preamble and thirty-three articles. The preamble is a ten-point statement outlining the convictions, hopes, and ideals of the member states. Its first sentence, beginning "We, the Heads of African States and Governments . . . ," emphasizes that the OAU is an organization of governments, not of peoples. The preamble stresses the inalienable right of all people to control their own destiny. As will be noted, the application of this noble principle is a different matter entirely. The preamble recognizes the territorial integrity of all African states. Thus, it ratifies the European establishment of boundaries despite the arbitrary methods by which the borders were determined. Self-determination by peoples thus seemed to receive short shrift from the self-styled African defenders of human rights.

The OAU charter established four main institutions. The first, the Assembly of Heads of State and Government, was designed to make and coordinate policy and to review all activities of the OAU. It met yearly and could convene extra sessions if necessary. Each member state had one vote, and a quorum was two-thirds of the OAU's total membership.

The Council of Ministers consisted of the foreign ministers or other persons designated by members. It implemented decisions of the assembly, prepared conferences, and coordinated inter-African cooperation. Meetings were twice yearly or as needed in extraordinary session. Each member state possessed one vote, and a quorum was two-thirds of the OAU's total membership.

The General Secretariat was directed by the administrative secretary-general, appointed by the assembly on the recommendation of the council (Diallo Telli was the first secretary-general of the OAU). A fourth body, the Commission of Mediation, Conciliation, and Arbitration, was intended to settle disputes by peaceful means. A separate agreement among the members would later define its composition, responsibilities, and functions.

SIGNIFICANCE

The founding fathers of the OAU overwhelmingly believed that their creation promised to advance pan-Africanism. Events that followed would show

Charter of the Organization of African Unity

The main points of the Charter of the Organization of African Unity follow:

We, the Heads of African States and Governments assembled in the City of Addis Ababa, Ethiopia;

Convinced that it is the inalienable right of all people to control their own destiny;

Conscious of the fact that freedom, equality, justice and dignity are essential objectives for the achievement of the legitimate aspirations of the African peoples;

Conscious of our responsibility to harness the natural and human resources of our continent for the total advancement of our peoples in spheres of human endeavour;

Inspired by a common determination to promote understanding among our people sand co-operation among our States in response to the aspirations of our peoples for brotherhood and solidarity, in a larger unity transcending ethnic and national differences;

Convinced that, in order to translate this determination into a dynamic force in the cause of human progress, conditions for peace and security must be established and maintained;

Determined to safeguard and consolidate the hard-won independence as well as the sovereignty and territorial integrity, of our States, and to fight against neocolonialism in all its forms;

Dedicated to the general progress of Africa; Persuaded that the Charter of the United Nations and the Universal Declaration of Human Rights, to the principles of which we reaffirm our adherence, provide a solid foundation for peaceful and positive co-operation among States;

Desirous that all African States should henceforth unite so that the welfare and well-being of their peoples can be assured;

Resolved to reinforce the links between our states by establishing and strengthening common institutions;

Have agreed to the present Charter.

The Organization shall have the following purposes: a. to promote the unity, and solidarity of the African States; b. to co-ordinate and intensify their co-operation and efforts to achieve a better life for the peoples of Africa; c. to defend their sovereignty, their territorial integrity and independence; d. to eradicate all forms of colonialism from Africa; and e. to promote international co-operation, having due regard to the Charter of the United Nations and the Universal Declaration of Human Rights. . . .

successes and failures, and eventually result in an even more intensive effort at pan-African cooperation as the OAU was replaced by the African Union in 2002. The OAU became the concrete manifestation of the spirit of pan-Africanism, featuring successes and failures in the realm of human rights in Africa. Certain of its actions reveal its idealism balanced against cynical pragmatism.

The OAU charter pledged the member states "to eradicate all forms of colonialism from Africa." Thus, action should spring against vestiges of European imperialism. The OAU chose to ignore human rights violations in many states; however, it did manage to promulgate one of the most progressive regional agreements on refugees in 1969, and most African countries proved to be reasonably generous hosts for asylum seekers. There was also an attempt to promote human rights through the promulgation of the African Charter on Human and Peoples' Rights of 1981, which though often ineffective, at least indicated a desire to recognize the importance of such rights.

The OAU, though perhaps not responsible for the decolonization of the continent, saw that goal largely achieved by the 1990's. The fall of the white apartheid regime in South Africa and the establishment of democratic majority rule there represented the triumph of yet another of its goals. Indeed, the reemergence of democratic regimes in the 1990's bodes well for the future of human rights on the continent. Finally, the momentum built through the emergence of the African Union as the successor to the OAU indicated that a variety of key global and continental trends bode well for the future of an Africa of greater stability, justice, and prosperity.

—*Erving E. Beauregard*

KING DELIVERS HIS "I HAVE A DREAM" SPEECH

August 28, 1963

Martin Luther King, Jr.'s "I Have a Dream" speech, delivered during the 1963 March on Washington, encapsulated the social vision of the nonviolent Civil Rights movement and elevated that movement in the American, and world, consciousness.

Also known as: March on Washington
Locale: Washington, D.C.
Categories: Civil rights and liberties; social issues and reform

KEY FIGURES

Martin Luther King, Jr. (1929-1968), president of the Southern Christian Leadership Conference

A. Philip Randolph (1889-1979), labor leader and civil rights activist, and a major organizer of the 1963 March on Washington

John Robert Lewis (b. 1940), Student Nonviolent Coordinating Committee leader who made a controversial speech during the 1963 March on Washington

John F. Kennedy (1917-1963), president of the United States, 1961-1963, who introduced the package of reforms that led to the 1964 Civil Rights Act

View from the Lincoln Memorial toward the Washington Monument on August 28, 1963

SUMMARY OF EVENT

The setting for Dr. Martin Luther King, Jr.'s best-remembered speech was the massive March on Washington, D.C., in late August, 1963. On August 28, he delivered the partly extemporaneous address from the steps of the Lincoln Memorial to more than 200,000 march participants and, through radio and television, to millions of others around the world. To many, it was his clearest expression of his vision for America's future.

His rhythmic repetition of "I have a dream" between each major point of the speech accounts for the attributed title and reflects the measured optimism he sought to project.

At the time of the March on Washington, both King and the nonviolent Civil Rights movement were under intense pressure from several directions. The settlement effected on May 10, 1963, after the massive Birmingham campaign was considered inadequate by some critics.

Birmingham officials and business leaders had made substantial concessions, including hiring and promoting more black personnel and desegregating public facilities, but there was little assurance that living conditions for African Americans would improve substantially.

The speech was released to the press on August 27, the day before the March on Washington, but was toned down somewhat before delivery and had little impact. Generally, the march was orderly and the speakers avoided direct attacks on the Kennedy administration.

Many speakers, including A. Philip Randolph, National Association for the Advancement of Colored People (NAACP) leader Roy Wilkins, labor leader Walter P. Reuther, Lewis, and others, spoke to the crowd of more than 200,000 that rallied near the Lincoln Memorial on August 28. It was a hot, sunny Wednesday afternoon, and the crowd was tiring when King came to the microphone. He had been introduced by the march's prime mover, Randolph, who had dreamed of this kind of massive display since 1941. King began slowly and deliberately, noting that he was happy to join with the marchers "in what will go down in history as the greatest demonstration of freedom in the history of our nation."

King spoke of the Declaration of Independence and its recognition of the rights of all citizens, as well as President Abraham Lincoln's Emancipation Proclamation of 1863. "But one hundred years later," King said, "the Negro still is not free." Instead, "the Negro lives on a lonely island of poverty in the midst of a vast ocean of material prosperity." African Americans were in Washington to "cash a check"—to demand their rights as American citizens.

The "promissory note" of the founding fathers had never been paid to the nation's black citizens, the SCLC president averred. King paid respect to those who had suffered in the quest for racial justice, noting that many had been jailed, beaten, and otherwise "battered by the storms of persecution." In the midst of such difficult times, King affirmed, "I still have a dream." With that, the crowd became excited. Repeating the "I have a dream" phrase, King outlined his fundamental hopes for the future. "It is a dream deeply rooted in the American Dream. I have a dream that one day this nation will rise up and live out the true meaning of its creed, 'We hold these truths to be self-evident, that all men are created equal.'"

From there, King proceeded through several of his specific dreams. One was that "one day on the red hills of Georgia, sons of former slaves and the sons of former slave owners will be able to sit down together at the table of brotherhood." For his own children, he dreamed of the day when they would not be judged "by the color of their skin, but by the content of their character."

In Alabama, Tennessee, and Georgia, and across the nation, King hoped, racial discrimination and tension would cease. Drawing upon Old Testament prophecy, as he often did, King cried out, I have a dream that one day "every valley shall be exalted and every hill and mountain shall be made low. The rough places will be made plain and the crooked places will be made straight, and the glory of the Lord shall be revealed, and all flesh shall see it together." The ending was dramatic and similarly charged with moral emphases. "So let freedom ring from the prodigious hilltops of New Hampshire; let freedom ring from the mighty mountains of New York. . . ." In his panoramic survey of the mountains of America, he included Stone Mountain of Georgia and Lookout Mountain of Tennessee, and "every hill and molehill of Mississippi.

From every mountain side, let freedom ring." If that happened, said King, Americans could speed up the day when all people, regardless of race, religion, or creed, could "join hands and sing in the words of the old Negro spiritual: 'Free at last. Free at last. Thank God Almighty, we are free at last.'" By then, the huge throng of marchers was electrified.

King walked quickly to a car provided by President Kennedy and met with the president, along with several other civil rights leaders, at the White House. The high emotion of the rally now had to give way to the reasoned discourse of political realities of the civil rights bill. No one was sure on August 28 whether it would pass, despite King's warmly received address.

SIGNIFICANCE

The initial impact of the "I Have a Dream" speech was to lift the spirits of the participants and to give the March on Washington a tone of historical importance. King's speech was to become his most famous, epitomizing for many people the essence of the nonviolent movement's social vision. It was heard, directly and indirectly, by millions of people, including hundreds of representatives and senators. One of them, Senator Hubert H. Humphrey, watched and heard the speech with some 150 other members of Congress and remarked that although it probably did not change anyone's vote on the pending civil rights bill, it was "a good thing for Washington and the nation and the world." That was generally the feeling among supporters. There were detractors as well, many of whom considered the whole affair histrionic and unrelated to the actual power struggle for civil rights reform.

There is little doubt that the march and the King speech contributed to support for civil rights reform, although resistance to the administration's bill continued for months and was not overcome until well after Kennedy's assassination in November, 1963. President Lyndon B. Johnson, Kennedy's successor, steered an enlarged version of the Kennedy bill through Congress in the spring of 1964, and on July 2 signed it into law. Most of the resistance was from senators. House passage on February 10, 1964, was much easier than the months-long process that led to a favorable Senate vote, seventy-three to twenty-seven, on June 19. The role played by the march and King's speech in that legislative struggle was to provide the example of a basically orderly demonstration and an articulate statement of African Americans' demands set in a traditional American value structure.

That the speech did not change attitudes widely is also evident. Violence and racial tensions continued. On September 15, 1963, just days after the speech, four young African American girls were killed by dynamite hurled into a window of the Sixteenth Street Baptist Church in Birmingham. In St. Augustine, Florida, and several other cities, there were other manifestations of racial violence in the months immediately following the events in Washington.

On balance, however, the speech did have significant impact on attitudes. In the address, King had retained continuity with his previous speeches and sermons on human relations. He understood that the task of building bridges between races and social classes would not be easy. That he emphasized the economic plight of African Americans and poor people in the United States assured that there would be controversy, but it also signaled one of the principal emphases of the movement in the period after passage of the Civil Rights Act of 1964 and the Voting Rights Act of 1965. The address was highly moral and religious in tone, while linked clearly to the American constitutional tradition.

This important aspect of the "I Have a Dream" speech made it adaptable to a variety of uses in churches and civil rights campaigns and in the political processes of civil rights reform. For the SCLC, it became the major symbol of its future programs. Keeping the dream alive was the prevailing theme of King's organization in his last years and well beyond.

—*Thomas R. Peake*

See also: Montgomery Bus Boycott; Three Civil Rights Workers Are Murdered; King Wins the Nobel Peace Prize; Selma-Montgomery March; Congress Passes the Voting Rights Act; Watts Riot; Assassination of Martin Luther King, Jr.; Fair Housing Act Outlaws Discrimination in Housing; Supreme Court Upholds Ban on Housing Discrimination.

UNITED NATIONS CONDEMNS RACIAL DISCRIMINATION

November 20, 1963

The United Nations adopted the Declaration on the Elimination of All Forms of Racial Discrimination to expedite the elimination of apartheid, segregation, and other forms of racial domination.

Also known as: Declaration on the Elimination of All Forms of Racial Discrimination
Locale: New York, New York

Categories: United Nations; civil rights and liberties; human rights; diplomacy and international relations

KEY FIGURES

Adlai E. Stevenson (1900-1965), U.S. ambassador to the United Nations, 1961-1965

Philippe de Seynes (1910-2003), French U.N. undersecretary of economic and social affairs

U Thant (1909-1974), Burmese U.N. secretary-general, 1961-1971

SUMMARY OF EVENT

After World War II, for the first time in history, the fundamental rights of individuals became an international concern. Before that time, the rights of individuals had been a matter exclusively of domestic jurisdiction of a state. With the exception of certain categories of persons such as diplomats, aliens, and refugees, international law and international organizations dealt directly only with nation-states. The massive inhuman treatment and torture of people at the hands of Nazis and Fascists both before and during World War II made the protection of rights derived from the inherent dignity and equality of a human person a matter of universal concern. Thus, the human rights of individuals were to find a place in the agenda of the newly established United Nations.

The United Nations took a major initiative by adopting the Universal Declaration of Human Rights on December 10, 1948. The declaration served as the basic document providing guidelines and goals about the rights of individuals before the community of nations.

The Universal Declaration was adopted in the General Assembly with forty-eight nations voting in its favor, none against, and eight abstaining. Although it lacked legal binding force over member states, it served as a model to be emulated, inspired the inclusion of guaranteed protections for individuals in many constitutions all over the world, and provided a yardstick against which the conduct of nations could be judged.

The Universal Declaration formally stipulated human rights of an individual related to liberty and spiritual integrity, political freedoms, and social, economic, and cultural independence. It became the basis for the adoption of a number of important U.N.-sponsored declarations and covenants in subsequent years. The spirit of this declaration was violated in varying measures by most members of the United Nations; however, despite frequent practices to the contrary, no government has ever publicly admitted the disregard of the declaration's provisions.

The United Nations' declarations are formalized statements of general principles. The United Nations Declaration on the Elimination of All Forms of Racial Discrimination of 1963 was an offshoot of the 1948 Universal Declaration. It received its main impetus from dual sources: the entry of a host of African and Asian states into the United Nations championing the cause of self-determination of nations, and the policy of apartheid, which extolled racial discrimination and racial superiority, practiced in South Africa. The racial problems in the United States, particularly the practice of segregation in the South, also provided impetus to the declaration.

The groundwork for the declaration on racial discrimination of 1963 was prepared as early as 1947, when the U.N. Commission on Human Rights established a subcommission to study and report on discrimination against and protection of minorities. A number of organs and procedures for the supervision of human rights were established by the United Nations in the following years. In 1963, the Subcommission on Prevention of Discrimination and Protection of Minorities, the Commission on Human Rights, the Economic and Social Council, and the General Assembly of the United Nations considered the question of the elimination of all forms of racial discrimination. After considerable debate and several amendments, on November 20, 1963, the General Assembly unanimously adopted the Declaration on the Elimination of All Forms of Racial Discrimination.

The purpose of the United Nations Declaration on the Elimination of All Forms of Racial Discrimination was to expedite the elimination of racial discrimination, which, despite international efforts, had continued to manifest itself in many parts of the world in the form of "apartheid, segregation and separation, as well as by the promotion and dissemination of doctrines of racial superiority and expansionism in certain areas." Under the provisions of the declaration, the practice of discrimination between human beings on the grounds of race, color, or ethnic origin was declared to be a denial of the principles of the charter of the United Nations, a violation of human rights, and an obstacle to friendly and peaceful relations among nations and peoples within nations.

States, institutions, groups, and individuals were all barred from practicing racial discrimination and the use of police powers and violence to oppress individuals on racial and related grounds. Moreover, prescription was made to adopt positive measures at the state level for the adequate protection of individuals belonging to certain racial groups in order to ensure their full enjoyment of human rights. The declaration on racial discrimination suggested speedy governmental action in reversing public policies of racial segregation and the policies of apartheid. It advocated effective steps to be taken by governments to promote teaching, education, and information, with the intent of eliminating racial discrimination and prejudice and promoting understanding, tolerance, and cooperation.

The General Assembly requested all states to undertake all necessary measures to implement fully, faithfully, and without delay the principles contained in the declaration. It also requested governments and nongovernmental organizations to publicize the text of the declaration as widely as possible. The U.N. secretary general and specialized U.N. agencies were given the responsibility of circulating the declaration in as many languages as possible.

The most important immediate outcome of the declaration on racial discrimination was the adoption of a resolution by the U.N. General Assembly to give absolute priority to the preparation of a Draft Convention on the Elimination of All Forms of Racial Discrimination to be considered by the General Assembly in 1964. The Convention on the Elimination of All Forms of Racial Discrimination was later adopted by the General Assembly in 1965, quickly garnering widespread international support.

A committee on the elimination of racial discrimination was also established to review the information placed before it by the convention's signatory states and to report directly to the General Assembly once a year. This body now is overseen by the U.N. Commission on Human Rights.

The Declaration on the Elimination of All Forms of Racial Discrimination was to have a strong impact on the future U.N. instruments related to human rights, which included the two International Covenants adopted by the U.N. General Assembly in 1966, the 1968 convention on the nonapplicability of statutory limitations to war crimes and crimes against humanity, the Convention on the Suppression and Punishment of the Crime of Apartheid (1973), the Convention on the Elimination of All Forms of Discrimination Against Women

(1979), the Declaration on the Elimination of All Forms of Intolerance and of Discrimination Based on Religion or Belief (1981), the Declaration on the Rights of All People to Peace (1984), and the Declaration on the Human Rights of Individuals Who Are Not Nationals of the Country in Which They Live (1985). Moreover, the General Assembly declared the period of 1973-1983 to be the "Decade Against Racial Discrimination." The declaration on elimination of racial discrimination also gave a boost to the activities of nongovernmental watchdog agencies such as Amnesty International in bringing to light the violation of human rights of racial and ethnic minorities within states.

On a limited scale, despite the approval of only a very few states, the committee on the elimination of racial discrimination deals with communications directly from individuals within these states. It comments upon particular situations involving racial discrimination and prepares proposals and recommendations regarding such acts. Although its jurisdiction is advisory in nature and without any legal force, the committee plays an important role in focusing world attention on racial issues and mobilizing worldwide public opinion.

SIGNIFICANCE
The Declaration on the Elimination of All Forms of Racial Discrimination of 1963 considerably increased worldwide public awareness of the human rights of individuals regardless of their race, color, or ethnicity. The declaration generated moral, rather than legal, pressure in the society of states, and thus, despite their record of violations, all governments pay lip service to the doctrine and deny its disregard.

The declaration on racial discrimination suffered from an inherent limitation. As a result of the sudden emergence of a multitude of Asian and African states as the new majority at the United Nations in the 1960's, the Universal Declaration of Human Rights was expanded by adding the right of self-determination of nations to its list, a right which had been conspicuously absent from the original list. The rights of racial groups or individuals began to be perceived in terms of the self-determination of nations and an ideological framework opposed to Western colonialism and Western imperialism. The rights of people within these postcolonial societies and elsewhere in the international state system continued to be regarded as a matter of state jurisdiction and sovereignty.

Furthermore, Cold War bloc politics and the superpower rivalry complicated the situation. The Soviet

Union, as the leader of the communist countries and a friend of the nonaligned developing nations, and the United States, as the leader of the Western bloc and an ally of the Western-aligned or anticommunist developing nations, introduced the system of bloc voting at the United Nations, a system that seriously undermined the cause of human rights. Political expediency caused the United States to vote with its allies on the side of such countries as South Africa to maintain the solidarity of the Western bloc. The United States' criticism and negative vote during the deliberations on the draft proposal of the 1963 declaration on racial discrimination related mainly to technical grounds and the use of certain phrases in the proposal. The declaration in its final form was unanimously adopted by the General Assembly.

The Soviet Union and other communist countries, as well as most of the developing countries, continued to violate the human rights of racial and ethnic minority groups within their respective states to varying degrees. Their rhetoric indicated a discrepancy of perceptions caused by their focus on colonialism and imperialism as the exclusive manifestations of racism.

The issue of racial discrimination at the United Nations remained heavily focused on South Africa,

which represented a unique, formally created political-legal system of racial discrimination. Israel, too, became a main target. As a result, racialist practices in the Western world, particularly in the form of institutional racism, escaped receiving similar criticism or denouncement. For example, in 1963, the year in which the declaration was made, the Civil Rights movement in the United States began to protest the practice of segregation in the South and violation of human rights of black Americans. Practices in the United States did not become a controversial issue at the United Nations.

The powers of the U.N. Commission on Human Rights have gradually expanded. The role of nongovernmental watchdog organizations, which closely collaborate with the U.N. agencies, has been impressive. These include Amnesty International, the International Commission of Jurists, the International League of Human Rights, the International Federation of Human Rights, and the World Council of Churches. In promoting their efforts and others, the U.N. Declaration on the Elimination of All Forms of Racial Discrimination played an important role within the structural limitations of its parent organization.

—Indu Vohra

TWENTY-FOURTH AMENDMENT
January 23, 1964

The poll tax was an arbitrary limitation on voting rights, particularly in the South, where it was often employed to deny the franchise to African Americans and poor whites.

On January 23, 1964, the South Dakota senate cast the deciding vote in the ratification process of the Twenty-fourth Amendment to the United States Constitution. The amendment ended the poll tax as a condition of voting in federal elections. The real function of the tax had been to deny civil rights to members of racial minorities, especially black southerners. The Twenty-fourth Amendment, passage of which began in 1962, was only one part of a larger campaign of civil rights reform that came to a head with the Civil Rights Act of 1964.

POLL TAXES
Civil rights issues were central to the social questions that surfaced during the 1950's and 1960's. Beginning with the *Brown v. Board of Education* case in 1954, which disallowed school segregation, both courts and legislatures were engaged in the resolution of such issues. John F. Kennedy assumed office as president in 1961, at a time when the Civil Rights movement was taking on a direct-action character—undertaking mass demonstrations, civil disobedience, and occasional acts of violence—and opposition to it was being manifested in mass arrests, intimidation, and even murder. This trend convinced the new administration and its liberal supporters in Congress that the time had come to use federal legislation as well as the courts to initiate civil rights reform. The first target was the poll tax.

The poll tax, a uniform, direct, and personal tax levied upon individuals, was not a new phenomenon. It had existed in some states since the early twentieth century and in others, such as New Hampshire, since colonial times, though not as a franchise prerequisite. All states with the poll tax allowed exceptions to it: officers and men on active militia duty, veterans, and persons with disabilities resulting from gainful occupation and whose taxable property did not exceed $500, for example. The tax was nominal in most cases for those who did have to pay, being only $1.50 or $2.00 per year. The tax was cumulative, however, so that voters who came to register after having not paid the tax for a number of years might find themselves having to pay what for many poor people would be a considerable sum. To civil rights advocates, the poll tax paralleled literacy tests as a device to limit voting rights, and they were determined that both should be abolished. Even in southern states where the poll tax was no longer used, literacy tests, closed registration lists, and straightforward intimidation were used to prevent African Americans from voting.

THE PROCESS OF REFORM

The process of reform had to begin somewhere, and northern Democrats, acting upon inspiration from the Kennedy administration, began with the anti-poll tax amendment process early in 1962. There was strong opposition from a southern bloc of conservatives, mostly Democrats led by Richard B. Russell, a Democrat from Georgia, but it was not as strong as might have been expected.

The Senate majority leader was Michael H. Mansfield, a Democrat from Montana, and it was his responsibility to shepherd the legislation through the Senate. The anti-poll tax amendment itself was sponsored by Spessard L. Holland, a Democrat from Florida, whose role might have appeared surprising, since he was part of the southern bloc. Holland, however, was no friend of the poll tax in any form and had led a successful campaign to abolish it in his own state in 1937.

The Senate Judiciary Committee, chaired by Senator James O. Eastland, a Democrat from Mississippi and part of the southern bloc, had conducted hearings on the poll tax and literacy tests for weeks to little avail. On March 14, Senator Mansfield moved for Senate consideration of a bill to establish Alexander Hamilton's New York home as a national monument, to which, it was suggested, the proposed constitutional amendment could be attached. The Senate Judiciary Committee, wherein, according to liberal senators, civil rights issues tended to get lost, was effectively bypassed, and the Hamilton motion, with the expectation of its being linked to the anti-poll tax amendment, was put before the Senate.

As soon as the motion appeared on the floor, the southern conservative bloc began a "friendly" filibuster, so termed because the southerners did not go all-out to prevent the Hamilton resolution from coming to a vote. It is conceivable that the vote was considered a foregone conclusion, and the filibuster was merely for form's sake. In any event, it endured for ten days, until, apparently, the participants had run out of words. Then Senator Holland introduced the preordained motion to substitute the language of the anti-poll tax amendment for the language of the Hamilton resolution. This brought Senator Russell to his feet in protest: "We are adopting an absurd, farfetched, irrational, unreasonable, and unconstitutional method to get this amendment," he charged. Others agreed, including Jacob K. Javits, a Republican from New York, who proposed that the Senate should act against the poll tax by simple legislation, and Paul H. Douglas, a Democrat from Illinois, who warned that, the questionable manner of the adoption notwithstanding, using the amendment process could itself prove the downfall of efforts to abolish the tax.

Nevertheless, the Holland motion was put to a vote, and on March 27 it passed the Senate by a margin of seventy-seven to sixteen. An amendment to the Constitution of the United States repealing the poll tax for all federal elections was then forwarded to the House of Representatives, where it was debated, dissected, promoted, and opposed in similar manner, until it passed that chamber in August, 1962. It was then up to the states to ratify the amendment by vote of their legislatures.

THE AMENDMENT GOES TO THE STATES

It was speculated widely during succeeding months that, on the premise that the poll-tax amendment would pass the states and greatly broaden the base of the southern electorate, the Democratic leadership would work to break the power of the southern bloc by promoting candidates who were more loyal to the national party to oppose the bloc's members in the primaries. At least thirteen congressional seats were thought to be on a target list. Needless to say, Republican Party leaders were delighted, convinced by the southerners' defiant attitude that the Democrats had outsmarted themselves.

Meanwhile, the poll-tax amendment was being considered by the states, and it was an uphill battle.

The Arizona house, for example, approved the amendment in 1963, but it died in the state senate. By the end of the year, however, momentum toward ratification gathered, and by January 5, 1964, the amendment needed to be approved by only two more states. A few days later the number dropped to one, and on January 23 South Dakota's senate voted thirty-four to zero in favor of ratification. The Twenty-fourth Amendment to the Constitution was law, requiring then only the further technicality of formal certification by the General Services Administration of the federal government. South Dakota was compelled to race through its vote in order to beat out Georgia as the deciding state. There was an irony in this, as Georgia was the home of Senator Richard Russell, the most outspoken opponent of the amendment in the early days of debate on the motion.

IMPACT

The poll-tax amendment symbolized the liberal determination to institute civil rights reform. There was, however, opposition of nearly equal intensity. Three political proposals made in 1963 were meant to redress—or so their advocates claimed—the eroding of states' rights by the federal government. In fact, this package aimed at countering the possible effects of impending civil rights legislation, including abolition of the poll tax. The first proposal sought to give the power to redraw congressional districts to state governments. Gerrymandering could then keep power out of the hands of members of racial minorities, even if minorities came to the polls in greater numbers after the Twenty-fourth Amendment was passed.

The second proposal placed the constitutional amendment process in the hands of the state legislatures, bypassing either Congress or a national convention. Under this plan, a two-thirds majority of the state legislatures could propose an amendment, and a three-fourths majority could make it part of the Constitution. The third proposal sought to create a "Court of the Union" that would review Supreme Court decisions on federal-state relations and would be made up of the chief justices of the fifty states. This court would have effectively nullified the Supreme Court as the final arbiter of constitutionality in matters touching upon civil rights, because most such matters touched in turn on federal-state relations.

None of these propositions came to fruition, but the Twenty-fourth Amendment did, abolishing the poll tax in federal elections. Within two months, however, Arkansas, one of the last states to cling to the poll tax, upheld in court the state constitution's requirement of a poll tax for state and local elections. Later, a private election oversight organization found at least seven irregularities in the primary election process in Arkansas, including the fact that unauthorized persons were permitted to help count ballots. The organization discovered that, while the poll tax was no longer required for federal elections, there were many other devices available to skew elections in the way segregationists wanted.

Various avenues were taken to limit the impact of the new amendment even for federal elections. In Mississippi, state officials cracked down on minor violations of little-used aspects of the civil code as a device to intimidate members of the Congress of Racial Equality and others who were involved in voter registration drives among African Americans. Violence was used as well when African Americans congregated in anticipation of a protest march in Canton, Mississippi, in 1963. In Georgia, support for segregationist presidential candidate George Wallace led to black-white confrontations and violence. In Virginia, on the eve of the 1964 presidential election, a federal court upheld a state law requiring payment of the poll tax for the right to vote in local and state elections. Two years later, however, in *Harper v. Virginia Board of Elections*, the Supreme Court concluded that poll taxes violated the equal protection clause of the Constitution, and the last such tax was swept away. Abolition of the poll tax was a step in the right direction, but there was a long road still to travel before voting rights for minority groups would be secure at all levels of American politics.

—Robert Cole

See also: Civil Rights Act of 1960; Civil Rights Act of 1964; Fifteenth Amendment; Politics and government; Poll taxes; Voting Rights Act of 1965; Voting Rights Act of 1975

POLL TAXES ARE OUTLAWED

January 23, 1964

The poll tax was an arbitrary limitation on voting rights, particularly in the South, where it was often employed to deny the franchise to African Americans and poor whites. With the ratification of the Twenty-fourth Amendment, the tax was abolished.

Also known as: Twenty-fourth Amendment to the U.S. Constitution
Locale: Washington, D.C.
Categories: Government and politics; laws, acts, and legal history; civil rights and liberties; social issues and reform

KEY FIGURES

John F. Kennedy (1917-1963), president of the United States, 1961-1963
Spessard L. Holland (1892-1971), U.S. senator from Florida, 1946-1971
Richard Russell, Jr. (1897-1971), U.S. senator from Georgia, 1933-1971, and leader of the Senate's Southern bloc
Mike Mansfield (1903-2001), U.S. senator from Montana, 1953-1977, and Senate majority leader, 1961-1977

SUMMARY OF EVENT

On January 23, 1964, the South Dakota Senate cast the deciding vote in the ratification process of the Twenty-fourth Amendment to the U.S. Constitution. The amendment ended the poll tax as a condition of voting in federal elections. The real function of the tax had been to deny civil rights to racial minorities, especially Southern blacks. The Twenty-fourth Amendment, passage of which began in 1962, was only one part of a larger campaign of civil rights reform that came to a head with the Civil Rights Act of 1964. Civil rights issues were central to the social questions that surfaced during the 1950's and 1960's. Beginning with the *Brown v. Board of Education* case in 1954, which disallowed school segregation, both courts and legislatures were engaged in the resolution of such issues.

John F. Kennedy assumed office as president in 1961, at a time when the Civil Rights movement was taking on a direct-action character—undertaking mass demonstrations, civil disobedience, and occasional acts of violence—and opposition to it was being manifested in mass arrests, intimidation, and even murder. This trend convinced the new administration and its liberal supporters in Congress that the time had come to use federal legislation as well as the courts to initiate civil rights reform. The first target was the poll tax.

The poll tax, a uniform, direct, and personal tax levied upon individuals, was not a new phenomenon. It had existed in some states since the early 1900's, and in others, such as New Hampshire, since colonial times, though not as a franchise prerequisite. All states with the poll tax allowed exceptions to it: military officers and men on active militia duty, veterans, and persons disabled as a result of gainful occupation and whose taxable property did not exceed $500, for example. The tax was nominal in most cases for those who did have to pay, being only $1.50 or $2.00 per year. The tax was cumulative, however, so that voters who came to register after having not paid the tax for a number of years might find themselves having to pay what for many poor people would be a considerable sum. To civil rights advocates, the poll tax paralleled literacy tests as a device to limit voting rights, and advocates were determined that both devices should be abolished. Even in Southern states where the poll tax was no longer used, literacy tests, closed registration lists, and straightforward intimidation were used to prevent African Americans from voting.

The process of reform had to begin somewhere, and Northern Democrats, acting upon inspiration from the Kennedy administration, began with the anti-poll-tax amendment process early in 1962. There was strong opposition from a Southern bloc of conservatives, mostly Democrats led by Richard Russell, Jr., a Democrat from Georgia, but it was not as strong as might have been expected. The Senate majority leader was Mike Mansfield, a Democrat from Montana, and it was his responsibility to shepherd the legislation through the Senate. The anti-polltax amendment itself was sponsored by Spessard L. Holland, a Democrat from Florida, whose role might have appeared surprising since he was part of the Southern bloc. Holland, however, was no friend of the poll tax in any form and had led a successful campaign to abolish it in his own state in 1937.

The Senate Judiciary Committee, chaired by Senator James Eastland, a Democrat from Mississippi and part of the Southern bloc, had conducted hearings on the poll tax and literacy tests for weeks, to little avail. On March 14, Senator Mansfield moved for Senate

457

consideration of a bill to establish Alexander Hamilton's New York home as a national monument, to which, it was suggested, the proposed constitutional amendment could be attached.

The Senate Judiciary Committee, wherein, according to liberal senators, civil rights issues tended to get lost, was effectively bypassed, and the Hamilton motion, with the expectation of its being linked to the anti-poll-tax amendment, was put before the Senate. As soon as it appeared on the floor, the Southern conservative bloc began a "friendly" filibuster, so termed because the Southerners did not go all out to prevent the Hamilton resolution from coming to a vote. It is conceivable that the vote was considered a foregone conclusion, and the filibuster was merely for form's sake. In any event, it endured for ten days, until, apparently, the participants ran out of words. Then Senator Holland introduced the preordained motion to substitute the language of the anti-poll-tax amendment for the language of the Hamilton resolution. This brought Senator Russell to his feet in protest: "We are adopting an absurd, farfetched, irrational, unreasonable, and unconstitutional method to get this amendment," he charged. Others agreed, including Jacob K. Javits, a Republican from New York, who proposed that the Senate should act against the poll tax by simple legislation, and Paul H. Douglas, a Democrat from Illinois, who warned that, the questionable manner of the adoption notwithstanding, using the amendment process could itself prove the downfall of efforts to abolish the tax.

Nevertheless, the Holland motion was put to a vote, and on March 27 it passed the Senate by a margin of seventy-seven to sixteen. An amendment to the Constitution of the United States repealing the poll tax for all federal elections was then forwarded to the House of Representatives, where it was debated, dissected, promoted, and opposed in similar manner, until it passed that chamber in August, 1962. It was then up to the states to ratify the amendment by vote of their legislatures.

It was speculated widely during succeeding months that, on the premise that the anti-poll-tax amendment would pass the states and greatly broaden the base of the Southern electorate, the Democratic leadership would work to break the power of the Southern bloc by promoting candidates who were more loyal to the national party to oppose the bloc's members in the primaries. At least thirteen congressional seats were thought to be on a target list. Republican Party leaders were delighted,

convinced by the Southerners' defiant attitude that the Democrats had outsmarted themselves.

Meanwhile, the anti-poll-tax amendment was being considered by the states, and it was an uphill battle. The Arizona house, for example, approved the amendment in 1963, but it died in the state senate. By the end of the year, however, momentum toward ratification gathered, and by January 5, 1964, the amendment needed to be approved by only two more states. A few days later the number dropped to one, and on January 23 South Dakota's senate voted thirty-four to zero in favor of ratification.

The Twenty-fourth Amendment to the Constitution was law, requiring then only the further technicality of formal certification by the General Services Administration of the federal government. South Dakota was compelled to race through its vote in order to beat out Georgia as the deciding state. There was an irony in this, as Georgia was the home of Senator Richard Russell, Jr., the most outspoken opponent of the amendment in the early days of debate on the motion.

SIGNIFICANCE

The anti-poll-tax amendment symbolized the liberal determination to institute civil rights reform. There was, however, opposition of nearly equal intensity. Three political proposals made in 1963 were meant to redress— or so their advocates claimed—the eroding of states' rights by the federal government. In fact, this package aimed at countering the possible effects of impending civil rights legislation, including abolition of the poll tax. The first proposal sought to give the power to redraw congressional districts to state governments. Gerrymandering could then keep power out of the hands of racial minorities, even if minorities came to the polls in greater numbers after the Twenty-fourth Amendment was passed.

The second proposal placed the constitutional amendment process in the hands of the state legislatures, bypassing either Congress or a national convention. Under this plan, a two-thirds majority of the state legislatures could propose an amendment, and a three-fourths majority could make it part of the Constitution. The third proposal sought to create a "Court of the Union" that would review Supreme Court decisions on federal-state relations and would be made up of the chief justices of the fifty states. This court would have effectively nullified the Supreme Court as the final arbiter of constitutionality in matters touching upon civil rights, because most such matters touched in turn on federal-state relations.

None of these propositions came to fruition, but the Twenty-fourth Amendment did, abolishing the poll tax in federal elections. Within two months, however, Arkansas, one of the last states to cling to the poll tax, upheld in court the state constitution's requirement of a poll tax for state and local elections. Later, a private election oversight organization found at least seven irregularities in the primary election process in Arkansas, including the fact that unauthorized persons were permitted to help count ballots. The organization discovered that, while the poll tax was no longer required for federal elections, there were many other devices available to skew elections in the way segregationists wanted.

Various avenues were taken to limit the impact of the new amendment even for federal elections. In Mississippi, state officials cracked down on minor violations of little-used aspects of the civil code as a device to intimidate members of the Congress of Racial Equality and others who were involved in voter registration drives among African Americans. Violence was used as well when African Americans congregated in anticipation of a protest march in Canton, Mississippi, in 1963. In Georgia, support for segregationist presidential candidate George C. Wallace led to black-white confrontations and violence. In Virginia, on the eve of the 1964 presidential election, a federal court upheld a state law requiring payment of the poll tax for the right to vote in local and state elections. Two years later, however, in *Harper v. Virginia Board of Elections*, the Supreme Court concluded that poll taxes violated the equal protection clause of the Constitution, and the last such tax was swept away. Abolition of the poll tax was a step in the right direction, but there was a long road still to travel before voting rights for minority groups would be secure at all levels of American politics.

—*Robert Cole*

See also: Supreme Court Rules African American Disenfranchisement Unconstitutional; Supreme Court Ends Public School Segregation; Civil Rights Protesters Attract International Attention; King Delivers His "I Have a Dream" Speech; Three Civil Rights Workers Are Murdered; Congress Passes the Civil Rights Act of 1964; Congress Passes the Voting Rights Act.

CLAY DEFEATS LISTON TO GAIN WORLD HEAVYWEIGHT BOXING TITLE

February 25, 1964

The storied career of one of the most legendary sports figures began when young boxer Cassius Clay overcame steep odds to defeat reigning heavyweight champion Sonny Liston. Clay changed his name to Muhammad Ali and his religion to Islam but never changed his boxing style during nearly two decades of fighting. He became one of the most recognizable figures in the world after his retirement, and he devotes his time to global humanitarian causes.

Also known as: Muhammad Ali
Locale: Miami Beach, Florida
Categories: Sports; popular culture

KEY FIGURES

Muhammad Ali (Cassius Clay; b. 1942), professional boxer, 1960-1981
Angelo Dundee (b. 1923), Ali's trainer
Sonny Liston (1932-1970), professional boxer, 1953-1970

SUMMARY OF EVENT

On February 25, 1964, one of the most legendary, successful, and controversial careers in professional sports was launched when heavyweight boxer Cassius Clay successfully dethroned the champion Sonny Liston. Shortly thereafter, Clay changed his name to Muhammad Ali and his religion to Islam and embarked on a twodecadelong career as one of the greatest prizefighters in the history of the sport and one of the most recognizable persons around the globe.

Ironically, prior to the fight, the twenty-two-year-old Clay had been considered an overwhelming underdog by most boxing sportswriters and other observers of the sport. The odds for the title fight were 7 to 1 against him, even though Clay had compiled an impressive overall record. His amateur mark was 108-8 and included six Kentucky Gold Glove titles, an International Gold Glove title, and a gold medal as the light heavyweight champion at the 1960 Olympics in Rome. He had also amassed nineteen professional victories.

Nevertheless, it was widely held that the brash young boxer from Louisville, Kentucky, was no match for the reigning heavyweight champion, thirty-two-year-old Sonny Liston. A scowling ex-convict, Liston was regarded as one of the fiercest fighters and most intimidating punchers of all time. He had become heavyweight champion by severely beating champion Floyd Patterson on September 25, 1962. He beat Patterson again on July 22, 1963, to retain the title. Both fights were short, brutal affairs that lasted less than one round each and ended with Patterson prone on the canvas. Liston was thought to be unstoppable, and many believed he would do to Clay what he did to Patterson, or worse.

Clay, who was nicknamed the Louisville Lip for his boastful antics, had a very different end in mind. Even before he signed for the fight, Clay had subjected Liston to an unceasing barrage of quips and quotes designed to undercut the champion's confidence while goading him enough that he had no choice but to fight Clay if he wanted peace. Clay heckled Liston while the champion was giving boxing exhibitions before the second Patterson fight. He harassed him at the dice tables in a Las Vegas casino. He climbed into the ring after Liston had won the second Patterson fight in convincing fashion and flourished a fake newspaper headline that announced how Liston would shut his mouth; Clay then tore up the paper.

Clay's hyperbole was rewarded in November, 1963, when he signed to fight the champion. If Liston thought that by agreeing to the fight, he would get Clay finally to leave him alone, he was sadly mistaken. Clay continued his campaign of torment by driving a bus to Liston's Denver, Colorado, home and honking the horn and screaming insults from the window—at 1:00 a.m. When Liston traveled to Miami to train for the fight against Clay, Clay met his plane on the tarmac and began verbally abusing him the instant he got off the plane. Clay drove after Liston's car as he left the airport, yelling and screaming at him. Clay drove to the house Liston had rented and performed his antics on the front lawn before reporters and television cameras.

Clay, however, saved his most outrageous behavior for the weigh-in on the morning of the fight. Shouting out that he was ready to "float like a butterfly, sting like a bee," Clay pounded the ground with an African walking stick and proclaimed, with shrieking hysteria, that he was going to whip Liston badly. He even predicted that the eighth round was when he would knock Liston out. Clay became so animated, and his behavior so outrageous, that the Miami Boxing Commission fined him $2,500 on the spot.

Shortly after the bout, when it was revealed that Clay had become a Muslim and had taken the name Muhammad Ali, American boxing fans realized that this new king was going to be unlike any who had come before.

SIGNIFICANCE

Clay's victory over Liston and his subsequent public embrace of Islam and new name heralded the Black Power movement of the 1960's, when African Americans began to demand their civil rights at the national level. Also, Clay's antics signaled the transformation of sport into spectacle, a form of public entertainment that transcended regional boundaries and appealed to a worldwide audience.

Finally, Clay's win launched the career of one of the most gifted and controversial athletes in the history of sport. In 1978 he became the first boxer to win the heavyweight championship of the world three times. In 1999, *Sports Illustrated* magazine named him Sportsman of the Century. He has spent much of his retirement time working for human rights around the world, and he was awarded the Presidential Medal of Freedom in 2005.

—*Russell Roberts*

DUTCHMAN DRAMATIZES RACIAL HATRED

March 24, 1964

Audiences were shocked by the language and ideas of Dutchman, *a venomous play by Le Roi Jones (who would soon be known as Amiri Baraka). The play was filled with the emotions of contempt, anger, and hatred, and it ended in emasculation and murder.*

Locale: New York, New York
Category: Theater

KEY FIGURES
LeRoi Jones (Amiri Baraka; b. 1934), African American playwright, director, writer, activist, and teacher

460

Lorraine Hansberry (1930-1965), African American playwright

SUMMARY OF EVENT

LeRoi Jones emerged as a leading American playwright in 1964, when his striking drama *Dutchman* (pr., pb. 1964) was produced Off-Broadway at New York's Village South Theatre. The play, which was widely acclaimed as one of the year's best after it opened on March 24, catapulted Jones into the front ranks of African American writers, and he soon became known as an uncompromising black militant. In the wake of his newfound prominence, he severed many of his ties with white American culture; in 1966, he renounced the name "Jones" and became known as Imamu Amiri Baraka (he later dropped the name "Imamu").

Baraka became the leading writer of militant black theater.

He articulated the African American condition. To support his work as a theater revolutionary, he founded the Black Arts Theatre and School in Harlem. Much of the subject matter of Baraka's works was designed to attack the "white establishment." The objective Baraka sought through his drama was not integration but the separation of whites and African Americans: He wished to drive a wedge between them. Throughout his career, Baraka continued to write drama that denounced whites and to express a militant philosophy, espousing the need for African Americans to force whites to redress the injustices of the past and present. He strongly advocated the creation of a separatist society for African Americans. These themes remained evident in his activities and playwriting.

Dutchman makes use of the techniques of Antonin Artaud's Theater of Cruelty. The play's major characters, Clay and Lula, force the audience to examine their prejudices through the violence of the dramatic action. Through them, Jones wanted to make audience members face and confront what he saw as the violent reality of the subconscious hatred buried in their psyches. He challenged his audiences to recognize that they created the moral standards by which they chose to live. Certainly, Jones wanted his viewers to see Clay and Lula as real people; at the same time, however, the play insists that these characters must be understood to be character types.

Dutchman is set in a New York City subway car, in which Clay and Lula are riding beneath the city. The action of the play thus takes place in the heart, the very infrastructure, of the city; the setting may be read as emblematic of the sociopolitical structure of the United States. As the dramatic action evolves, it is possible to see the "true" feelings of the characters as demonstrated by their language and gestures. The play's action seems intended to represent the class struggle going on in society.

Clay wants to be a man, but Lula hatefully attacks his attempts toward manhood; she asks him, accusingly, "What right do you have to be wearing a three-button suit and striped tie? Your grandfather was a slave, he didn't go to Harvard." Racial stereotypes are revealed in the play's dialogue; Lula, for example, remarks on the black male's supposed sexual ability.

The play's title is metaphorical. The word "Dutchman" does not appear in the dialogue of the play. It could be a reference to the myth of the *Flying Dutchman*, the phantom ship forever doomed to sail the seas. The title may also allude to the Dutch ship that brought the first African slaves to the Americas. Whichever interpretation one prefers, the play is clearly a study of the black-white experience. Clay represents African Americans who are trying to live and survive in a white-controlled society; Lula stands for white efforts to prevent African Americans from achieving equal status in the United States.

The play is a blend of realism, expressionism, and absurdism. Jones successfully brought together realism in the play's structure and characters, expressionism in the juxtaposition of the emasculation and the emancipation of Clay, and absurdism in the play's dialogue. Moreover, Jones successfully pulled together emotions that represented frightening savagery. Jones's anger toward, contempt for, and hatred of white culture was forcefully portrayed in the play's raw, ugly, and repelling dramatic action.

Dutchman was powerful and compelling in its statement. Ritualistic violence underscored the representation of the conflict between African Americans and whites. It became representative of a genre of African American literature known as the Black Arts movement. Younger black writers, including Don L. Lee (Haki Madhubuti), Ed Bullins, Sonia Sanchez, Marvin X, and Larry Neal, soon produced a torrent of African American-themed work that sought to establish the artistic validity of African American cultural idioms and that was often openly antiwhite. *Dutchman* was the opening shot in this volley of militant 1960's works. With *Dutchman*, Jones opened the doors for African American writers to deal with a broad range of political, racial, and social themes. These works included examinations of the lives and times of African American historical figures, of race relations in the United States, and of the African American bourgeoisie. The African American plays of the 1960's included African American militant dramas, comedies, allegories, ritual dramas, and even musicals.

Amiri Baraka's influence on the drama of the 1960's made him one of the cultural and spiritual leaders of the era. His leadership was best demonstrated by his revolutionary theater. Such prominent later African American playwrights as Ed Bullins, August Wilson, and Charles Fuller seemed to receive an impetus to excel as a result of the force Baraka brought to the ethnic theater. Moreover, Baraka's revolutionary theater was a

major factor in the appearance and success of agitprop street plays in the 1960's and 1970's. In recognition of his success as a playwright, director, poet, novelist, and activist, Baraka in 1972 received an honorary doctorate from Malcolm X College in Chicago, Illinois.

—Willis M. Watt

See also: Ellison's *Invisible Man* Is Published; Hansberry's *A Raisin in the Sun* Debuts on Broadway; Baldwin Voices Black Rage in *The Fire Next Time*; *The Autobiography of Malcolm X* Is Published.

MISSISSIPPI FREEDOM DEMOCRATIC PARTY

Founded on April 24, 1964

Its aim was to enable African Americans to participate fully in the Mississippi state political process.

Identification: Alternative political party
Place: Jackson, Mississippi

Mississippi's 1890 constitution had disfranchised its African American citizens, allowing only a tiny percent to register to vote. Potential voters were prevented from exercising their rights through intimidation and taxes at the polls and registration laws requiring applicants to read and copy any section of the state constitution on request, give a "reasonable" interpretation of the section, and demonstrate a "reasonable" understanding of the duties and obligations of citizenship under a constitutional form of government. Illiterate whites often passed by just "signing the book," however, African Americans were often told they had failed but were not permitted to see test results. In the mid-1950's, an effort to restrict registration even further by adding a "good moral character" requirement was initiated in response to the U.S. Supreme Court school desegregation ruling; this amendment was successful in 1962.

The Mississippi Freedom Democratic Party (MFDP) was founded in April, 1964, in Jackson, Mississippi, by African Americans as an alternative to a segregationist state Democratic Party. Profoundly grassroots in both promise and practice, the MFDP was chaired by Lawrence Guyot with vice chair Ed King; its legal council was attorney Arthur Kinoy. It pledged

loyalty to the National Democratic Party and sought its base among poor Mississippians of all races.

In the summer and fall of 1964, MFDP "freedom registrars," building on a fall, 1963, voter registration campaign, collected more than sixty thousand registrations on simplified unofficial forms. The MFDP and others also worked under the umbrella of the Council of Federated Organizations (COFO) to help people register on official rolls. Prevented from participating in the regular Democratic state convention, the MFDP held its own state convention on July 26, 1964, and elected delegates and alternates to the Democratic National Convention. The MFDP also nominated the first African American candidates to run for Congress since Reconstruction: Fannie Lou Hamer, Second District; Annie Devine, Fourth District; and Victoria Gray, Fifth District.

THE DEMOCRATIC NATIONAL CONVENTION

At the Democratic National Convention in Atlantic City in August, the MFDP challenged seating of the official delegation from Mississippi. Televised coverage of the MFDP's activities at the Democratic National Convention favorably affected public perception of the justice of the group's challenge. However, its challenge was rejected by the party's credentials committee. In turn, the MFDP rejected a proposed compromise, linked to Hubert Humphrey, that promised that the Democratic Party would seat a racially balanced Mississippi delegation in 1968.

In January, 1965, the MFDP challenged the seating of Mississippi's newly elected congressional delegation. Depositions about voting irregularities collected in support of that challenge during the following months further publicly disgraced the state's segregationist political leadership although the MFDP's congressional challenge finally died in a House vote on September 17, 1965.

The MFDP failed to unseat the official delegation at the 1964 Democratic National Convention but was effective in local consciousness raising and in increasing national disaffection with Mississippi's segregationist voter registration practices. In April, 1965, a federal court injunction ordered Sunflower County's registrar to operate on a nondiscriminatory basis. In August, 1965, Mississippi reformed its voter registration application process. Mississippians of all races began to register with increasing success, and racial diversity increased among elected officials. In 1968, a racially integrated Mississippi delegation was seated, as promised, at the Democratic National Convention. The MFDP was absorbed into a liberal coalition known as the Mississippi Loyal Democrats in 1968. By the late 1970's, there were more African Americans registered in Mississippi than in any other state.

—Barbara Roos

See also: Civil Rights movement; Council of Federated Organizations; Freedom Summer; Student Nonviolent Coordinating Committee; Voting Rights Act of 1965

FREEDOM SUMMER

1964

With the help of one thousand volunteers from all over the country, African Americans in Mississippi endured many jailings and some deaths to break barriers and alert the nation to the reality of a social system maintained by terror.

The Event: Summer-long voter-registration campaign in a state in which African Americans had long been excluded from voting
Place: Mississippi

In the early 1960's, Mississippi's elected officials were determined to preserve white supremacy and segregation. Several African Americans who attempted to register to vote or to challenge the status quo were murdered. In 1961, leaders of the National Association for the Advancement of Colored People (NAACP), Student Nonviolent Coordinating Committee (SNCC), Congress of Racial Equality (CORE), and the Southern Christian Leadership Conference (SCLC) formed the Council of Federated Organizations (COFO) to further the cause of civil rights in Mississippi.

CHALLENGES
The COFO planned to register voters; set up freedom schools to teach African Americans job skills, African American history, and the rights of citizens under the U.S. Constitution; form community centers from which to launch challenges to segregation under the Civil Rights Act of 1964, and canvass for the newly established Mississippi Freedom Democratic Party (MFDP), which had no standing under Mississippi law. Organizing began in especially difficult towns such as McComb in southwest Mississippi. Stokely Carmichael moved SNCC headquarters to Greenwood in the Delta area of the state, where local businessperson Amzie Moore and SNCC organizer Robert P. Moses began planning for a massive effort for the summer of 1964, which would follow the violent resistance to the enrollment of James H. Meredith at the University of Mississippi in 1962 and the murder of NAACP leader Medgar Evers in 1963. Recruitment of volunteers of all races took place, mostly on college campuses, and civil rights workers began arriving long before the summer began. Many underwent orientation in Oxford, Ohio.

Three COFO volunteers—James Chaney, Michael Schwerner, and Andrew Goodman—were murdered in Neshoba County by a mob led by Sheriff Lawrence Ramey and including Ku Klux Klan members on June 21, 1964. However, the violence did not stop the COFO from carrying out its plans for community centers, freedom schools, and voter registration drives. White volunteers got most of the publicity, and their presence protected local African Americans to some extent, but permanent change was achieved by local people working in their own behalf, using the volunteers as a catalyst.

463

Volunteers averaged slightly more than one arrest each by local authorities during the summer, and many were beaten or otherwise harassed. Publicity for the project had a major national impact. A reluctant Federal Bureau of Investigation and other agencies were forced into action to protect volunteers and local people, a role that has been much exaggerated in films such as *Mississippi Burning* (1988).

The MFDP challenge to regular Mississippi Democrats at the 1964 Democratic National Convention provided a showcase for local leaders such as Fannie Lou Hamer of Ruleville. Some disputes arose between Moses, who believed that local people should lead the movement for their own freedom, and Allard Lowenstein, who believed the COFO should form a close alliance with the liberal wing of the Democratic Party; however, COFO remained united until the summer project was over. Many volunteers stayed on to work with SNCC and other organizations that flourished in the wake of the pioneering 1964 effort.

ACHIEVEMENTS

Freedom Summer was successful in opening the eyes of the American public to the inequities suffered by black residents of Mississippi; however, the public's concern with the state of affairs in Mississippi itself did not last much longer than the summer. The white volunteers gained considerable experience during the summer, and many of them continued to be active in other organizations. Within the COFO, the divisions between black and white activists and local and outsiders grew, causing it to disband in 1965.

The MFDP gained considerable publicity when it challenged the seating of the "regular" Democratic Party delegates from Mississippi at the party's national convention in 1964. Although the MFDP was unable to replace the official delegates with any of its own, it had a lasting effect: The 1968 Democratic National Convention featured a racially integrated Mississippi delegation.

Although Freedom Summer ended without any marked improvements in the state, by the 1990's, Mississippi had more elected African American officials than any other state, social relations among the races did not differ greatly from those in other parts of the country, and educational opportunities for African Americans had greatly improved. However, tensions between whites and African Americans remained and the poverty of the majority of the African American community was largely unabated.

—*J. Quinn Brisben*

See also: Civil Rights Act of 1964; Civil rights worker murders; Congress of Racial Equality; Ku Klux Klan; Mississippi Freedom Democratic Party; National Association for the Advancement of Colored People; Southern Christian Leadership Conference; Student Nonviolent Coordinating Committee; University of Mississippi desegregation

THREE CIVIL RIGHTS WORKERS ARE MURDERED

June 21-22, 1964

A group of white supremacists attacked and murdered three civil rights workers in the Deep South. The three men were missing for weeks, capturing national headlines even before their bodies were discovered and focusing renewed attention on the struggle for civil rights in southern United States.

Locale: Neshoba County, Mississippi
Categories: Civil rights and liberties; terrorism

KEY FIGURES

Michael Henry Schwerner (1939-1964), Jewish American civil rights activist and a member of the Congress of Racial Equality

James Earl Chaney (1943-1964), African American plasterer and civil rights activist

Andrew Goodman (1943-1964), Caucasian American student and civil rights activist

Cecil Ray Price (c. 1937-2001), Neshoba County deputy sheriff and a member of the Mississippi Ku Klux Klan

J. Edgar Hoover (1895-1972), FBI director, 1924-1972

Robert F. Kennedy (1925-1968), U.S. attorney general, 1961-1964

SUMMARY OF EVENT

The struggle for black equality reached its crest in the two years after the August, 1963, March on Washington.

During that period, the last elements of legal segregation died. More important, black disenfranchisement, the key to maintaining the old, dual system of life in the South, also ended. The registration and enfranchisement of African Americans came, however, at a heavy cost. Three young civil rights workers, for example, were killed for their efforts to give the right to vote to those who had been denied it since the end of Reconstruction in the 1870's. The murders of James Earl Chaney, Andrew Goodman, and Michael Henry Schwerner focused international attention on the Civil Rights movement and brought a commitment from the federal government to bring to justice those responsible for the crime.

After judicial decisions had ended the tradition of separate schools and facilities in the South, civil rights organizations turned their attention to registering African Americans as voters. Believing that access to the ballot box was the key to empowering the disenfranchised, organizations such as the Student Nonviolent Coordinating Committee (SNCC) and the Congress of Racial Equality (CORE) sought to organize massive voter registration drives in the Deep South. In particular, leaders targeted the state of Mississippi, the poorest and least literate in the nation.

During the winter of 1963-1964, the Council of Federated Organizations (COFO), a confederation of civil rights organizations, planned for the Mississippi Freedom Summer, which had as its goal the registration of as many African Americans as possible. More than one thousand white college students volunteered to spend their summers organizing community centers and teaching reading, writing, and civics to rural African Americans who wanted to become voters. In the area of Neshoba County, Mississippi, COFO's plans were unpopular with most white citizens. For the first time since the end of Reconstruction, the national Ku Klux Klan organized local klaverns in the area.

Michael Schwerner, a graduate of Cornell University, and his wife had moved to Meridian, Mississippi, during the winter to begin the preparations for the Freedom Summer. A committed believer in racial equality, Schwerner quickly became a target for the white supremacists of Neshoba County. Various plans to eliminate him were discussed in Klan meetings. James Chaney was a native of the area and had become a paid COFO staff member a few months before he was murdered. Andrew Goodman was one of the Freedom Summer volunteers who was scheduled to work in Neshoba County. He arrived in the area on June 20 and was killed one day later.

The events surrounding the murder of the three civil rights workers began on June 16, when a group of armed white men beat the lay leaders of the Mount Zion Methodist Church in Longdale, a small, all-black community in Neshoba County. Later that night, several of the whites returned and set fire to the church, which was to have housed one of the Freedom Schools. On June 21, Chaney, Goodman, and Schwerner drove to Longdale from Meridian to examine the church's remains. On their return from Neshoba County, Deputy Sheriff Cecil Ray Price stopped their car for speeding. After arresting Chaney for driving sixty-five miles per hour in a thirty-five-mile-per-hour zone, Price arrested Goodman and Schwerner for suspicion of arson in the Mount Zion church fire. He then placed the three in the Neshoba County jail, where they remained for more than five hours.

At about the time that the three were placed in jail, COFO was activating its procedures for locating fieldworkers who had not returned or phoned by 4:00 p.m. In addition to telephoning all of the area hospitals, COFO staff placed calls to all the jails. When the Neshoba County jail was called by the Meridian COFO office, however, the person who answered the phone flatly denied having seen any of the three.

On August 4, the bodies of Chaney, Goodman, and Schwerner were unearthed from the new dam. Despite autopsies that unequivocally showed that Goodman and Schwerner had been shot to death and that Chaney had suffered an "inhuman beating" before dying from three gunshot wounds, a Neshoba County coroner's jury ruled on August 25 that it was unable to determine the cause of death for any of the three.

On December 4, Hoover announced the arrests of eighteen men on federal conspiracy charges in connection with the murders, including Price and his superior, the Neshoba County sheriff. The FBI focused on the role of the Klan in the deaths, and more than sixty agents infiltrated the Mississippi Klan to obtain evidence. More than 1,000 Mississippians, including 480 Klan members, were interviewed during the investigation.

SIGNIFICANCE

The murders of James Chaney, Andrew Goodman, and Michael Schwerner brought profound changes to the Deep South generally and to Neshoba County, Mississippi, specifically. Eventually, those directly involved were tried and convicted, and the cause for which the three men died, black enfranchisement, became a reality.

When the 1964 Neshoba County Fair opened six days after the bodies had been recovered, the mood was subdued and tense. Arizona senator Barry Goldwater, the Republican nominee for president, canceled a planned appearance at the event, even though it had been an obligatory stop for politicians in the past. The discovery of the corpses also ended most of the discussions of a COFO-arranged hoax. Instead, the FBI used the discovery as a lever to secure information from Klansmen who mistrusted each other and feared arrest in the case. Since the FBI learned the precise location of the bodies, it was clear that agents were receiving very reliable information.

A number of those involved suspected that more than just the burial location had been passed to the federal government, and the Klan's code of silence was broken as several members sought to save themselves by cooperating with the investigation.

Using laws passed as part of the Civil Rights Act of 1870, the federal government obtained grand jury indictments charging those involved with conspiracy to deny Chaney, Goodman, and Schwerner their civil rights. No substantive local investigation of the crime ever took place, and no murder charges were ever filed by the state of Mississippi. On October 20, 1967, a federal jury in Meridian convicted Cecil Ray Price and six codefendants of the charges, marking the first successful prosecution in Mississippi history of white officials and Klansmen for crimes against African Americans or civil rights workers. After unsuccessful appeals, all of the defendants entered federal custody on March 19, 1970, five and one-half years after the three murders. The impact on the fight for civil rights was less clear.

On July 2, 1964, Congress enacted the Civil Rights Act of 1964, which prohibited discrimination in public accommodations, publicly owned facilities, federally funded programs. and union membership. It also created the Equal Employment Opportunity Commission to end discrimination in employment. In November, 1964, President Johnson won a landslide reelection, capturing 61 percent of the popular vote and 94 percent of the African American vote. Two million more African Americans voted in that election than had in 1960.

Following the discovery of the bodies and the revelation that Chaney had been beaten before his murder, unlike Schwerner and Goodman, the trend toward self-segregation within the Civil Rights movement came to the fore. Some African Americans had come to believe that they needed to lead their own fight and that whites could not be part of it. As the 1960's progressed, these differences of opinion within the Civil Rights movement became more acute, and the movement became more diffuse as a result. Some, like Martin Luther King, Jr., rejected the idea of a movement for racial equality practicing segregation within itself. Others, like the leadership of SNCC, assumed a more radical position and eventually expelled all nonblacks from its projects. By then, enfranchisement for all was no longer a dream but instead a reality, and the Civil Rights movement was a success in ending legal segregation.

—*E. A. Reed*

See also: Supreme Court Rules African American Disenfranchisement Unconstitutional; SCLC Forms to Link Civil Rights Groups; Civil Rights Act of 1960; Council of Federated Organizations Registers African Americans to Vote; Civil Rights Protesters Attract International Attention; Poll Taxes Are Outlawed; Congress Passes the Civil Rights Act of 1964; Congress Passes the Voting Rights Act.

CONGRESS PASSES THE CIVIL RIGHTS ACT OF 1964

July 2, 1964

Congress passed comprehensive civil rights legislation, giving life to the constitutional principle of "colorblind" equal protection of the law.

Also known as: Public Law 352, 88th Congress; U.S. Code Title 42, sections 1971 (amended) and 2000 et seq.
Locale: Washington, D.C.

Categories: Laws, acts, and legal history; civil rights and liberties; social issues and reform

KEY FIGURES
Everett Dirksen (1896-1969), U.S. senator from Illinois, 1951-1969, and minority leader, *1959-1969*

Hubert H. Humphrey (1911-1978), U.S. senator from Minnesota, 1949-1964 and 1971-1978, majority whip, 1961-1964, and later vice president of the United State*s, 1965-1969*

*Lyndo*n B. Johnson (1908-1973), president of the United States, 1963-1969

John F. Kennedy (1917-1963), president of the United States, 1961-1963

Emanuel Celler (1888-1981), U.S. representative from New York, 1923-1973, and chair of the House Judiciary Committee, 1949-1952 and 1955-1972

Richard Russell, Jr. (1897-1971), U.S. senator from Georgia, 1933-1971, and leader of the Senate's Southern bloc

SUMMARY OF EVENT

After the Civil War and after ratification of the Thirteenth, Fourteenth, and Fifteenth Amendments to the Constitution, commonly referred to as the "Civil War Amendments," Congress did little to enforce, by statute, the provisions of those amendments, particularly as they applied to voting and equal access to and protection of the law. Although some important advances were initiated by passage of the Civil Rights Acts of 1957 and 1960, most human rights observers agree that most of the provisions found in those laws did little if anything to eradicate the sometimes blatant discrimination suffered by many African Americans prior to 1964.

On February 28, 1963, President John F. Kennedy, perceived by most at the time as being a strong advocate of civil rights, proposed to Congress the need for strengthened civil rights legislation. Although Kennedy was in favor of greater gains for minorities, his civil rights agenda included only minor cosmetic additions to the civil rights laws already on the books. The agenda was conspicuous in its failure to advance fair employment guarantees.

Kennedy understood that a proposal for a stronger civil rights bill would be doomed to failure before ever reaching the floors of the House and Senate for debate. Kennedy recognized the barriers which a bill would have to cross before it came to a roll-call vote in either house of Congress. Two powerful anti-civil rights legislators stood in its way: Virginia Democrat Howard W. Smith, chair of the House Rules Committee, and Mississippi Democrat James Eastland, chair of the Senate Judiciary Committee.

President Kennedy was keenly aware that his foreign policy initiatives regarding Cuba, Berlin, Vietnam, and the Soviet Union required maximum public support and

President Lyndon B. Johnson signs the 1964 Civil Rights Act as Martin Luther King, Jr., and others, look on. By Cecil Stoughton, White House Press Office (WHPO)

congressional unity. He initially conceded to the powerful Democratic "Southern bloc" and advanced proposals that would not antagonize its members and therefore jeopardize his foreign policy program in Congress. He hoped that these halfway measures would indicate to his black constituents that he was at least doing something.

Black leaders at the time understandably believed that they had been betrayed. The Black Leadership Conference on Civil Rights suggested that Kennedy had sacrificed domestic civil rights on the altar of foreign relations and re-election politics.

Not long after the president had sent his civil rights message to Congress, the issue of civil rights manifested itself to the American public as an issue involving violations of fundamental human rights. In May of 1963, the Southern Christian Leadership Conference, led by the Reverend Martin Luther King, Jr., began sit-in demonstrations across the South protesting segregation of public facilities and accommodations. The American public, only vaguely aware of the human rights violations taking place in some sections of their own country, were outraged and appalled as they viewed on the nightly news the likes of Birmingham, Alabama, Commissioner of Public Safety Bull Connor unleashing his dogs and opening up fire hoses to disperse peaceful protesters. The United States' sense of justice required that President Kennedy take a leadership role to abolish these violations of human rights and to achieve civil rights for all American citizens.

President Kennedy, responding to that mandate as a matter of duty as well as political necessity, commissioned his brother, Attorney General Robert F. Kennedy, to draft a comprehensive civil rights bill to submit to Congress. Sent to Congress on June 19, 1963, the bill was originally referred to the House Judiciary

Committee. It was "reported out" to the full House on November 20, 1963, and included, as an amendment, a fair employment proviso, thanks in large part to the leadership of committee chair Emanuel Cellar and his partner on the committee, Republican William McColloch. Normally, the next hurdle in the House would be to get the bill past the House Rules Committee, which had killed many past civil rights initiatives before they could come to a vote on the floor. Committee chair Smith had promised to utilize that strategy again.

It is difficult to ascertain the effect that John F. Kennedy's assassination on November 23, 1963, had on the success of the civil rights bill as it entered the Rules Committee phase. Most analysts concede that this unfortunate accident of history paradoxically set in motion a series of events supportive of the bill. Support might easily have not been as strong had the young president not been killed.

There are two strong arguments to support this theory. First, Lyndon B. Johnson became president. As a Southern Democrat with a questionable civil rights voting record as a member of the Senate, Johnson needed to dispel his "Southern" image among Northern liberals in Congress. In a more general sense, he needed to establish himself as a decisive and compassionate leader to the grief-stricken nation, a nation that would be going to the polls in less than a year. To accomplish these goals, and perhaps because he sincerely believed in the need to pass the civil rights legislation, President Johnson made passage of the civil rights bill his highest priority.

Kennedy had been martyred, and Congress quickly learned that any legislation introduced "in memory of " the slain president would be tough to vote against. When President Johnson addressed a joint session of Congress on November 28, 1963, it was within this context that he appealed for quick passage of the former president's bill.

It was also in this spirit that a majority of the House signed a discharge petition, filed on December 9, 1963, by Judiciary Committee chair Emanuel Cellar. This petition would get the bill to move directly from Howard Smith's Rules Committee to the House floor for debate, without the addition of debilitating features likely to be tacked on by Smith. On January 30, 1963, the Rules Committee, yielding to the pressure of the petition and the president, allowed the bill to be reported out to the floor under an "open debate" rule. The floor debate took only nine days.

On February 10, 1964, with bipartisan support of Republicans and Northern Democrats, the House passed its version of the civil rights bill by a 290-130 roll-call vote. Following in the footsteps of the House, the Senate put the bill on a fast track. On February 26, 1964, it voted fifty-four to thirty-seven to bypass referring the bill to James Eastland's Senate Judiciary Committee, where it could have been stalled or mortally wounded, and voted instead to place the bill directly on the Senate calendar for debate. It was resolved that the actual debate would commence on March 30, 1964.

In an attempt to kill the measure outright, or at least to gain crippling amendments to the bill, a Southern Democratic filibuster was initiated on March 26, 1964, by Richard Russell, Jr., the Georgian leader of the Southern Democratic coalition. It was Russell's belief that the only way for the bill's supporters to bring the filibuster to a close would be to vote for cloture. This type of cloture required that two-thirds of those present and voting had to vote to end the filibuster. Russell was confident that the opposition would have to accept the Southern amendments to the bill on his terms. He and his supporters called the bluff of the rest of the Senate and lost.

Behind the bipartisan leadership and political maneuvering of the Senate majority floor leader for the bill, Hubert H. Humphrey, and Senate minority leader Everett Dirksen, a coalition of votes was put together to challenge the "Southern Strategy." On June 10, 1964, the cloture measure came up for a vote. With all one hundred members present, the Senate voted seventy-one to twenty-nine to shut down the civil rights filibuster. For all intents and purposes, any opposition to the civil rights legislation was dead.

After accepting a number of primarily technical amendments by Dirksen dealing with the enforcement sections of the public accommodations and employment provisions, the Senate, on June 19, 1964, passed by a roll-call vote of seventy-three to twenty-seven the so-called "Mansfield-Dirksen" substitute version of the civil rights bill. Fearing a renewed Senate filibuster, Representatives Celler and McColluch accepted in principle the Senate version of the bill. The House formally agreed to the Senate compromise bill by a roll-call vote of 289-126 on July 2, 1964, thus concluding congressional action on the bill. Later that evening, President Johnson, in the presence of many of the bill's sponsors and civil rights leaders, signed into law the most comprehensive and meaningful piece of civil rights legislation in American history.

SIGNIFICANCE

The Civil Rights Act of 1964, the most comprehensive piece of civil rights legislation to be enacted into law in the twentieth century, put statutory "teeth" into the "color blind" language enunciated in the dissenting opinion of *Plessy v. Ferguson* (1896) and the majority opinion of *Brown v. Board of Education* (1954). Congress invoked its authority to enact civil rights legislation under the commerce clause of the U.S. Constitution rather than the equal protection clause of the same document. This allowed Congress wider authority to eliminate, among other things, discrimination in public accommodations and facilities, the symbolic focal point of the black civil rights movement, and job discrimination, which was viewed as a national problem. The Civil Rights Act of 1964 requires that determinations made within its jurisdiction be made without regard to race, color, religion, sex, or national origin. The major effect of the act has been to cast aside the legal barriers of segregation as they relate to voting, public education, public accommodations and facilities, federally assisted programs, and private employment.

Although it has certainly expanded opportunities of those affected in a legal sense, the Civil Rights Act of 1964 has generated controversy over its enforcement and effects. Civil rights leaders and organizations have held since the inception of the law that the Civil Rights Act is a hollow promise, given that the law has done nothing to dispel the institutional forms of discrimination prevalent in society.

Statistical evidence suggests that the employment rate, mortality rate, education level, and living conditions among minorities have in fact worsened since 1964. On the other hand, nonminorities have become increasingly alienated by what they see as a gross transformation of the intent and letter of the Civil Rights Act. They cite, for example, disregard for a section of the act which expressly holds that preferential treatment in employment cannot be granted for the purpose of balancing a workforce by race or sex, and for another section which expressly guarantees that desegregation of schools will not be implemented in order to overcome racial imbalance. It is widely agreed, even in light of these concerns, that the Civil Rights Act of 1964 has gone a long way in guaranteeing the rights of minorities and in advancing the human rights atmosphere within the United States, setting an example for democratic nations worldwide.

—*Frank W. Andritzky*

Civil Rights Act of 1964

The "heart" of the Civil Rights Act of 1964, Title II, addressed the rights of all persons to public accommodations:
Title II
Sec. 201.

(a) All persons shall be entitled to the full and equal enjoyment of the goods, services, facilities, privileges, advantages, and accommodations of any place of public accommodation, as defined in this section, without discrimination or segregation on the ground of race, color, religion, or national origin.

(b) Each of the following establishments which serves the public is a place of public accommodation within the meaning of this title if its operations affect commerce, or if discrimination or segregation by it is supported by State action:

(1) any inn, hotel, motel, or other establishment which provides lodging to transient guests, other than an establishment located within a building which contains not more than five rooms for rent or hire and which is actually occupied by the proprietor of such establishment as his residence;

(2) any restaurant, cafeteria, lunchroom, lunch counter, soda fountain, or other facility principally engaged in selling food for consumption on the premises, including, but not limited to, any such facility located on the premises of any retail establishment; or any gasoline station;

(3) any motion picture house, theater, concert hall, sports arena, stadium or other place of exhibition or entertainment; . . .

(e) The provisions of this title shall not apply to a private club or other establishment not in fact open to the public, except to the extent that the facilities of such establishment are made available to the customers or patrons of an establishment within the scope of subsection (b).

Sec. 202.

All persons shall be entitled to be free, at any establishment or place, from discrimination or segregation of any kind on the ground of race, color, religion, or national origin, if such discrimination or segregation is or purports to be required by any law, statute, ordinance, regulation, rule, or order of a State or any agency or political subdivision thereof.

See also: Supreme Court Ends Public School Segregation; Congress Creates the Commission on Civil Rights; Civil Rights Act of 1960; Civil Rights

Protesters Attract International Attention; Poll
Taxes Are Outlawed; Three Civil Rights Workers Are Murdered; Supreme Court Prohibits Racial

Discrimination in Public Accommodations; Congress
Passes the Voting Rights Act.

KATZENBACH V. MCCLUNG
December 14, 1964

*Case upholding Title II of the Civil Rights Act of 1964
as applied to a restaurant.*
*Enforcement of the ruling speeded the end of racial
segregation.*

The Case: U.S. Supreme Court ruling on segregation
    in public accommodations

The U.S. Congress has no constitutionally delegat-
ed power to regulate local business practices. If such
practices can be shown to affect interstate commerce,
however, Congress can reach them under its powers
regulating commerce. In this way, Congress can use its
authority to control interstate commerce to address social and economic problems. After five months of committee hearings and seven months of debate, Congress
passed the Civil Rights Act of 1964. The act represented
Congress's most sweeping attack on race discrimination
since the Civil Rights Act of 1875. *Katzenbach v. Mc-
Clung* involved a challenge to the constitutionality of
Title II of the act and raised the question of whether
Congress could use its authority to regulate interstate
commerce to ban racial discrimination in public accommodations. The case was argued along with *Heart of
Atlanta Motel v. United States*, in which the U.S. Supreme Court upheld the constitutionality of Title II's
prohibitions of race discrimination in the hotel and motel industry.

Katzenbach v. McClung centered on Ollie's Bar-
becue, a small family-owned restaurant in Birmingham, Alabama, that provided sit-down service for
whites but only take-out service for African Americans. If the discrimination practiced at this restaurant
involved the state of Alabama, courts could intervene
to enforce the Fourteenth Amendment's equal protection clause. In this case, however, no one claimed that
the state supported the restaurant's practice. If large
numbers of interstate travelers frequented the restaurant, Congress could intervene by using its power to
regulate interstate commerce. However, Ollie's Barbe

cue seemed to be a local operation rarely visited by
interstate travelers.

Writing for the unanimous Court, Justice Thomas
Clark ruled on December 14, 1964, that Congress could
regulate this restaurant because a substantial portion
of the food served there had moved in interstate commerce. Clark mentioned congressional testimony that
discrimination in restaurants restricted interstate travel
by African Americans: "One can hardly travel without
eating." He reasoned that such discrimination likewise
deterred skilled professionals from moving into areas
where such practices occurred. If viewed in isolation,
discriminatory practices at this single restaurant would
appear to have an insignificant impact on interstate
commerce. However, if other "similarly situated" restaurants engaged in such practices, the cumulative effect would impose "a substantial economic effect on
interstate commerce." Congress could regulate this apparently local business because it had a "rational basis"
for concluding that racial discrimination in restaurants
has a "direct and adverse effect on the free flow of interstate commerce." Justices Hugo Black, William O.
Douglas, and Arthur Goldberg wrote separate concurring opinions.

The Supreme Court permitted Congress to use
its substantial powers to regulate interstate commerce in the battle against racial discrimination
practiced by private parties. This ruling, along with
the Court's decision in *Heart of Atlanta Motel v.
United States*, helped end lingering segregation in
the southern United States by enabling legislation
to be enforced.

—Joseph A. Melusky

See also: Civil Rights Act of 1960; Civil Rights Act of
1964; Civil Rights Act of 1968; *Heart of Atlanta Motel
v. United States*; *Patterson v. McLean Credit Union*;
Voting Rights Act of 1965.

KING WINS THE NOBEL PEACE PRIZE

December 10, 1964

Martin Luther King, Jr.'s nonviolent struggle for racial equality in the United States was recognized with a Nobel Peace Prize. King was the first major leader in the West to advocate social change without violence.

Locale: Oslo, Norway
Categories: Civil rights and liberties; social issues and reform; organizations and institutions

KEY FIGURES

Martin Luther King, Jr. (1929-1968), 1964 Nobel laureate in peace, minister, and civil rights leader
Rosa Parks (1913-2005), Montgomery, Alabama, resident who sparked King's first major civil rights campaign

SUMMARY OF EVENT

Martin Luther King, Jr., ascended to national prominence in the United States during a struggle for civil rights that had its roots in a period of racial justice-seeking between the American Revolution and the Civil War. However, the struggles were not over. More needed to be done to bring about rapid racial integration within all sectors of American society to combat the violently repressive economic, political, and social atmosphere faced by black Americans. Moreover, African Americans needed leadership to offset a growing sense of apathy, divisiveness, and helplessness.

King, pastor of the Dexter Avenue Baptist Church in Montgomery, Alabama, became visible in African American politics on a national level during the Montgomery bus boycott, which began as a minor racial incident on December 1, 1955, when Rosa Parks refused to give up her seat to a white male passenger. The boycott evolved into a major strike by African Americans lasting 382 days and resulting in desegregation of Alabama buses.

King was elected the first president of the Montgomery Improvement Association (MIA), the organization responsible for leading the boycott. A resistance movement throughout the South grew out of the victory of the boycott, coalescing into the Southern Christian Leadership Conference (SCLC) in 1957. King became the first president of the SCLC, and his voice began to be heard worldwide.

Between 1957 and 1968, King led voter registration drives and protest marches, traveled more than six million miles, and gave more than twenty-five hundred lectures and speeches. A charismatic speaker and scholar well versed in the philosophical works of great thinkers, King valued and embodied religious concepts. He pledged his life as a champion of the downtrodden in society and embraced and inspired nonviolent civil disobedience through direct action as espoused through the life and teaching of Mahatma Gandhi of India. Before the eyes of the world, King led protest marches in which marchers met with police dogs, water hoses, and police brutality. During his own incarceration following a Birmingham protest march, King inspired his followers with his classic treatise "Letter from a Birmingham Jail." He also wrote several books and was jailed many times; his life was threatened often.

As a result of the efforts of King and those who were led by him, other events also took place that helped transform King and the entire American society. On the national level, the Dwight D. Eisenhower administration enacted the 1957 Civil Rights Act, which affirmed the rights of all Americans to vote in all elections. President John F. Kennedy, elected in 1960, received overwhelming support in his election bid from King and his supporters. Following his election, Kennedy pledged support for the Civil Rights movement to support racial equality. One tangible result of Kennedy's pledge was the dynamic cooperation of the Justice Department and the Civil Rights Commission in enforcing neglected voting rights laws. There was a tremendous upsurge in the number of voting rights suits initiated, from six during the entire Eisenhower administration to fifty-eight by 1963, when Kennedy was assassinated.

On August 28, 1963, King directed the largest demonstration that the U.S. capital had ever seen, the historic March on Washington to demand jobs and freedom for all unemployed Americans, especially African Americans. Moreover, the march was staged to support a civil rights bill pending in the U.S. Congress and to support the movement's economic goals. King delivered his famous "I Have a Dream" speech at the march.

In 1964, when King was nominated for the Nobel Peace Prize, the conditions faced by African Americans had improved on some levels with regard to human rights. There were fewer "whites only" signs throughout the South as more public facilities such as restaurants, movie theaters, schools, and hotels had become desegregated.

471

Less-blatant forms of racial discrimination persisted, as reflected, for example, by the common phrase that African Americans were "the last to be hired and the first to be fired." Thus, the interaction between abject poverty and racial discrimination was identified by King as an enduring destructive force that was crippling the entire society and exacerbating the ordinary survival problems among underprivileged African Americans.

The Nobel Prize committee lauded King not because he had led a racial minority in its struggle for equality but for the way in which he waged his struggle. King was the first person in the Western world to show that a struggle could be waged without violence. He called the award a recognition of nonviolence as the answer to the crucial political and moral question of our time—the need for humankind to overcome oppression and violence without the use of oppression and violence. King praised the real heroes and heroines of the freedom struggle and shared his prize money among his various organizations. In his acceptance speech, King reflected upon the problems of humankind worldwide: racial injustice, poverty, and war. In a mere four years, he would be dead of an assassin's bullet.

SIGNIFICANCE

King's untiring leadership supported the election of President Lyndon B. Johnson, whose administration passed two major civil rights laws—the 1964 Civil Rights Act and the 1965 Voting Rights Act—which provided the nation's minorities legal protection to vote. King perceived, however, that these measures did not go far enough in reversing the hopeless plight of millions of blacks in northern city ghettos who suffered from racism and deprivation.

Through its nonviolent approach, King's movement stirred the conscience of the American people and caused irrevocable changes in American society. Further, King's objectives and principles strengthened and united minorities seeking freedom, justice, and racial integration.

Leadership in the African American community has changed since the King era. Subsequent leaders seldom possessed the stamina, organizational ability, and charisma of King, and civil rights marches and delegations became sporadic and often did not involve direct participation of the masses.

—*B. Mawiyah Clayborne*

See also: Montgomery Bus Boycott; SCLC Forms to Link Civil Rights Groups; Civil Rights Protesters Attract International Attention; King Delivers His "I Have a Dream" Speech; Three Civil Rights Workers Are Murdered; Selma-Montgomery March; Congress Passes the Voting Rights Act; Watts Riot; Assassination of Martin Luther King, Jr; Fair Housing Act Outlaws Discrimination in Housing; Supreme Court Upholds Ban on Housing Discrimination.

HEART OF ATLANTA MOTEL V. UNITED STATES
Date: December 14, 1964

In this ruling the U.S. Supreme Court endorsed laws forbidding private discrimination by hotels, restaurants, and other places of public accommodation in this case.

The Case: U.S. Supreme Court ruling on segregation in public accommodations

The Fourteenth Amendment to the United States Constitution was enacted in 1868 to provide protection for the newly freed slaves. After the Civil War, Congress passed several broad statutes aimed at protecting African Americans against racial discrimination in housing and contracts. These laws were needed because, although they were freed from slavery, African Americans still suffered from severe discrimination in all aspects of American life. The Supreme Court took a narrow view of congressional power in 1883, however, and issued a decision that prevented Congress from attempting to stop private individuals and companies from engaging in racial discrimination. The Supreme Court said that Congress could enact laws aimed only at governmental discrimination. In effect, the Supreme Court declared that African Americans could be victims of blatant discrimination by private entities without any interference from the law. As a result, many African Americans' lives changed little from their experience as slaves. They were still forced to work as agricultural laborers because they were not permitted to be trained and hired for other jobs.

THE LEGACY OF SEGREGATION

Because no federal laws could prevent private discrimination, until 1964 African Americans were deprived of many opportunities readily enjoyed by white people. If they wished to travel, black people frequently could not find motels that would accept them or restaurants that would serve them. African Americans were forced to carry their own food if they went on bus trips and often had to knock on doors in black neighborhoods in order to find families that would put them up for the night in private homes. For example, when professional baseball teams had spring training in Florida every year, the white players stayed in hotels while their black teammates rented rooms in the homes of local black families.

Similar circumstances arose when northern college sports teams traveled to the South for games. Racial segregation and discrimination were so severe that bus stations had separate waiting rooms, rest rooms, and drinking fountains for black passengers. In many cities, black and white friends could dine together only in black-owned restaurants because African Americans were not allowed to eat in white-owned establishments. In sum, it was very difficult for African Americans to travel and shop because they were denied access to so many business establishments.

Beginning in the 1940's, members of Congress made repeated attempts to enact antidiscrimination legislation. The structure of Congress, however, gave members power according to seniority. Because southerners had the most seniority, they controlled many of the legislative committees. Thus, by keeping bills tied up in committee hearings, they could prevent Congress from considering proposed legislation. Southern congress people were very successful in ensuring that only weak civil rights laws, if any, were enacted by Congress.

Beginning in the 1940's and 1950's, many African Americans organized boycotts, marches, and other protests to challenge racial discrimination. Peaceful protesters were often met by violent mobs of whites or were attacked, beaten, and arrested by all-white police forces. Shortly after highly publicized demonstrations against racial discrimination in Alabama during May, 1963, President John F. Kennedy decided to send a major civil rights bill to Congress.

THE CIVIL RIGHTS ACT OF 1964

Title II of the proposed legislation that eventually became the Civil Rights Act of 1964 prohibited private discrimination in places of public accommodation, including hotels, motels, restaurants, and theaters. President Kennedy was assassinated in November, 1963, while the bill was working its way through Congress. Upon succeeding to the presidency, Lyndon Johnson made the civil rights bill his major legislative priority. Within days of Kennedy's assassination, President Johnson asked a joint session of Congress to enact the Civil Rights Act as a memorial to the late President Kennedy.

When the Senate held hearings to consider the proposed legislation, questions arose concerning congressional power to outlaw private discrimination. The Supreme Court had clearly stated in 1883 that Congress lacked such power under the Fourteenth Amendment. Attorney General Robert F. Kennedy testified that Congress possessed the power to outlaw discrimination in public accommodations through its constitutional authority to regulate interstate commerce. Kennedy and his assistants argued that racial discrimination in public accommodations hampered the national economy because it prevented African Americans from traveling freely. Moreover, it deterred northern companies from expanding into the South because they did not wish to subject their black employees to severe discrimination.

Senator Strom Thurmond of South Carolina, one of the consistent opponents of civil rights legislation, questioned Attorney General Kennedy closely. From the repeated questioning, it was clear that the Civil Rights Act's supporters were not completely certain about precisely which private businesses would be prevented from discriminating under the law. Although a national bus company could clearly be regulated under congressional power over interstate commerce, it was not clear whether establishments such as neighborhood diners and barbershops were subject to federal laws governing commerce. If these small businesses were involved only in the local economy and did not affect interstate commerce, then Congress presumably would be unable to prevent them from engaging in racial discrimination.

THE SUPREME COURT INTERVENES

When the Civil Rights Act was enacted in 1964, it was immediately challenged by southern businesses that wished to continue engaging in racial discrimination. The Heart of Atlanta Motel claimed that it was not engaged in interstate commerce because it provided services at one location inside Georgia. The motel wished to continue its practice of refusing to rent rooms to black customers, so it filed a legal action seeking to have federal judges declare that the Civil Rights Act was invalid. Although it usually takes several years for cases to work their way through the judicial system in order to reach the Supreme Court, the high court took up the issue of discrimination in public accommodations without delay in late 1964. In opposition to the motel's arguments, Archibald Cox, the solicitor general of the United States, argued to the Supreme Court that congressional power to regulate interstate commerce should be construed broadly to cover all businesses which affect commerce in any way. Even if a business appeared to be limited to local customers, Cox argued that it would have links to interstate commerce. For example, a neighborhood barbershop's equipment inevitably includes a chair, a pair of scissors, or other equipment that was manufactured in another state.

On December 14, 1964, only two months after hearing oral arguments, the Supreme Court issued a unanimous decision that endorsed congressional power to outlaw private discrimination in public accommodations. The Court's opinion in *Heart of Atlanta Motel, Inc. v. United States*, written by Justice Tom C. Clark, acknowledged that racial discrimination had prevented African Americans from enjoying their right to travel. Because the Heart of Atlanta Motel served many travelers from outside Georgia, it was found to affect interstate commerce and therefore to come under the antidiscrimination laws. In this and other decisions concerning Title II of the Civil Rights Act, the Supreme Court interpreted congressional power to regulate interstate commerce so broadly that virtually every private business, no matter how localized in nature, was barred from engaging in racial discrimination. Scholars argue that the Court dispensed with legal arguments concerning technical limitations on congressional power because the justices were committed to endorsing all governmental efforts to combat racial discrimination.

IMPACT OF THE COURT'S DECISION

After the Supreme Court's decision in *Heart of Atlanta Motel*, the United States Department of Justice initiated hundreds of investigations into racial discrimination complaints concerning places of public accommodation. The Court's decision clearly confirmed the federal government's authority to prosecute businesses that failed to end discriminatory practices. Through the combined efforts of Congress, the president, and the Supreme Court, African Americans could finally enjoy access to theaters, motels, and restaurants. The deeply entrenched practices of racial discrimination had been dealt a powerful blow by the federal government. As a result, black people who traveled could find motels and restaurants that would serve them. Many proprietors of public accommodations businesses initially resisted implementation of the antidiscrimination law by declining to serve African Americans or by being rude to black customers. Over time, however, the American public, including business owners in the South, accepted the idea that all people should have equal access to public accommodations. Only a tiny number of businesses were so opposed to desegregation that they turned themselves into private clubs in order to avoid having to conform to the terms of the Civil Rights Act.

Title II of the Civil Rights Act of 1964 is regarded as one of the most effective civil rights laws ever enacted. Unlike laws concerning employment, in which there are controversies concerning proof of discrimination, Title II addresses a very straight-forward subject. In the employment context, there might be many legally acceptable reasons why a particular individual did not receive a particular job. Thus, a minority applicant may find it difficult to discover whether illegal racial discrimination played a role in the hiring decision. In public accommodations, the question is much simpler. Were the customers provided with the services that they requested and for which they were willing to pay? Because discrimination in public accommodations, unlike that in employment, is very difficult to disguise, businesses throughout the United States have generally eliminated any vestiges of the formal discrimination that was previously so prevalent. In fact, proprietors of restaurants and other places of public accommodation have discovered that it is good for their businesses to seek African American customers. Previously, they not only deprived black people of services and the ability to travel but also deprived themselves of customers in a growing segment of the American population. Eventually, racial discrimination in public accommodations was pushed so firmly into the past that many establishments owned or controlled by whites developed advertising campaigns aimed specifically at black consumers.

The Supreme Court's decision in the *Heart of Atlanta Motel* case indicated that all three branches of the federal government were committed to dismantling racial discrimination and segregation. The message sent by this decision not only warned segregationist interests that their power had been diminished but also helped to mobilize and encourage civil rights supporters to pursue actively additional antidiscrimination statutes and favorable judicial decisions in areas such as housing and voting.

—*Christopher E. Smith*

See also: *Katzenbach v. McClung*; Segregation; *Shelley v. Kraemer*

BLACK IS BEAUTIFUL MOVEMENT

Mid-1960's-1970's

Part of a broader drive to change political, economic, and social conditions for African Americans, the Black Is Beautiful movement emphasized the importance of countering stereotyped representations.

Identification: Movement which supported the study of African customs and history and celebrated the uniqueness of African American culture

The Black Is Beautiful movement, part of a broader drive to change political, economic, and social conditions for African Americans, emphasized the importance of countering stereotyped representations. Originating in the Black Power movement of 1965–1975, the phrase "black is beautiful" appealed to large segments of the black community not directly involved with movement organizations. Music and visual arts were central to this appeal: James Brown's "Say It Loud, I'm Black and I'm Proud" and Aretha Franklin's "Respect" signified the change in spirit from earlier integrationist phrases of the movement. Movement theorists, including Kwanza founder Ron (Maulana) Karenga, declared the necessity of an art connected with the African American community and committed to its well-being and proposed that black art should "praise the people" as well as "expose the enemy" and "support the revolution."

The Black Is Beautiful movement initiated sustained investigations of African traditions and history and celebrated the distinctiveness of African American culture. The success of evocations of "soul" in black music, food, speech, physical beauty, body language, and clothing inspired the creation of independent presses and bookstores and student demands for African American studies departments. Though the Black Power movement lost most of its impetus by 1975, the Black Is Beautiful ethos exerts a continuing influence on the struggles for multicultural, feminist, and homosexual self-definition.

—*Trudi D. Witonsky*

See also: African Liberation Day; Afrocentrism; Black nationalism; Black Power movement; Pan-Africanism; Stereotypes

ASSASSINATION OF MALCOLM X

February 21, 1965

Malcolm X, a radical African American civil rights activist and spokesman, broke with the Nation of Islam, a group of which he had been a leading member. Shortly after this break, he was assassinated, probably by members of the group.

Locale: Harlem, New York
Categories: Terrorism; social issues and reform

KEY FIGURES
Elijah Muhammad (1897-1975), leader of the Nation of Islam
Malcolm X (Malcolm Little; 1925-1965), spokesman for the Nation of Islam
Marcus Garvey (1887-1940), early African American nationalist and leader of the Universal Negro Improvement Association

Talmadge Hayer (fl. late twentieth century), *Norman 3X Butler* (fl. late twentieth century), and
Thomas 15X Johnson (fl. late twentieth century), convicted assassins of Malcolm X

SUMMARY OF EVENT

Perhaps no twentieth century African American leader better expressed the anger and frustrations of urban African Americans than did Malcolm X. During the 1960's Civil Rights movement, Malcolm X, the national spokesman of a black separatist Muslim sect known as the Nation of Islam, articulated in militant language the effects of the nation's historical pattern of racism against African Americans and the social consequences the country faced if significant change did not occur. Before his assassination in 1965, Malcolm X had come to symbolize the disenchantment of African American ghetto residents, a group who were disillusioned about the benefits of racial integration and becoming increasingly impatient with the dominant nonviolent philosophy of the Civil Rights movement.

Malcolm X was born Malcolm Little on May 19, 1925, in Omaha, Nebraska, to Louise Norton Little and J. Early Little. His father, a Baptist preacher, worked as an organizer for the Universal Negro Improvement Association, the black nationalist organization led by Marcus Garvey. In his later life, Malcolm too, would consider himself a black nationalist. In 1931, Malcolm's father died mysteriously in East Lansing, Michigan, where the family had relocated. Thereafter, Malcolm's life was marked by a series of crises.

The impoverished family, now comprising Malcolm, his mother, and six siblings, was soon separated: Malcolm's mother was committed to a mental hospital and no longer influenced his development. Malcolm was placed in a foster home and began to get into trouble as he grew older. Hoping to change the direction of the troubled teen's life, Ella, an older half sister, brought him to live with her in Boston, Massachusetts. Although he possessed a good mind, he did not find school rewarding and dropped out to work at odd jobs. An attraction to street life overcame his interest in legitimate employment, however, and he gradually gravitated toward hustling, drugs, and petty crime.

For a time, Malcolm loved the culture of urban street life and seemed to flourish in it. In the 1940's, he wore the zoot suit and wide hat popular among young African American and Hispanic hipsters and patronized the night spots in Boston's Roxbury and New York's Harlem ghettoes. The seedy side of this life proved to be his downfall. His graduation to the more serious crime of burglary eventually landed him in prison, and at twenty years of age, he began serving six years of a ten-year sentence in Massachusetts's Charlestown and Norfolk penitentiaries.

Initially, Malcolm was hardly a model prisoner. In many ways, however, prison proved to be his redemption, for it was in prison that Malcolm converted to a version of Islam that changed his life. Largely through the efforts of his sisters and brothers, who visited him regularly, Malcolm was introduced to the ideas and philosophy of a little-known Muslim sect, the Nation of Islam, headed by Elijah Muhammad. Gradually, Malcolm abandoned his aggressive behavior, adopted Muslim prayer and life practices, and enmeshed himself in the teachings of Muhammad.

Malcolm absorbed the Muslim interpretation of the history of races, an interpretation that explained how and why white people came to be regarded as "devils" and the oppressors of black people throughout the world. Based on Muhammad's teaching, Malcolm's own life experiences, and wide reading in history, politics, and economics, Malcolm came to understand how central the role of white people had been in causing the lowly conditions of African Americans. Muhammad could not have found another adherent with a wider breadth of knowledge about black and white race relations than Malcolm. Their attraction to each other and Malcolm's commitment to spreading Muhammad's message placed Malcolm in an ideal position for elevation to a more visible role in the Islamic organization.

Shortly after his parole in 1952, Malcolm was appointed minister of Temple No. 7 in Harlem by the Muslim leader. Articulate and intellectually gifted, Malcolm undertook his duties with a passion and energy unmatched by his peers. He increased the membership in his own temple and traveled throughout the country organizing new mosques. By 1959, the sect could boast of forty-nine temples nationwide and more than forty thousand members. In six years, temple establishment increased nearly tenfold, and Malcolm almost single-handedly accounted for this. By 1960, Malcolm clearly had emerged as the second most influential man in the Nation of Islam, and was the national spokesman for Elijah Muhammad. Malcolm was heard on the radio and seen on national television.

Converts and sympathizers read about his views through the columns of the newspaper that he established, *Muhammad Speaks*, and in other African American urban newspapers for which he regularly wrote.

In his Harlem street meetings, he railed against police brutality, and he quelled potentially explosive confrontations between African Americans and law enforcement officials. He continued to "fish" on the ghetto streets for new converts, appealing to them with a mastery of oratory that condemned white racism and the failure of liberal black and white leaders to address the real needs of the African American community. In no uncertain terms, he told listeners that African American men sought to present and defend themselves as men, violently if necessary. Change would occur in the United States, he said, either by the ballot or by the bullet.

In the span of a few short years, Malcolm's name was as familiar as that of Martin Luther King, Jr. Malcolm's national notoriety and influence sparked rivalry and jealousy within the ranks of the Nation of Islam, however. Even Elijah Muhammad, who had warned Malcolm of potential internal dangers from becoming too powerful, grew envious of his national prominence. Rival factions looked for ways to bring him down.

The opportunity occurred in December, 1963, following President John F. Kennedy's assassination, when Malcolm violated Muhammad's order for Muslims to remain silent about the murder. In an interview, Malcolm equated the president's death to "chickens coming home to roost," an impolitic remark that provided the excuse for Muhammad to punish him. Discredited and officially silenced for ninety days, Malcolm's influence within the Nation of Islam waned precipitously.

Unable to forge an effective reconciliation with Muhammad and increasingly determined to speak more broadly for African Americans independent of Nation of Islam constraints, Malcolm left the organization in early 1964 to form his own group, Muslim Mosque, Inc. A pilgrimage to Mecca, the Hajj, and subsequent travel to Africa expanded his understanding about the true nature of Islam, validated his status as an international personality, and helped him to define new agendas in his fight for black people worldwide. A new Malcolm with a new Islamic name, El-Hajj Malik El-Shabazz, hoped to accomplish his agenda through a more politically oriented organization of his making, the Organization of Afro-American Unity.

Malcolm remained a marked man, however, and was unable to escape the vilification of enemies in the Nation of Islam. Privately and publicly, they denounced him as a traitor to Elijah Muhammad and placed him under surveillance. From many quarters, those threatened by Malcolm's mass appeal and influence called for violent retribution. In February, 1964, he and his family escaped death from a bomb that destroyed their home. Malcolm's pleas for peace with the Nation of Islam could not stave off another attempt on his life. On February 21, 1965, while speaking before a crowd of several hundred followers in Harlem's Audubon Ballroom, Malcolm was felled by a fusillade of bullets. In March, 1966, a racially mixed jury found three men—Talmadge Hayer, Norman 3X Butler, and Thomas 15X Johnson—guilty of first-degree murder in Malcolm's death. Despite their conviction, conspiracy theories about Malcolm's death have remained, including theories implicating non-Muslims and even the federal government.

SIGNIFICANCE

For the many African Americans who regarded him as their champion, Malcolm X's death was a devastating psychological blow. For those who felt disenfranchised, lost in an uncaring system tainted by the historical effects of racism, Malcolm's death silenced a voice that articulated their anger, frustrations, and aspirations. The urban ghetto had forged his life and he understood its victims; they understood him, too, and drew from his aggressive spirit. Malcolm's loss also had meaning for whites, as it stilled a voice that effectively raised whites' consciousness about their role in the plight of African Americans. In the harshest of language and the fiercest of manners, Malcolm had sought to ensure white accountability for past deeds and to encourage remedies.

—*Robert L. Jenkins*

See also: *The Autobiography of Malcolm X* Is Published; Assassination of Martin Luther King, Jr.

SELMA-MONTGOMERY MARCH

March 21-25, 1965

The civil rights march from Selma to Montgomery, Alabama, led by Martin Luther King, Jr., was a significant factor in the passage of the 1965 Voting Rights Act and marked increased pressures toward both political and economic reforms in the United States.

Also known as: Voting Rights March

Locale: Selma, Alabama; Highway 80 between Selma and Montgomery, Alabama

Categories: Civil rights and liberties; social issues and reform

KEY FIGURES

Martin Luther King, Jr. (1929-1968), president of the Southern Christian Leadership Conference and one of the principal leaders of the march

Hosea Williams (1926-2000), an SCLC field organizer and one of the leaders of the first attempted march on March 7, 1965

John Robert Lewis (b. 1940), activist who, along with Hosea Williams, led the attempted march on March 7

James G. Clark (fl. mid-twentieth century), sheriff of Dallas County who was known for adamant resistance to integration and black voting rights

Lyndon B. Johnson (1908-1973), president of the United States, 1963-1969

George C. Wallace (1919-1998), governor of Alabama during the Selma campaign, who resisted racial integration and banned the march to Montgomery

SUMMARY OF EVENT

The Selma-Montgomery march of 1965 is often viewed as one of the most decisive events in the history of the

Bloody Sunday-Alabama police attack Selma-to-Montgomery Marchers, 1965, by Federal Bureau of Investigation

American Civil Rights movement. It was marked by considerable violent resistance, a high degree of emotional intensity for those who participated, and political impact not often matched. Its basic purpose was to extend voting rights to black Americans in a period when many southern white leaders adamantly resisted broadening the franchise. The Civil Rights Act of 1964, signed by President Lyndon B. Johnson on July 2, 1964, did contain provisions for minority voting rights. Its eleven titles spanned the spectrum of basic rights, including equal access to public accommodations, schools, and employment.

Title VI gave the federal government the power to cut off funds from state or local authorities that discriminated, but there was little increased authority in the voting rights provisions of Title I. Nor was it certain that any of the desegregation mandates would be respected in the Deep South.

Although Selma was a small city in an essentially rural part of Alabama, it was in the highly segregated Dallas County region that some civil rights leaders believed would be a good place to launch a concerted voter registration drive. In February, 1963, well before the 1964

Civil Rights Act, Student Nonviolent Coordinating Committee (SNCC) field workers such as Bernard and Colia Lafayette, John Love, Worth Long, and others began to work with local black leaders. The results were meager because of intense resistance by the forces of Sheriff James G. Clark and the entrenched white power structure. On the other hand, Clark's roughness provided the kind of focus needed to stir a grassroots movement.

Throughout 1963 and 1964, SNCC and the Dallas County Voters' League held monthly voter registration clinics and occasional mass rallies. Southern Christian Leadership Conference (SCLC) organizers such as James Bevel, C. T. Vivian, Harry Boyte, and Eric Kindberg participated in some of these activities and began to consider the Dallas County area as a possible target for the SCLC's heightened voter registration drive begun in earnest after the Civil Rights Act.

If voter registration was the chief focus of Dallas County black leaders such as Albert Turner, Amelia Boynton, and Voters' League president Frederick D. Reese, it was by no means the only issue with which they were concerned. There was widespread concern among African Americans about police roughness, barriers to school integration, and widespread poverty because of job discrimination. They believed that gaining the vote

would open the door to other reforms in the local communities.

The Johnson administration had already introduced a voting rights act in Congress by late 1964, but passage was uncertain and some of its terms were considered weak by the SCLC, SNCC, the National Association for the Advancement of Colored People (NAACP), and other advocacy groups. Martin Luther King, Jr., the SCLC's president, shared these concerns and came into Selma in January, 1965, to spur the voter registration effort.

King met forceful resistance, as did several others. He was slightly injured when a white detractor attacked him as he tried to integrate Hotel Albert. On January 19, Sheriff Clark roughly shoved Amelia Boynton as she participated in a march to the courthouse on behalf of black voter registration. That incident was pictured in the national and international media and drew the world's attention to Selma, a city in south central Alabama that had fewer than thirty thousand residents. It became obvious that voting rights were tied to other basic American constitutional rights. When King, by then a Nobel Peace Prize recipient, was jailed in early February, a new wave of activists poured into Selma to give aid to the effort.

Many of them were students, but ministers, workers, and others were also attracted to the increasingly dramatic Selma campaign. Even Malcolm X, just days before his assassination on February 21 in Harlem, went to Selma to support King. The fatal shooting of young Jimmie Lee Jackson by police in nearby Marion added to the determination to continue the voting rights drive and the effort to deal with the various violations of rights that blacks faced. The original plan for a motorcade from Selma to Montgomery was abandoned in favor of a walking demonstration along the rural highway leading to the state's capital. This brought to light a complex pattern of racial segregation that reached all the way to the governor's office and state laws.

The first effort to march from Selma to Montgomery was made on Sunday, March 7. King and Ralph Abernathy were at their churches preaching. The SCLC's Hosea Williams and SNCC Chairman John Robert Lewis led a crowd of more than five hundred people out of Brown Chapel to the Edmund Pettus Bridge and toward Montgomery, along Highway 80. Governor George C. Wallace had banned the march the previous day, and Clark was expected to try to stop it, but no one anticipated the military-like force that waited to confront the marchers. Across the bridge, a large volunteer posse put together by Sheriff Clark waited, along with well-quipped state troopers under Colonel Albert Lingo. As the marchers approached the bridge, they were ordered to stop and told to disband within two minutes. Before the short warning period had ended, the police began to attack. Some were on horseback, swinging billy clubs and whips that lashed into the marchers' bodies. Tear gas canisters were fired as the crowd began to scatter. Some troopers pursued the fleeing demonstrators as they tried to find refuge. The Selma march had suddenly become a rout that would be remembered as "Bloody Sunday" by many people. About eighty injured people were treated at the Good Samaritan Hospital, seventeen of whom were admitted for more treatment and observation.

The Bloody Sunday attack was publicized widely, both in the United States and abroad. King rushed back to the city and prepared for another attempt on Tuesday, March 9, appealing for help from around the nation. Public concern deepened, and within two days about 450 white members of the clergy and a wave of other supporters poured into Selma. This time, a federal injunction prohibited the march, and President Johnson requested a postponement. Local Selma and Dallas County officials disagreed on how to approach any renewed effort to march to Montgomery. Public Safety Director Wilson Baker had opposed the use of force against the first attempted march, and now he urged compromise to avoid a repetition of its violence. Behind the scenes, federal and local officials worked with King and other leaders to arrange a symbolic march across the Edmund Pettus Bridge, with promises that police would let marchers pass. The march would then halt without continuing to Montgomery. Few people knew of these arrangements, however, so that the March 9 trek caused confusion and some disillusionment.

A crowd of about nine hundred people left Brown Chapel once again. The number swelled to more than fifteen hundred as they neared the bridge. King told them, "We must let them know that nothing can stop us, not even death itself." Most assumed that they were on their way to the capital. As the marchers crossed the bridge, the police lines widened to let them pass. The marchers paused to sing "We Shall Overcome," and then the march leaders turned the group around and headed back into town.

Despite this ostensible retreat, the events in Selma were important in the history of civil rights activism in the United States. The week following the second attempted march was filled with significant legal and political moves. A federal court declared the Alabama bans on demonstrations invalid, and President Johnson spoke out forcefully to Congress and the nation on March 15 in support of the effort in Selma. He declared what had happened on March 7 to be "an American tragedy," and said that the Selma campaign was important to all Americans.

In Johnson's words, "Their cause must be our cause, too." No president had ever taken this bold a public stand on civil rights. The fact that Johnson ended his address by saying, "And we shall overcome!" won wide applause from black activists.

On March 17, Judge Frank M. Johnson authorized the march to Montgomery and ordered Governor Wallace not to interfere. The same day, President Johnson sent his completed voting rights bill to Congress. Certain restrictions were placed on the march, such as a limit of three hundred on the number of marchers on two-lane sections of the road, but it would proceed with police protection to its destination. About eight thousand people started out of Selma on Sunday, March 21. It took five days to complete the trip. Along the way, a number of prominent entertainers and political figures participated, among them Harry Belafonte and Leonard Bernstein. King left on Wednesday, March 24, to fly to Cleveland for a speech, but rejoined the march as it entered Montgomery on Thursday, its final day. About thirty thousand people had taken part in the march. There were some violent eruptions in places, but the march proceeded in an orderly way without major incident.

After the march, however, a white Michigan housewife and mother, Mrs. Viola Liuzzo, was shot to death in her car as she drove black marchers back home from Montgomery. When the SCLC board of directors met in Baltimore in early April, they considered a boycott campaign against the state of Alabama in response to that and other violence.

SIGNIFICANCE

The Selma march has a significant place in civil rights history. It helped convince Congress that a voting rights act was necessary. Such a bill was passed by Congress in May, 1965, and signed into law by President Johnson on August 6. It covered all states where screening devices such as literacy tests were used to restrict voting and states in which either fewer than half of the voting-age citizens were registered as of November 1, 1964, or fewer than 50 percent voted in the 1964 presidential election.

In another major sense, this march was historically significant. After Selma, the Civil Rights movement gave more attention to the socioeconomic conditions of racial minorities and poor people in the United States. It seemed imperative after 1965 to exercise the right to vote and thereby seek to bring about some of the reforms that were impossible when black Americans were systematically prohibited from voting. The Selma march was also psychologically important. It boosted confidence and energized new enthusiasm for future changes. King biographer Stephen B. Oates concluded that, "In truth, Selma was the movement's finest hour, was King's finest hour." There is much truth in this estimation. The Selma experience not only effected political changes but also infused the movement with a new confidence. Some scholars see in it the culmination of the trend from nonviolent persuasion to nonviolent coercion, that is, the transition from using marches and other demonstrations to win support to using them to bring higher legal and political authority to bear on local opposition. This distinction is not absolute since, from the beginning, both elements were present.

At the personal level, Selma is remembered as an inspirational experience. Marchers were resisted violently, yet they persisted. Many children and young people who witnessed the March 7 confrontation recalled years later being helped to safety by the adults. Voter registration efforts, furthermore, were thereafter regarded by increasing numbers of individuals as important direct action contributions to social reform in the United States. After Selma, the nonviolent Civil Rights movement in the United States began to venture out of the South into places such as Chicago, Cleveland, and Louisville.

—*Thomas R. Peake*

See also: Supreme Court Ends Public School Segregation; Montgomery Bus Boycott; SCLC Forms to Link Civil Rights Groups; Civil Rights Protesters Attract International Attention; King Delivers His "I Have a Dream" Speech; Congress Passes the Civil Rights Act of 1964; Supreme Court Prohibits Racial Discrimination in Public Accommodations.

HEAD START IS ESTABLISHED TO AID POOR CHILDREN

May 18, 1965

Project Head Start was established to help ensure the rights of poor and otherwise disadvantaged preschool children and their families in the United States to adequate health care, nutrition, and education. It is the longest-running school readiness program in the United States.

Locale: Washington, D.C.
Categories: Education; health and medicine; organizations and institutions; government and politics

KEY FIGURES

Lyndon B. Johnson (1908-1973), president of the United States, 1963-1969, who authorized the establishment of Head Start
Sargent Shriver (b. 1915), first director of the Office of Economic Opportunity and originator of the idea of Head Start
Michael Harrington (1928-1989), author of *The Other America*, which heightened the nation's awareness of poverty in the United States

Benjamin Bloom (1913-1999), author of *Stability and Change in Human Characteristics*, which argued that a child's early years are critical to the learning process
John F. Kennedy (1917-1963), president of the United States, 1961-1963, who began the federal government's War on Poverty
Julius Richmond (b. 1916), first director of Head Start

SUMMARY OF EVENT

The United Nations Declaration of the Rights of the Child (1959) entitles all children to adequate nutrition, accessible medical services, free education, and lives of freedom and dignity. Project Head Start was inaugurated by President Lyndon B. Johnson in Washington, D.C., on May 18, 1965, and as the first comprehensive federal effort at early childhood intervention stands as a significant contribution to the fulfillment of this declaration. Head Start is the product of historical, intellectual, political, and personal influences.

Many British immigrants arrived in North America in the seventeenth and eighteenth centuries convinced of the importance of education to the political, socio-economic, and spiritual success of their colonial experiment. By the early nineteenth century, education became a birthright of U.S. citizens. This conviction fueled the common school movement of the 1820's and 1830's. By the end of the century, educational reformers had turned their attention to the early childhood years, hoping that public orphanages, day-care centers, and kindergartens would safeguard the rights of disadvantaged children, especially those of urban immigrant parents.

The first White House Conference on Children, convened by President Theodore Roosevelt in 1909, signaled the first major federal attempt at protecting children's rights. President Franklin D. Roosevelt's New Deal of the 1930's further addressed early childhood concerns. The Works Progress Administration built nursery schools for low-income children, and the Lanham Act created day-care centers administered by local communities.

The 1950's and early 1960's provided the intellectual foundations for Head Start. Rejecting twentieth century conventional wisdom, J. McVicker Hunt argued that environment, and not heredity, primarily governs human behavior. Oscar Lewis, from his studies of the poor in Latin America, identified a global culture of poverty characterized by matriarchal authoritarian families, early maturation of children, and feelings of helplessness among individuals. Benjamin Bloom concluded that a child develops half of his or her intelligence by age four and 80 percent by age eight. Early education therefore offers a potential escape from poverty.

Journalists joined these scholars in heightening public awareness of the children of the poor. Michael Harrington's The Other America (1962) defined poverty as deprivation of minimal levels of health, housing, food, and education. He contended that as many as one in four Americans fit this definition, and that the other three in four largely refused to acknowledge the existence of poverty in an increasingly affluent society. Dwight Macdonald's article "The Invisible Poor" (The New Yorker, January 19, 1963) critiqued Harrington's and others' contributions to the emerging literature on poverty. Macdonald, while finding fault with specific pieces of evidence advanced in these works, nevertheless concurred with their general conclusion that poverty was a dire national problem in need of a prompt national solution. He even forwarded his own antipoverty

proposal: a minimum income for all, guaranteed by the federal government.

The 1960's also offered the political opportunity for Head Start. President John F. Kennedy addressed poverty in the 1960 West Virginia presidential primary. He coined the phrase "war on poverty" in an August campaign speech and presided over the civil rights revolution, which would mobilize many poor people of all races. After reading Harrington's and Macdonald's indictments of federal inaction toward the poor, he ordered Walter W. Heller, chairman of the Council of Economic Advisers, to launch a national antipoverty effort. On November 23, 1963, the day after Kennedy's assassination, Heller presented the martyred president's antipoverty plan to his successor, Lyndon B. Johnson.

Johnson's own background added a personal influence to the creation of Head Start. After working his way through Southwest Texas State Teachers College, Johnson had commenced his teaching career in Cotulla, Texas, at a school for disadvantaged Mexican children. On January 8, 1964, Johnson resurrected the term "war on poverty" in his state of the union address. On January 20, he sent Heller's report to Congress. On February 1, Sargent Shriver, the first director of the Peace Corps, agreed to become Johnson's special assistant in the War on Poverty and to head a task force to draft legislation.

The Economic Opportunity Act of August 30, 1964, created the Office of Economic Opportunity (OEO), a federal antipoverty agency whose programs would be directed by Shriver but locally administered by the poor themselves. The OEO soon incurred criticism for this latter "community action" feature, which, by enlisting the poor, often bypassed local administrators. The agency, while furthering the rights of the disadvantaged through work-study, job training, and volunteer programs, overlooked the rights of the children of the disadvantaged.

About 17 percent of the nation's poor, or nearly six million, were under six years old. Shriver moved to address both of these concerns. He believed that because children were the most tragic victims and the most potentially sympathetic symbols of poverty, a program to ensure their basic human rights would provide a political justification for community action and a moral underpinning for the War on Poverty.

Building on his experience with his wife Eunice Kennedy in early intervention programs for the mentally disabled, Shriver appointed a committee of child-development specialists led by Robert Cooke, pediatrician-in-chief at Johns Hopkins Hospital, to draft an extensive federal program of early childhood intervention for the socioeconomically deprived. On May 18, 1965, President Johnson presented the result of the committee's deliberations.

Project Head Start (OEO staffer Judah Drob suggested the name) would be a summer program for disadvantaged children who were to enter kindergarten or the first grade in the fall of 1965. It would provide an intellectual, medical, nutritional, and psychological head start for children in their lifelong quest for the full enjoyment of their fundamental human rights. It would encourage considerable involvement by parents and community leaders. The OEO would finance up to 90 percent of the cost of the programs; the local community would cover the rest.

The first director of the program would be Julius Richmond, dean of the medical faculty at the State University Upstate Medical Center in Syracuse, New York. Although Head Start would offer no respite from a summer of civil rights demonstrations and race riots, it would enroll almost 560,000 children at 13,400 centers in 2,500 communities and would provide paid summer employment for about 100,000 people. It engendered such hope that Johnson announced on August 31 that it would become a year-round program for more than 350,000 disadvantaged preschool children three years old and older. A summer session with follow-through

programs such as special classes, home visits, and field trips would be available for those children excluded from the year-round classes.

SIGNIFICANCE

Preschool children living in poverty are too often the victims of inadequate health services, incomplete immunizations, and uncorrected or unattended physical disabilities. They lack communication skills; they have little opportunity to enjoy reading, art, or music; and they distrust strangers. They reach school age with low self-esteem and little motivation to learn. Project Head Start has made great progress in attacking these symptoms of early childhood poverty.

Head Start grew to enroll nearly 500,000 children in 24,000 classrooms by 1991. A decade later, enrollments had grown to more than 900,000 students in more than 48,000 classrooms, while the 2004 budget for the program reached an all-time high of nearly $6.8 billion.

Studies show that every dollar spent on Head Start saves six dollars in health care, welfare payments, and crime control, justifying the U.S. government's steady increases in financial support for the program over the years. Head Start has won wide acclaim as a significant step in the quest for human rights in the United States.

—Lawrence J. McAndrews

CONGRESS PASSES THE VOTING RIGHTS ACT

August 6, 1965

The Voting Rights Act of 1965, passed by Congress, was the most significant extension of voting rights to African Americans since the passage of the Fifteenth Amendment to the U.S. Constitution.

Locale: Washington, D.C.
Categories: Laws, acts, and legal history; civil rights and liberties; social issues and reform

KEY FIGURES

Lyndon B. Johnson (1908-1973), president of the United States, 1963-1969
Martin Luther King, Jr. (1929-1968), civil rights leader and adviser to President Johnson on civil rights reforms
Nicholas de Belleville Katzenbach (b. 1922), U.S. attorney general who drafted the Voting Rights Act

SUMMARY OF EVENT

The Voting Rights Act was the culmination of a ninety-five-year effort to extend voting rights to all Americans regardless of "race, color, or previous condition of servitude." These words are from the Fifteenth Amendment to the U.S. Constitution, which gave Congress the power to pass "appropriate legislation" to ensure voting rights. Although this amendment was ratified on March 30, 1870, it was not until 1965 that the U.S. Congress exercised that power in a significant fashion. Congress had indeed proposed the Twenty-fourth Amendment, outlawing poll taxes for federal elections, but that measure required ratification by the states. In less than two years, thirty-eight states had ratified this amendment, making it part of the Constitution on January 23, 1964. This action was important but did not reflect the kind of positive congressional response called for by civil rights leaders.

Poll taxes had been merely one of many devices used in the South to discourage blacks from exercising their constitutional right to vote. Literacy tests, examinations, and errors or omissions on applications were also used to deny suffrage to blacks. The Twenty-fourth Amendment had symbolic importance, but it did not provide the kind of sweeping reforms that were needed. This was accomplished by the Voting Rights Act of 1965.

It is difficult to pinpoint what brought the voting rights issue into focus in 1965, but it was only one part of the larger civil rights issue. The voting rights sections of the Civil Rights Act of 1964 were among the least controversial aspects of that legislation. In the eyes of most civil rights advocates, greater electoral strength was the appropriate means of allowing black Americans to secure their rights. This was the position of the Mississippi Freedom Democratic Party in 1964. Its actions, together with the 1965 Freedom March from Selma to Montgomery, Alabama, seem to have been pivotal events in the voting rights movement in the United States.

The Mississippi Freedom Democratic Party (MFDP) began as a grassroots effort to forge a political union among blacks, labor, and poor whites. The party's efforts to participate in regular Democratic party meetings throughout the state met with little success. After meeting with numerous obstacles, the MFDP decided to challenge the all-white delegation that the Mississippi Democrats were sending to the 1964 Democratic convention. Using the rules set by the Democratic National Committee, the MFDP chose forty-four delegates and twenty-two alternates to attend the national convention in Atlantic City.

President Lyndon B. Johnson was concerned about the plight of the MFDP, but he wanted to keep as many mainstream southern votes as possible. He attempted to work out a compromise between Mississippi's regular delegation and the MFDP at the convention, but the nationally televised battle before the Credentials Committee gave many Democratic Party officials a clearer picture of the extent and nature of voter discrimination in the South. In this respect, the actions of the MFDP greatly advanced the cause of voting rights reform.

As soon as his reelection was secured, President Johnson started exploring legislative options for removing obstacles to voter registration and participation. Attorney General Nicholas de Belleville Katzenbach presented the president with a variety of approaches. One was a constitutional amendment limiting the requirements states could impose for voter registration, including age, residency, felony convictions, and mental stability. The primary objective of this approach was to remove literacy requirements. Another proposal was to create a federal commission to handle registration for all federal elections. Katzenbach also proposed using federal agents to supervise and monitor registration in states and regions where voter discrimination could be verified. As President Johnson pondered these legislative options, others pressed for fast and decisive action.

In early 1965, voting rights activists focused the nation's attention on Alabama. Dallas County was one of the most obvious examples of voter discrimination in America. The population in Dallas County was 57.6 percent black, yet only 335 of its 9,542 registered voters were black. The registration process in Dallas County was one of the most cumbersome in the nation, and there were only two days each month when one could attempt to register. The Student Nonviolent Coordinating Committee (SNCC) led demonstrations on the steps of the courthouse in Selma, the county seat, in order to attract attention. After Jimmie Lee Jackson was killed in a similar demonstration in nearby Marion, the Southern Christian Leadership Conference (SCLC) planned a march from Selma to Montgomery, the state capital. Alabama state troopers turned the marchers back on their first attempt, using violence and tear gas to restrain the marchers. A limited march eventually took place.

The sheer brutality of events in Selma produced a national outcry for swift action to protect the voting rights of all Americans. On March 17, President Johnson, after consulting with Martin Luther King, Jr., submitted a comprehensive voting rights bill to the U.S. Congress. Johnson's bill called for federal monitoring of registration and voting in states with a clear history of discrimination.

In the Senate, there were sixty-six cosponsors to the bill but there was also considerable opposition from some key southerners. One of the most controversial issues during the floor debate in the Senate was whether to ban poll taxes in state and local elections. The Senate passed a version of the bill with the poll tax ban removed on May 26, by a vote of 77-19.

In the House of Representatives, the Republicans offered a substitute bill that allowed poll taxes but also permitted judicial proceedings when such taxes were found to be discriminatory. Southern Democrats started defending it as the lesser of the evils. On July 9, the House passed the bill by a vote of 333-85. In less than a month, the conference report had passed both houses.

On August 6, Johnson signed the Voting Rights Act of 1965.

SIGNIFICANCE

Two key provisions in the act were the creation of federal examiners to determine an individual's qualifications to vote and the abolition of literacy tests. An aggressive Justice Department, under Attorney General Katzenbach, moved swiftly to implement the new law. On August 7, the department suspended literacy tests and other discriminatory measures in seven states. The entire states of Alabama, Alaska, Georgia, Louisiana, Mississippi, South Carolina, and Virginia were affected. Suspension or investigations occurred within certain counties in Arizona, Idaho, Maine, and North Carolina. By August 9, the first groups of federal examiners were assigned to help blacks register in Alabama, Louisiana, and Mississippi. In fewer than three weeks, 27,385 blacks were added to the voter registration rolls in those three states alone.

From 1964 to 1969, voter registration among blacks in the South rose by almost 30 percent, while registration for whites increased by 10 percent. The most significant change for blacks occurred in Mississippi, where only 6.7 percent of adult blacks had been registered in 1964. By 1969, that figure had risen to 66.5 percent. The act was not without controversy. South Carolina challenged the constitutionality of the "triggering" provision, which authorized federal examiners for a state or political subdivision if the attorney general determined that there had been discriminatory devices in place on November 1, 1964, and if the director of the census determined that less than 50 percent of the voting-age residents in that area either were not registered or did not vote in the 1964 presidential election. South Carolina argued that such a provision denied the states equal protection, violated the due process clause, constituted a bill of attainder, and violated the separation of powers provision. The U.S. Supreme Court, in *South Carolina v. Katzenbach* (1966), found the Voting Rights Act to be a logical and consistent expression of the Fifteenth Amendment.

There has been some disappointment over the long-term effect of this act. By the late 1960's and early 1970's, the progress toward enfranchisement had lost its steam. Removing legal barriers was a necessary but not always sufficient means to ensure citizen participation. Katzenbach observed that the presence of examiners was not enough. Local efforts had to organize registration campaigns actively. Individuals who had been

The Right to Vote

Fifteenth Amendment (1870)

The right of [male] citizens of the United States to vote shall not be denied or abridged by the United States or by any State on account of race, color, or previous condition of servitude.

Voting Rights Act (1965)

No voting qualification or prerequisite to voting, or standard, practice, or procedure shall be imposed or applied by any State or political subdivision to deny or abridge the right of any citizen of the United States to vote on account of race or color.

Understanding tests

Understanding tests were used to practice racial discrimination in voter registration. The Supreme Court ruled on such tests several times before they were prohibited by the Voting Rights Act of 1965.

In an effort to circumvent the Fifteenth Amendment, which gave the right to vote to African Americans, many southern states, beginning in the latter part of the nineteenth century, used poll taxes and literacy requirements to prevent African Americans from registering to vote. Part of the literacy requirement in some states was the passing of understanding tests, which commonly required prospective voters to read and explain a provision of the U.S. Constitution or the state constitution. Voting registrars sometimes had discretion to choose the passage to be interpreted and judge the adequacy of the explanation given. The discretion vested in registrars provided the opportunity for widespread discrimination against African American voters.

The Supreme Court confronted the issue of literacy tests several times. In *Lassiter v. Northampton County Board of Elections* (1959), the Court upheld the use of literacy tests on the grounds that they had some relationship to intelligent voter choices. The Court did say, however, that should a state law give election officials complete discretion to determine whether prospective voters understood the constitutional passages they were given to interpret, that law might be unconstitutional. The Court subsequently did hold such a law unconstitutional in *Louisiana v. United States* (1965). Because of the difficulty in determining when literacy tests were being used to perpetuate racial discrimination, Congress suspended their use in the Voting Rights Act of 1965.

excluded from the political process needed experience and political education before they could exercise their new political clout.

—Donald V. Weatherman

See also: Supreme Court Rules African American Disenfranchisement Unconstitutional; Supreme Court

Ends Public School Segregation; Congress Creates the Commission on Civil Rights; Civil Rights Act of 1960; Council of Federated Organizations Registers African Americans to Vote; Poll Taxes Are Outlawed; Three Civil Rights Workers Are Murdered; July Congress Passes the Civil Rights Act of 1964

WATTS RIOT

August 11-17, 1965

Days after the enactment of the Voting Rights Act of 1965, the African American community in Los Angeles began to riot, burning, looting, and attacking white persons and their property.

Locale: Los Angeles, California
Categories: Social issues and reform; wars, uprisings, and civil unrest

KEY FIGURES

Edmund G. Brown, Sr. (1905-1996), governor of California, 1959-1967

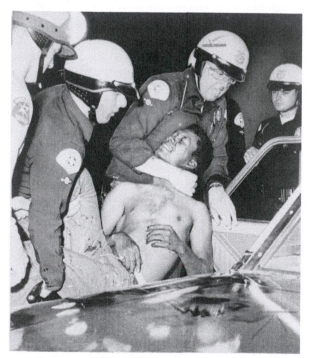

Police arrest a man during the riots on August 12, by New York World-Telegram

Samuel Yorty (1909-1998), mayor of Los Angeles, 1961-1973
Martin Luther King, Jr. (1929-1968), African American reverend and civil rights leader

SUMMARY OF EVENT

On the evening of August 11, 1965, on one of the hottest days of the year in Los Angeles, California, the black community erupted in what has come to be called the "Watts riot." Thirty-four people were killed, approximately four thousand were arrested, and more than $40 million in property damage was caused by the riot. It was estimated that ten thousand people participated.

It came as a surprise to many that Los Angeles would be the scene of one of the most violent conflicts in the United States during the twentieth century. Most visitors to the black community in Los Angeles remarked on the fact that the community did not have the physical ugliness and dilapidated conditions of ghettos in the East, Midwest, and South. Moreover, black Los Angeles did not have the tension-ridden history of other areas; for example, by 1741 New York City had experienced two major slave rebellions in which blacks had tried to burn down the entire city and had almost succeeded. Although blacks had participated in the founding of Los Angeles in 1781, an 1880 census showed that there were only about one hundred African Americans in the city. The black population of Los Angeles began to expand dramatically during World War II, when a need for labor in the area led to large-scale black migration.

A turning point came when the Japanese American community was interned; "Little Tokyo" became "Bronzeville," and the first black ghetto in Los Angeles was born. Watts itself was known as "Mudtown" and was multiracial until the war, when black migrants from

Texas, Oklahoma, and Louisiana particularly began to pour into the city. Although Los Angeles was viewed by some as a sunny paradise, African Americans there encountered restrictive racial covenants that limited their ability to leave the ghetto, police brutality, employment discrimination, and many of the ills that they had hoped to leave behind. The riot itself was a culmination of the accumulated anger, disappointment, and pain encountered by African Americans in Los Angeles.

The riot was precipitated by the stopping of Marquette Frye, an African American male, by the California Highway Patrol. Frye was stopped for speeding and appeared intoxicated. As he was being questioned, a crowd gathered, and the officers decided to call for reinforcements. To that point, Frye had complied with the officers' requests, but then his mother appeared on the scene and began to berate him. Frye then became unruly, and the decision was made to arrest him and take him away.

A highway patrolman—apparently mistakenly—struck a bystander with his billy club. A young African American woman, who was accused of spitting on an officer, was dragged into the middle of the street. A rumor circulated that a pregnant woman had been attacked by the officers (actually, the woman in question was not pregnant but happened to be wearing a barber's smock). When the officers departed with the Fryes, the crowd erupted. Rocks and other missiles were hurled at passing cars. White motorists were pulled from their cars and beaten, and their cars were set on fire. Law enforcement authorities reacted hesitantly at first, overwhelmed and stunned by the ferocity of the crowd.

The following day, the area was calm, but that evening the pattern of violence was repeated; however, not until almost thirty hours after the initial flare-up did window smashing, looting, and arson begin. These events were concentrated in Watts, two miles from the location of the original disturbance. The looting and arson spread rapidly throughout the black community of Los Angeles, eventually encompassing a 46.5-square-mile region.

The pattern of the riot shifted over time from random attacks on whites to attacks on property, particularly large stores that were viewed as exploiting the community. A number of black-owned businesses escaped damage by conspicuously posting "Blood Brother," or similarly worded signs. A number of small businesses that were not perceived as being exploitative managed to escape damage.

The riot was not helpful to the political career of Governor Brown; the riot and the student protests at Berkeley in 1964 were major factors in Brown's defeat at the hands of Ronald Reagan in 1966 in Reagan's first effort to attain political office. Governor Reagan was essential in reviving the conservative movement in the United States, which had suffered what some had seen as a maiming blow when Barry Goldwater was soundly defeated for the presidency in 1964. The Reagan victory in turn underscored the importance of the "crime in the streets" theme as a riveting one for many U.S. voters—a theme that was utilized skillfully by Richard M. Nixon during his victorious presidential campaign of 1968. The riot also had a significant impact on African Americans in California. A hospital was built in South-Central Los Angeles; the absence of such a facility had been a primary complaint of the area's residents. A shopping center was built so that residents did not have to travel miles simply to buy groceries. Housing units were built. The University of California and the University of Southern California began to admit more African American students. Local businesspeople and local government initiated programs to address the problem of black unemployment. The riot also highlighted the ongoing issue of police brutality.

The cultural arena may have been most significantly affected by the riot. Budd Schulberg, a well-known screenwriter and novelist and the son of a major film industry executive, initiated a writers' workshop that helped produce a number of prominent African American writers. There was a general cultural renaissance in black Los Angeles that spread across the nation. The fact that the riot took place in Los Angeles meant that the entertainment industry based there was affected. From August, 1965, it was possible to discern an increased employment of African American actors, technical personnel, and themes in film and television.

—*Gerald Horne*

I Spy Debuts to Controversy
September 15, 1965

I Spy, a television espionage drama, was controversial because it featured Bill Cosby, a black actor, in a starring role. It was the first drama mainstream television history to starring an African American actor.

Locale: United States
Categories: Radio and television; social issues and reform

Key Figures
Bill Cosby (b. 1937), African American comedian and actor
Robert Culp (b. 1930- 2010), American stage and television actor
Sheldon Leonard (1907-1997), American film and television producer

Summary of Event
The early 1960's was a tense time in the United States. The Cuban Missile Crisis, U.S. military involvement in Vietnam, and the intensified Cold War produced a spate of books and articles that made the American public aware that the Central Intelligence Agency (CIA) was carrying on a secret war against foreign countries and rulers. This awareness was in sharp contrast to the American public's traditional view of the United States as the open and honest "good guy" of world affairs, but world conditions convinced most Americans that the CIA's covert actions were necessary.

Television responded to this public interest by introducing spy programs, which fed on the mood of a public that believed that the United States was under a secret attack and should respond in kind. Many of these shows were jingoistic and were unrealistic in the schemes they plotted for their characters. The National Broadcasting Company (NBC) broke out of this mold by developing *I Spy*, an hour-long weekly show to be filmed on location around the world. *I Spy* followed the exploits of two American intelligence agents, Kelly Robinson, played by Robert Culp, and Alexander Scott, played by Bill Cosby. Robinson was a pro tennis player, and Scott was his trainer; their travels on the international tennis circuit provided the cover the pair needed to perform secret missions for the United States government. The cool, sophisticated nature of the acting, plots, and settings made the show a popular favorite during its three-season run.

The executive producer of the show, Sheldon Leonard, came to television after having achieved success as an actor in 1940's and 1950's films. His television record was impressive; he had produced and co-owned such hits as *Gomer Pyle, U.S.M.C.*, *The Dick Van Dyke Show*, and *The Andy Griffith Show*. Leonard had already contracted with NBC to produce *I Spy* and was looking for actors.

The role of Alexander Scott was not written specifically for an African American, and Leonard actually had Dane Clark, a white actor, in mind for the role. Leonard, however, saw Cosby perform on late-night television and decided that he would be perfect for the part. Leonard was especially attracted by Cosby's athletic agility and his sense of humor.

At the time, however, no black performer had had a starring role in a U.S. television series. Reflecting on Leonard's decision to cast him, Cosby later remarked that "no other producer would have had the guts to cast a Negro as Alexander Scott." Indeed, it took guts. Civil rights was a divisive issue in the United States at the time; large-scale demonstrations were the order of the day, and massive civil rights legislation was moving through Congress. In the midst of this, Bill Cosby was about to become the first black star of an integrated program on national television. As Cosby said, "This is the first time they called [a Negro] up to play a spy instead of a problem." The script for the show called for the characters played by Culp and Cosby to live, eat, and work together as complete equals. Culp summed up the attitude of the actors and the point of view of the show when he said, "We are two guys who don't know the difference between a colored and White." The deliberate determination not to make an overt racial statement with the show was followed. In its three-year run, *I Spy* made only a handful of racial references. People were simply people, so far as the show's scripts were concerned.

That decision did not guarantee a dramatic hit. The first episode of the show was set in Hong Kong. Following the broadcast, a critic for *The New York Times* noted that "the setting was the real star. The actors wavered between strained suspense and a flirtation with James Bond. The show is searching for an attitude and the style to go with it." Part of this initial problem was that Cosby was not yet a good actor. He had not made the transition from performing as a comic working alone to being a member of a team.

I Spy helped change the public image of blacks in entertainment. When first offered the role of Alexander Scott, the trainer to a white tennis player, Cosby was hesitant; he feared that the role would prove to be merely another sidekick part. He was assured by Leonard, though, that he would play a character with special skills, would have equal prominence, and would be allowed to develop romantic interests. Once Cosby settled into the role, his performances were virtuoso, and his part became one of the most significant in television history. Cosby himself said of his character that Alexander Scott was " the first Negro champion on TV. He is working for goodness and the law; a multi-lingual, highly educated man who is not the Negro stereotype." The old stereotype would never again be believable.

I Spy's success was largely the product of the charming on-screen interplay of its stars, who ad-libbed much of their dialogue. Together, Culp and Cosby brought a light touch to the show, even as the plots revolved around shootouts and superpower confrontation. Cosby's blackness made the series groundbreaking, but it was his skill as an actor that helped make the show a success. Having broken television's color line, Cosby opened the door for other serious black performers.

I Spy had an enormous impact on Cosby's career. For each season the show was on the air, 1965-1966, 1966-1967, and 1967-1968, Cosby won an Emmy Award for "outstanding continuous performance by an actor in a leading role in a dramatic series." Of course, such success brought other roles his way and boosted his earnings. He began to command $25,000 a week as a nightclub comic, and sales of record albums containing his comedy routines tripled. The experience on *I Spy* also turned Cosby into an accomplished actor. Before the series began, one television critic commented that seeing Cosby tied to a structured script and working with other actors would be like seeing Thelonious Monk play piano for Lawrence Welk. By the end of *I Spy*'s first season, no one doubted that Cosby could both improvise and work with a group.

—*Michael R. Bradley*

See also: *Stormy Weather* Offers New Film Roles to African Americans; Poitier Emerges as a Film Star in *The Blackboard Jungle;* Berry's "Maybellene" Popularizes Rock and Roll

AFFIRMATIVE ACTION IS EXPANDED
September 24, 1965

The U.S. government's evolving commitment to nondiscrimination was expanded with the signing of an executive order prohibiting discriminatory employment practices. Proactive efforts were mandated in the hiring of racial minorities and women in businesses holding federal contracts.

Also known as: Executive Order 11246
Locale: Washington, D.C.
Categories: Government and politics; social issues and reform; business and labor; women's issues

KEY FIGURES
Lyndon B. Johnson (1908-1973), president of the United States, 1963-1969
John F. Kennedy (1917-1963), president of the United States, 1961-1963
Dwight D. Eisenhower (1890-1969), president of the United States, 1953-1961

Franklin D. Roosevelt (1882-1945), president of the United States, 1933-1945

SUMMARY OF EVENT
Affirmative action, as developed through executive orders, has a long history, beginning with defense contractors in World War II. President Lyndon B. Johnson's executive order of 1965 was an important milestone, best understood as an expansion of an evolving governmental commitment to nondiscrimination, which enjoyed bipartisan support until the 1980's. In the mid-1990's, affirmative action would become a lightning rod for discontent over class, race, ethnic, and gender differences in the United States in a time of shrinking economic and educational opportunities.

The term itself has many definitions. Some consider affirmative action to be merely a way to produce nondiscrimination and equal employment opportunity. Others characterize it as preferential treatment or quota hiring: choosing people solely because of a race or gender identity, with little or no reference to their qualifications or actual disadvantage. Affirmative action can refer to recruitment efforts at colleges and training for apprenticeships, government mandates that a percentage of contracts or radio licenses go to minorities, voluntary efforts on the part of employers to diversify the workforce, or court-ordered remedies for proven cases of unlawful discrimination. All the preceding examples of affirmative action have been subjected to judicial scrutiny by the U.S. Supreme Court to see if they violate the Fourteenth Amendment's constitutional guarantee of the equal protection of the laws. Those who seek a definitive answer to the legal status of affirmative action are often frustrated and confused.

The Court has spoken with many voices on the subject and changed its position over time. Perhaps even more confusing is the public debate over affirmative action, which often fails to articulate carefully which of the many incarnations of affirmative action is being debated, but instead lumps them all together.

The development of affirmative action through executive orders has its origins in the conviction of Franklin D. Roosevelt's administration that companies receiving federal government defense contracts should open their doors to workers who were not white. The idea was that government money should not be spent to discriminate against people because of race, color, religion, or national origin, specifically, by closing jobs to African American workers. President Dwight D. Eisenhower extended the purpose beyond ensuring that racism not hinder national defense to a more general commitment to equal employment opportunity.

Eisenhower's Government Contracts Committee, chaired by then-vice president Richard M. Nixon, recommended that government overcome private employers' indifference by requiring them to take positive steps to ensure nondiscrimination. It was President John F. Kennedy in 1961, with Executive Order 10925, who mandated that government contractors have an equal employment opportunity clause in all contracts, that they implement affirmative action, and that the ultimate sanction for noncompliance would be loss of the contract. Kennedy's order was the first to use the term "affirmative action."

President Johnson continued the bipartisan support for nondiscrimination in government contracts when he issued Executive Order 11246, on September 24, 1965. While the first part of the order prohibited employment discrimination based on a person's race, creed, color,

or national origin, and mandated equal opportunity in federal employment, the second part of the executive order prohibited federal contractors and subcontractors from discriminating and required them to take "affirmative action." Johnson moved responsibility for the program from the Office of the President to the Department of Labor. With Executive Order 11375 on October 13, 1967, he added "sex," or gender, to the list of prohibited categories of discrimination. In 1975, when the executive order program was extended to disabled and Vietnam War veterans, the office was renamed the Office of Federal Contract Compliance Programs (OFCCP). President Jimmy Carter later consolidated governmental efforts in the OFCCP and stepped up enforcement.

Regulations issued in 1968 and modified in 1970 defined affirmative action as "specific and result-oriented procedures designed to achieve prompt and full utilization of minorities and women at all levels and in all segments of the contractor's workforce where

Affirmative Action

Executive Order 11246 (1965) prohibits discriminatory employment practices. With Executive Order 11375 (1967), "gender" was added to the list of "categories" protected against discrimination. The main points of each order follow:

Executive Order 11246

It is the policy of the Government of the United States to provide equal opportunity in Federal employment for all qualified persons, to prohibit discrimination in employment because of race, creed, color, or national origin, and to promote the full realization of equal employment opportunity through a positive continuing program in each executive department and agency.

The policy of equal opportunity applies to every aspect of Federal employment policy and practice.

Executive Order 11375

Executive Order No. 11246 1 of September 24, 1965, carried forward a program of equal employment opportunity in Government employment, employment by Federal contractors and subcontractors and employment under Federally assisted construction contracts regardless of race, creed, color or national origin. It is desirable that the equal employment opportunity programs provided for in Executive Order No. 11246 expressly embrace discrimination on account of sex.

deficiencies exist." All contractors who employed fifty or more employees and had a contract worth more than $50,000 were forbidden to discriminate and were required to develop an affirmative action plan. Not only were contractors required to monitor and report on the composition of their workforces, but they also were to identify problem areas and develop goals and timetables to rectify them.

SIGNIFICANCE

Affirmative action was implemented as a method to dismantle discriminatory policies, practices, and procedures in hiring and employment. Insofar as affirmative action was understood to mean the inclusion of ethnic groups and women in occupations from which they were traditionally excluded, employers were tempted to provide only token responses, such as hiring just one African American or one woman for a particular job. This form of tokenism was, and still is, vigorously protested. As an increasing number of women and racial minorities were hired, some men began to complain of reverse discrimination. Furthermore,

employers began to complain of the costs of collecting, organizing, and analyzing masses of statistics on employees.

After a 1978 case before the Supreme Court, in which the Court ruled against using segregated pools of applicants in determining university admissions but ruled for considering racial diversity instead, "diversity" began to replace "affirmative action" as a civil rights goal.

In the late 1990's, President Bill Clinton announced standards for "mending" affirmative action. Affirmative action should not establish quotas or preferences for the unqualified, involve reverse discrimination, or continue beyond a point where there is a demonstrable need.

—Sally J. Kenney

See also: Supreme Court Rules African American Disenfranchisement Unconstitutional; Truman Orders Desegregation of U.S. Armed Forces; Congress Creates the Commission on Civil Rights; Civil Rights Act of 1960; Congress Passes the Civil Rights Act of 1964

BLACK CHRISTIAN NATIONALIST MOVEMENT

Late 1960's

The movement correlated black Protestantism in the United States with African American heritage, culture, and political values.

Identification: Religious movement emphasizing the ethnic characteristics of African Americans

African American Protestants have often had a sense of separation from other Christians in the United States, mostly because of slavery, segregation, and the formation of African American churches and denominations within the black community. This separation led to belief systems that stressed the history of oppression among African Americans and often likened them to the ancient Israelites living in slavery. This biblical analogy allowed African American Christians to interpret themselves as a religious people who were distinct, a people with their own national characteristics. The interpretation was supported in the 1960's and later by nationalistic political movements among African Americans who were secular but dependent on the support of churches and religious organizations.

The movement termed Black Christian Nationalism is not one event but a series of occurrences including the establishment of congregations based on Black Christian Nationalist ideology, the publication of writings by major African American theologians, and the dissemination of the movement's ideas, which found varying levels of receptivity among religious African Americans. The most institutionalized example of Black Christian Nationalism was the formation during the 1960's of churches called The Shrine of the Black Madonna in Detroit, Michigan, and some southern cities by the Reverend Albert Cleage. The foremost African American theologian promoting these ideas was Professor James Cone of Union Theological Seminary in New York City, author of *Black Theology and Black Power* (1969) and *Black Theology of Liberation* (1970). These explicit examples, however, do not capture the much broader dissemination of Black Christian Nationalist ideas.

Younger, more formally educated pastors of African American Protestant congregations—denominations such as Methodists, Presbyterians, and Baptists—had been influenced by both biblical analogies and current events of the 1960's. These pastors preached sermons comparing the plight of African Americans to the Israelites, stressing that African Americans in the United States were a separate nation that had been conquered by the larger surrounding white nation. They called for obedience to a God who was on the side of oppressed people, a Jesus who was dark skinned and non-European, and for identification with the nation of African Americans. The less-educated, more evangelical holiness and Pentecostal ministers were less influenced by the ideas of Black Christian Nationalism. Some black Catholic priests interpreted Black Christians as a religious group for a separate "nation" of African Americans within the United States.

IMPACT

The somewhat disassociated congregations, writings, and dissemination of ideas by young educated pastors that make up Black Christian Nationalism drew on two resources: an interpretation of the Bible associating African Americans with the enslaved people of God, the Israelites, and the Civil Rights and Black Power movements of the 1960's that clarified what constituted an oppressed nation within a nation. As Black Christian Nationalist views began to influence pastors and congregations, churches often abandoned the idea of the separation of church and state, and politics were considered a part of religious commitment. Being African American was identified as distinct from being any other sort of American, and religious organizations were perceived as the appropriate place to announce the religious-political ideology of Black Christian Nationalism.

—*William Osborne Max C. E. Orezzoli*

See also: Black church; Black nationalism; Black Power movement; Church bombings; Nation of Islam; Republic of New Africa; Southern Christian Leadership Conference

THE AUTOBIOGRAPHY OF MALCOLM X IS PUBLISHED

November, 1965

The Autobiography of Malcolm X *offered white Americans revealing insights into life in the nation's black ghettos and helped explain the attraction of the racially exclusive Nation of Islam for African Americans.*

Locale: New York, New York
Categories: Literature; social issues and reform

KEY FIGURES

Malcolm X (Malcolm Little; 1925-1965), African American activist and leader of the Nation of Islam
Elijah Muhammad (1897-1975), African American founder of the Nation of Islam
Marcus Garvey (1887-1940), Jamaican American founder of the Universal Negro Improvement Association
Alex Haley (1921-1992), African American writer who collaborated with Malcolm X in composing the latter's autobiography
Betty Shabazz (1936-1997), African American activist and wife of Malcolm X

SUMMARY OF EVENT

Malcolm Little, better known by his adopted name of Malcolm X, was assassinated in the Audubon Ballroom in Harlem on February 21, 1965, shortly after leaving the Black Muslim movement. In November of that year, his autobiography (coauthored by Alex Haley) was published. The cultural and political significance of *The Autobiography of Malcolm X*, the memoir of one of the most controversial leaders of the Civil Rights movement in the United States, should be approached from several perspectives. In the immediate context of the Civil Rights movement of the mid-1960's, Malcolm X's account of the various stages of his life was quite significant. This was true because his autobiography represented personal insights into different aspects of black life in the United States that many Americans knew something about but could not picture accurately in their minds in relation to their own experience.

One very important aspect of his book was Malcolm X's description of the family life of African Americans. His family, like so many of their generation, had left the traditional rural setting of the southern

United States to implant themselves in the very different environment of the northern states, first in Omaha, Nebraska, then in Milwaukee, Wisconsin, and Lansing, Michigan. The autobiography depicted elements of racism in small towns.

Until Malcolm X's book, few had any understanding of their rigorous code of ethics. Something similar could be said for Malcolm's explanation of the place of women in the community of Black Muslims. His emphasis was on their extreme pride in propriety of appearance and behavior. This code was meant to belie widespread popular images of the depravity of ghetto existence in the 1960's.

Malcolm X's ultimate message concerning race relations, however, would turn away from the exclusivism of the mainly U.S.-based Nation of Islam movement and call for a much wider view of the problems of injustice in the United States and in other areas of the world. He came to espouse, for example, what he believed were the universal principles of brotherhood contained in orthodox Islam, which rejected race as a form of identity in favor of an ideology calling for human justice in all societies and among all races.

At the time of its publication, then, the autobiography became something more than an exposé of the American Black Nationalist movement: It was a personal witnessing by a black militant of the tenets of universal faith to which he, at least, attributed the potential to resolve the increasingly divisive struggle for civil rights all over the world. Possibly because his autobiography ended with a disavowal of the Black Power movement that was then gaining momentum, both in the Nation of Islam and in more radical violence-oriented groups such as the Black Panthers, he fell to assassins' bullets fired by African American rivals.

SIGNIFICANCE

Whatever readers throughout the world may have learned from the diverse contents of Malcolm X's autobiography, whether these concerned "inside details" of black ghetto existence, the inequities of open or latent racism, or the declared principles behind the Nation of Islam movement, the book symbolized the unresolved dilemma his career seemed to represent. Stated succinctly, the question remained: Which way should the Civil Rights movement turn?

Only months before Malcolm X's assassination, black leaders associated with the nonviolent Civil Rights movement, most prominently Martin Luther King, Jr., of the Southern Christian Leadership Conference, had

riveted the attention of the world on their determined efforts to exercise the civil rights of thousands of demonstrators on a march between Selma and Montgomery, Alabama. Malcolm X, then still a fervent believer in the Nation of Islam, withheld his support from such movements, which were perceived to be a form of begging for the white majority's help in defending minority rights. Instead, at that time Malcolm X preferred to support what he considered to be the courage of a different sort of champion of black rights, represented by the heavyweight boxing champion Cassius Clay. Clay, who had taken on the name Muhammad Ali when he joined the Nation of Islam, drew attention to the strength of conscious, but still pacifist, civil disobedience when he refused to be inducted into the armed forces as a statement of his opposition to the U.S. interventionist policy in Vietnam.

Malcolm X's declared militancy on the issue of active application of black rights raised the question of appropriate boundaries and ethical as well as legal legitimacy. Before his "conversion" from the Black Muslims, he would have argued that black ethics existed as part of the identity of black people; no reference to a more universalist source of justice was necessary. In fact, what was not part of the Nation of Islam was by definition unjust through its suppression of black identity. The concept of "enemy" loomed large.

By his espousal of more universalist concepts of ethics in the orthodox Islamic religion, Malcolm's impact on the late 1960's and the decades that would follow cannot be said to have been clear. To the degree that African Americans chose to disavow the narrowness of Nation of Islam definitions and to search beyond extremist stands for more universal perceptions, his impact has had two sides: clarification of the true nature of Islam and increasing disinclination to couch all racial justice questions in terms of "us against them."

There seem, therefore, to have been several longer-term results that stemmed from Malcolm X's unique involvement in the Civil Rights movement. His autobiography opened a new, necessarily disconcerting world for the majority of Americans who had very little inkling of what black culture signified to those who lived it. This world contained both positive and negative features, although the latter tended to outweigh the former. Rejection of continuation of the status quo of racism assumed that these negative factors had to be eradicated, but few knew how to proceed.

Because the last stages of Malcolm X's career opened him to a philosophy that was based more on universal concepts of justice for oppressed peoples than on specific theories of racial inequities, there was some hope that there might be a gathering together of at least some of the many militant movements of the mid-1960's around a single positive social reform theme. The major drawback that promised to complicate such a drawing together was connected to the fact that Malcolm X's revised views reflected a clear association with the Islamic religion. Even though his eventual views espoused an Islam that was a reflection of a principal world religion, not a "devised" faith along the lines of the Nation of Islam movement, they were nevertheless religious views. This had two repercussions for those who might have considered, if he had lived, recognition of his leadership within a circle of civil rights movements and activist political reform groups.

On the black side, there definitely remained a strong insistence, at least among the more radical groups, on Black Power, which depended on a continuing exclusivist and confrontational perception of social justice. These African Americans would have rejected Malcolm X's last messages on racial bases. On the other hand, less racially radical, integrationist movements such as the Southern Christian Leadership Conference very obviously depended on their identification with specifically Christian religious principles as the basis of their racial reform policies. Here, Malcolm X's specific identification with Islam would have prevented, at least in the short run, a coming together of such integrationist groups around altered philosophical and religious principles. Finally, one must consider that another aspect of Malcolm X's controversial position by 1965 would surge to the forefront in the year of his death and become, for the next five years at least, the overwhelming focal point of American political activists' efforts. That was the question of American involvement in Vietnam, which became a catalyst for racial and political ferment. Although it took Malcolm X's messages into consideration, activism tended to rush into a number of different ideological and organizational directions. His message and his ideals remained part of American culture, however, as exemplified by the positive response to Spike Lee's 1992 film *Malcolm X* and by the fact that such a film even was made.

—*Byron D. Cannon*

"A Human Being First and Foremost"

Malcolm X, in his autobiography (1965), told his readers that seeing the interracial cooperation among Muslims outside the United States was eye opening for him. Upon his return to America, he attempted to convince not only his friends and followers but also the "white press" of his changed perspective:

My thinking had been opened up wide in Mecca. In the long letters I wrote to friends, I tried to convey to them my new insights into the American black man's struggle and his problems, as well as the depths of my search for truth and justice.

"I've had enough of someone else's propaganda," I had written to these friends. "I'm for truth, no matter who tells it. I'm for justice, no matter who it is for or against. I'm a human being first and foremost, and as such I'm for whoever and whatever benefits humanity *as a whole.*"

Largely, the American white man's press refused to convey that I was now attempting to teach Negroes a new direction. With the 1964 "long, hot summer" steadily producing new incidents, I was constantly accused of "stirring up the Negroes." Every time I had another radio or television microphone at my mouth, when I was asked about "stirring up Negroes" or "inciting violence," I'd get hot. "It takes no one to stir up the sociological dynamite that stems from the unemployment, bad housing, and inferior education already in the ghettoes. . . . "

They called me "the angriest Negro in America." I wouldn't deny that charge. I spoke exactly as I felt. "I *believe* in anger. The Bible says there is a *time* for anger."